Literary Hypertext:

The Electronic Attempt to Break Textual Norms

By Hava Ritter-Cohen, Ph.D.

ISBN 978-965-572-642-8

Table of Contents

Preface and Acknowledges

I began this book in the era of print, the final stage of the 20th century. Many a times I thought that this book should be written and issued in an electronic format. Since the book was meant as a doctoral thesis it had to be written and published in print. Yet, today, in the digital era, I'm publishing it as it should – in an electronic format, even though it is extremely unconventional (yet) of academic publications.

I must first acknowledge my debt to Prof. Hannah Naveh, Tel Aviv University, without whom this volume would not have been penned. Thank you for your counsel, encouragement, criticism, and faith. Thank you for all the time you spent reading and re-reading all those drafts and thank you for your insights and suggestions that opened my eyes and helped broaden the work into a full-fledged research.

Last, but not least, I wish to thank my family for all their love and encouragement: my husband Dr. Zvika Cohen and my three sons, Tomer, Erez and Dana, and Oren. Thank you for all the patience and support that you bestowed upon me throughout the long years in which this research was written.

The work is dedicated to my beloved parents who did not live to see it, the late Lea and Nissan Ritter, who taught me to pursue my dreams as they did.

Dr. Hava Ritter Cohen

Introduction

> We look at the present through the rear-view mirror.
> We march backwards into the future. (Marshall
> McLuhan)

McLuhan wrote the above quotation in 1967, the midst of the turbulent sixties. Those years were characterized by political, social and cultural restlessness and by technological innovations. In the USA, nine political assassinations were carried out, social movements and students protested daily against the Vietnam War, feminism rose, ethnic minority groups were demanding equality and civil rights. Space race started and many technological inventions were born: satellite broadcasting, home video recorder, the computer mouse, word processor, the modem [Weiss], the prototype of the internet – ARPANET,[1] hypertext[2] and the personal computer (1973) [Pool].

The personal computer caused a revolution in economics, sociology, education, lifestyle and many other areas of life (Wells. 1997). Adding a modem to the PC allowed decentralized computers

---

[1] The Defense Advanced Research Projects Agency (DARPA) is an agency of the United States Department of Defense responsible for the development of new military technologies. It is responsible for funding the development of technologies which have had a major effect on the world, including computer networking, as well as NLS, which was the first hypertext system.

[2] The term was coined by Theodor Nelson in 1965.

to communicate with each other. Then came the Internet, which is a network of powerful servers, scattered around the world, available to the public 24/7 from any site. These servers store different kinds of digital media: text, sound, pictures, animation, video, and other multimedia files. All Internet users can address these servers and view, on their own personal computer screen, the stored materials; the best newspapers, art museums, literary art and research papers, TV shows, all can be reached and viewed with no need to leave the house, or even getting up from the armchair.

The technological inventions enabled a new way of communication – a digital one – and influenced civilization in later years. The word-processor gradually replaced the typewriter thus creating a text that could be stored as a digital object without being printed on paper [Haigh, 2006). While the word-processor turned the computer into a writing tool, networks turned it into a reading machine as well. The internet's prototype, ARPANET, enabled the realization of a new text format, hypertext, envisioned about twenty years earlier by Vannenvar Bush (1945).

This development, along with the easiness with which a file is sent from one computer to another, brought on the transition from print publishing to digital publishing as a form of dissemination. The decision whether or not to print a document was left entirely to the addressee, and even without printing – publishing of a sort occurred on multiple screens with great speed and with less cost.

On the Internet, information is presented by the hypertext format, which is a digital format that links together various nodes into one text. The node and the link, both, can be any digital object: a word, a sentence, a paragraph, a whole document, a picture, a sound file, a video film etc. Hypertext was invented by two American researchers working separately, Nelson (1980) and Engelbart (1984). Though arriving at the same outcome, they began their research from different starting points. While Nelson was seeking for an authorial-tool, which will facilitate writing, Engelbart was looking for a communication-tool, which will enable the sharing of resources. These two starting points are relevant to this study, since they encompass the dyad of author and reader.

Hypertext enables not only the linking of separate files and different media on a single page but it eliminates the problem of distance in linking objects from around the world as well. When the Internet became graphical, in the early nineties, hypertext became the *de facto* standard of writing and reading, and with time, got its multimedia characteristics. (Berners-Lee, 1993)

These two main developments, the computer becoming a writing/reading machine, in conjunction with the option of linking different texts, brought on the development of a new literary format, which is the focus of this dissertation: **hyper-literature**. Hyper-literature is the generic name for literary works that are written in hypertext format. These works differ from print literature in many properties, but the most obvious one is the difference between the book – the physical container of the work – and the digital object.

The book is a tangible object that has a materialistic presence and is perceived as a cultural object as Petroski (1999, 4) observes while talking about the bookshelf, "The bookshelf, like the book, has become an integral part of civilization as we know it, its presence in a home practically defining what it means to be civilized, educated, and refined" (4).

Bourdieu (1984), while talking about different forms of capital, regards the book as an object of cultural capital. He defines three forms of capital: economic, cultural and social. The cultural capital exists in three states: the embodied, the objectified and the institutionalized. The embodied capital is closely connected with a person and the cultivation of his mind and body hence, it "cannot be transmitted instantaneously (unlike money, property rights, or even titles of nobility) by gift or bequest, purchase or exchange" (85). This cultural capital is transmitted in two main ways: hereditary and educational.

The objectified capital is,

> Material objects and media, such as writings, paintings, monuments, instruments, etc., is transmissible in its materiality. A collection of paintings, for example, can be transmitted as well as economic capital (if not better, because the capital

transfer is more disguised). But what is transmissible is legal ownership and not (or not necessarily) what constitutes the precondition for specific appropriation, namely, the possession of the means of 'consuming' a painting or using a machine, which, being nothing other than embodied capital, are subject to the same laws of transmission (87).

The objectified state of cultural capital is cultural objects such as books, monuments and paintings, because of its materiality, its being a body. The ability to understand a painting or read a book is the embodied state of cultural capital which is very different from merely owing a painting or a book.

The third state is the institutional one, which is academic recognition, sanctioning, of competence and qualification, "a certificate of cultural competence which confers on its holder a conventional, constant, legally guaranteed value with respect to culture" (88), enabling the comparison and exchange of their holders.

A fourth category is the symbolic capital, defined by Bourdieu, "all forms of symbolic capital – prestige, charisma, charm - and the relations of exchange through which this capital accumulates – the exchange of services, gifts, attention, care, affection – are particularly vulnerable to the destructive effect of words which expose and disenchant" (1991, 28). The symbolic capital is created by conversion of cultural capital and economic capital by sociological capital. For instance,

> Of all the conversion techniques designed to create
> and accumulate symbolic capital, the purchase of
> works of art, objectified evidence of 'personal taste',
> is the one which is closest to the most irreproachable
> and inimitable form of accumulation, that is, the
> internalization of distinctive signs and symbols of
> power in the form of natural 'distinction', personal
> 'authority' or 'culture' (1984, 282).

The book, like works of art, has economic value, even if it's worth is degenerating since print invention, because the reproduction of books had become so easy and somewhat cheap. The accumulation of books answers the same "evidence of 'personal taste'" and testifies about its holder's economic status on the one hand, and on the other hand on his cultural capital, his intellectuality, scholarliness and his symbolic capital expressed as prestige.

The materiality of the book is one of its merits as a cultural capital. Hyper-literature has no substance; it is digital code, which has no meaning or direct access for the reader and requires an electronic device, a computer or any electronic reader, for its decoding and presentation – turning the code into text. Its cultural meaning does not stem from the artistic field like literature and books, but from the technological domain and gaming culture.

More importantly hyper-literature varies from print literature in its structure. The book has a single, evident and fixed entering point, "first page", a fixed and undisputed exit point – the end of the book –

and one defined pathway between them, which is fixed and pre-arranged by the writer. This enforced linearity of presentation and of reading may be de-stabled by non-linearity of the narrated content but a strong basic sense of linearity remains stable: we read page after page, from beginning to end. Hyper-literature may have multiple points of entry, multiple points of exit and multiple pathways to navigate among, thus abandoning any linearity, opening and closure. Those multi-pathways create multi-stories in one literary work, all of them packaged inside and raising the question: what is the "real" story?

In order to form those multi-pathways, the text is segmented – each node includes some text (or other media) and is connected by links to one or many other nodes. Thus, the reading is always disturbed by the decisions that the reader has to make – as to where she wants to go – and by the need to bind the nodes narratively. These are decisions and this is an "activity" which the reader of a book never comes across. In fact, this format of storytelling calls to mind Barthes' "writerly texts," (1974, 4), only in a most fundamental way. Barthes idealistic story is the one that causes the reader to be active; she has to find out the codes, or voices, that make up the text and see how they are intertwined, how they create an endless network.

The communication point of view questions the roles and relations of the author and the reader, which are distinct in print; the author paves the reader's way and the reader is following passively. Calvi (1999, 101) portrays the author and the reader as working from two different poles: while the author is making the exclusion of words and scenes according to the effect he wants to achieve, what is referred as 'Calvino's garbage axiom,' and the selection of what will be presented to the reader, the reader is selecting within the presented text to make a coherent interpretation. This selection is called by Calvino (1987) "the labyrinth challenge". Eco reformulate the labyrinth challenge into a dichotomy of two reading strategies: the first is the "first-order model reader" that tries out all the feasible ways to reach a predefined goal (e.g. finding the murderer) and the second one is the "second-order model reader" that aims at understanding the labyrinth itself, the author's implicit strategy, what Eco (1994, 57-60) calls the Model Author. In hyper-fiction, as in print fiction, the first-order model reader corresponds to the user who only wants to come to a plausible version of the work. The second-order reader tries to identify the Model Author that she is interacting with, the fabula of the story.

Aarseth (1997) regards print reader as a passive one, she cannot influence the text, and she is safe. This passive attitude is relative as the reader may be "doing" a mental, interpretive and emotional work, but she is passive in her dictated processes of consuming the story: page by page, line by line. The cybertext reader is not safe,

> The effort and energy demanded by the cybertext of
> its reader raise the stakes of interpretation to those
> of intervention. Trying to know a cybertext is an
> investment of personal improvisation that can result

in either intimacy or failure. The tensions at work in a cybertext, while not incompatible with those of narrative desire, are also something more: a struggle not merely for interpretative insight but also for narrative control: I want this text to tell my story; the story that could not be without me" (4)

In hypertext the author serves the reader with choices – created by the linkage device thus making the reader more active – she must make decisions as to which link to choose and find her way through the text incessantly, on top of the regular need for interpretation or unveiling the codes. The so-called reading process when done by assembling of nodes blurs the boundaries between the reader and the author and contaminates their two separate roles. Instead of the distinct role of the author as a master of words, the one who creates the literary work art, and determines every aspect of the "given text" and the reader's distinct role as his follower, the pursuer of the paths prepared for him, the consumer, the reader becomes a semi-author since by her assembling the nodes she is actually "creating" the literary work. Every reader, instead of being the passive consumer of the book and the narrative, is thus turned into an authority – the one that is responsible for its creation. This intertwinement and interdependence of roles affirmed the notion of the "death of the author" that was raised by Roland Barthes (1977, 142-149), though in a way which was far from what Barthes could have imagined and much more radical in fact.

Barthes, in his *The Death of the Author* essay regards the author as a limiting entity,

> The removal of the Author (one could talk here with Brecht of a veritable 'distancing', the Author diminishing like a figurine at the far end of the literary stage) is not merely an historical fact or an act of writing; it utterly transforms the modern text (or - which is the same thing - the text is henceforth made and read in such a way that at all its levels the author is absent) (145).

For him the text "is not a line of words releasing a single 'theological' meaning (the 'message' of the Author-God) but a multi-dimensional space in which a variety of writings, none of them original, blend and clash." The "death" of the author raises the status of its counter entity, the reader, who becomes the,

> Place where this multiplicity is focused and that place is the reader, not, as was hitherto said, the author. The reader is the space on which all the quotations that make up a writing are inscribed without any of them being lost; a text's unity lies not in its origin but in its destination. Yet this destination cannot any longer be personal: the reader is without history, biography, psychology; he is simply that someone who holds together in a single field all the traces by which the written text is constituted (147).

The power of the reader who unites the text is even greater in hypertext than what Barthes envisioned. While the printed book is finalized by the writer, his editor and publisher, in hyper-literature even typography is not final and the reader can change it, for instance: font style and size, which causes a change in the book's layout and pagination thus the reader is gaining some sort of control over the text. This procedure along with the assembling of nodes raise the question of who is the real writer of the work – the one who paved the pathways or the one to choose and concretize it.

The first hyper-literature work is considered to be Michael Joyce's "*afternoon, a story*," written in 1986 as the "test file" for *Storyspace*.[3] This work and the ones that followed it in a flurry of some 15 years will be the object of this inquiry.

While some literature scholars[4] embraced the new format expectantly as early as 1984, others resisted it for diversified reasons,

---

[3] *Storyspace* is a hypertext writing environment that is considered the first software program specifically developed for creating, editing, and reading hypertext literature. Storyspace was first created by Michael Joyce, Jay David Bolter, and John B. Smith and then licensed to Mark Bernstein of Eastgate Systems, who has improved, extended, and maintained it. [Hayles, 2007].

[4] Michael Joyce, a writer and a scholar, met Jay David Bolter, a scholar of the classics that had a M.S. degree in Computer Science, at the Yale Artificial Intelligence Lab and they began work on *Storyspace* in 1984.

some of them quite general.[5] Birkets (1995), an American essayist and literary critic, fears, for instance, that the electronic age will cause language erosion, a flattening of historical perspectives and the waning of the private self (117-133). Tolva (1995), while referring to hypertext as a textual format, observes a similarity between the ancient fear that what is essentially a means of storage will not organize thought but stifle, disperse, or worst of all, control it and today's fear of hypertext. He claims,

> Today, faced with the possibility that huge matrices of scholarly data will be available to any neophyte with a computer terminal, modern critiques of text-based computing often reveal their rhetorical substratum, namely, an aversion to the democratizing potential of the digital word.

The resistances were of practical, technological, and personal reading habits. There was the technological difficulty of reading from the screen along with readers' long-standing habits of reading place and reading posture. The screen's resolution and brightness[6] caused a practical problem of reading (Landow 1997, 5). Computer display did

---

[5] Moulthrop, (1995), 55-77. Bernstein, 1999.

[6] The screen that is lighted from within brings to mind McLuhan's reference to the change that print brought about, "Scribal culture and Gothic architecture were both concerned with light through, not light on." (McLuhan1965 (1962), 105).

not achieve at that time the quality needed to enable the same ease of reading as printed documents, and although this "ease" is culturally obtained and internalized, it has, nevertheless, a strong hold on book lovers to this day. People reported miscellaneous physical ailments after a long reading session by the screen. Screen manufacturers' on-going attempts to improve monitors' quality is the best testimony for that problem. The variety of screen sizes and font sizes is also a testament to the uneasiness in reading from screen and to the manufacturers' attempts to overcome it. Much progress in the direction of improving the screen's quality has meanwhile been achieved with the introduction of LCD and other high-definition monitors and electronic ink that is applied by reading's gadgets like Amazon's Kindle and Barnes & Noble's Nook.

Second, there is the issue of people's reading habits that were, and still are – to read from paper if the amount of documents that are still being printed out is anything to go by.[7] The same goes for book

---

[7] "Paper consumption has been growing despite predictions that the spread of information technology, in particular the widespread use of computers, would lead to the paperless office. However, about 95 per cent of business information is still stored on paper, while the greater availability of copying machines, printers and fax machines, as well as personal computers and desktop printers, has produced an increase rather than a decrease in demand for paper." In *Australian Screen: Australia's audiovisual heritage online.* <http://aso.gov.au/titles/documentaries/paper-trail/clip1/>, 24.7.2016. See also Gladwell, 2002, 92-96. And Sellen, 2002. The future does not look any better: "Global production in the pulp, paper and publishing sector is expected to increase by

production, as Barbara Fister (2011) explains the present status of books and reading, in the description of her course "Books and Culture," and says that though everyone is talking and prophesizing about the extinction of books, "Yet over a million books were published in the US last year and the number of people using public libraries has doubled in the past decade."

Included in this habit of reading from paper is the customary reading site, or as Landow (1994, 4-5) calls it "the issue of portability." While a book can be read anywhere, at home, at work, on the bus, in bed and in the bathtub, hyper-literature required a computer of some kind, and usually a sit-down position at a desk and (before wireless) a proximity to electric and electronic sources. It does seem a trivial issue, yet most people do not read books while sitting at a table and those that do are complaining that it is uncomfortable. Portable reading devices[8] as well as wired environments solve this difficulty nowadays, and people are getting - and have gotten - used to reading from screens.

A psychological resistance to the electronic text arose out of the lack of the book's materiality, which helps the reader feel at home

---

77% from 1995 to 2020" (OECD Environmental Outlook. Paris: OECD, 2001, 215). See also Smith, 1997, 170.

[8] For a survey of these new "portable musings," see Birkerts, 1998. For second generation e-Books see Rosa Golijan, 2010. These gadgets, in their turn, brought other expectations. For example, see, Johnson, 2009.

with the work as a whole, a feeling of alienation caused by the lack of "object-hood." Meaning, the reader of a printed text can "feel and smell" the bounded volume as she can touch the page and even smear the letters, the physical marks on a physical surface; she can smell the scent of freshly printed pages, not yet explored by anyone, or the smell of old ones that were loved by many. The reader of hypertext can touch the screen, but not the text, the "page" nor the fonts.[9] Nevertheless the book is not merely a commodity and a material possession but has a legacy of manifold associations and cultural meanings.[10]

The electronic reader has to give up the psychology of passivity that is one of the reasons why people love reading. While hypertext

---

[9] The verbal difference between "letters" and "fonts" denotes the difference between the printed book and the electronic one.

[10] Johanna Drucker, [1994] addressing the subject of artists' books says: "The "Book" invokes the Book of Life, of Law, of Nature, Divine Purpose and Plan, and the whole other host of images resonating with theological purpose. The Book is at once an image of prescription, delineation, and control; of inscription and inclusion, expansion and exclusion; the repository of minute particulars of rules that prohibit and circumscribe the permitted, the transgressive, the sacred and the profane, the named and the unnamable, the written and the unspeakable. The book is the record of secret knowledge, the repository of ancient wisdom, the gift of insight and revelation, the testimony and confession. It is kept in the ark and burnt in the public square, sold in the supermarket and under the table, arrives in a plain brown wrapper or is bound in animal skins and gilded, is the site of the mundane and sacred, the secular and spectacular." (14)

needs a reader response or choices, the book can be used for reflexive leisure and relaxation. Virginia Woolf (1929) indicates in her article *The Love of Reading* that pleasure is the primary reason for reading,

> The true reason remains the inscrutable one - we get pleasure from reading. It is a complex pleasure and a difficult pleasure. It varies from age to age and book to book. But that pleasure is enough. Indeed that pleasure is so great that one cannot doubt that without it the world would be a far different and a far inferior place from what it is (274).

Spontaneous pleasure and relaxation reading is referred by Nell (1988, 6-50) as ludic reading: "Ludic reading (from the Latin ludo, I play: Stephenson, 1964) is therefore a useful descriptor of pleasure reading, reminding one that it is at root a play activity, and usually paratelic, that is, pursued for its own sake (Apter 1979)" (7).

The passive reading can cause absorption and entrancement that has the power to transport the reader from her real life into imaginary, interesting, better, and different worlds, which is called by researchers "transportation into a narrative-world."[11] This

---

[11] "Narratives have the power to sweep readers away to different places and times or to alternative universes. Readers of compelling stories may lose track of time, fail to observe events going on around them, and feel that they are completely immersed in the world of the narrative." (Green 2004, 247-266).

transportation can turn into addiction as Leavis (1932), in his research about the 18th century reading public says, "This, along with the information volunteered by a public librarian that many take out two or three novels by Edgar Wallace a week, and the only other books they borrow are 'Sapper's or other 'thrillers' suggests that the reading habit is now often a form of the drug habit" (7). He refers to reading also as 'mental relaxation' (50), which cannot refer to hypertext who needs a mental keenness since it, not only destroys linearity, but its segmented nature poses even a bigger challenge to print readers seeking relaxation. It takes quite an effort and a change of habits to assemble hypertext segments into a coherent narrative as a way of reading.

The parting from such an important, pleasurable and cultural icon is challenging and takes time. The electronic text is a virtual entity: it cannot be handled, it cannot be placed on a shelf, it cannot be gift-wrapped, and it has no touchable physical dimensions and no cultural heritage.

Finally, the physical and culturally embedded conventions of linearity of the book in face of hypertext's order – nonlinearity or multi-sequentiality – was new and unnatural and needed significant reading adaptations. This resistance toward hypertext is much more profound since it has to do with the way the brain functions. Readers are used to linear writing, reading and deciphering texts. Hypertext breaks away from this sequentiality and offers parallel reading paths that break away from linearity. Nevertheless, linearity is not a habit that can be modified, transformed or moderated; it is implanted as the procedure with which the normal human brain process information, as in reading.

The human brain has two hemispheres, the right one and the left one, which are mostly symmetrical in terms of function. One very important exception to this symmetry lies in information processing. While the right hemisphere is responsible for the spatial and creative cognition, the left is responsible for language and logic processing (Wong 2009, 16). The left hemisphere processes information in a "more slowly acting, linear, sequentially active, temporal (time-dependent) processes."[12] Thus, linearity is the normal manner in which the brain's language-system operates and any deviation is regarded as a disorder (as for instance, dyslexia is a reading disorder.) This biological phenomenon may be responsible, in part, for the reader's abstention and reluctance to change to the electronic format in general and to hypertext in particular.

In addition, there is a difference between women and men's brain functions[13] as "different segments of the brain are often

---

[12] Siegel, 1999, 179. Also, Shaywitz, 1998.

[13] The subject is the hot topic of neurology and psychiatry, so much that many popular yet scientific books are being written about this new-found difference. For instance, Louann Brizendine's two books: *The Female Brain*, 2006 and *The Male Brain*, 2011 or Carol Tavris' *The Mismeasure of Woman*, 1993 and authors like Judith Hall and Leslie Brody to mention only a few.

activated in males and females, even when both are exposed to identical external stimuli" (Ponder 1997). It is possible to pinpoint the difference since research indicates, "men and women do in fact have different structures and wiring in the brain, and men and women may also use their brains differently. In some cases, this may explain some of the stereotypes that we may not like to acknowledge about the genders" (Edmonds 2008). Hence, men process information linearly, vertical thinking, since that is the way the left hemisphere works and women process more laterally.[14] This scientific observation causes feminists to regard the way women communicate as different,

> [...] women have never depended on what appears before them. On the contrary, they have persisted in communicating with each other and their environment in ways which the patriarch has been unable to comprehend, and so has often been interpreted as mad, or hysterical. Now these lines of communication between women, long repressed, are returning in a technological form. Hypertext destroys linearity, allowing the user to enter the density of writing, and disrupting every conception of the straightforward narrative (Plant 1993, 12-17).

---

[14] The terms "vertical thinking" and "lateral thinking" originated by De Bono (1973). While the vertical thinking is the logical hierarchical one, the lateral thinking is the provocative, investigative and nonlinear way of thinking.

Taking into account that women are approximately 62% of fiction readers (Tepper 1998) it seemed that hyper-literature will become the "new fiction" of the 21th century. However, women are not going to be the torch carriers of hypertext since it needs a technological gadget for its presentation and it is a well-known fact that woman have more negative feelings toward technology than man (Broos 2005, also Imhof, 2007, Lindsay H., 2004). Thus they will prefer books over hyper-literature. Not only that, but there is an "Optional Thinking Deficiency" that can be found in some psychological syndromes and is measured by a special test: "The Optional Thinking Test (Platt & Spivak, 1977) is an outcome measure of interpersonal problem-solving ability that assesses respondents' capacity to generate alternative possibilities for overcoming real-life interpersonal problems" (McAuliffe 2008). Other narrative works like movies, prefer what Nitzan Ben Shaul (2012) calls "the close state of mind" over the "optional thinking" in order to provide the spectators with closure and by that "biasing our cognitive processes toward a reductive and selective attention to incoming data" (1). Hence, hypertext is leaning a-priory on a special manner of thinking that is not suitable to all, does not provide closure and is innovative.

Scholars' statements declaring the "death of the book"[15] escorted the emergence of the new medium. McLuhan, in *The*

---

[15] According to Evans, (1979) "the 1980s will see the book as we know it, and as our ancestors created and cherished it, begin a

Gutenberg Galaxy, described the changes that caused his world to become a print galaxy and remarks that, "Consistently, the twentieth century has worked to free itself from the conditions of passivity, which is to say, from the Gutenberg heritage itself" (278). For him the Gutenberg Galaxy dissolved in 1905 with the discovery of Einstein's curved space. Such remarks and his disposition towards electronic media combined well with Derrida's ideas in *Of Grammatology* (1976),

> The end of linear writing is indeed the end of the book, even if, even today, it is within the form of a book that new writings – literary or theoretical – allow themselves to be, for better or for worse, encased. It is less a question of confiding new writings to the envelope of a book than of finally reading what wrote itself between the lines in the volumes. That is why, beginning to write without the line, one begins also to reread past writing according to a different organization of space. If today the problem of reading occupies the forefront of science, it is because of this suspense between two ages of writing (86-87).

There is a big difference between the two thoughts. While McLuhan refers to the book as a technology, Derrida refers to the

---

slow but steady slide into oblivion." Also, Mims, 2010, Coover, 1992.

reading/writing process. His "death of the book" brings to mind Marinetti (1972, 130-134) and his futuristic manifest about the cinema, which was his generation new technology,

> The book, a wholly passéist means of preserving and communicating thought, has for a long time been fated to disappear like cathedrals, towers, crenellated walls, museums, and the pacifist ideal. The book, static companion of the sedentary, the nostalgic, the neutralist, cannot entertain or exalt the new Futurist generations intoxicated with revolutionary and bellicose dynamism (130).

Though the book survived this prophecy, the appearance of the hypertext format rekindled the idea of the death of the book, and it caught the imagination of writers and scholars and is still one of the topics discussed in literature history and criticism.[16] As late as 2011

---

[16] Some samples for the popularity of the subject: Mash, David. "The Death of the Book." In *Mars Hill Review*, Web document: <http://www.marshillreview.com/extracts/mash.shtm>, 24.7.2016. Neumann, Fritz-Wilhelm. "Information Society and the Text: The Predicament of Literary Culture in the Age of Electronic Communication." In *Erfurt Electronic Studies in English*, strategy statement no. 6 (1999). Kurzweil, Ray. *The Future of Libraries, Part 2: The End of Books*. KurzweilAI.net August 6, 2001 (1992). <http://www.kurzweilai.net/the-future-of-libraries-part-2-the-end-of-books>, 24.7.2016. Bolter, Jay David. *Degrees of Freedom*. Web document: <http://www.uv.es/~fores/programa/bolter_freedom.html>, 24.7.2016.

Ben Ehrenreich (2011) is still dealing with that subject, though ironically, and says,

> Pity the book. It's dead again. Last I checked, Googling "death of the book" produced 11.8 million matches. The day before it was 11.6 million. It's getting unseemly. Books were once such handsome things. Suddenly they seem clunky, heavy, almost fleshy in their gross materiality. Their pages grow brittle. Their ink fades. Their spines collapse. They are so pitiful, they might as well be human.

We have seen thus, that some new medium raises hope and expectations for the 'death of the book' as an information and communication medium as the futuristic movement declared with the introduction of the cinema, hence it is only expected that the same will happen with the introduction of the new format – hypertext.

Though this dissertation is written after the hypertext medium seems to have reached its peak in literature, we may not have yet the needed perspective to fully understand the changes that it might yet bring on, and therefore the inquiry into its specific characteristics and proclaimed innovative nature is still called for. McLuhan (1962)

Evans, Christopher., 1979. Price, Leah. "Introduction: Reading Matter." *PMLA* (2006). Also: <http://scholar.harvard.edu/leahprice/files/introduction_-_reading_matter.pdf>, 24.7.2016. Price refers to the birth of Amazon that computers and networks enabled and that sell books.

describes the changes engendered by the advent of print, and says, that only today, after five hundred years of use, we can fully appreciate and understand these changes. Febvre & Martin (1999) though writing in 1958 still regard print as "a relative newcomer in western society" (10). Perhaps the hypertext medium failed to acquire the central place that it was predicted to get in literature, nevertheless we should inquire into the works that were created at the time and confront them with the "great expectations" that the new medium generated.

This dissertation is neither about hypertext development nor its meaning as an innovative tool that will bring change into text writing, publishing, and reading. This study does not offer any theories, hypotheses or predictions, about the sociological and cultural role hypertext will have in the near future, meaning the 21st century, or the far future, in centuries to come. It is rather an attempt to take a historical view and look back at the 15 years in which hypertext literature thrived, academically and creatively, and analyze the works, which were produced in terms of their general and detailed innovative and radical departure from print literature, as was proclaimed for the genre. In 1986, Joyce wrote his *afternoon, a story*, so this will be the initial time border. The decision as to the exact time of hyper-literature's disappearance is problematic since there was no specific event that can be set as a final date. Hyper-literature dissolved into the academic discourse both analytically and creatively, and it was the gaming community,[17] which adopted it in the beginning of the 21st century thus removing it away from literary discourse.

This inquiry will therefore try to examine the many predictions and various hypotheses, proclaimed by researchers and critics alike, which regarded hypertext as a mean for change in literature poetics. Many are the books dealing with hypertext's origin, its potential, and its future contribution to the cultural development of humanity.[18] However, there is no comparative analysis of the poetics of hypertext literary works that ascertains whether those great expectations were realized in the literary domain. Thus, this dissertation will use a comparative methodology to examine and compare a broad front of poetic values and means of hypertext literary works and print literature works. The analyses and comparison will be the basis for determining whether the hypertext format had a potential for a radical revolutionary change, as many researchers seem to prophesize and anticipate in literature's history.

---

[17] Hypertext did not vanish. It can still be found on the Internet, but it lost focus of the academic research. It is assumable that the new reading gadgets, which allow for a comfortable digital-reading and for links' activation while reading, will bring the issue of hyper-literature into academic attention again. Researchers regard computer games as the format's successor. See Jones, 2009, 264–272. Tosca, 2003. Jones, 1997.

[18] Such as Yellowlees Douglas, 2000. Murray, 1999. Aarseth, 1997. Birkerts, 1995. Lanham, 1994. Landow, 1997. Nelson, 1992. McKnight et al., 1991. Bolter, 1991. Ryan, 1991.

The novelty of the hypertext medium turned the term 'hypertext' into a buzzword. It was used in many different contexts and had many different definitions – a form, an approach, a technique, a style, a system, a way of writing – so much so that a poetic definition is called for in order to delimit the phenomenon on the one side, and to distinguish it from other non-literary objects on the other side. Thus, my first chapter, after this introduction, will be a short survey of hypertext's origin and its various definitions including an operative definition that will be used in this work.

Standing between the new electronic era and the conclusion perhaps of print age we are in the midst of a cultural collision, thus we are prone to generalization. Those general prospects and expectations are the issue of the second chapter, respectively called *Great Expectations*. McLuhan sees generalization as an advantage, "Another basic advantage of cultural clash and transition is that people on the frontier between different modes of experience develop a great power of generalization" (142). Thus, I will examine those generalizations interlaced with expectations that hyper-literature gave rise to from two points of view in order to figure out whether they are realistic or at least plausible. The first point stems from hypertext's digital nature and the second arises from the linkage device, though it is present, in a form, in print literature as well.[19] Yet, in the hypertext

---

[19] Nelson's (1992) remarks about the Talmud: "This is an extraordinary hypertext, a body of accumulated comment and controversy, mostly on the Torah (the Hebrew Old

medium, the link feels natural, while in print it feels incongruous and out of the ordinary – a disturbance to the natural order of reading.

All the following chapters after "great expectations," will deal with hyper- literature and compare it with print literature in order to examine if hypertext's poetics, as it is embodied in the works themselves, realize those expectations. This comparison will be the basis for concluding if this new 'literature' is actually new: is it a significant novelty or maybe it is only an expansion of the experimental printed literary tradition,[20] written in an electronic

---

Testament) and on life in general, by scholars of old. It has been accreted over centuries with commentaries on commentaries. This hypertext is a fundamental document of Jewish religion and culture, and the Talmudic scholar is one who knows many of its pathways" 1/16. Nelson refers to the Talmud as a printed hypertext because of the structure of the Talmudic page - blocks of commentary arranged in concentric rectangles around the text itself. Landow (1997, 80- 81) regards allusion in printed literature as a way to turn print into hypertext, since allusion is a linkage device among texts, which cancels the text's borders as in hypertext.

[20] For instance, Marc Saporta's *Composition No 1* which is actually a deck of cards which could be shuffled to produce different texts or Raymond Queneau's *Cent mille milliards de poems*, where by combining strips of papers the reader creates the sonnets. Milorad Pavić *Dictionary of the Khazars* which is a lexicon novel based on the Khazars' conversion to Judaism, yet this book is fictional and as Pavić writes in the introduction, "No chronology will be observed here, nor is one necessary. Hence each reader will put together the book for himself, as in a game of dominoes or cards, and, as with a mirror, he will get out of this dictionary as much as he puts into it, for you [...] cannot get more out of the truth than what you put into it" (13).

medium? How does the physical breakage of the text into nodes affect the linear structure of the text, the literary work, the process of reading and the relations between author and reader? Is there a compensation mechanism for this tearing apart (segmenting) of the literary work, and if so, what devices make up this compensation?

The third chapter inspects the new tools, with which the hypertext medium furnishes the reader and will question the supposition that the digital medium, in which hypertext literature is written, is supposed to change textual norms and navigation and orientation tools.

One of the major topics that hypertext theorist of computer science as well as authors and literature scholars expected, hoped for and tried to foresee is the effects and affects of hypertext's fragmented nature. The fourth chapter queries the assumption that hypertext nature is fragmented, by defining fragmentation in relation to segmentation as they are in hypertext literature in comparison with print literature. The embodiment of the terms will be studied in various levels; at the typographical level, the textual levels – the volume's, the chapter's and the paragraph's – and narrative ones like the structure of episodes, the temporal organization, multi points of view, interceptive events etc.

The fifth chapter will query hypertext's narrative structure as a 'whole', how does it begin, where is it leading to, and how does it end. Scholars' argument that in hypertext there is no beginning and no end will be inspected in fact, again in comparison with print literature.

Hypertext, whether as an authorial tool or as a collaborative one (author-reader), is a method for combing segments. Hypertext's main combinatorial device is the linkage, which creates the path and the notion of a network. The use of a three-dimensional object, the network, in order to describe a two-dimensional object inevitably creates numerous concepts for different scholars. This combinatorial device and its outcome – the path and the 'network' – will be the main issue of the sixth chapter, which will compare it in hypertext literature and in print literature.

In the concluding chapter, I will sum up the findings of previous chapters, while trying to answer the main question of this study: Was the new medium a revolutionary format for literature? Did it offer a new set of poetic devices and means that changed the experience of "reading" (consuming) a story in a meaningful way? Did it fulfill the great expectations it raised, for instance, did it change the relations between reader and author?

The research studies hypertext works from the beginning of the medium in 1986 to 2000. Hyper-literature was written mainly in two ways; A dedicated application, named *Storyspace*, created by Eastgate System Inc., which slogan is "we create new hypertext technologies and publish serious hypertext, fiction and non-fiction: **serious, interactive writing**." The other way is by writing web hyper-literature using the internet standard language named HTML. One of the biggest differences between those two methods is that there are no navigation tools like maps or lists of nodes on the Internet, yet it is more graphical.

Thus, the corpus refers to the early electronic literary hypertexts, Joyce's *after noon, a story* (1986) and Moulthrop's *Victory Garden* (1991), later works like Larsen's *Samplers* (1997). Those works were written with *Storyspace* application. One of the latest - Coverley's *Califia* (2000), was written with *Toolbook* application.[21] The study refers also to web hypertexts like Geoff Rymam *253* (1996) and Moulthrop's *Hegirascope* (1997 [1995]). The study leans heavily on Moulthrop's hypertext *Victory Garden*, which was first written in *Hypercard*,[22] as an etude for checking hypertexts potential as a literary machine. The work is quite huge in comparison with the other works. It contains 993 nodes and 2,804 links thus it presents wide possibilities for poetic observation and analysis.[23]

These works were chosen because they represent the whole spectrum of possibilities in hyper-literature. First, they represent the

---

[21] *ToolBook* was a multimedia authoring system created by Asymetrix that provides an object-oriented environment for developing Windows applications.

[22] *Hypercard* is an application program that was created by Apple, where each node is a card.

[23] While *afternoon, a story* holds "only" 539 nodes and 956 links.

main two ways to create hyper-literature: by HTML language or by a dedicated application: *ToolBook* and *Stoyspace*. I tried to present the whole timeline of hyper-literature: Two of the works present the beginning of hyper-literature, and one presents its end. Most of the works are dated from 1995-7, the format's peak. Since hyper-literature is mostly in novel length, one work differs, Larsen's *Samplers*, and is a collection of short stories. I chose works that were written by male and female writers alike.

Some notes regarding methods of reference and citations:

(1) In all the works that were written with the *Storyspace* application the node's label enables the reader to locate it through the search utility found in the software's menus. Nodes' names are in Italics and when functioning as a reference it is encased in square brackets. The *ToolBook* application does not allow for any search thus it is referred to with the nodes name and the section in which it resides. Internet hypertexts are referenced by their file name.

(2) I kept the original typography of citations. Thus, if not indicated otherwise, the use of Italics or Bold letters is in the original.

(3) I decided to refer to the reader as "she" and to the author as "he" in order to equalize the use of gender in the work. There are no hidden or overt motives to that decision and each role can be played by any species.

1   What is Hypertext?

In this chapter, I will briefly sketch the origin of hypertext[24] as an electronic medium and analyze some of its most prevalent definitions in computer science and literary study, with their different methodologies. I will define and explain some of the main technological terms and concepts that are relevant to hypertext, such as *system*, *information*, and *network*, as they were perceived in both computer science and poetics. Equipped with these terms, I will tackle communication theory as was practiced in both disciplines. Finally, the chapter will not be complete without thoroughly discussing Aarseth's research *Cybertext* that attempts to distinguish between print literature and the electronic text through a typology of textual communication.

My survey of hypertext's history and its definitions is primarily intended to establish a definition of hypertext, which will serve as a basis for this study.

---

[24] The discussion of hypertext origin will not be a full survey of hypertext development, but a brief description of its origin and the two different approaches underlying it.

1.1 Hypertext's Cradle

Vannevar Bush is traditionally considered[25] the first to envision hypertext, although he did not call it by its present name. Bush was Director of the Office of Scientific Research and Development of the USA and, during the Second World War, coordinated the activities of some six thousand leading American scientists involved in the application of science to warfare. His most significant article "As We May Think," published in the July 1945 issue of *The Atlantic Monthly*, is regarded by all hypertext scholars[26] as the prediction of the Internet in general and hypertext in particular. In this article, written after the Second World War, Bush presents a new challenge to scientists. He saw as a crucial issue the problem of the overflow of knowledge, nowadays called "the explosion of information," resulting in the problem of the availability (or unavailability) of data and scholarship to researchers. The overflow of information was the result of transformations in the Academy's domain. Universities' role turned from being exclusive qualification centers into research organizations that were available to all. The academic instruction shifted too, from "laborious teaching and recitation to primary research and publication" (370).[27] Academic need to publish created academic

---

[25] Nyce, 1991.

[26] Joyce 2000, 213-238. Yellowlees 2000, 23-25. Landow 1997, 7. Bolter 1991, 23-24.

[27] Rüegg, 2004. Also, Konrad, 1983. Rudy, 1984.

journals, series of monographs and established the universities presses. These transformations of the 19th century along with the growing specifications of academic subjects were the causes for the excess of information that Bush is referring to.

Bush provides an example of the problem of getting access to scholarly records:

> Mendel's concept of the laws of genetics was lost to the world for a generation because his publication did not reach the few who were capable of grasping and extending it; and this sort of catastrophe is undoubtedly being repeated all about us, as truly significant attainments become lost in the mass of the inconsequential.

Namely Bush points at the problem of dissemination on the one hand ("did not reach" in the sense of distribution) and the problem of overflow which drowns the significant ("mass of the inconsequential") on the other hand.

In response, Bush suggested a device, which he called "memex" – a memory extender. His memory extender brings to mind Plato's dialogue, Phaedrus, in which Socrates discusses with Phaedrus the invention of writing and relates an ancient tale about the Egyptian god Theuth who invented, among other things, the alphabet and writing. Presenting his inventions to Ammon, king of Egypt, the god says it "will make the Egyptians wiser and give them better memories; it is a specific both for the memory and for the wit" (2010, 69). Nevertheless, Ammon, while praising his other inventions, answered:

> This discovery of yours will create forgetfulness in the learners' souls, because they will not use their memories; they will trust to the external written characters and not remember of themselves.

Indeed, the ability to write and save information (to store in writing) frees the memory, loosens its requisiteness as a way of controlling information, and reduces the criticality of the individual agent that is an expert, as a mediator and a teacher (mnemotechnique) (Yates, 1966).

However, before the digital era, people with phenomenal memory were reputed with a desirable competence for research and the production of new knowledge. Writing, and later on print, procreated a wealth / flooding / overflow of texts that became inaccessible in their entirety, unsorted, and uncategorized in any way thus preventing their efficient utilization by scholars and scientists, as well as by the general readers.

In the beginning of academic research, scholars' knowledge bases (libraries, private documents and copied documents) were regarded as a private treasure and the learning place was the scholars' private library and manuscript collections (Grafton, 1997. See for instance p. 113, where Grafton refers to the keeper of the Royal Library behavior towards a young researcher). Only in the end of the nineteenth century, primary sources became available to everyone.[28]

The dramatic increase in information and knowledge in the 20th century made such and even institutional libraries an inadequate tool. Bush is looking for an additional device for storing and sorting knowledge, one that may be consulted with speed, flexibility and universality. Its main advantage should be the associative linkage among items, in the same way that the human mind operates "by association. With one item in its grasp, it snaps instantly to the next that is suggested by the association of thoughts, in accordance with some intricate **web** of trails carried by the cells of the brain."

In Bush's opinion, a "web of trails" that will join items together will make a storage system capable of presenting and accessing knowledge. Through it,

> numerous items [...] can be reviewed in turn, rapidly
> or slowly, by deflecting a lever like that used for

---

[28] Grafton's description of the change: "In the late nineteenth and twentieth centuries, finally, the sources needed to produce footnotes became readily accessible to young men – and women – who did not come from families rich enough to provide them with private research libraries. The archives of the major European states opened reading rooms where scholars could work regularly, making all – or almost all – of their documents available to accredited readers. National libraries, similarly, made the published collections of primary sources available in their domed, public reading rooms to men and women of letters who would never have had the money or the social credentials to use them in the private libraries of previous centuries" 226.

turning the pages of a book. It is exactly as though the physical items had been gathered together to form a new book. It is more than this, for any item can be joined into numerous trails.

Bush's ideas were applied in the 1960's by two American researchers working independently of each other: Ted Nelson, who, in 1965, coined the term "hypertext" (Nielsen 1995, 37) and Douglas Engelbart, nowadays credited with inventing of "word processing," "screen windows," the mouse as a pointing device, E-mail, and many other digital technological inventions (Myers 1998, 44-54).

Nelson (1992)[29] regarded himself as the realizer of Bush's ideas: "I say Bush was right, and so this book describes a new electronic form of the memex, and offers it to the world" (1/5). His book sketches the ideas that led him to develop *Xanadu*, a hypertext system, whose main use is indicated by the book's title, *Literary Machines*, or "as an authorial tool." He defines hypertext as, *"non-sequential writing* -- text that branches and allows choices to the reader, best read at an interactive screen" (0/2). This was a huge revolution in the

---

[29] Nelson, 1992. The book's page numbering follows 'User manuals' standards of the computer industry. This pagination is meant to facilitate and reduce costs of revisions by allowing for a revision of one chapter without disrupting the whole numbering of the book's units. The chapters are numbered sequentially, starting with chapter zero, and so are pages within chapters, though they each start with page number one. Hence, the sign (1/15) refers to chapter one, page 15.

concept of reading/writing texts. He wanted to "unify and organize in the *right* way, so as to clarify and simplify our computer and working lives, and indeed to bring literature, science, art and civilization to new heights of understanding" (0/4).

Nelson distinguishes two types of "hypertext" according to the textual source. The first is the *chunk style hypertext*, where one source is cut up into sections, connected by a multiple choice-choosing device:

> The most obvious [nonsequential form] is that which simply connects chunks of text by alternative choices - we may call these links, of which more later - presented to the user. I call this simply chunk style hypertext. The user, or reader, moves through it by reading one chunk, then choosing the next (1/15).

The second style of hypertext, which he calls "windowing style hypertext," is the linking of different sources. It involves a

> compound text, where materials are viewed and combined with others. (This term too has recently become common.) A good way of visualizing this is as a set of windows to original materials from the compound texts themselves. Thus, I prefer to call this windowing text (1/15-16).

These hypertext styles enable non-linear associative composing (reading and writing) of text. Nelson thinks that it is unfortunate that for thousands of years people turned their ideas into a linear sequence, unnatural to the thinking processes. A true disciple of Bush, he regards hypertext as a way to realize the association of ideas in writing:

> The structure of ideas is never sequential; and indeed, our thought processes are not very sequential either. True, only a few thoughts at a time pass across the central screen of the mind; but as you consider a thing, your thoughts crisscross it constantly, reviewing first one connection, then another (1/16).

Nelson's words recall Wittgenstein's (1968) preface to his *Philosophical Investigations*, where he complains that the attempt to "force" the spatial associative thoughts into a linear order "crippled" them:

> But the essential thing was that the thoughts should proceed from one subject to another in a natural order and without breaks. [...] After several unsuccessful attempts to weld my results together into such a whole, I realized that I should never succeed. [...] My thoughts were soon crippled if I tried to force them on in any simple direction against their natural inclination (vii).

He was concerned with thoughts' "natural inclinations," which needed a new method for linking/combining. Not finding it anywhere, Wittgenstein founded a segmented/fragmented new genre of writing. Wittgenstein's *Philosophical Investigations* is written in short numbered segments, as Shawver explains,

> He often begins an aphorism with a quoted passage. For example, he begins the first aphorism with a quotation from Augustine. Most quoted passages are not actual quotes, however, but rather Wittgenstein's construction of a kind of interlocutor. This interlocutor might be thought of in terms of Augustine, Plato, characters in Plato, Bertrand Russell or even early Wittgenstein, or perhaps just a vague composite of these various figures. At any rate, this voice (and it is not always in quotes) represents the problem that Wittgenstein tries to think through. I will call this the voice of tradition and symbolize it at times as "T".
>
> It is useful to think of there being two additional voices. One is the voice that discovers perplexities or aporia. This voice is often, but not always, introduced with a dash and it often, but again not always, begins with the word "But". I will call this the voice of aporia and symbolize it at times as "A".
>
> Then, there is a third voice in which Wittgenstein makes an incisive point in the face of the tradition

and aporia. Wittgenstein wanted this voice to be completely clear. I will symbolize it at times as "C".

Nelson's main concern with hypertext is thus as a tool for personal writing. The hypertext system allows the associative connection of ideas, whether by connecting *chunks* of text or by presenting multiple sources in multiple windows. He regards footnotes as a possible way for associative writing in print. Thus, for him, the Talmud is the only printed book that is not sequential:

> [The Talmud is] an extraordinary hypertext, a body of accumulated comment and controversy, mostly on the Torah [...]. It has been accreted over centuries with commentaries. This hypertext is a fundamental document of Jewish religion and culture, and the Talmudic scholar is one who knows many of its pathways (1/16).

The Talmud, for Nelson, is like a screen with multiple windows. The description of it, having "accreted over centuries with commentaries," can be interpreted as a reference to blocks of commentaries that were added along generations, each in its own corner, or place, which is similar to the look and function of a window on the screen.

The Talmud is a very old example of the marginalia tradition that provides authors and readers with a way of writing personal comments, notes and bibliographical material linked to the main text. The mass practice of marginalia started at the time of the scrolls and continues to this day, as Jackson (2001) remarks,

> Readers continue to this day to do what readers did in the Middle Ages, besides doing much more in the way of recording individual impression. They mark up their books as a way of learning and remembering what they contain, and improve them by correcting errors and adding useful relevant information (51).

The marginalia practice was and still is a way for personal multi-voices in print tradition that allows for such a level of personal writing that it can be used as a method of revenge.

Engelbart (1968) reached a similar technological solution, the *NLS* system, which stands for "oNLine System" (later renamed as AUGMENT) and is a hypermedia—groupware system that facilitated the creation of digital libraries and storage and retrieval of electronic documents as a group communication tool,

> In other words we are concentrating fully upon reaching the point where we can do all of our work on line--placing in computer store all of our specifications, plans, designs, programs, documentation, reports, memos, bibliography and reference notes, etc., and doing all of our scratch work, planning, designing, debugging, etc., and a

good deal of our intercommunication, via the consoles.

Engelbart, too, read Bush's article, but he was more influenced by Benjamin Whorf's letter written in 1927 yet not published until 1956. Whorf addressed Dr. English, who just published a dictionary of psychological terms, and asked for his help in finding a term:

> [A term] to denote a kind of connection or relation, approximation, closeness, allied character, between ideas. The only psychological term I know of that expresses connection between ideas is "association",[30] but this has quite a definite meaning and one that will not do for the meaning I have in mind. The "connection" of ideas, as I call it in the absence of any other term, is quite another thing from the "association" of ideas. In making experiments on the connecting of ideas, it is necessary to eliminate the "associations", which have an accidental character not possessed by the "connections" (35).

Whorf wants to differentiate between "connection" and "association." The second involves a kind of personal link, not necessarily intelligible to everyone, "accidental" and free of logic,

---

[30] In the continuum of the letter, Whorf refers to "free association" a method that was developed by Freud as a replacement for hypnosis. See his direct reference - 71.

reason and causality, while the first is "important from a linguistic standpoint because it is bound up with the communication of ideas" (36). The term "communication" attests to the socio-collective and inter-personal character of the idea. The connection pertains "to the social or collective experience which is embodied in the common linguistic stock of concepts" (36). Connection is a way of communication hence it is bounded and conditioned by collective knowledge base, while association is a personal process.

Engelbart (1983) describes his system, AUGMENT, and the goals he seeks to achieve as follows:

> The architecture and general character of AUGMENT were directly oriented toward augmenting the capability of humans to deal with tough knowledge work and to process effectively the large volumes of information that burden the modern office. An explicit sub-goal was to support close, active collaboration among groups of workers (1).

The difference between the two pioneers is summarized by Bardini (1997) concisely and accurately:

> For Nelson, hypertext is a fundamental tool for individual creativity, and for Engelbart, hypertext is a necessary capability of a system designed to improve communication. These two alternatives parallel two different conceptions of the user, seen

either as a creative individual or as a member of a community in a human organization.

There were thus two different approaches, two points of view, indeed two cultures at the basis of hypertext. Ted Nelson and his *Xanadu* Project, which aimed to facilitate individual nonsequential literary writing, represent the first approach. Douglas Engelbart and his *oNLine System* represent the second, which regarded hypertext as a tool for group collaboration and dissemination. The opposition between "association" and "connection" mirrors the difference between these two projects as two trends[31] of future hypertext systems.[32]

1.2 *Definitions of Hypertext*

Nelson and Engelbart came up with the same technological apparatus in spite of their two polar conceptual starting points. This

---

[31] See also McKnight et al. 1991, 8-9, who regard Bush's idea of hypertext as a third approach, point of view, to hypertext, which is natural, modeling the mind intuitive tool.

[32] For an informal fascinating meeting between Engelbart and Nelson see Howard Rheingold's video: *Doug Engelbart & Ted Nelson come to dinner*, <https://www.youtube.com/watch?v=zCLCIw-HSJc>, 24.7.2016.

was a new digital medium that enables the linking of text, or texts, in an easy way, which allows for many different readings, each according to a different concept, focus, or point-of-view.

Gygi, in her article, "Recognizing the symptoms of hypertext" (1990), summarizes hypertext's definitions by classifying them into two groups; group I holds the "broad-spectrum" definitions, found in the popular press, advertising and marketing, and group II, the "more clinical variety," which is common in technical journals and in research endeavoring to develop computer-supported hypertext systems.

The "broad-spectrum" definitions refer mainly to hypertext's a-linear structure since it is hypertext's most obvious trait from the user's point of view,

> Hypertext works by association rather than indexing.
> Hypertext is a format for nonsequential representation of ideas.
> Hypertext is the abolition of the traditional, linear approach to information display and processing.
>
> Hypertext is nonlinear and dynamic.
> In hypertext, content is not bound by structure and organization (282).

The definitions of the "more clinical variety" present the viewpoint of computer-science scholars and vary according to the writer's field of interest. In the late 1980's computer-science researchers defined the new textual medium - hypertext - in ways such as,

> Hypertext is: 1) a **form** of electronic document; 2) an **approach** to information management in which data is stored in a network of nodes and links." (Smith & Weiss 1988, 816, emphasis is mine)

> "Hypertext connotes a **technique** for organizing textual information in a complex, nonlinear way to facilitate the rapid exploration of large bodies of knowledge (Weiland & Shneiderman 1988, 23, emphasis is mine).

These definitions refer to hypertext as a form, an approach, a technique, or in other words, as a new means of writing, presenting, and publishing textual information. They take for granted the a-linearity of hypertext ("network" refers to this aspect) and they allude to the collaborative and communal aspect by using terms such as "information management" and "organizing."

Hypertext developers as well, regard hypertext as a style for building information systems, which allow linking, presenting, and managing information in a new way. For instance, Frank Halasz was one of the team that developed the *NoteCard* hypertext system (1988). *NoteCard* was a network-based information-structuring tool. The nodes were called 'cards' and contained pieces of text, graphics, etc.

and were connected by typed links. Its strength was its tailoring ability, "the capacity for users to extend the system in ways appropriate for their application and personal style" (Randall, 40). Halasz broadens hypertext definition to include sound, image and animation - hypermedia in general. For him,

> Hypermedia is a **style** of building **systems** for information representation and management around a network of nodes connected together by typed links (Halasz, 836, emphasis is mine).

Nicole Yankelovich and her team developed (1988) a hypertext system called *Intermedia* that was first used for an English course at Brown University. Their definition of hypertext is pragmatic and refers to the system's potential:

> Hypertext system allows authors or groups of authors to link information together, create paths through a body of related material, annotate existing texts, and create notes that direct readers to either bibliographic data or the body of the referenced text (81).

Jakob Nielsen defines hypertext (1990) as nonsequential writing that gives its reader the feeling of a free reading path:

> Hypertext is non-sequential writing: a directed graph, where each node contains some amount of text or other information. [...] True hypertext should

also make users feel that they can move freely through the information according to their own needs (298).

Computer-oriented definitions regard hypertext as a style, a form, an approach, a technique, a structure, a digital presentational tool, and a means for linking information by a single user or a group of users or, for non-sequential writing that allows the reader free navigation. The multiple definitions and the variety of attitudes attest to the fluidity of the concept and to its wide usages, but they do not blur its basic nature of an electronic reading/writing medium that allows for connecting various kinds of media in an interactive and non-linear way.

While computer researchers and system developers take for granted hypertext's dependency on computers, literature researchers are used to regard the medium of their study as print, since till that point it was the main medium for writing, reading and publication. Thus, literature-oriented definitions primarily refer to hypertext's electronic nature, which requires a computer as an intermediate between the text and its display. For instance, Bukatman (1995), who compares hypertext with Virtual Reality,[33] defines both as "interface

---

[33] Virtual Reality is "a computer simulation that creates an image of a world that appears to our senses in much the same way we perceive the real world, or "physical" reality. In order to convince the brain that the synthetic world is authentic, the computer simulation monitors the movements of the participant and adjusts the sensory displays in a manner that

50

technologies" since the information stored on a computer is digitally coded and unavailable to the user, unless there is an interface that decodes the code into a material intelligible to human beings, like text, image, sound, 3D space etc. Thus, hypertext and Virtual Reality function as the intermediate, the decoder, between the user and the computer. He defines hypertext as, "texts that utilize non-linear (or multi-linear) structures through their composition and display on computer terminals," thus emphasizing, again, hypertext's dependence on the computer. Bukatman argues that hypertext, though it is entirely based on "the sign," is thought to be a space as well, for writing and reading.

Stuart Moulthrop, not only a scholar of hypermedia and communication but a hypertext author as well, also stresses hypertext's dependence on computers, while defining it as "a scheme for producing articulated, multi-dimensional writing by means of interactive computer systems" (1997). In an earlier essay (1989), Moulthrop[34] established a resemblance between hypertext and the structure of an encyclopedia, in order to clarify what hypertext is:

---

gives the feeling of being immersed or being present in the simulation. Concisely, virtual reality is a means of letting participants physically engage in some simulated environment that is distinct from their physical reality" Craig et al. 2009, 1.

[34] Moulthrop was an artist and a scholar in the Department of English

of the University of Wisconsin-Milwaukee and the author of hypertexts, *Victory Garden* (1991), *Hegirascope* - a web

A collection of writings through which the reader is
free to move in almost any sequence. But unlike a
printed encyclopedia, the hypertext does not come
to the reader with a predefined structure. The
'articles' in a hypertext are not arranged by title or
subject; instead each passage contains links or
reference markers that point toward other passages.

All the various definitions are based on the two main
approaches[35] to hypertext (Nelson and Engelbart), which are latent in
hypertext's foundations in the 1940's. Computer-oriented definitions,
for instance Yankelovich who refers to "authors or groups of authors,"
regard hypertext as a technique for communication and a tool for
collaborative work as Engelbart envisioned hypertext. Literature-
oriented definitions as seen in the Nielsen and Bukatman citations

hypertext (1997), "Reagan Library" (1999), "Pax" (2003),
"Deep Surface" (2007), "Under Language" (2008) and many
articles about digital literature and communication. See his
latest website
<https://pantherfile.uwm.edu/moulthro/index.htm>,
24.7.2016.

[35] Bardini said that "Engelbart's and Nelson's visions of hypertext
reveal two cultures deeply embedded in the technology, but
organized on the same operating principle. Their perspectives
take two views on the user: An individual or a member of a
community. Engelbart and Nelson are the prophets of these
two trends deeply intertwined and absolutely indivisible, for
which each of us is defined as a potential user, a class in itself
or a member of an entity of greater importance. Both of them
address the question of our relationship to the act of creation
from diametrically--and therefore complementary and
irremediably opposite, points of view."

foreground hypertext's non-sequential nature, thus referring to hypertext as a writing/reading method, after Nelson.

1.3 Hypertext's Main Terms

The key words of the computer-oriented definitions are *system*, *information*, and *network*. As hypertext reflects and combines two fields of academic interest I will somewhat elaborate on these terms from both fields' points of view, though this work is about literature. I will start with the term system. A quick look at the lexical definitions of the term *system* in OED reveals that each field defines the term somewhat differently, as Ackoff (1971) explains:

> Despite the importance of systems concepts and the attention that they have received and are receiving, we do not yet have a unified or integrated set (i.e., a system) of such concepts. Different terms are used to refer to the same thing and the same term is used to refer to different things. This state is aggravated by the fact that the literature of systems research is widely dispersed and is therefore difficult to track. Researchers in a wide variety of disciplines and interdisciplines are contributing to the conceptual development of the systems sciences but these

contributions are not as interactive and additive as
they might be (661).

By its lexical and general meaning according to the OED a
system is "an organized or connected group of objects." The Merriam-
Webster dictionary defines system as "a regularly interacting or
interdependent groups of items forming a unified whole." Hence, a
system is a group of items (more than one) that are connected
somehow to each other. The concept of "system" was introduced to
the scientific world by von Bertalanffy (1950) in response to past
centuries, where:

> [...] science tried to explain phenomena by reducing
> them to an interplay of elementary units which could
> be investigated independently of each other. In
> contemporary modern science, we find in all fields
> conceptions of what is rather vaguely termed
> 'wholeness' (134).

This 'wholeness,' which is found in many diverse fields, such
as psychology, environment, biology etc. has collective traits: "There
exist therefore *general system laws* which apply to any system of a
certain type, irrespective of the particular properties of the system or
the elements involved" (138). Von Bertalanffy called

> To postulate a new basic scientific discipline which
> we call General System Theory. It is a
> logicomathematical field, the subject matter of
> which is the formulation and deduction of those

principles which are valid for 'systems' in general. There are principles which apply to systems in general, whatever the nature of their component elements or the relations or 'forces' between them (139).

System theory that was formalized by von Bertalanffy since 1950 has many types, some of them referring to their field of reference like "Developmental Systems Theory and psychology." There are general types like a 'closed system', which is self-sufficient and there is an 'open system' that interact with other systems. There is a 'dynamical system' and there is a 'static system' etc.[36]

Both approaches to system theory, poetics and computer science, use the term *system* as denoting connected items. Literature-oriented definitions refer to linguistic and semantic systems for instance, "the English language itself is a system, consisting of syntactic, phonological, and semantic systems, which in turn contain other systems (e.g. the vowel and consonant systems)" (Chalker, 1998). Hence, literature is a polysystem, a system composed of various internal systems like the linguistic system, the prosodic system, the semiotic system etc. (Even-Zohar, 1979).

The computer-oriented citations refer to computer systems and hypertext software. In computer science, the computer itself is

---

[36] For other disciplines' points of view and general systems theory see: Ackoff, 2006. Bailey, 1994. Laszlo, 1996.

regarded as a hardware system, which functions with the aid of an operating system and other software systems. Therefore there is no real difference between the two fields' conception of *system*, but naturally, each refers to the system's parts according to its area of interest. Hypertext combines the poetic parts along with the computational parts to create a new polysystem.

The term *information* is also in use by the two disciplines, computer science and poetics. While we are used to think of information as facts or data, information theory, as developed by Claude Shannon (1948), does not refer to the message's meaning or content, but to the message as a collection of signals and signifiers, with no regard to its meaning. In his most famous article "A Mathematical Theory of Communication," published in 1948, but still the basis for communication theory[37] at large and specifically for the Internet, Shannon says:

> The fundamental problem of communication is that of reproducing at one point either exactly or approximately a message selected at another point. Frequently the messages have meaning; that is they

---

[37] Under the name "Communication Theory" one can find many traditions and much debate, so much so that Robert Craig (1999) wrote an essay that summarizes the different approaches which he finds "mutually relevant" and questions whether they are not ripe to make up "an identifiable field of study." See also its rich bibliography that sums the research on the subject.

> refer to or are correlated according to some system with certain physical or conceptual entities. These semantic aspects of communication are irrelevant to the engineering problem (379).

The 'engineering problem,' as Shannon calls it, refers to five obligatory 'players' in a communication system: an information source, a transmitter, a channel, a receiver, and a destination source. The information source, which is responsible for the beginning of the process, produces a message or sequence of messages to be communicated to the receiving terminal, which is the destination source. The transmitter operates on the message in order to produce a signal suitable for transmission over the channel. The channel is merely the medium used to transmit the signal from transmitter to receiver like a telephone line, a light ray, air etc. The receiver ordinarily performs the inverse operation of that done by the transmitter, reconstructing the message from the signal. The destination is the person (or thing) for which the message is intended signifying the end of the process, in both meanings of the word, as the goal of the communication and as its termination point.[38]

The signal, which is the transmitted entity, the message, is not obligatory for a communication system though it is essential for a communication process. Shannon regards information as something

---

[38] This model was copied into literature research by many literary scholars most notable is Seymour Chatman 1980.

that is transmitted over a channel, mainly the phone lines on which he was working at Bell Labs. Thus, information is the signal and not semantic content, which may be verbal objects, light, sound etc. This concept of the signal explains why for Shannon the semantic aspect of meaning is irrelevant.

The same is true in the process of communication between two computers via a phone line, for instance, where the sender (a computer) transmits digital signs. The phone line, which functions as the channel, cannot transfer digital signs therefore a modem (modulator) is needed to code the digital signals into tones. The phone line transmits the tones to the addressee (a computer), where another modem (demodulator) decodes the tonal signals into digital ones, which the computers can receive. See Shannon's schematic communication process in Figure 1.

The main emphasis of computer science is on the safe arrival of the signals while overcoming the channel's limitations and noises, interrupting elements, and does not refer to the semantic aspect of information. Phone lines, for instance, have two main limitations as channel in computer communication. The first is the difference between the signals that are used by computers and the signals that can be transmitted through the channel. The second problem, which is called 'noise,' has to do with the quality of the channel, which depends on its properties.

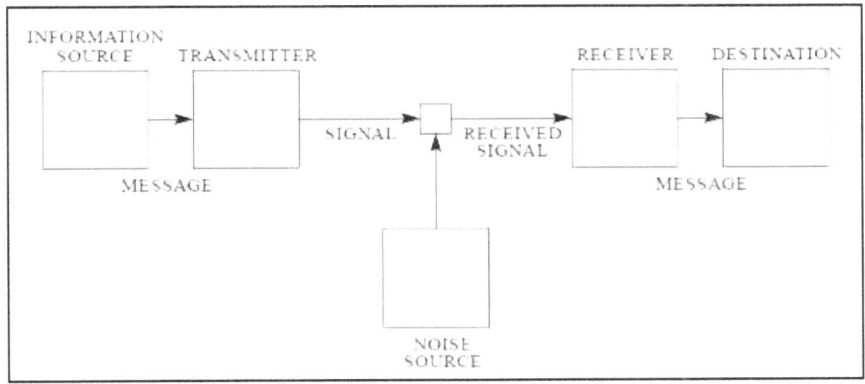

Figure 1 – Shannon's schematic diagram of communication system (381)

Thus, 'meaning of information' is precisely the main point of difference between communication as regarded by engineering and computer science, and communication as perceived by language and literary scholars. Engineering and computer sciences are interested in the safe delivery of the transmission process while poetics generally focuses on the decoding process. Safe delivery includes the decoding process, but only in the technical sense of duplicating at the receiving end exactly or approximately the same message that was transmitted from the other end. Thus, since the subject of this work is literary hypertexts there is a need for a communication theory that takes into account the semantic aspects of communication.

Hypertext takes advantage of the technological communication process for poetical use. The main interest of poetics, deriving from linguistics and semiotics, is in the semantic aspect of communication as it is structured by the linguistic system, which is a special system of signals. Jakobson's well-known paper *Linguistics and Poetics* (1960)[39] describes the linguistic communication process with much the same 'players' (constitutive factors) as Shannon (See Figure 2). The addresser that sends the message and the addressee that receives it should both know the code – the language, and there should be a physical and psychological channel between them, which he calls 'contact'. The information source and transmitter in Shannon's scheme equals Jakobson's addresser and the receiver and destination equals his addressee. Shannon's channel is Jakobson's contact and both of them refer to the message. Yet, while Shannon sees the message as a transmitted signal, Jakobson regards the signal, first as a verbal entity, language in his case, and second, merely as code. For Jakobson the message is a different entity than the code because of its meaning. Another player that Jakobson adds is the "context," which he thinks is required for the message to be operative.

Figure 2 – Jakobson's schematic communication model (p. 35)

---

[39] Jakobson, 1960, 350–377. This "closing statements" was a milestone as "It had an incalculable effect in bringing to the attention of Anglo-American critics the rich-ness of the structuralist tradition of poetics and textual analysis that originated in Eastern and Central Europe." Lodge 2008, 141.

Figure 1 and Figure 2 show quite clearly the distinction between the two theories, stemming from the difference in focus. The variance is in the additional players, context and message, which hold the semantic and contextual aspect of communication. Jakobson, as a linguist, is interested in the coding/decoding process and its relation to the message meaning, while engineering and computer science sees the coding/decoding merely as means for the safe delivery of signals, meaning the producing of the same signal at the destination end. Consequently, Jakobson's communication model is focused on linguistic communication, namely meaning, while Shannon's communication theory, though it is more general, regards language as a collection of neutral signs without any regard for it content.

Each factor in Jakobson's communication model presents different functions of language (Figure 3). Thus, he assigns six functions to language: referential, emotive, conative, phatic, metalingual and poetic. The *emotive* function is focused on the addresser, on the direct expression of the speaker's attitude towards what he is speaking about. It tends to produce an impression of a certain emotion whether true or feigned. The *conative* function is oriented toward the addressee, its purest grammatical expression is in vocative and imperative words. The third function is the *referential*, the context in the communication scheme, and is centered on someone or something that is spoken of. The *phatic* function serves to establish, prolong or discontinue communication, to check whether the channel works and is oriented towards the contact. The *metalinguistic* function is used whenever the user needs to check whether the addresser and the addressee use the same code. The *poetic* function promotes the palpability of signs, deepens the dichotomy between signs and objects. All texts have a dominant function, and in literature, the poetic function is the dominant since it is focused on the message.

Emotive	Referential Poetic Phatic Metalingual	Conative

Figure 3 - Jakobson's scheme of functions (38)

Chatman presented a narrative-communication model which can be associated to Jakobson's addresser and addressee. He regards narrative as a communication, thus he presents the sender and receiver as a three-layer personage: the outer players (to the text) who are the real flesh and blood author and its reader; the first inter-textual players are the *Implied author* and its *Implied reader*, which are constructed by the *Real author* and *Real reader*; and an inner layer where the overt narrator and its reader are presenting the story.

Thus, while the term *system* has a similar meaning in poetics and computer science, considering the difference of the research objects, the term *information* has a different significance. In computer science, the term denotes a collection of signals and signifiers, with no regard to its meaning, yet in poetics meaning is its main focal point, so much so that Jakobson adds two constitutive factors: context and code. The differentiation between the code and the message emphasizes poetics interest in the semantics of the message. This difference will bear significantly on the analysis in my work.

The third term that is used by the two academic fields involved in defining hypertext is the portrayal of hypertext as a *network*. A network, by its lexicographical definition is an openwork fabric or structure in which cords, threads, or wires cross at regular intervals. The concept of the term net is most probably from nature, and the spider's web is probably what inspired hunters and fishermen to build their own nets as hunting appliances in the spider's web format.[40] Thus, the term is used in a metaphorical way to describe "a large system consisting of many similar parts that are connected together to allow movement or communication between or along the parts or between the parts and a control center." (Cambridge Dictionaries On-line) While the original net or web is palpable and has equal spaces between the nodes, computer science and poetics refers to its conceptual model, its scheme.

In computer science, the metaphoric uses of the term refer to the general scheme, the visual similarity between a network (a web, a net) layout. A computer network consists of many computers that are connected together, via cables or any other channel, thus allowing for

---

[40] Fishermen utilize real spider webs see Gabriel 2005, 352.

sharing of resources and information. In a schematic diagram, it actually looks like a network (see Figure 4) (*Microsoft Encarta* 1996).

The diagram in Figure 4 shows the two most common types of computer networks: the LAN and the WAN. On the left side, enclosed by the rectangle, we can see the LAN (Local Area Network) type, which is used mostly for sharing information and resources, for instance printers, within an organization. This type of network consists of multiple computers, workstations, permanently connected to each other and to various shared resources through fixed cables or wireless devices. The diagram as a whole shows the WAN (Wide Area Network) type, which connects LAN type networks to a wider network. The Internet is the ultimate example for a WAN type network. Computer science regards hypertext as a WAN, distributed, yet connected, texts that may be used or connected in any order.

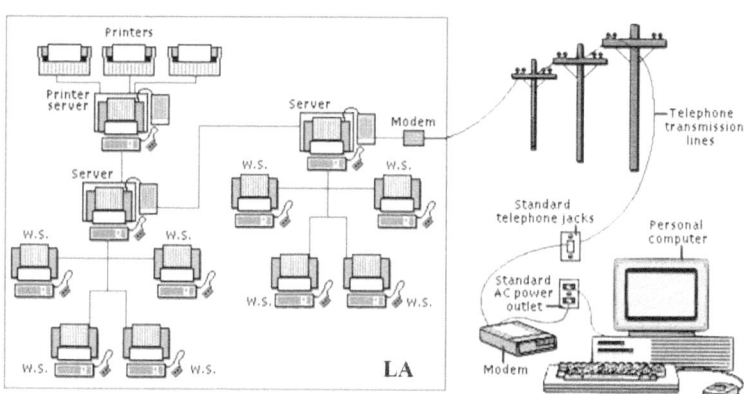

Figure 4 - A computer network

The use of the term *network* in poetics is even more abstract. While there is a visual resemblance between the layout of computer networks and a net, the resemblance involved in the poetic use of the term is purely metaphorical and many times is interchanged with the term *system*. De Sausssure (1959) defines language: "Language is a system of interdependent terms in which the value of each term results solely from the simultaneous presence of the others" (114). Though De Saussure does not use the term network explicitly, his description of the two axes of linguistics, the diachronic and synchronic, portrays a network, where the word is the node that combines between the axes, "Everywhere distinctions should be made, according to the following illustration, between (1) the axis of simultaneities (AB), which stands for the relations of coexisting things and from which the intervention of time is excluded; and (2) the axis of successions (CD), on which only one thing can be considered at a time but upon which are located all the things on the first axis together with their changes" (80). Hudson (2001) declares explicitly that the whole of language is a network, "a collection of units linked pair-wise by relations" (49).

According to Linguistics, language is a grammatical and structural web of words, each defined by its functions in a specific discourse and by its relations with other members in the web. Semantics regards language as a web of meanings, in which analogical or oppositional relations define each of its members. Barthes (1974), for example, observes five different codes of meaning. The *hermeneutic code*, which denotes an enigma that moves the narrative forward; the *semic code* which refer to the unit of the signifier; the *proairetic* code that refers to actions; the *symbolic code* are constitutive meanings, which renders the text open to different interpretations; the *cultural code* is the references to science or wisdom that are external to the text. These codes, or structures of meaning, are weaved into a meaningful text,

> The five codes create a kind of network, a topos through which the entire text passes (or rather, in passing, becomes text). Thus, if we make no effort to structure each code, or five codes among themselves, we do so deliberately, in order to assume the multivalence of the text, its partial reversibility. We are, in fact, concerned not to manifest a structure but to produce a structuration (20).

Poetics perceives the linguistic and semantic networks as artistic devices for conveying meaning. Jakobson refers, in *Linguistics and Poetics*, to poetics in its relation to linguistics and says:

> Poetics deals primarily with the question, What makes a verbal message a work of art? Because the main subject of poetics is the differentia specifica of verbal art in relation to other arts and in relation to other kinds of verbal behavior, poetics is entitled to the leading place in literary studies.

Poetics deals with problems of verbal structure, just as the analysis of painting is concerned with pictorial structure. Since linguistics is the global science of verbal structure, poetics may be regarded as an integral part of linguistics (350).

Jakobson regards "verbal structures" as poetics' field of interest, its matter, and distinguishes two "basic modes of arrangement, *selection* and *combination*" (358) in verbal behavior. By *selection,* he means the contingency to select a specific word out of an equivalent stack of synonyms, thus having the special semantic effect that the writer wishes to convey. By *combination* he refers to the positioning of one word in accordance with the other, thus creating a linguistic contiguity. Hence, the poetic function "projects the principle of equivalence from the axis of selection into the axis of combination."

The numerous approaches to the network metaphor in both fields, computer science and poetics, create ambiguity when used to define hypertext's distinctive features. A unique and pragmatic approach to defining hypertext's singularity, which looks at the text from its communication function, is Espen Aarseth's (1997), who characterized digital narratives by a typology of textual communication. He looks for a way to widen the definition of literature so that the electronic texts, including hypertext, which was then considered "new" and "revolutionary," will be included. Aarseth does not discern between electronic literature and print literature,

> ... to show what the functional differences and similarities among the various textual media imply about the theories and practices of literature. The exploration is based on the concepts and perspectives of narratology and rhetoric but is not limited to these two disciplines (17).

Aarseth is one of the first to introduce the idea of proximity between hypertext and computer games: "To claim that there is no difference between games and narratives is to ignore essential qualities of both categories. And yet, [...] the difference is not clear-cut, and there is significant overlap between the two" (5). His words may have been a prophecy since hypertext-literature had eventually collapsed into the gaming world.

Aarseth differentiates between the text and the information it transmits: whereas information is a string of signs, as Shannon defined it earlier, text is, "any object with primary function to relay verbal information" (62). Therefore, a text cannot operate independently of some material medium, which influences its behavior. For instance, oral literature is characterized by repetition, which helps the story-teller to remember the story and to emphasize certain ideas on one side and on the other, helps the listener to concentrate and remember the story (Lord 1973, 89). Hence, oral literature will be different from print literature and print literature, in turn, will be different from digital literature: "Most literary theorists take their object medium as a given, in spite of the blatant historical differences between, for instance, oral and written literature" (15). Aarseth continues to say that print literature was always the privileged medium and just "At this point, [1997] in the age of dual ontology of everyday textuality (screen or paper), this ideological blindness is no longer possible."

Aarseth divides literature into two categories according to the requirements from the reader: ergodic and linear. Linear literature requires merely "eye movement and the periodic or arbitrary turning of pages" (2) therefore the reader is a spectator and his only function in the text is interpretative, which is common to all literary readers, print and electronic alike.

'Ergodic' is a term borrowed from physics, which "derives from the Greek words *ergon* and *hados*, meaning 'work' and 'path.' In ergodic literature, nontrivial effort is required to allow the reader to traverse the text" (1). Hence, the ergodic literature reader's function is not merely interpretative, but may be 'explorative', 'configurative', and 'textonic'. The functions of the reader, according to Aarseth, are accumulative; 'linear literature' has only one reader function, the interpretative. Hypertext, which belongs to the 'ergodic literature,' but is static, since it has a fixed number of scriptons[41] has two reader

---

[41] Aarseth perceives the text as built out of strings of words, which he distinguishes into two modes of existence: "strings as they appear to readers," (62) which he calls "scriptons" and "strings as they exist in the text," which is called "textons." The distinction is mainly between the raw material (textons) and its possible combinations (scriptons). The mechanism that

functions, the interpretative and the 'explorative'. He defines the explorative function as a function "in which the user must decide which path to take" (64).[42] When 'ergodic literature' is dynamic, meaning the content of scriptons may change, the reader might be required to a more significant effort. The pure dynamic text he calls 'cybertext' which he defines as, "texts that involve calculation in their production of scriptons" (75), and the reader activity may be just 'configurative,' in which "scriptons are in part chosen or created by the user" or 'textonic' as well, when "textons or traversal functions can be (permanently) added to the text" (64).

Aarseth's taxonomy comprises more than 20 texts, old and new, print works, computer software generating narrative, computer games, hypertexts, electronic presentations of text etc. that are classified according to seven categories: dynamics, determinability, transiency, perspective, access, linking and user functions. The value and interest of this typology is his intersection between categories that is sharpened when he applies digital network's terms on print texts and creates a system of conceptual analogies. Aarseth places hypertext between 'linear literature' and 'cybertext' since he regards it as an ergodic text, which requires the reader to activate links in order to explore them, yet he does not regard it as dynamic like computer

---

generates scriptons out of the given textons he calls "the traversal function," carried out by the reader.

[42] Aarseth's explorative function is like the "Optional Thinking" to which I referred in the introduction.

games, "The reader's level of involvement is much closer to that of traditional fiction" (102).

Aarseth (2004) does not ignore the latent playfulness in the reading process:

> When we try to guess the murderer in a Poirot novel, we are adding a coincidental game to the story. The guessing game is not necessary, and the narrator doesn't care whether we play or not. If we happen to guess correctly early on, nothing different happens in the novel. Worse, we may even stop reading prematurely, since the ending has become obvious and boring. These novels are games only in a metaphorical sense; they tease us, but we are not real players. In the case of hypertext fictions, we are explorers, but without recognizable rules, there is no real game. To equalize these metaphorical games with a real game is to marginalize an already (academically) marginal phenomenon, to privilege the illusion of play over real play. And for game scholars, that is a poor strategy. (Web document)

However, the print reader's playfulness is only part of her involvement in the reading process. The reader, except from the technical activity of reading and turning pages, is mentally occupied in deciphering the text and turning it into meaningful narrative. Taking for granted that the reader can read and has command of the language, there is the higher level of meaning-creation in the dynamic process of reading stories. The reader, who interprets the story, creates its meaning, throughout the reading process according to the order in which she encounters the text and to her previous experiences, memories, culture and religion, gender, age, class etc. As she encounters new information along the reading process she constantly qualifies it, reframes its meaning, renames its significance, and in short: participates in an extremely serious interpretation process.

1.4 Defining hypertext

Sub-chapter *Definitions of Hypertext* (1.2) offered various definitions of hypertext, each from a different academic approach. However, these definitions differ so much from each other that a short explanation of how hypertext works is called for. Thus, in order to choose a definition that will serve as this study's working assumption, (as it was known at the time, a time of vast changes,) I will try first, to illustrate what it is by comparison to print.

The standard printed book contains paper pages, arranged sequentially, on which the words that make up the text are visible. When the reader finishes reading a page, line after line, she turns to the next one, by the order that the pages are bound together, namely the order they are lined up. This reading order is usually called "linear" and its linearity refers both to the lines and the movement from each line to the next, as if they were printed in one long (very long) "line"; and to the movement from page to page, as if they were lined up one after (at the bottom of) another.[43]

Hypertext is an electronic medium, which replaces traditional paper with a computer screen, though there are researchers (Bolter, Landow) that find hyper-textual structures in print literature too.[44] As the term 'hypertext' was invented for the digital medium, in this study it will be reserved for electronic texts alone (though not all electronic texts are hypertexts). Hypertext is made up of "nodes," which are linked according to the author's decisions. One node can be linked to one other node or to a number of different nodes. Each node can contain a variety of media: text, image, video and animation - either

---

[43] Schematically this order looks like this:

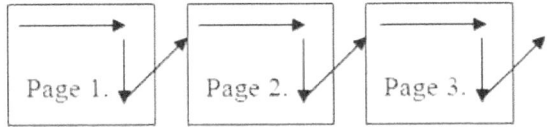

[44] Bolter (1991) says: "Ulysses and particularly Finnegans Wake are themselves hypertexts that have been flattened out to fit on the printed page. [...] A historian might choose to write an essay in which each paragraph or section is a topic in hypertextual network. The connections would indicate possible orders in which topics could be assembled and read, and each order of reading might produce a different literary and analytic result" (24). The flattening of the text is in the real and metaphorical sense and loses its dynamic connectivity.

separately or in different combinations. Schematically drawn this "text" looks as follows:

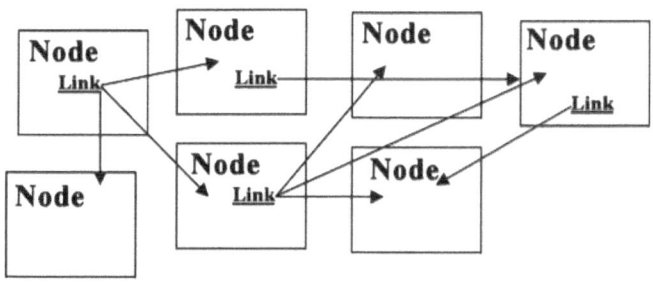

Figure 5 – Optional presentation order of hypertext.

Though the term "node" has come up repeatedly in our discussion, it is still quite a vague entity. In the foregoing citations, only one researcher (Nielsen) has tried to explain what he means by this term, while all the others referred to it as an obvious term that does not require defining or explaining. Nielsen (1990, 298) says that "each node contains some amount of text or other information," an explanation which is so general on the one hand and may be correct for a paper page as well, that it does not contribute to the understanding of what is actually a node. Landow (1994) uses the words "blocks of text" and "passage of verbal discourse" in relation to the node and likens it to Barthes's *lexias*. Barthes (1970) defined *lexias* as "a series of brief, contiguous fragments" (13). Nevertheless, Barthes' definition stresses only the small scale and the contiguousness of this brief fragment. The problem of scale will be discussed later, but the requirement of contiguousness is relevant only to the printed text, with its fixed sequential order. In hypertext, nodes that within reading seem to be contiguous may change and lose their necessary connectedness.

The dictionary definition for node is twofold: it is a knob, knot, protuberance, or swelling (The American Heritage Dictionary of the English Language), or a junction of some type (*Bookshelf 2000*, Computer and Internet Dictionary). Though these two definitions seem remote from our subject matter, together they explain the origin of the term. The node is a junction, from which the links branch out; to use computer science terms, the concept of the node is like a knot in a network. The node is the writing or inscription space from which the links branch out to other nodes. However, this does not yet answer the question of scale: how long is this block, discourse, message, or writing space? and not surprisingly so. The node has so many aspects that it is quite difficult to define.

From one aspect, the node bears a resemblance to the printed page, though its digital medium endows it with some additional and unique traits. As in print literature, where the reader has to turn the page in order to continue reading, in hypertext the reader/user has to hit a key (if she chooses to read by default,[45] which is a kind of linear

---

[45] The term "default" is used throughout the work as a generic term meaning - what happens when the reader is not activating any built-in links.

reading) or to choose (by clicking or writing) a link to get to another node. The printed page is limited by its physical boundaries, though it can have various sizes. And yet one page, like a news-paper, can hold "several pages" in the form of columns or in any other form, each presenting separated and noticeable chunks of text, images etc. in its fixed size.[46] The electronic "page" - the node - is limitless by the properties of the medium. John Slatin[47] (1991) defines the node as,

---

[46] Children oriented print fiction is more radical, avant-garde if you will, than literature written for adults. Starting with the books' size that is fixed in adults, between certain boundaries, yet varies largely in children's fiction as can be seen in Kathleen Hale's *Orlando (The Marmalade Cat) Buys a Farm* that is big - over 12" - 15" tall to Maurice Sendak's miniature books *Nutshell Library (Caldecott Collection)*, which is 2.8 x 1.8 x 4 inches tall. The use of colors, pictures, interactivity of pop-ups, transformations, tunnel books, volvelles, flaps, pull-tabs, pop-outs, pull-downs, and "Where's Waldo?" series, though started in adult literature turned into the children's unique realm since the 18th century. See for example the exhibition that was held at the *University of Virginia Library* between May 12 - August 18, 2000 by the name "Pop Goes the Page: Movable and Mechanical Books from the Brenda Forman Collection," curated by Johanna Drucker, Robertson Professor of Media Studies. The exhibition's site: <http://explore.lib.virginia.edu/exhibits/show/popgoesthepage /walkthrough>, 24.7.2016. The Most similar to hypertext is the "Choose Your Own Adventure" stories, which is actually a hypertext in print, where the reader has to choose her way through the narrative by choosing the next episode out of a number of options.

[47] Slatin was a literature professor in the English department at UT Austin. He was suffering from an eye disease that eventually caused blindness. Thus, he was one of the first to see how the new technologies could help him and others. He became the first director of the innovative Computer Writing

"any object which is linked to another object" (162). The object can be any digital medium: text in various lengths, sound, images, video etc. Nevertheless, this definition is not quite accurate, as a node can hold more than one object, for instance text and graphics, and there can be more than one link in a node. However, his definition rules out any delimitation of the node's size; the node, he argues, "may be as large as an entire book or as small as a single character." Theoretically speaking, the node can hold one dot, one paragraph, one chapter, or even a whole volume, although in practice, nodes are quite short. The complete electronic version of Balzac's *Père Goriot* can be looked at as one node, and each of the 208 chapters making up Fieldings's *Tom Jones* can be considered as nodes too. Moulthrop's first node of *Victory Garden* labeled *Come In*, on the other hand, holds only four words. Slatin likens the node to a paragraph in the printed book, either being "a way of structuring attention," with the boundaries "somewhat arbitrary" (162). However, as a node can contain more than one paragraph, it cannot be defined by its scale.

A somewhat better operational definition can be found in *The Electronic Labyrinth*, (1995) which is the result of a research project mostly undertaken in 1993 by Canada's Hypertext Fiction Research Group and carried out by Christopher Keep and Tim McLaughlin. In a node labeled "Node," they say:

---

and Research Lab in the Department of Rhetoric and Writing, and subsequently director of UT's Accessibility Institute. <https://currents.dwrl.utexas.edu/2009.html>, 24.7.2016.

A node is an integrated and self-sufficient unit of information, small relative to the complete document. In electronic instances, nodes are often thought of as being small enough to fit on one computer screen. Janet Fiderio states that they "consist of a single concept or idea". Other, grander schemes (such as Xanadu) make allowances for nodes the size of books.

Contrasting these definitions highlights the question of scale. In an essay, a node might be the size of a paragraph or two; in a library, each book might be a node. Fiderio's assertion that "the information contained in a node can usually be displayed on one computer screen" is true only at a certain scale. (hfl0046.html)

The citations exemplify the problem of defining the node. However, in practice, the node's length in the hyper-literature is most often smaller than the size of the screen in length and width, simulating the printed book's page on the one hand, and on the other hand, taking into consideration the text's legibility and readers' comfort in reading from a computer screen. Thus, Fiderio's typographic assertion is the most acceptable to define what a node is. Though the scale can differ from node to node and the computer screen is hardly a principled measure, in a digital medium, it can become a practical measure. A node is a unit of information, textual or graphical, which can be scrolled-up on one screen, without the reader's intervention (except for the scrolling, of course) that is, without activating any link. The link is the binding device between the nodes, enabled by the electronic medium.

The two unique and novel properties of hypertext are its use of an electronic medium and the new device, which the electronic medium enables, the link. Thus, I will define hypertext as an electronic system of nodes and links. My definition is the broadest possible, so that it will not influence the study in any way and allow for an in-depth comparison between print and hypertext literature.

In summation, this chapter describes hypertext origin as a device that will allow interactive and collaborative work and for a quick and free access to information thus becoming a common memory extender. Hypertext has various definitions according to the academic field within which it is discussed, and even within the same field, like a style, a form, an approach, a technique, a structure, a system, a network, or in other words, an application for writing, storing, and publishing textual information.

I discussed the three terms that were common in the definitions: system, information and network from two points of view that are relevant to this research, computer science and poetics. The conclusion of the chapter is a description of the hypertext format, its components and structure and, in light of the multitude of definitions, a simple working definition that will serve as the basis for this research and its application to narrative is presented. This broad definition takes into account the two properties that distinguish hypertext from print and the electronic medium that enables the use of various kinds of media and the linkage device that allows the creation of an interactive and non-sequential narrative that causes the reader to choose his navigation through the text.

In light of my hypertext definition, it is understandable that the medium raised great expectations for a change in textual norms. Literature is considered a temporal art, sequential, linear, and unfolding in time, in contrast to the visual arts, which are spatial. Literature is supposed to posit the reader in a relatively passive position (despite the constant "data processing" in the reader's mind), yet hypertext requires active decisions in reading-time. Narrative is based on language, a sequential practice of combination; hence, its sequential character is an inherent principle, while a work of visual art is seen in its entirety in a single moment. To cite Lessing (1962) who compares visual art with the written one:

> I grant that since the signs of speech are arbitrary, it is very possible by their means to delineate the different parts of a body, one after the other, with the same precision as they are found combined in nature (165).

Hence, the possibility of overriding language limitations fascinated narrative and literature researchers and ignited a hope for a new genre, one which will cause a re-examination of poetical and rhetorical issues. The following chapter will hold detailed descriptions of those "great expectations" and the reasons for them.

2   Great Expectations

Many literary scholars find the electronic hypertext too disparate from the printed text to be compared or considered with the same tools that are common in print literature as Lanham remarks: "Obviously our poetics will require some basic non-Aristotelian adjustments" (7). Slatin opens his article *Reading Hypertext: Order and Coherence in a New Medium* with the following statement, "The basic point I have to make is almost embarrassingly simple: hypertext is very different from more traditional forms of text" (153). His embarrassment stems from a feeling of obviousness: being a literary scholar, he feels that the difference between the computer's screen and the printed page is so vast that it is self-evident and resists comparison. He, too, feels the need for some new poetics that will suit the new medium: "A new medium involves both a new practice and a new rhetoric, a new body of theory." Bolter (1991) says: "Electronic writing forces us to recast the familiar questions of literary criticism and theory by redefining both the critical object (the text) and the act of reading itself. [...] As it restores a theoretical innocence to the making of literary texts, electronic writing will require a simpler, more positive literary theory" (147).

Bostad (1994) claims that writing is a way to organize, store, and present information no matter what tool we use, a pen, a typewriter, or an electronic information-processing tool. The organization of information is done according to known conventions, whether print or electronic. He claims that these conventions, differing from technology to technology, leave their mark on the text and on the mode in which it is organized and realized. He argues that since writing is a certain interaction between the writer and the technology he uses, "No matter what technology a writer makes use of, it influences the process and product of writing, and adds something to what is being written." Thus electronic literature will be different from printed one because of the specific import of the technology. Hence, while Bostad belittles the effect that technology will have on poetics, Lanham, Slatin and Bolter think that technology will have a vast effect on literary production and hence also on literature criticism.

There is no dispute that the technology used for writing effects the text. For instance, the method of hand copying the bible resulted in spelling mistakes that, in time, changed some of the original meaning of the Scripture, thus effecting, and over time even reversing, the meaning of the original text.[48] McLuhan, in his book *The Gutenberg Galaxy*, (1965) associates the whole of human evolution with the development of literacy, from the oral through print to the new electronic age. He analyzes liturgical, economical, and sociological transitions as an outcome of the developments in text production, literacy, and publishing. Although this extensive view can be disputed, there is a general consent that print-literacy transformed

---

[48] Tov, Emanuel. *Textual Criticism of the Hebrew Bible*, Minneapolis: Fortress Press, 2001, 8.

literature. First, print created the format of the book as the new container for communication, writing, and presentation (78). Secondly, it enabled a quick and cheap duplication, so that the book became affordable and available to a wide range of readers. Oral texts were within reach only to their audience, and even the written manuscripts, which used to be the main tool for literacy, were confined to traditional scholars. The printed book, however, is an accessible and democratic commodity that transfers ideas quickly and to wide communities. Thus, the book created the "public," the reading public and communities of readers. The creation of the public resulted in its turn, in a change in literature's subjects, taking literature out of the realm of religion and scholarship and into the domain of the secular. (275-276)

Books becoming a commodity in the print age reversed the process of literary creation and writing. McLuhan (100) explains that in early ages the patron was the one to dictate to the artist many literary elements, including the work's subject. The print era brought a change in patronage - the public and publishers became the patron and "Art reversed its role from guide for perception into convenient amenity or package. But the producer or artist was compelled, as never before, to study the effect of his art." (275). Thus, the writing of literature turned into an artist's "planned production." McLuhan sketches the demands involved in this production:

> Planned production means that the total process
> must be worked out in exact stages, backwards, like

a detective story. In the first great age of mass production of commodities, and of literature as a commodity for the market, it became necessary to examine the effect of art and literature before producing anything at all. This is the literal entrance to the world of myth.

It was Edgar Allan Poe who first worked out the rationale of this ultimate awareness of the poetic process and who saw that instead of directing the work to the reader, it was necessary to incorporate the reader in the work (276).

McLuhan refers to Edgar Allan Poe's much-debated essay, *The Philosophy of Composition* (1846), in which Poe writes about the common mode of constructing a story,

Either history affords a thesis - or one is suggested by an incident of the day - or, at best, the author sets himself to work in the combination of striking events to form merely the basis of his narrative - designing, generally, to fill in with description, dialogue, or authorial comment, whatever crevices of fact or action may, from page to page, render themselves apparent (259).

Poe refers to the literature that preceded his time, literature that used to present itself as a 'history' to claim plausibility and realism. For instance, Fielding's work *Joseph Andrews*, (1742) which full name, as was written on the title page of the first addition is, *The History of the Adventures of Joseph Andrews, and of his Friend Mr. Abraham Adams*. Stern's *Tristram Shandy*'s (1759-1769) full title, written some twenty years later, is *The Life and Opinions of Tristram Shandy, Gent.* As in a historical work novels were constructed of the "striking events" in the protagonist's life namely, his "history" or biography. The first review to appear at *Tristram Shandy*'s publication (1759-60) was an unsigned survey in the *Monthly Review*,[49] which begins with the proclamation:

> Lives and Adventures the public have had enough, and, perhaps, more than enough, long ago. A consideration that probably induced the droll Mr. Tristram Shandy to entitle the performance before us, his Life and Opinions (471-2).[50]

This review goes to show that the public had become more and more important and came to have a say about the preferred literary subjects and should be taken into account when the author plans a new work.

Thus, Poe does not begin planning his poem by plotting the

---

[49] *Monthly Review: or Literary Journal* was an English periodical founded by the publisher Ralph Griffiths.

[50] Kenrick, William. "Review of Tristram Shandy." 1759 in Stern, Laurence. *Tristram Shandy*. Ed. Howard Anderson, New York, London: W. W. Norton & Company, 1980.

events. He takes into account his reader by establishing the effect he strives to elicit. Describing the *modus operandi* of the creation process and reasoning of his poem *The Raven*, Poe asks the reader to dismiss the circumstance "which, in the first place, gave rise to the intention of composing *a* poem that should suit at once the popular and the critical taste" (260). For him, the basic postulation for creating the poem was its effect on its readers.

Though the example of the change in the writer's focus is a trivial one, referring exclusively to literature, McLuhan finds many other alterations, concerning all areas of the human existence (art, ethnography, sociology, politics etc.), stemming from changes in the medium with which the text is conceived. No wonder that the new electronic medium, which is different from all previous media, led to so many expectations for innovation of unforeseen measures.

Landow (1994) professor of English and Art History, predicts that hypertext, as a new literacy technique, "has the power to reconfigure our culture's basic assumptions about textuality, authorship, creative property, education, and a range of other issues" (32). Other scholars of literature, art and culture claim that we do not yet have the adequate tools for criticizing this new hyper-literature genre, but agree that it will definitely influence cultural and artistic criticism. This claim is supported by McLuhan's statements that, "This somnambulist conforming of beholder to the new form or structure renders those most deeply immersed in a revolution the least aware of its dynamic" (272).

Since the declarations about hypertext as a new medium, at the time of its advent, were quite general in nature, though raising great expectations, it stirred researchers into studying it closely. They explored hypertext characteristics by contrasting it with printed literature poetic topics, as they tried to envision the future of literature and foresee the changes expected in the creative processes and reading procedures alike, which may involve new procedures for interpretation and analysis, and change the basic paradigm for the study of literature, and at the same time to re-examine traditional poetics matters.

This chapter will sketch the great expectations that the medium, or genre if you will, gave rise to when introduced into the literary domain and applied by several authors. It is interesting to note that those authors,[51] applying the hypertext format in their literary works, are mainly literature scholars as well. [52] This fact might imply that the first literary hypertexts were created as an exercise, a writing experiment in a new textual medium by academic experts of the old, conventional (written printed) genre. On the one hand, they were made to examine the new medium's potential as a literary tool, and on the other hand, since the authors were literary scholars as well, they

---

[51] Like Michael Joyce, Stuart Moulthrop, Janet Yellowlees Douglas and M.D. Coverley.

[52] The fact that the authors of those new-media texts were mostly academic researchers bears witness to the exercises' experimental and empirical nature.

could professionally evaluate the differences between the old and the new. They could re-access conventional paradigms that were predominant in the field of "Understanding Literature."[53]

Although different scholars have different expectations and hopes, they all stem from two main distinctive traits of hypertext: the electronic medium and the linking device. Thus, they can be classed into two groups, albeit interconnected ones. The first group of expectations deals with the new electronic format versus the format of the book; the second group contends with the new structural element, the link.

The new electronic medium raises questions about the traditional roles of the book as a storage vehicle, a presentation tool, and an organizational method. How will the lack of a tangible container change the organization and presentation of text? What effect will the change have on the literary work? What will be the effect on its relations with other art forms, and with non-artistic texts?

---

[53] Two academic books that appeared in the thirties and the forties of the last century in America by Cleanth Brooks and Robert Penn Warren were regarded as the "bible" for understanding literature. *Understanding Poetry* (1938) and *Understanding Fiction* (1943) had an immense effect in the field as they defined the constitutive forms of literature and its basic concepts, distinguished between literature from other forms of communicative activity, interpretive paradigms etc. The books' influence was unprecedented and they set up the discipline. See also Jancovich, Mark. *The Cultural Politics of the New Criticism*. Cambridge University Press, 1993, 81-89.

Will the new medium call for new textual norms, norms that differ from the ones we know and use today?

The new structural element, the link, eliminates the material borders of the book as a differentiated object, and binds it to other objects. In David Bolter's (1991) words, "An electronic book is a structure that reaches out to other structures, not only metaphorically, as does a printed book, but operationally" (87). If the linkage allows for an infinite looping and connecting, will the literary work retain its closure? Will the text become fluid, temporary, episodic, and changeable? Will there be one authoritative text and reading that can be interpreted and scholarly analyzed and debated? What is the text, the basic work and what is the story: is there a basic, stable narrative? What is the role of the creative artist? What control will he have on his work? etc.

2.1 The new medium

Printed letters are displayed on the page by a fixed order of small dots outlining them. It is possible to touch the printed letter, even to smear it on the page, it being the tactile presentation of the alphabet, while blinking, passing and vanishing points of light display the electronic letters.

Historically speaking, this change in the source and role of light can be found already in the Middle Ages, though in reverse. McLuhan (1965), referring to the stained-glass windows of churches says, "Scribal culture and Gothic architecture were both concerned with light *through* not light *on*" (120). He cites Otto von Simson (1962) that describes the interior of the Gothic cathedral after the invention of print as inadequate, since the light was unsatisfactory for reading:

> "Not that Gothic interiors are particularly bright [...] in fact, the stained-glass windows were such inadequate sources of light that a subsequent and blinder age replaced many of them by grisaille or white windows that today convey a most misleading impression" (3).

The stained-glass windows served to intensify the believer's religious experience while the service was conducted orally, but "After Gutenberg the new visual intensity will require light *on* everything" (123). The Gutenberg age changed the use of light; the electronic era is changing it yet again.

2.1.1 The Book as an Object

Books are mainly material objects, "Primarily a bound volume of printed pages, it may also be a division within a book (as in the

Bible) or a statement of accounts."54 The book comprises pages on which words and/or graphical elements are printed, fastened together and bound. The book's cover is thus one of its important features, marking its beginning and end, its borders, and actually separating it from other objects – and from other letter filled pages – by turning it into a container, a privileged discrete vehicle for text.

Rosello (1994) sees the value of hypertext in its calling attention to the object:

> Whether it becomes dominant or goes down in history as a failed experiment, hypertextuality will have had the merit of questioning the status of the book as a privileged vehicle for narratives, by raising ideological and practical issues (123).

In other words, Rosello refers to the book as a physical presence, a tangible object, and to its materialistic entity, which turned it into an object of cultural, symbolic and sentimental capital. Though being so important, "privileged," it turned to be transparent and self-evident to the reader since up till the emergence of the digital text there was no other feasible "container."

Bostad too, looks upon the book as a storage object, thus

---

[54] "book" *World Encyclopedia*. Philip's, 2008. *Oxford Reference Online*. Oxford University Press. <http://www.oxfordreference.com>, 24.7.2016.

envisaging the transition from the material object to the digital object, and the change in the way the text is stored as hypertext's main innovation:

> The most obvious change may be that our texts are no longer necessarily the physical objects of the written paper, but as often electronically stored binary codes of which we might fetch copies and convert to recognizable signs in the form of pixels displayed on a computer screen.

Bostad agrees with Rosello about the loss of materiality but he stresses the digital nature of the new text and it being displayed on a screen.

Bukatman says, "On screen, the text is separated from its physical existence on a hard disk, and becomes a malleable, 'virtual' text" (web document). However, as the material entity that is stored on the hard drive is not the text, but magnetic signs, the text proper is unavailable to the reader as an object, virtual or material. Even if the reader can touch the magnetic media or view it, it is not hypertext that he sees, or any text for that matter, but a plastic matter. The digital magnetic signs are indecipherable by human beings, as Bolter (1991) has discerned, "The most unusual feature is that these new electronic hard structures are not directly accessible either to the writer or the reader. The bits of the text are simply not on a human scale" (42). Hypertext not only requires the presence of a computer, which will decode the binary codes, it requires a special application too, which will present it to the reader on the computer monitor, thus turning the digital signs into the notion of text. "Text" loses thus its fixed and object-ly nature.

Hypertext's need of an intermediate agent for its existence as a text, earned it a place in what Ong (1982) and other researchers call the *Second Orality*, referring to all electronic communication media, such as television, telephone, video and audio recording, and the computer. There, the audience experiences the text through a mediator, a technological device that presents the text. Oral literature, as defined by Milton Parry's pupil and follower Lord, (1995) "consists of the songs and stories, and other sayings that people have heard and listened to, sung and told, without any intervention of writing" (1). Thus, oral literature requires a human intermediate, the singer or story teller, which conveys the text and without whom there is no text at all. The computer and its software have in hypertext literature the same function as the singer or the storyteller in oral literature. They are the performers, without which there is no text at all. In a previous book, (1973) Lord argues that, "Our singer of tales is composer of tales" (13) as well, which most of the technological devices referred to don't do, but that feature is no longer evident in print literature either.[55]

---

[55] A machine which runs Artificial Intelligence programs can compose stories. The most primitive composition program is Eliza, which was written at MIT by Joseph Weizenbaum between 1964 to 1966. Nowadays most of the video games run some form of AI and Siri, which is the virtual personal

There is not much to add to this simple fact that the electronic text is not a material object, however it is a crucial fact that raised researchers' expectations[56] for far reaching changes in the literary work and communication processes. While trying to read and write in the new medium, they noticed other changes like a difference in textual norms, a potentiality for a conversion in typographic conventions by using visual signs, and the feasibility of blurring traditional art categories, like image, sound and animation. I will now address these concerns.

2.1.2 Textual norms

Textual norms are the social dimension of the text, and they refer to how users apply and respond to text. Usually norms are the outcome of a developmental process that ends when the norms become accepted to such an extent that they are practiced automatically, and taken for granted. In cultural terms, they become transparent to the user.

Researchers claimed that the obvious, acute, and pressing consequences that the lack of the book's materiality will bring about are changes in the textual norms surrounding its usage. Acute, since

---

assistant on the iPhone 4S and thereafter, is based on it: "What Makes Siri Special?" in *PCWorld*, 25.1.2010.

[56] To name a few: McLuhan (1965), Rosello (1994), Landow (1997), Lanham (1994), Bostad (1994).

the change between a material object and the virtual text is (rather) distinctive so much so that it cannot be ignored as the reader feels disorientated and confused as soon as she encounters it, because it is very different from print; and pressing, as it concerns the basic process of reading, which is the first step of encountering the literary work.

Rosello (121-122) describes a futuristic scenario: in the year 2048 there will arise a need to explain what we see nowadays as elementary actions and conventional aspects in connection with writing and reading like, "a book, to read, to browse," because they will be so changed by then. Nowadays, readers know how to navigate through a book by browsing and by means of table of contents, indexes, and pagination, but if these all will disappear, it may be hard to recall what they meant. At the time of Rosello's observation (1994), not many readers were familiar with electronic texts, but that changed rapidly since.

The electronic textual norms have not crystallized into binding standards in the days of hyper-literature's peak, and they never actually became transparent to date. The novelty of the medium, the great dissimilarity from the book as we know it and the need for "filters," or intermediates, that will turn the binary code into a readable text, produced many applications, each with its own standards unlike the book (any book), which all readers know how to "use". This situation is similar to the state in which the software industry was in the eighties and nineties of the previous century, before Microsoft's *Windows* standardized the field. Every application had its own commands and key-combinations, and users had to study separately each application in order to work with it. As there are no common regulations for electronic texts, they may vary from application to application, thus, the writer should provide some directions as to the available navigation options and ways of "reading" for the specific application in which the text is written and read and for the specific work. This feature or 'state of the art' is responsible for the "un-naturalness" of reading hypertext, vs. the naturalness of reading print literature.

This is valid not only for electronic texts, but to all *unusual* texts, texts that stray from ordinary print standards. Julio Cortázar's novel *Hopscotch* (1966) is a good example of a printed book with unusual textual norms. The author declares plainly, "In its own way, this book consists of many books, but two books above all."[57] The 'two books above all' of this printed book stems from two[58] possible coherent ways of reading embedded in this novel. The one is reading one page after the other till chapter 56 and then stopping although there is more. The second is by following the instruction at the bottom of the page, which sends the reader to a new chapter, not the next one in pages' sequence. The author outlines two ways of reading, each

---

[57] Cortázar (1966) Table of Instruction, (not numbered).

[58] There is a third way for reading, the *regular* linear way of reading from the first page to the last, but as this reading does not create coherency, at least not in the second part of the book, I will ignore it.

making its own *book,*

> The first [book] can be read in a normal fashion and it ends with Chapter 56, at the close of which there are three garish little stars which stand for the words The End. Consequently the reader may ignore what follows with a clean conscious.

> The second [book] should be read by beginning with Chapter 73 and then following the sequence indicated at the end of each chapter. In case of confusion or forgetfulness, one need only to consult the following list:

> [73 – 1 – 2 – 116 – 3 – 84 ...]

> Each chapter has its number at the top of every right-hand page to facilitate the search. (Table of Instruction)

The author's feeling that a *Table of Instruction* is called for, in substitution of the conventional *Table of contents*, and the last line, which refers to facilitating "the search," emphasizes the fact that the book deviates from regular textual standards: we normally need no instructions to read a book, and the instructions we actually follow are transparent to us. The author's providing a list of his preferred chapters-sequence of reading (see chapters' sequence in the square brackets), which overrides the chapters' ordinal numbering as is conventional, accentuates his apprehension that he might be misunderstood, a feeling resulting from his acquaintance with conventional textual standards, which he consciously breaks. The "confusion" and "forgetfulness" he mentions are not experiences book readers normally encounter vis-à-vis the sequence of reading.

A year later (1967), McLuhan's book *The Medium is the Massage*[59] was published. The book is a scholarly manifest of the new electronic media, its present implications, and its revolutionary potential. "Our time is a time for processing barriers, for erasing old categories - for probing around" (10), says McLuhan. His book is as good as his word and though it's medium is print, the old medium, it is an example of possible ways for breaking print-conventions in print. Not only does the book dwell on the new possibilities in which the electronic medium can and will change the ways with which texts are composed and presented; it is a performative exhibit of it.

Interestingly, though referring to various aspects of change that the electronic media will bring about, the most notable issue that McLuhan's book exhibits is a change in typography. The first sign the reader has of the irregularity of the book is in the way the book embeds images. The first page is a picture, bearing the words "Good morning!" The picture is explained in the pictures' index – "A trademark is printed on a raw egg yolk by a no-contact, no-pressure

---

[59] The title of the book has attracted criticism and is supposed to be a print error. Yet Mcluhan liked the typo and decided to leave it as it can be read as parodied his famous saying: "The medium is the message" or like *Mass Age.*

printing technique. Imagine the possibilities to which this device will give birth!" This statement defines the relations between the book's text and its accompanying typography, a presentation of possibilities.

McLuhan's book is crowded with images; some of them hold a whole page and some are spread over several pages in sequence. This too runs against books' texture conventions. Some retain their traditional illustrative function as they reside along the text, but some have additional functions like serving as a background for the text, thus questioning the traditional and standard white color of paper and the clean "empty" surface of it, which privileges the literary text over other types of text/ures. There is a variety of visual genres; though most of the pictures are photographs, some are much diversified: some caricatures, some paintings, and some are geometric designs. Although all the visual objects are in black and white, they vary in style. Some are regular photos, some are enlargements or distortions of common objects, some are cut off, some are realistic, and some are abstract. This variety demonstrates McLuhan's statement, "When two seemingly disparate elements are imaginatively poised, put in opposition in new and unique ways, startling discoveries often result" (10). This theme runs along the book. McLuhan regards the juxtaposition as the way to perceive, understand and discover new media and even as the preferred way for education. This mélange of pictures is unusual in a book. Usually embedded visual objects in a single volume keep within the same type and serve to illustrate the text's meaning. The use of pictures as background for the text, in the first place, is usually the norm of children's books and can seldom be found in standard literature, let alone academic publications. Thus this print book itself is an example of innovations and media's power.

The juxtaposing of elements expands the conventions of print typography: the pagination, the coherence of letters styles, size and color, and letters directions. In McLuhan's book the break in pagination's unity is not obvious to the reader until page 26. Up to page 24, page numbers are written at the bottom of the page, on the right side, as is conventional, page 25 is not numbered, and page 26 numbering is written at the right side of the page, but at the top. On page 69, the numbering is printed on the left side at the top and on page 70 it is printed on the top right side. The deviation from the pagination's standard questions pagination norms, which dictates a unity of location. Such variations make our norms of reading visible, apparent, and not at all natural.

Most books keep a coherence of letter's style, size, and color. Only if the author desires to stress a point or a word, will he change the chosen letters' style. Academic research papers have fixed and binding typographical rules, which turn McLuhan's deviations from them even more noticeable.

Figure 6 is a sample from McLuhan that presents a paragraph that uses intermittently two fonts styles (regular and bold letters) without any poetical justification; words that are written only with capital letters together with regular ones without any standard order;

underlined words along with regular ones without any intelligible reason. This sample says:

> Reminders – (relics of the past) – in a world of the printed word – efforts to introduce an auditory dimension onto the visual organization of the page: all effect information, rhythm, infliction, pauses. Until recent years, these effects were quite elaborate – they allowed for all sorts of changes of type faces. The newspaper layout provides more variety of auditory effects from typography than the ordinary book page does.

Reminders—(relics of the past)—in a world of the PRINTED word—efforts to introduce an AUDITORY dimension onto the visual organization of the PAGE: all effect information, RHYTHM, inflection, pauses. Until recent years, these EFFECTS were quite elaborate—they allowed for all sorts of CHANGES of type faces. The NEWSPAPER layout provides more variety of AUDITORY effects from typography than the ordinary book page does.

Figure 6 – McLuhan, page 117 – the lack of letters' style coherence

In this sample McLuhan refers to the printed word as "relics of the past" where changes of typefaces (as is illustrated) could be a way to endow the text with auditory effects, beside rhythm and punctuation marks and yet they were hardly in use and even newspapers, in comparison, were more diversified than literature.

McLuhan's deviations from the textual norms raise attention to them and that is his intention. He questions the unified norms of print, as has been shown in Figure 6 and he does it in print. Hence, no wonder that researcher's expectations of the hypertext medium were for innovative typography and textual norms.

Unless the text is written originally in short lines, like poetry, it is conventional to justify the volume of the text in relation to the page margins. McLuhan breaks this convention as well, sometimes by creating one-word lines, and sometimes by stretching a sentence along some pages. The sentence "the book is an extension of the eye…" begins on page 34[60] and ends on page 38. These four pages contain two pictures. The cutting or stretching of sentences turns the reader's attention to the text's message, like the phenomenon of enjambment in poetry, on the one hand, and on the other hand, it questions, once again, the norms of pagination and typography.

While the regular printed book keeps the direction of reading and alignment of lines in relation to the page throughout the book, this book uses all possible directions and alignments. As the book is

---

[60] Pages with pictures are not numbered, so my reference is deductive.

written in English, which is written from left to right, we would expect that the text would be aligned to the left, as is the norm. However, in this book sometimes the alignment is to the middle of the page or even to the right.

Nevertheless, McLuhan does not stop with letters' alignment. He is questioning even the conventional direction of lines in relation to the page. On pages 56-57 we find the text upside down and rotated in an angle (Figure 7):

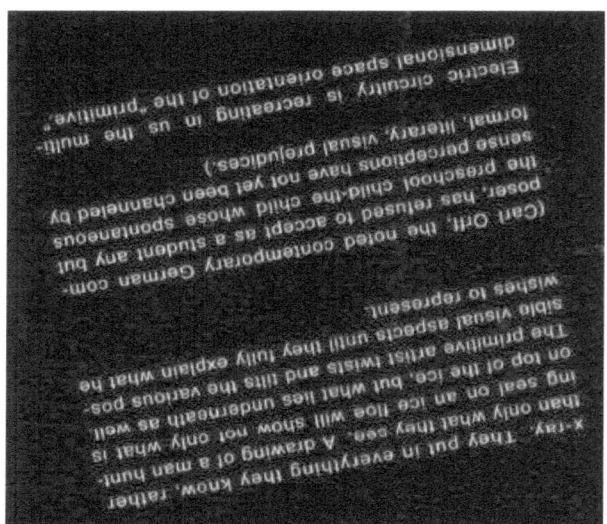

Figure 7 – McLuhan, page 56

The most bizarre typology can be found on pages 54-55, (as can be seen in Figure 8, where the text is mirrored. In order to read the text, the reader has to use a mirror.

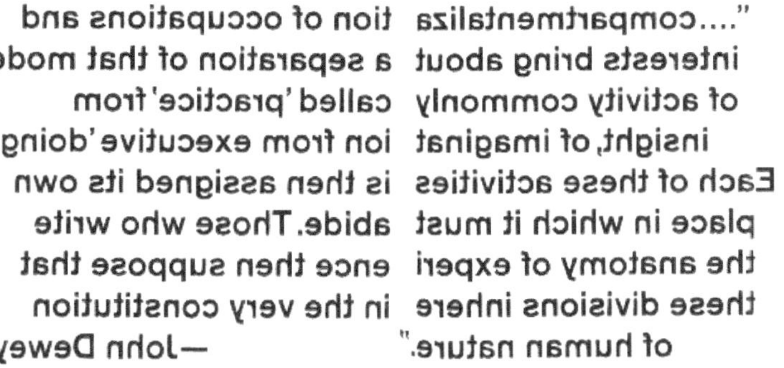

"....compartmentaliza
tion of occupations and
interests bring about
a separation of that mode
of activity commonly
called 'practice,' from
insight, of imaginat
ion from executive 'doing.'
Each of these activities
is then assigned its own
place in which it must
abide. Those who write
the anatomy of experi
ence then suppose that
these divisions inhere
in the very constitution
of human nature."
—John Dewey

Figure 8 – McLuhan, mirrored text – pages 54-55

Pages 78-79 are white and empty except for one continuous sentence at the top of each page, in very small letters, saying: "Environments are invisible. Their ground rules pervasive structure and overall patterns elude easy perception." The empty page is an illustration of the illusiveness of the environments, while raising the question – whether a book/page "eludes easy perception?" These pages are enclosed in four other pages, two on each side, showing a picture of The Fairmount Water Works in Philadelphia, Penn. The first pages, 82-83 present only the upper side of a picture showing some buildings in a Greek temple style, and the upper half of the letters "enviro." Only after the two "empty" pages, the reader receives the full picture (or maybe not) and an explanation of it, accompanied with the letters "nment." These letters, combined with their other part, two pages before, create the word "environment," but still, only the upper part of it, which raises doubts whether we are presented with the whole picture on the last two pages. This constitutes an illustration of the elusiveness of the environment in two senses: the word and the image (reality). Although McLuhan talks against imposing "the new media to do the work of the old" (81), he does exactly that but with a twist. He shows new ways to use the old media. Thus, he is actually imposing the old medium of print to do the work of the new media. He accomplishes precisely the opposite if what he supposedly preaches and, furthermore, he shows that print format is not exhausted yet. In fact, let alone actually interfacing with an active reader (inter-activity), McLuhan comes close to exhausting the repertoire of digital mode options (though not of linking).

McLuhan's book raised scholars' expectations for a typographical change with the introduction of the digital text. Bolter (1991)[61] argues that "Printing is a frozen medium in more ways than one: its letters forms stabilized between the 16th and 18th centuries and have since changed only a little" (65). He does not predict what will be the typographic changes that the electronic medium will attain, but presents the electronic medium as enabling change, "depending upon its use as an auxiliary to printing or as an alternative writing space, the computer can either reinforce this stability or sweep away the whole tradition of typography," which McLuhan actually does, in an irregular print book. Landow (1997) encompasses typography under the general graphical design of the book and calls it "the visual appearance" of text which is part of textual norms. He conceives a

---

[61] Especially Chapter 5, 64 - 81.

"good deal of visual information" in print, all of which composes our textual norms quite unnoticeably:

> The visual components of writing and print technology include spacing between words, paragraphing, changes of type style and size, formatting to indicate passages quoted from other works, assigning specific locations on the page or at the end of sections or of the entire document to indicate reference materials (foot- and endnotes) (61-62).

He argues that "Hypertextuality inevitably includes a far higher percentage of nonverbal information than does print; the comparative ease with which such material can be appended encourages its inclusion" (59). This ease causes him to see the electronic space as a system "that centrally involves nonverbal information – visual information in the form of symbols and representational elements as well as other forms of information," (61), in which he includes images and sound. He surmises that the lack of such implementing is a result of a general human resistance to change, namely – perseverance of the "old" textual norms.

Lanham[62] while trying to outline the ways in which computers, "fulfill the expressive agenda of twentieth-century art," asks "what

---

[62] As print became the regular way of writing and reading many

happens when text moves from page to screen?" (31) He observes an ongoing struggle between icon and alphabet, which he perceives as inherent to the calligraphic tradition. In his opinion, "Electronic display both invites manipulating the icon/alphabet mixture and makes it much easier to write" (34). What is more, he perceives text on screen as a picture that the artist can change the scale of, "to turn transparent attention to opaque contemplation, especially, as we begin by noting, in regard to the typographical conventions" (50).

Bostad (1994) talks about the semiotics of communication where text is a sign. He refers to Hjelmslev (1970) who claimed that signs have two sides, the first is the content they carry, and the second is their visual expressiveness. The expressive potential of signs derives from the technology with which they are communicated, however, as Finn discerned, "The electronic writing and presentation technology has, however, introduced new media and a wider range of non-linguistic signs." He differentiates "ten non-linguistic signs used in writing when using a specific hypertextual multimedia writing tool." The ten non-linguistic signs are: space, nodes, links, views, colors, sound, graphics, icons, video and animation, and text norms. Though this list is not specific for hypertext or multimedia writing, since print technology enables the use of most of these signs,[63] the

---

[63] Lately print technology enables even the implanting of sound by use of small pre-recorded chips. This is used mostly in greeting cards and the amount of sound that can be recorded on the chips is quiet limited, not to mention its sound quality.

fact that researchers perceive those traits as specific for hypertext and multimedia confirms the high hopes and expectations for a change in textual norms and typographic presentation that accompanied the emergence of hypertext. If McLuhan's examples of the possible new textual norms can be applied in print, then the electronic medium will surely be much more elaborate and fascinating.

2.1.3   The relations between literature and art

The encoded nature of the electronic text blurs the distinctions between the verbal medium and other kinds of media. The mixture of various media is regarded by Bolter (1991) as "true" writing: "True electronic writing is not limited to verbal text: the writeable elements may be words, images, sounds, or even actions that the computer is directed to perform" (113). Since the encoded electronic sign is contextually sensitive, as has been argued previously in this chapter, the electronic text can embed sound, animation, and video with ease. Some researchers, like Theall (1992), regard the tendency to blur the boundaries between the arts as part of modern and post-modern artistic tendency, giving as an example Duchamp's works:

> Duchamp, for example, became an early leading figure in splitting apart the presumed generic boundaries of painting and sculpture to explore arts of motion, light, movement, gesture, and concept, exemplified in his Large Glass and the serial publication of his accompanying notes from The

Box of 1914 through The Green Box to A l'infinitif.
(Theall, 1992)

Thus, literary critics foresaw the emergence of a new genre, the multimedia, or the hypermedia work, as Bolter defines, "A hypermedia display is still a text, a weaving together of elements treated symbolically. Hypermedia simply extends the principles of electronic writing into the domain of sound and image" (27). Landow (1997, 167-177) refers to this mélange and calls it *collage*, though he does not condition it to hold an assortment of different media; it can be a textual collage. His main point, like McLuhan's, is the juxtaposing of materials. Lanham agrees with Landow that hypertext operates by "an aesthetic of collage" (40), and goes even further to say that, "electronic writing brings a complete renegotiation of the alphabet/icon upon which print-based thought is built" (34).

This vision refers to the old controversial relations between literature and the visual arts. The study of the relations between literary texts and pictures has its roots in the classic rhetoric.[64] Lund (1992) in an attempt to draw "clear and well-defined lines between the different relations of verbal texts to optical pictures" (5),

---

[64] For an historic review of the relationships between text and picture, see James Heffernan, *Museum of Words: The Poetics of Ekphrasis from Homer to Ashbery*. Chicago: University of Chicago Press, 1993. The rivalry between the arts is so old that it got a term of its own: paragone. See Goddard, Linda. *Aesthetic rivalries: word and image in France, 1880-1926*. Oxford and New York: Peter Lang, 2012.

differentiates three categories of relations between pictures and printed text: combination, integration, and transformation.

He defines combination as "coexistence, at best a cooperation between words and pictures. It is, then, a question of bi-medial communication, where the media are intended to add to and comment on each other" (8). For instance, Sterne's *"mis on page"* as Fanning calls Sterne's spatial layout, which includes various graphical elements. There are some paintings that illustrate the text in which they reside, like Hogarth's engraving of Tristram's baptism in Vol. II, XX and the "marble page" in Vol. III, XXXVII which is more symbolic, as Sterne himself declares: "motley emblem of my work!" Sterne uses graphical illustrative sketches to demonstrate his narrative intentions as in Vol. VI, XL or to clarify his description of the Corporal's flourish in Vol. IX, IV and the "black rectangle" that is the symbol and lamentation for Yorick's death (Vol. I, VII). But the most unusual graphic phenomenon in the book is 'the blank page' in Vol. VI, XXXVIII, which Sterne left for the reader to paint Widow Wadman. His plea to the reader:

> TO conceive this right,—call for pen and ink— here's paper ready to your hand.——Sit down, Sir, paint her to your own mind——as like your mistress as you can——as unlike your wife as your conscience will let you—'tis all one to me—— please but your own fancy in it.

The continuum, after the blank page that follows these directions and the blank pages that await the reader's painting, is the applause the reader receives for his painting:

> ——Was ever any thing in Nature so sweet!—so exquisite!
>
> ——Then, dear Sir, how could my uncle Toby resist it?
>
> Thrice happy book! thou wilt have one page, at least, within thy covers, which MALICE will not blacken, and which IGNORANCE cannot misrepresent.

To this category, Lund relates William Blake, Dante, Gabriel Rossetti, and Günter Grass. They are characterized as "Authors who combine and to a certain degree master the literary as well as the pictorial medium." (Lund, 8) He adds to this category works that are the results of a creative cooperation between a writer and a pictorial artist, like the partnership between Dickens and Phiz.[65] This category can be related also to poems that are written in view of paintings or sculptures[66] and vice versa - painting and sculptures created after a literary model.

---

[65] Hablot Knight Browne was an English artist, famous by the name of Phiz. He met Dickens as the later was looking for an illustrator for *The Pickwick Papers* after his illustrator, Robert Seymour, committed suicide, in 1837.

[66] As an example, see Paul Durcan, 1994. The poems are inspired by paintings from the National Gallery in London.

In integration, says Lund, there is a closer connection between text and pictures based on the typesetting. The picture is created by the textual signs,

> Integration means that verbal and visual elements constitute an overall unity which is not reducible to the shape of a goblet or an hour-glass and the like in the pattern poems of baroque poetry as well as Apollinaire's Calligrammes and the concrete poetry of Modernism (9).

An example to Lund's integration is Concrete poetry that not only refers or describes something verbally, it takes advantage of the typographical properties of letters and presents it figuratively.

The third category is transformation, which is equal to the rhetorical phenomenon known in academic professional vocabulary as *ekphrasis*, "verbal and visual texts function in an intertextuality" (11-12). Namely, the picture, factual or fictitious, is transformed into text. Unlike the first two categories, in this category there is no picture or a graphical layout in the text, but rather the literal text substitutes the picture. The text describes, in detail or fleetingly, the picture or parts of it or other features such as its compositional characteristics and so forth, according to the effect the text desires. Lanham argues that "the struggle between the icon and alphabet" is quite old, since the Greeks' time, the 4th century B.C. He regards the transition from oral rhetoric to the written one as the cause for *ekphrasis*, "When the rich vocal and gestural language of oral rhetoric was constricted into writing, and then print, the effort to preserve it was concentrated into something classic rhetoricians called *ecphrasis*, dynamic speaking-pictures in words" (34).

All three categories Lund proposes are applicable in hypertext as in literature; however, it is easier to embed pictures in the electronic text than in print, thus why describe a picture if you can just present it? In hypertext, we may see the reversed procedure of the *ekphrasis* phenomenon; instead of a description of any kind, readers will be presented with pictures and other visual objects, as Lanham predicts,

> Through the infinite resources of digital image recall and manipulation, ecphrasis is once again coming into its own, and the pictures and sounds suppressed into verbal rhetorical figures are now reassuming their native places in the human sensorium. The complex icon/word interaction of oral rhetoric is returning, albeit *per ambages* (34).

All three traits of hypertext discussed above, the lack of a material object, the lack of textual norms, and the option to embed various kinds of media, gave rise to a change in the concept of the page and of the book as a vehicle for text, as a linear two-dimensional object, which will be substituted by an electronic writing space.

2.2 The new device

On top of all the above, the uniqueness of hypertext over and vis-a-vis texts is in its structure, or actually it's so called 'no structure.' The structural device which enables a meaningful reading of some sort is the linkage. This device elicited various expectations such as a transformation in the traditional roles of the participants in the literary communication process, a structural change that will change the way in which we read and understand texts, and for the elimination of the text's borders and the boundaries between the different arts and the privileged role of the author – his authority, his authorial position.

The linkage device can be, and usually is, used more than once in one node, thus creating multi-optional sequences of reading, which are basically created by the author and would/could be realized by the reader. This optional multi-sequentiality[67] raised questions such as what roles do the writer and the reader have in hypertext? Is the author, the writer, the creator of the work, and the reader is its consumer, recipient, or interpreter? Or maybe, we are witnessing a

---

[67] There is indeterminacy between "multi-sequentiality" and "ambiguity." To cite Aarseth (1997): "Since literary theorists are trained to uncover literary ambivalence in texts with linear expression, they evidently mistook texts with variable expression for texts with ambiguous meaning. When confronted with a forking text such as a hypertext, they claimed that all texts are produced as a linear sequence during reading" (3), and thus tried to overcome the full effect of multi-sequentiality.

historical change; the reader is turned in hypertext into a writer and an author, as some researchers claim.

The linkage device raised researchers' expectations for a change in the traditional structure of the book, its sequential order and linearity. Bolter (1991) says that "A hypertext has no canonical order. Every path defines an equally convincing and appropriate reading, and in that simple fact the reader's relationship to the text changes radically" (25). Indeed, this feature positions the reader as creator of a sort.

Aarseth distinguishes two readers; the print reader, "A reader, however strongly engaged in the unfolding of a narrative, is powerless. Like a spectator at a soccer game, he may speculate, conjecture, extrapolate, even shout abuse, but he is not a player" (4). The hypertext reader, on the other hand, is struggling to control the story:

> The cybertext reader, on the other hand, is not safe, and therefore, it can be argued, she is not a reader. The cybertext puts its would-be reader at risk: the risk of rejection. The effort and energy demanded by the cybertext of its reader raise the stakes of interpretation to those of intervention. Trying to know a cybertext is an investment of personal improvisation that can result in either intimacy or failure. The tensions at work in a cybertext, while not incompatible with those of narrative desire, are

also something more: a struggle not merely for interpretative insight but also for narrative control: "I want this text to tell my story; the story that could not be without me." In some cases this is literally true. In other cases, perhaps most, the sense of individual outcome is illusory, but nevertheless the aspect of coercion and manipulation is real.

The notion of the reader as the one to "control" the story raised hope that hypertext will enable the realization of modernistic and post modernistic text theories, especially Barthes's writerly text, for a text that is composed of many un-hierarchical and interacting networks that may have multi entrances and is produced by the reader who is assembling it, also: Derrida's notion of de-centering[68] the text – a de-centered text. Moreover, scholars hoped that the elimination of the container's materiality, the book, will eliminate its structural influence and will erase boundaries between the various arts and between them and non-artistic communications. This sub-chapter will look into all these anticipations in order to understand their motivation on the one hand, and on the other hand, to prepare the ground for an in-depth examination whether hypertext realized these expectations.

[68] Derrida, Jacques. "Structure, Sign, and Play in the Discourse of the Human Sciences," In *The Structuralist Controversy: The language of Criticism and the Sciences of Man*. Eds. Richard Macksey and Eugenio Donato, Baltimore: John Hopkins Press, 1972.

2.2.1 Reader, writer and what's between them

In print, the literary work appears before the reader as a finalized object, which does not allow any changes. The publisher prearranges its form; the author premeditates its content of sequence according to his needs, by conventions, tradition, style and culture. The reader is buying, or loaning, a product, which has a certain look, a fixed typography, and a fixed sequence of pages and narration, starting with page one and ending on the final page, starting with episode one and ending with the last, though this may not be a chronological sequence of represented events of the fictive world. The reader also assumes there is a "messenger" (an author, a narrator) behind the "message" (the book, the story). The book is a shelf product, an "as is" commodity; the reader cannot change its pagination, choose another cover,[69] or read in a different order than is presented in the book. Of course, the reader can decide to skip some pages, read backwards, or skim through, what Barthes (1975) calls

---

[69] Mostly, a book has one specific cover, yet there are cases when the book is published with two covers, for instance, one for children and the other for adults, as in the first edition of the *Harry Potter* series. The cover is regarded in the modern world as enhancing sales; hence, the two different cover addressing two different consumers. The same may be the case when there are different versions, reprints or different publishers, or after a film was created by the book – the publisher might change the cover in order to create an association between the book and the film. However, it is not a change by the reader or purchaser.

tmesis, [70] however, this kind of reading bypasses and / or goes against textual norms, or according to Barthes it is incorporated in them.

Aarseth (1997) describes print reader status quite pictorially:

> A reader, however strongly engaged in the unfolding of a narrative, is powerless. Like a spectator at a soccer game, he may speculate, conjecture, extrapolate, even shout abuse, but he is not a player. Like a passenger on a train, he can study and interpret the shifting landscape, he may rest his eyes wherever he pleases, even release the emergency brake and step off, but he is not free to move the tracks in a different direction (4).

As print became the regular way of writing and reading many

---

[70] By "tmesis", which means "cutting," Barthes refers to the flow of reading and takes for granted that no one has ever read the whole of *War and Peace* and acknowledges the skipping of paragraphs or pages as a kind of a reader's pleasure: "Yet the most classical narrative (a novel by Zola or Balzac or Dickens or Tolstoy) bears within it a sort of diluted tmesis: we do not read everything with the same intensity of reading; a rhythm is established, casual, unconcerned with the *integrity* of the text; our very avidity for knowledge impels us to skim or skip certain passages (anticipated as "boring") in order to get more quickly to the warmer parts of the anecdote. [...] Tmesis is a seam or flaw resulting from simple principle of functionality; it does not occur at the level of the structure of languages but only at the moment of their consumption; the author cannot predict tmesis: he cannot choose to write *what will not be read*" (10-11).

typographic norms became transparent to the reader. The reader usually does not pay attention to the intermediate system of production: pagination, the quality of paper, letters size and style, margins etc. Postmodernist literature tried to direct the reader's attention to this system by de-familiarization: turning pages upside down, various letters' style, sizes and colors in the same word, paragraph etc. The electronic text presents the reader the power to change, maybe even invites changes and interventions. The reader can control how the text is displayed on her computer's screen[71] by changing fonts' format, style, size, and color. The reader can change the size of the text's window, thus changing the book's layout and pagination.[72] Those potentialities gave rise to the notion of the reader

---

[71] Though it is feasible, not all applications allow it, i.e. the *ToolBook* software does not allow the reader to change anything, while the *Storyspace* software allows the change of fonts and windows' size, and Internet browsers allow all possible changes including editing though it's allowed only of the reader's personal copy. Those two softwares are hardly in use today, though Eastgate, the developers of the *Storyspace* software said that they are working on a Windows 7 compatible version right now (2012). Asymetric Inc. the creators of ToolBook, became in 2004 part of SumTotal Systems turning the multimedia authoring *ToolBook* into a course development software.

[72] Since there is no limit to the electronic page, War and Peace can be one very long page. This causes a problem in referencing pages. For instance, Kindle, Amazon E-reader did not have any page numbering and the only way the reader could find his place in the text was a percentage meter at the bottom of the page. In light of users complains Amazon produced a repair patch which is supposed to solve the problem. One way to solve the problem, which is used in

as an author, or a co-author, or an intervening active publisher and graphic designer.

Hypertext characteristic of linking reinforces this concept of the reader as author or co-author. The linkage enables each reader to "compose"[73] her own text and narrative, by "linking information together." Though literary hypertexts in the studied corpus here, did not allow the readers to create new links, re-link, to add information, or any other editing activities, researchers still regarded the reader as an author or co-author as Landow (1997) explains and provides examples from the Bible and Borges:

> As readers move through a web or network of texts, they continually shift the center - and hence the focus or organizing principle - of their investigation and experience. Hypertext, in other words, provides an infinitely recenterable system whose provisional point of focus depends upon the reader, who becomes a truly active reader in yet another sense (36).

Landow sees the function of the "active reader" as two folded:

---

academic publication, is to mark page's end in square brackets that encase the page number, in the original print text, even if it is not a real page end.

[73] I enclose the word "compose" in brackets because I do not think that this is really the case, but this issue will be discussed in detail later on in this book.

she paves her own path in the story by choosing to activate or ignore certain links, available to her in the text, or/and as the one that determines the center of the work, its focus, hence its topic and theme – its meaning. Thus, the notion is that every reader is an author, composing a new and unique narrative. Landow (1994) declares, "Hypertext readers, who chose their own paths, each read different texts and, in some cases, can never read all the available text" (34). This is a huge difference from the printed book: the book has an assumption of finality – the reader can and must read everything, which is almost impossible in hypertext unless it is very primitive (dogmatic).

Aarseth seconds this view and says that the electronic text reader is given the power not merely to make typographical changes, but to create the structure (and structure creates meaning) of the literary work by assembling it out of nodes, blocks of text, and through links woven into the text thus suggesting to the reader options of branching. This activity of the hypertext reader raised great expectations for a new reader, whose role will not be like the football's spectator, but an active one, as described by Landow:

> As a reader, you must decide whether to return to my argument, pursue some of the connections I suggest by links, or, using other capacities of the system, search for connections I have not suggested. The multiplicity of hypertext, which appears in

multiple links to individual blocks of text, calls for
an active reader (6).

Thus, the "active" reader's choices are responsible for the final sequence, while the author is responsible only for a "potentiality" of sequences as Bolter claims – and even replaces the term "text" by "a set of potential texts":

> The new medium reifies the metaphor of reader response, for the reader participates in the making of the text as a sequence of words. Even if the author has written all the words, the reader must call them up and determine the order of presentation by the choices made or the commands issued. There is no single univocal text apart from the reader; the author writes a set of potential texts, from which the reader chooses (158).

Since the reader is the one to choose the "order of presentation" she is structuring, composing if you will, which have an overwhelming weight in determining the work's meaning as we have learnt from the effect of the beginning, ending, surprise etc.

This new division of author/reader responsibility, due to the nature of the reader's activity, vis-à-vis the texts potentiality causes Landow to declare that the two distinct roles of the author and the reader are almost merged,

> The figure of the hypertext author approaches, even
> if it does not entirely merge with that of the reader,
> the functions of reader and writer become more
> deeply entwined with each other than ever before.
> This transformation and near merging of roles is but
> the latest stage in the convergence of what had once
> been two very different activities (90).

Thus, in a hypertext style narrative the reader is invited to "compose" the story and not to read it.

Lanham takes the concept of an "active reader" even further and turns the reader into an "interactive reader":

> The interactive reader of the electronic word
> incarnates the responsive reader of whom we make
> so much. Electronic readers can do all the things that
> are claimed for them – or choose not to do them.
> They can genuflect before the text or spit on its altar,
> add to a text or subtract from it, rearrange it, revise
> it, suffuse it with commentary. The boundary
> between creator and critic (another current vexation)
> simply vanishes (6).

Lanham's concept of an "interactive reader" is based on the electronic medium as scholars envisioned it, where the reader can quite easily edit the text as in a word processor, add or subtract, rearrange it and determine the sequence of reading, which is not finalized ahead of the reading process. Though Lanham's vision is technically correct and feasible, as I have said above, the hypertext works of the time this study is concerned with, did not allow, or did not easily allow, for these kinds of activities and the reader had to be a skilled computer programmer in order to realize most of them.

The innovation in expected and stated reader's place and his role in relation to the narrative work should be viewed in light of the "reader-response" theory that gained focus in the 1970s as a reaction to the New Criticism movement that saw the text as the only source of meaning (McHale 2005, 484-486). The theory investigates "the reader's contribution to the meaning of a narrative (and, in fact, any text), assuming an interaction to take place between them" (484). This theory was adopted by several schools of criticism thus creating various points of view under this theme.

Jane Tompkins (1988) says in her article, *The Reader in History: The Changing Shape of Literary Response* that although the classical literary theorists were already taken with narrative's effect on its readers or audience (for instance the Aristotelian catharsis), the new or revived interest is different:

> One soon discovers that it is not what Wolfgang Iser, Stanley Fish, Michael Riffaterre, and their contemporaries have in mind. [...] In fact, despite initial appearances, the "affective" criticism practiced by critics in the second half of the twentieth century owes nothing to the ancient rhetorical tradition it seems at first to resemble, and

almost everything to the formalist doctrines it claims
to have overturned" (202).

The essays collected in Tompkins' seminal book provide a wide range of opinions regarding the place and role of the reader and assembles the main contributors to the "reader-response" theory. Wolfgang Iser (1988) thinks that the nature of the written text leaves gaps that the reader's imagination and articulation has to fill; hence there is a dynamic process of interaction between the reader and the text. The reader is engaged in a constant interweaving of anticipation and retrospection in order to come out with the narrative's consistent pattern, "gestalt." Culler (1988) presents a social model of reading by defining the procedures and conventions readers use to make sense of literary texts thus he describes an "ideal reader," one that is competent enough to make sense of the narrative. A psychological approach to the reader-response theory was developed by Holland (1988) and Bleich (1988) who emphasized the "individual" reader that expresses his identity in reading. Fish (1988) presents another point of view of the reading process when assuming that a reader's approach to a text is not completely subjective, and that an internalized understanding of language shared by the native speakers of that given language makes possible the creation of normative boundaries for one's experience with language, and hence creating an "interpretive community." Perry (1979)[74] sees the reader as a theoretical construct,

---

[74] See also and Perry, Menahem and Sternberg, Meir. "The King through Ironic Eyes: Biblical Narrative and the Literary

an implied reader that matches the implied author, who constructs the text while reading and has to make adjustments throughout the reading in accordance to the information that the text divulge. All the reader's activities that were described thus far refer to the various activities of interpretations of texts.

Barthes (1974) finds two kinds of readers: the first and the prevalent is the consumer, whose activities are pretty much like Aarseth's football watcher, the passive reader, idle:

> This reader is thereby plunged into a kind of idleness – he is intransitive; he is, in short, serious: instead of functioning himself, instead of gaining access to the magic of the signifier, to the pleasure of writing, he is left with no more than the poor freedom either to accept or reject the text: reading is nothing more than a referendum (4).

Opposite this reader, the consumer, there is the one who is the producer of the text. The production of the text does not depend on personal qualities of the reader but on the text's properties. Barthes refers to a "writerly text," a text that weaves the five codes found[75] in the text, the "five voices," into "*writing, a stereographic space*" (21).

Reading Process." *Poetics Today*, Vol. 7:2, 1986, pp. 275-322. Also: <http://www.jstor.org/stable/1772762>, 24.7.2016.

[75] The five codes: hermeneutic, semic, proairetic, symbolic, and cultural.

Thus, the reader has to dissect the text into lexias, chunks of text, each holding one code, and then to weave them into a coherent whole. This writerly text requires as well, a mental activity of its reader, of reorganization and interpretation, and not that of rewriting of the text or of composing it.

Derrida too refers to the text's attributes and thinks that the reader has to deconstruct the text as an attribute of the reading process. "Deconstruction" has received a great number of definitions. Barbara Johnson (1980) tries to understand the term by referring to its etymology and says:

> Deconstruction is not synonymous with destruction, however. It is in fact much closer to the original meaning of the word analysis, which etymologically means 'to undo' – a virtual synonym for 'to de-construct'. The de-construction of a text does not proceed by random doubt or arbitrary subversion, but by the careful teasing out of warring forces of signification within the text itself. If anything is destroyed in a deconstructive reading, it is not the text, but the claim to unequivocal domination of one mode of signifying over specificity of a text's critical difference from itself (5).

Culler (1982) in his book *On Deconstruction* describes deconstruction as:

> A practice of reading and writing attuned to the aporias[76] that arise in attempts to tell us the truth. It does not develop a new philosophical framework or solution but moves back and forth, with a nimbleness it hopes will prove strategic, between non synthesizable moments of a general economy (155).

Hence, Culler regards deconstruction not only as a method of reading, but of writing and interpreting texts and yet the text is left "as is."

In a book that presents practices of reading novels, Alsop and Walsh (1999) summarize deconstruction and say: "So one way in which deconstruction can be understood is to see it as a particular kind of theorized praxis, as a reflective practice of reading which attends as closely as possible to the text itself, and which proceeds by careful, vigilant analysis" (97). When referring to the role of the reader and the practice of reading in general and reading of novels in particular, they describe the reader's actions:

> So, rather like those reader-response theorists and critics who, as we have seen, conceive of the reader's role in terms of filling the textual gaps or

---

[76] Aporia denotes a perplexity. In philosophy it is used for a philosophical puzzle and in rhetoric as an expression of doubt and impasse.

lacunae, the deconstructive reader also reads 'between the lines' or 'against the grain', to use two common metaphors. And what such a reader searches for are those moments (we are back to the temporal nature of the reading process) when the text appears to unwittingly transgress its own laws of construction. Typically, the deconstructive reader seeks to unpack those oppositions which make up the text's ideological baggage (98).

We can sum up the discussion thus far and conclude that the reader, in print literature scholarship, has always been assigned a role: be it a role of emotional and moral reaction (catharsis) or a role of intellectual reasoning and sense making. The reader has to fulfill the gaps, to make sense, to interpret, to organize, to reframe, to come to conclusions, to unveil hidden messages, to detect etc. in any text let alone a fragmented or de-centered text.

Referring back to the electronic reader in light of the discussion above we see many similarities. The reader's activity in print texts is two faceted: physical and mental. On the physical side of the reading process, she has to turn the book's pages in order to continue her reading. The mental side of the reading process necessitates a constant crisscrossing of the present with the past into a coherent narrative (data processing, materialization of the text). Namely, all that is pertinent to "interpretation" and "deconstruction." The hypertext reader performs the same operations. Physically she "turns the pages" though Ryan (2001)[77] objects to the use of this phrase in hypertext practice, by choosing a link, that will lead her to the next node, and mentally, she tries to create a coherent and meaningful whole. These textual norms are maintained in both literary-textual forms.

However, there is a critical difference between print reader and hypertext reader. While the print reader is merely responding to the text, be it as active and creative and "writerly" response as it may, the hypertext reader is an interactive and participating one. She is actually participating in the creation and construction of the hypertext narrative, namely: making selection and composition decisions which are completely resisted and rejected in print literature, and not merely on its mode of presentation.

The writing process, which is traditionally the author's role, is two faceted too: physically there is the act of writing (by pencil, pen, computer keyboard etc.) and mentally, the author constructs the fictive world, the fictive characters, the mode of their presentation and the plot. He is in control of inventing the full picture or the potential full pictures, while neither print-reader nor hypertext-reader has any control over it. And even if we will accept that by activating links the reader is creating or constructing the narration and the components of the represented world, since the hypertext linking device creates many

---

[77] Ryan objects to this metaphor of "turning pages" because it belongs to the codex's terms and she is right (218). Yet, because there is no other term available, I use it here only as an analogical metaphor, to illustrate my point.

possible stories, the hyper-literature reader can have control only over one of the possibilities, the one she realized (which was potentially there beforehand, controlled by the author).[78]

Landow (1997) consents that the hypertext reader is different from the print reader and says: "The multiplicity of hypertext, which appears in multiple links to individual blocks of text, calls for an active reader" (6). And yet, he presented at the 1987' first Hypertext convention his conclusions of testing an *Intermedia* system, a hypertext application, which was developed at Brown University. One of his conclusions was that there is a need for "rhetoric of linking" as "simply linking one text to another in some cases fails to achieve the expected benefits of a hypertext system and even alienates the user" (331). He refers to the "blind date" that the link has with its reader. The reader chooses between enigmatic possibilities as she does not know where the link will take her, or what is awaiting her on the next page or node, so that she is not really intentionally constructing the text, but rather trying to find her way through the text by trial and error, if we agree not to regard expectations as knowledge and if we recognize that in this aspect both types of literature readers' are alike. In order for the reader to become active in any other sense Landow asks "to indicate the destination of links." Thus, he is not blind to the illusion of regarding the reader of hypertext as its author.

---

[78] Obviously, each reading of a hypertext narrative is different from the previous one, as is in print literature as well.

Ryan thinks this claim of the hypertext reader becoming an author to be a gross illusion, as though by reading a hypertext the reader will be granted with "the gift of literary creativity,"

> Call this writing if you want; but if working one's way through the maze of an interactive text is suddenly called writing, we will need a new word for retrieving words from one's mind to encode meanings, and the difference with reading will remain (9).

Thus, Ryan transfers the activity or interactivity from the reader to the medium. She regards hypertext as an interactive medium, which requires and makes use of the reader's response,

> Technically speaking, an interactive text is one that makes use of reader input; but we will be much closer to the spirit of interactivity, at least as it is conceived by most hypermedia theorists, if we associate the concept with a second feature. To label this feature I borrow from Espen Aarseth the term ergodic design (206).

Ryan says that reader's "input" is not enough to define the uniqueness of an interactive text; the text needs an *ergodic design*, which she conceives as a "built-in reading protocol involving a feedback loop that enables the text to modify itself, so that the reader will encounter different sequences of signs during different reading sessions" (206). The term *ergodic literature* as noted above was coined by Aarseth in his book *Cybertext* as: "nontrivial effort is required to allow the reader to traverse the text" (1). Ryan distinguishes between three types of texts: *Ergodic*, *Interactive* and *Electronic* (210). Each is a text by itself yet there are texts that combine two or more of these texts' properties. Ergodic text proper is defined by as "texts, or installations, that produce ever-new outputs by simply reacting to their environment without intervention from the appreciator: chimes and aeolian flutes operated by the force of the wind, mobiles and mechanized sculptures" (208). The most likely hypertext to fulfill that definition may be Moulthrop's *Hegirascope*, where pages change by themselves every 15 minutes. Ryan sees the shift, or alleged shift, which hypertext theories expect in the relationship between the reader and the writer, as a shift in textuality combined with the reader's input and I agree with her.

To sum: the expectations for the "death of the author" in its literal meaning (unlike Barthes' use of the phrase) and the birth of the reader as author were exaggerated. First, by definition a reader is the counterpart entity of the writer, thus the two entities' roles cannot be simply inverted. Second, the reader can have control over the editing of the electronic text: its fonts, pages layout and other editorial options, or she can have control over the way she is realizing the text: skim through, read it meticulously etc. or she can respond to the text: to fill gaps, assemble, speculate, interpret, organize textual sequentiality etc. (the last two options are partially available to print readers as well). What the electronic reader cannot do, thus she cannot be the author, is to invent the whole picture and layout of the paths, the story, the available story. The interactive reader is following the paths laid for her by the text's author, exactly as in print.

Since the author lays out the alternative and optional paths, it seemed to infer an illusion/feeling/effect of controlling the production of the story. But, de facto the reader cannot produce what is not potentially latent in the electronic text. Furthermore, as Ryan claims, the electronic texts have evolved towards the ergodic planning and design, which steered the reader purposefully and decreased the reader's creative (alleged) freedom.

2.2.2 The book as an organization tool

The hypertext medium provides an opportunity for a renewed consideration of the relations between the material structure of the book and the narrative structure of the literary work. Thus it invites a study of how the change of the "container," or the lack of a bounded volume, would affect the structure of the literary work, the reading process and the structure of narration.

The physical organization of the book, sequential pages bounded together, invites the reader to read in a pre-fixed order, from the top of the page to the bottom, from left to right and then from one page to the next etc. At the same time, the writer takes advantage of this pre-determined linear path of reading to achieve his artistic goals and the effects he desires. Reading textual norms "prohibit" readings in a different order. Thus, the presentation of data is bound to an order of reading, and the author has the option/s of miss-matching the two orders. For instance, if the author decides to attain an effect of surprise, he omits some crucial data from its natural location, thus creating an informational gap, and by exploiting the conventional reading sequence he springs it on the reader where it serves his artistic aims.[79] This is true in the opposite cases as well. In cases of analepsis and prolepsis the author shatters the chronological order by providing past information into the present situation, like in a flashback, or he foreshadows information in order to create tension, like in a prophecy.

Effects such as ambiguity, surprise, tension, fear, anxiety are created and manipulated by authors by ordering the presentation in types of dissonance with the single uni-directional chronology. Thus

---

[79] The exploitation of the linear sequence in order to create surprise is a well-known device in poetics. For instance, the delayed recognition of his father and mother-wife in Oedipus Rex; in Fielding's Tom Jones – the concealment of Tom's origin of birth is one of the factors that motivates the plot; Guy de Maupassant and O. Henry based many of theirs short stories on omitting information that when found out turns over the stories meanings, e.g. The Necklace and The Cop and the Anthem respectively. The gap is usually found in the beginning of the story, the exposition – see Sternberg, Meir. *Expositional Modes and Temporal Ordering in Fiction.* Bloomington & Indianapolis: Indiana University Press, 1978. The phenomenon of concealment or omission gave rise to a whole genre that is based on this device - the detective novel, which discloses the identity of the murderer, the details of the murder and its reasons at the end of the textual sequence although it conventionally precedes the narrative.

the book secures these manipulations by binding the reader to its order of presentation and promising the author's control of effects.

This trait does not seem to be shared by Hyper-literature. According to some of hypertext's definitions that have been discussed in the previous chapter, hypertext is referred to as a system. The definition, stemming from the computer domain, alludes to the way in which hypertext documents or nodes are stored in individual files that create a database. Their true position in the hypertext database is irrelevant to the literary work since it does not create any obligatory reading sequence as opposed to the text's sequence in the printed book. The link is the structural device that creates the narrative structure in hypertext. The reader chooses her next node out of the optional linkages, and does not need to know, and should not care what is the node's actual position or placement, storage place, in the hypertext database.

The use of nodes and links[80] inevitably results in a segmented structure, not characteristic of literary narrative. This structure became one of hypertext most powerful attractions to the literary world, authors, critics, readers and scholars alike. It was considered as the realization and application of post-modernistic text theories, which sought to divorce the linearity inherent, in their opinion, in

---

[80] In print the writer is working on the text as a whole, while in hypertext the writer creates nodes that are linked to other nodes. The need that one node will fit into different sequences inevitably causes some fragmentations in those sequences.

print, to remove the closure of the narrative work, its hierarchical order and distinct center, its preordained manipulations and create a borderless and centerless text.

The segmented text of hypertext brings to mind, again, Barthes' *lexia* (1974) and Derrida's (1976) deconstruction. Barthes describes the lexias as "units of reading" (13) and stars the text in order to interpret it. Derrida wants to use deconstruction in order to reveal the oppositions and incongruities that are latent in the narration. Hypertext, on the other hand, uses the node as a pragmatic structural unit that builds up, constructs or composes the text.

The first to observe hypertext as the embodiment of Barthes' concepts about text, according to his theory presented in his book *S/Z*, were David Bolter and George P. Landow. Bolter writes in his article *Degrees of Freedom*:

> They [hypertexts] enact the indeterminacy, the flexibility, and the interactivity that poststructuralists have ascribed to all texts. Yet, what the poststructuralists discovered in printed texts only by the subtlest and most extreme rhetorical analysis, hypertexts lay open for the most casual reader.

Landow's (1997) views and opinions of hypertext second this view:

In S/Z, Roland Barthes describes an ideal textuality that precisely matches that which in computing has come to be called hypertext - text composed of blocks of words (or images) linked electronically by multiple paths, chains, or trails in an open-ended, perpetually unfinished textuality described by the terms link, node, network, web and path (3).

Landow refers to Barthes' "ideal textuality," which is similar to hypertext. Barthes distinguishes in *S/Z* between two kinds of texts, the "readerly text" and the "writerly text." Although the readerly text is prevalent in literature, Barthes prefers the "writerly text," because he perceives "the goal of literary work (of literature as work) is to make the reader no longer a consumer, but a producer of the text" (1974, 4). From this concept of the reader as producer to describing the Barthes' ideal text as the way is short:

In this ideal text the networks are many and interact, without any one of them being able to surpass the rest; this text is a galaxy of signifiers, not a structure of signifieds; it has no beginning; it is reversible; we gain access to it by several entrances, none of which can be authoritatively declared to the main one; the codes it mobilizes extend as far as the eye can reach, they are indeterminable (meaning here is never subject to a principle of determination, unless by throwing dice); the systems of meaning can take over this absolutely plural text, but their number is

never closed, based as it is on the infinity of
language (5-6).

In order to analyze the text Barthes suggests a "step-by-step"
examination, which first step is to "star" the text, to "cut up into a
series of brief, contiguous fragments, which we shall call *lexia*, since
they are units of reading" (13).[81] The lexias have no "methodological
responsibility" because they are set arbitrarily, by convenience: "it
will suffice that the lexia be the best possible space in which we can
observe meanings" (13). The minimum requirement for establishing
the boundaries of lexia is "that each lexia should have at most three
or four meanings to be enumerated" (13-14). Barthes uses as a tutor
text Balzac's story *Sarrazine*, which he regards as "a classic, readerly
writing" (15).

After the text has been cut up, it should be separated into the
plural voices ("codes") making up the text. Barthes's inventory of
voices is made up of five unhierarchical codes: The *hermeneutic* code,
"the various (formal) terms by which an enigma can be distinguished"
(19). The *semes*, which is a semantic code, "it is the signifier par
excellence because of its connotation, in the usual meaning of the

---

[81] An example for the way Barthes stars the text: "(1)
SARRAZINE * (2) I was in one of those daydreams * (3)
which overtake even the shallowest of men, in the midst of
the most tumultuous parties. *" (17) The title is one lexia, and
the first sentence of the tale is starred into two lexias. After
each asterisk Barthes presents his interpretation and the code
to which he connects the lexia.

word." (17) The *symbolic* code, "the place for multivalence and for reversibility; the main task is always to demonstrate that this field can be entered from any number of points, thereby making depth and secrecy problematic" (19). The *proairetic* code refers to actions, "In Aristotelian terms, in which *praxis* is linked to *proairesis*, or the ability rationally to determine the result of an action" (18). The *cultural* code, the last one is "references to a science or a body of knowledge referred to, without going so far as to construct the culture they express" (20). The codes, or voices, turn the readerly into the writerly, "in their interweaving these voices, (whose origin is "lost" in the vast perspective of the *already-written*) de-originate the utterance: the convergence of the voices (of the codes) becomes *writing*, a stereographic space where the five codes, the five voices, intersect" (21). by the use of the combination "de-originate" Barthes regards the text created by the inter-linking of the codes as a way to change the origin of the utterance and to create a new text.

Although Bolter and Landow see hypertext as Barthes's writerly text, Barthes himself is not looking for a new technology or a new way of writing. He is trying to present a new way of reading, which turns the reading process from a relatively passive activity into an active and responsive response-able one, thus turning the reader from a consumer into a producer or co-producer of the text in its entirety including its hidden components. This new way of reading, "This new operation is interpretation (in the Nietzschean sense of the word). To interpret a text is not to give it a […] meaning, but on the contrary to appreciate what plural constitutes it" (5).

Kurtz (1997) provides a different view of Barthes' theory and explains the difference between *work* and *text* in Barthes terms:

> The difference that Barthes draws between a work and a text is not the result of a technological transformation; it is not a material difference between modes of writing; and it is not a stylistic difference, a quality of the writing itself. The difference consists instead in a change in attitude, a shift in perspective, a redistribution of roles.
>
> I understand Barthes's distinction in these terms: a "work" is a literary product viewed with reference to the author, while a "text" is a literary object viewed with reference to the reader.

The dominance of Landow's theory, which resides in the background, is implied by Kurtz' choice of language, even if not explicitly declared. I agree with Kurtz' explanation: while some of Barthes's terms (the text as many interacting networks, unhierarchical, has several entrances, there's no 'whole' of the text) can be applied in describing the way hypertexts seem to be structured, Barthes did not refer to the manner in which texts are structured, but to the way in which they are read. The use of Barthes's term "lexia" in equivalence to "node" is inappropriate for at least two reasons.

First, Barthes coined this term as an interpretive segmentation device and not as an authorial structural device. Second, as has been shown above, the lexia's boundaries are distinct by a minimum of requirements and the interpreter's "convenience," but, there are no such requirements of the "node." What is more, the node's boundaries are set up by the author and not by the interpreter. However, the primary reason why Barthes cannot be referring, albeit unwittingly to hypertext is that the main characteristic feature of hypertext does not exist in Barthes's theory - the link, the structural element, which turns a text into hypertext. The "weaving of voices," to which Barthes refers takes place in the reader's mind and not in the structure of the text or in its presentation.

Still, a most important feature that researchers adopted from the Barthezian theory is the concept of hypertext as a network, of mental linking possibilities, namely its multi-connections and multi-entrances (a certain idea of the lack of the final materiality of the book.) Barthes invites the reader to take charge of performing the text's writerly-ness in his imagination and in his interpretation. Thus interpretation becomes a super-active activity, but its interactive dimension remains in the realm of the reader. Hypertext, on the other hand, necessitates the reader's actual activity and inter-activity in order to perform its potential, in order to create its narrativeness. Thus, hypertext necessitates a different, or a preliminary activity of creating the specific version of the text that the reader will be able to "perform."

Thus, we had a lot of similarity and a lot of variance between print literature and the hypertext format. Variance produced great expectations, which were fairly exaggerated since there is much more resemblance than expected. The variance was actually trivial and uninteresting in a way that creates a too far-away category from the concept of literature as art and the author stayed in control despite all.

2.2.3 Borders, boundaries and the web

The lack of a physical storage container in hypertext, jointly with its links, gave rise to a renewed discussion as to the texts' frame, the boundaries between literary works, and between literature and other textual and non-textual materials and literature as a web.

Keep's Hypertext Fiction Research Group contends that viewing the book as a tool, as a neutral container to the fictive output of the writer, is wrong. It shows a disregard to the immense influence that the idea of the book had on literature, from the Bible to the post-modernistic novel and even on hypertext literature. In the group's opinion, "…the idea of the book as a totality […] was the model for our understanding of the world itself, for the way in which people try to make sense of the irreducible complexity of what we call nature, or reality" (*The Book of Nature*, hfl0247.html). They regard the book as an answer to human needs, "More abstractly, a book, with its front and back cover, its first page and last, is a model of our desire for completion, wholeness, and closure" (*The Book*, hfl0246.html). Since hypertext is perceived as a borderless text, without a cover and without a front-page or a last page, without a beginning or an end, and with potential "entrances" for importing external texts and materials, scholars expected it to bring about an examination of these concepts.

The perception of hypertext literature as a narrative without borders, without a fixed beginning and with no end has been much discussed in theoretical writings about the new medium and not surprisingly so. The beginning and the end of a book (or of a story) are so distinct in the printed book, that the first thing a hypertext reader encounters is their lack. Landow, one of the first literary scholars to realize hypertext's importance to literature research and especially to narrative theory, wrote, as early as 1992:

> The concept (and experiences) of beginning and ending imply linearity. What happens to them in a form of texuality not governed chiefly by linearity? If we regard hypertextuality as possessing multiple sequences rather than lacking linearity and sequence entirely, then one answer to this query must be that it provides multiple beginnings and endings rather than single ones (77).

Lanham expresses the need to transform Aristotelian Western based poetics: "The Aristotelian categories of beginning, middle, and end, it turns out, are based on fixed texts" (125). Douglas addresses this very issue:

145

> We are accustomed to dealing with texts that end more prematurely than their stories would seem to, but what do we do with a text that, a bit like a book made of sand,[82] has pages we cannot properly count and nothing like end titles or hard covers to contain it? And, when you stop reading, what is really finished: the stories – or you? (62)

One norm of print literature is the matching between the end of the narrative and the physical boundaries of the book, thus creating two types of closure: the narrative one and the material one. This was one of the issues that scholars hoped hypertext would challenge. The fact that the reader does not know if she read all the text raises many poetic questions like: When is the hypertext reading process finished? Is reading all the print-text, namely from page one to the last one, obligatory? Moreover, how do we know, in hypertext, that we have read all there is to read? And if we don't, how can we presume to interpret a literary work if we are not sure that we have read all the narrative? In addition, what becomes of closure? What structure can this narrative have and can there be a perception of closure to the text? Herrnstein Smith (1970) differentiates "between concluding and merely stopping or ceasing" (1). Thus, she sees two endings: the end

---

[82] The metaphor, "a book made of sand," refers to Borges' story *The Book of Sand* that describes a sacred book whose pages are always changing, thus there's no one fixed page that can be referred to as beginning or one page that functions as an end.

of the book, the last page, which causes the "stopping," and the end of narrative, where the story concludes. For her the basis for closure is latent in structure, "the sense of closure is a function of the perception of structure" (4). How then can hypertext create a sense of closure if it does not have a pre-conceived and pre-determined structure and perhaps no one point of departure (end)? As Douglas observes:

> Unlike print narratives, where each chapter builds upon the preceding one and leads to a single, determinate conclusion, the narrative strands in hypertexts can lead to numerous points of closure without satisfying the reader. Or the reader can be satisfied without reaching any point of closure at all (42).

While the Aristotelian requirement of the text is for three distinct functions: beginning, middle, and end, hypertext presents a new concept of "numerous points of closure" for what Douglas calls the "narrative strands" and on the contrary, she can see a text without any closure, and yet the reader may be satisfied. Thus Douglas sees hypertext's potential to conceptually deviate, revolutionize if you will, the Aristotelian concept that requires one distinct end. The same goes for concepts of middle and beginning.

Landow (1997) proclaims that hypertextual materials "by definition are open-ended, expandable, and incomplete" (79). Thus, for him "If one put a work conventionally considered complete, such as *Ulysses*, into a hypertext format, it would immediately become "incomplete"." But, this is a useless observation since *Ulysses* in a hypertext format will not be *Ulysses* at all.

Nelson, who is a computer expert in the first place, expects hypertext to be open-ended because of its revision potential as he declares in his well-known book *Literary Machines 93.1*: "There is no Final Word. There can be no final version, no last thought" (2/61). Not merely that, but the option of modification causes hypertext to be endless and the documents to become 'live': "The free-flowing, live documents on the network are subject to constant new use and linkage, and those new links continually become interactively available" (2/48).

In summation, the hypertext literature has the potential to break away from the Aristotelian traditional distinction of beginning, middle and end, by two opposite options: the text can have multi-points of closure or no point of closure at all. Hypertext can start anywhere in the text and the beginning can be different any time the reader starts a reading. Though these possibilities are feasible most of the hypertexts in the chosen corpus have a unique beginning and what can be regarded as a distinct end. Hypertext changes the middle according to the author's pre-organized possibilities that are presented to the reader to choose from.

Hypertext also breaks down the boundaries forced by the

materiality of the book and turns it into a decentered object.[83] The book's format allows an easy discerning, not merely between the margins of the page and its center, between its first page and its last page, but also between a single work, one text, and others. When holding a book in our hand we can feel it as a distinct, independent, and single object. However, in hypertext, the text's links can lead the reader to other texts, which might be outside the present literary work thus canceling the text's boundaries on the one hand and shifting the reader's interest, hence decentering the text.

Landow (1997) says:

> As readers move through a web or network of texts, they continually shift the center – and hence the focus or organizing principle – of their investigation and experience. Hypertext in other words, provides an infinitely recenterable system whose provisional point of focus depends upon the reader, who becomes a truly active reader in yet another sense (36).

The linkage device in hypertext literature creates a networked text, which shakes the privileged status of the main text. The question is whether there is a privileged first text? The famous "original" of

---

[83] This decentering is different from Derrida's use of the term. Derrida is decentering the reading, hence deconstructing, while the use of the term here is about the decentering of the text, a changeable focus of the text.

privileged status that all readers can relate to? In this hew decentered text everything can be the first and everything can be the secondary.

The possibility to electronically link diversified texts not only causes the blur of the individual text's boundaries but also may obscure the boundaries between different traditional genres and various domains. Landow predicts, in a sub-chapter named *Boundaries of the Borderless Text* (79-83):

> In hypertext systems, links within and without a text
> – intratextual and intertextual connections between
> points of text (lexias, including images) – become
> equivalent, thus bringing texts closer together and
> weakening or reconfiguring the boundaries among
> them (80).

Landow's main reason for this observation is the possibility to move in hypertext with ease and speed between passages and texts: "One change comes from this ability to move with equal facility to points within a text and to those outside it" (82). For instance, if Moulthrop, instead of citing from Barthes' *From Work to Text* in node *Wadi* in his hypertext *Victory Garden*, had transferred the reader to a full digital version of Barthes' book, what would have been the status of these two distinctive books? Would we say that Barthes' text has become part of *Victory Garden*? While in print literature a citation or allusion is a distinct reference to another text, in hyper-literature the whole work, not only one concept or one idea, can be integrated into the work itself. This issue, though referring to the boundaries of a literary work, is a theoretical problem as nowadays authorship is protected by copyright laws. Thus, even if Moulthrop had incorporated Barthes' work in his, he would have to distinguish it from his own work by law, obtain permission or warn his readers, and give Barthes due credit. Landow regards the option of embedding one literary work within another with a double perspective: "the weakening of the boundaries of the text, can be thought of either as correcting the artificial isolation of a text from its contexts or as violating one of the chief qualities of the book." Meaning from one point of view the artificial isolation of each work will be eliminated and all the literary works will be turned into a huge collage, and from the other point this collage will desecrate the text's most cherished trait which is its uniqueness, autonomy, individuality and at the same time its copyright and artistic genius.

The choice between these two views reflects a cultural position. Landow chooses the first view and suggests that "all that the hypertext linking of texts does is embody the way one actually experiences texts in the act of reading" (80). thus referring to the literary device, allusion and intertextuality, which is based on the virtual activation of texts previously known to the reader by use of words, sentences, scenes, and characters taken from these texts. The allusion aims at bringing together two texts, the text that is being read, and the text that has been read or is been referred to, hence, creating an analogue and connection (linkage) of some kind between them. In this sense

Landow regards the print-text's so-called isolation as a concept which needs "correction" which hypertext provides.

In summation, the great expectation of the new medium revolved around two points: the expectation for the contestation of the single work's conventions on the one hand, and clouding the boundaries between different works, genres, and artistic domains on the other hand. This anticipation stems from the electronic format, the "storage" system and especially the linking device, which discerns hypertext from other electronic texts. This device caused scholars to describe and treat hypertext as a network, after Barthes. The option that a single narrative will have multi-beginnings and multi-closures and different ones or no closure and yet the reader will feel satisfied, might be a real change. These options disputed intense norms and powerful conventions that were deeply rooted in narrative culture.

3   Textual Norms and Orientation tools

The new digital medium was at the time, mainly the nineties of the 20th century, fairly innovative to most literature readers, writers and critics alike.   While there is a five centuries tradition of writing, publishing and reading printed-books, hypertext as an electronic medium was available to writers, publishers and readers since the late eighties. In this chapter I will sketch the textual norms of hypertext that are overtly different from print norms in order to find whether they are radically different and revolutionary. In other words, are they "erasing old categories" as McLuhan (1967, 10) had anticipated.

By "textual norms" I refer to the

> Socio-cultural conventions which define the "well-formedness" of a text. Such norms prescribe how a text should be structured if it is to be accepted as a "well-formed" text in a certain community, and in specific situations and types of situation in that communicative community (Berge, Kjell Lars, 129).

Thus, I will confront the claim of many researchers that hypertext, being an electronic object, was expected to have different/new textual norms than the printed text, by closely inspecting Joyce's *afternoon, a story*, Moulthrop's *Victory Garden*, Geoff Ryman's *"two five three"*, Deena Larsen's *Samplers*, Moulthrop's *Hegirascope*, and Coverly's *Califia*. These seven narratives were chosen for several reasons: they provide a wide range of timeline capsulating the decade of flourish of the genre, they characterize different writing applications, common at the time, and they represent two literary genres: the novel and the short story.

The first textual norm I shall examine is the physical-material aspect of printed works (books). The lack of hypertext's physical existence and tangibility is unquestionable, thus raising the question whether there is really no cover or envelope to the work, no apparent boundaries, which separate the work from other physical or virtual objects, and if so, is there no traditional *title page* that announces its identity as well? Is there no table of contents and page numbering too? If so, is this a deficiency and does it change textual norms that derive from the printed book's tangibility? Are the topographic norms of the book broken? Moreover, if so, are there no substitutes or compensations for this lack?

In light of the excessive variance of hypertext compared to print literature authors guided and directed the "new reader" how to "read" the work. I will examine the reading directions that authors provided their readers with, in order to start and guide them on their reading. Through these directions, I will ascertain how the new textual norms are considered by the authors, what they see as imperative instructions for the reader, and what they expect of the "new" reader.

The lack of a physical entity in hypertext, its lack of structure, and the lack of generic organizational structures cause a problem, known in computer science technical terms, as the *disorientation problem.*[84] Though this is a computerization problem, it concerns the reader as well, hence the on-going debate in the early years of hypertext's development of its seriousness and the ways to solve it. With time, all software developers became aware of it and even authors considered it when creating hypertexts. For instance, Coverley in her work *Califia* created the *KitBag*, "The KitBag has items you may need to take bearings along the paths of *Califia*" (*Calvin's KitBag*). In this chapter, I will describe the problem and its common solutions in the form of *orientation tools,* which are supposed to facilitate hypertext-readers' orientation in the text, solve some of its consequences and compensate for the lack of a content list and page numbering. The *orientation tools* satisfy two of the readers' needs, which are part of the familiar and traditional textual norms: the need to locate a specific place in the work for further or returning inspection and the need to grasp the work as a whole. These tools satisfy the need for finding out "where am I?" and the need for crisscrossing back and forth, thus they can be classified as searching tools and navigation tools, and in short, *orientation tools*. I will refer to two main hypertext applications and theirs tools. The first is the *Storyspace* Reader application, which creates a closed, stand-alone

---

[84] The term *disorientation problem* was coined by Jeff Conklin (1987 17-41). See also Landow, (1997, 115-123). A later discussion with reference can be found in Michael Bernstein's article *Hypertext Gardens*, (1998), available at <http://www.eastgate.com/garden/NavTech.html>, 24.7.2016.

network.[85] The second application is Microsoft's *Internet Explorer* browser, an application for viewing hypertext documents on the Internet, which is a borderless space. I chose Microsoft's *Internet Explorer* because of its being the most popular browser at the time, yet most browsers allow the same navigational options, albeit under different names.

As all hypertext research expects a change in textual norms and expresses its inevitability and obviousness, there is no examination of what actually happens in the available hypertexts, and there is no investigation of *orientation tools,* or inspection of typographical layout, from the poetics point of view. Namely, up until today no research has been done to compare deferential diagnostic textual norms with new hypertext ones.

---

[85] The term 'stand-alone' is a term deriving from computer science, and means a system that is self-contained and independent. Hence, a stand-alone application is a self-sufficient software, which does not require any other device, for instance a network, for its operation. A stand-alone hypertext is a work that operates on a computer from a diskette or a CD-ROM without any help from other devices. By "closed" I mean that the reader cannot change the text, albeit she can write down personal notes, which will be kept by the software, along with her reading only if she will save her reading under a different file name, hence without actually changing the original text.

3.1 The electronic setting

Although the typography of a text is influenced by the medium in which it is written, it is influenced by older textual models as well, thus the first printed books preserved the typography of the manuscripts and even older models stemming from scrolls.[86] Martin (1958) sums up this tendency, "The earliest incunabula[37] looked exactly like manuscript. The first printers, far from being innovative, took extreme care to produce exact imitations" (77). Eisenstein (1998) agrees with this proclamation in her book *The Printing Revolution in Early Modern Europe* and brings visual examples for this

---

[86] Similar phenomena are found in innovative objects as explained by Johna Berger in *"'Think Different' is Bad Advice."* Web document, <http://www.nirandfar.com/2016/07/think-different-is-bad-advice.html?goal=0_9f67e23487-476f4a1319-97818197&mc_cid=476f4a1319&mc_eid=a54cb0c2fa>, 24.7.2016.

[87] The term "incunabula" was first used by Bernhard von Mallinckrodt (1591-1664), a German philologist. In his book *De ortu ac progressu artis typographicae dissertatio historica*, published in Cologne, 1640 referring to the early period of printing prior to 1501. The word "incunabula" is Latin for "swaddling clothes," as these books are from the infancy of European printing, typeset and printed by hard from moveable type. Incunabula reflect the transitional phase between the manuscript and print traditions. "incunabula". *Encyclopedia Britannica. Encyclopedia Britannica Online.* Encyclopedia Britannica Inc., 2013. Also: <http://www.britannica.com/EBchecked/topic/284960/incunabula>, 24.7.2016. See also National Diet Library, Japan <http://www.ndl.go.jp/incunabula/e/chapter1/chapter1_04.html>, 24.7.2016.

conservatism and conservation (18-22). The typographic preservation concerns every aspect of printed books, as attested by Martin:

> The 42-line Bible for example was printed in a letter-type which faithfully reproduced the handwriting of the Rhenish missals.[88] For a long time printers did not merely use the same individual characters but also groups of letters linked by the same ligatures as those used in manuscripts. For an even longer time initials in printed books were rubricated by the same calligraphers and illuminated by the same artists who worked on manuscripts. So much is this the case that the layman sometimes has to examine a book very carefully before deciding whether or not it is printed or handwritten (77).

Martin rejects the various explanations used to account for this conservatism, like the desire to deceive the buyers "who might distrust the new mechanical process" or the fear of offending the *Guilds* of copyists.[89] He argues that the "15th-century eye" will have

---

[88] An artistic style of painting, calligraphy and manuscripts illustration by artists from the Rhine region of 15th- and 16th-century, which is regarded as a genuine golden age for Rhenish artists.

[89] "Copying books became a trade, and the men who did that work were called copyists. In time these men joined together in a guild. In those years all skilled workers had to belong to guilds." Eaton, Jeanette. *Leaders in Other Lands*. Lexington MA: Heath, 1950, 42.

easily spotted the deceit and that the same people who dealt with manuscripts were dealing with printed-books, which were sold side by side with manuscripts. Instead, he provides a very simple and banal reason for this conservatism: "How could they have imagined a printed book other than in the form of the manuscripts on which they were in fact modelled?" (78) Thus, according to Martin the first printers adopted the format of columns, after that of ancient scrolls, for lack of imagination and for disregard for innovation.

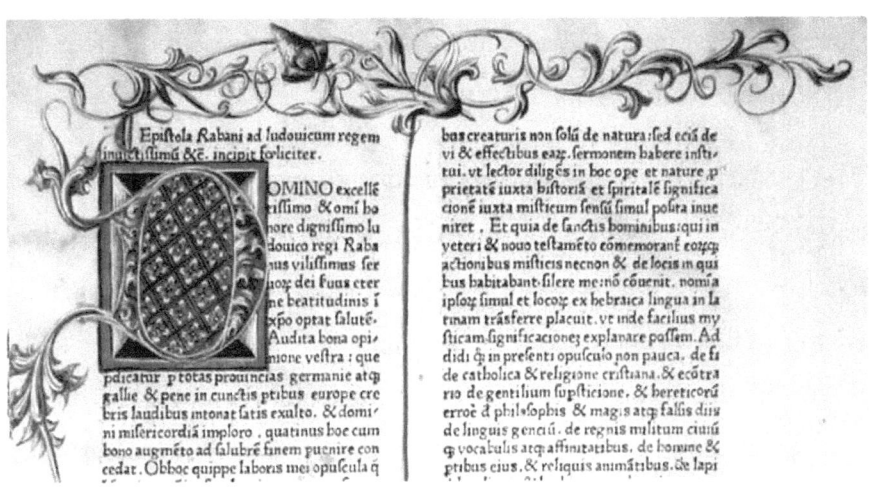

Figure 9 - Hrabanus Maurus, *Opus de Universo* (Strassburg), 1467.[90]

---

[90] An example of the two columns format that characterized the incunabula. The OU [Oklahoma University] History of Science Collections, <http://hos.ou.edu/galleries/03Medieval/Maurus/1467/Maurus -1467-Pi2r-image/10in/>, 24.7.2016.

The columns format was adopted in scrolls for practical reasons. The scroll was one very long piece of papyrus, parchment, vellum, or cloth that was rolled from side to side in order to read. In order to ease the reading, the text had been "cut up" into columns, so that the reader could see one column in its entirety in order to read without keeping scrolling all the time. Although the page of a book was much smaller, and the reader could see the entire page without any effort, so that there was no practical reason for the use of columns on a single page, the columns format was preserved on book pages.[91] Not until "roman script came into general use, was the presentation of the text modified" (Martin, 87).

Martin says that another residue from the manuscript was the placing of the book's information at the end of the book in the 'colophon': "it was there that he [the reader] could expect to find the name of the printer, place of publication, perhaps the title and the name of the author" (84). However, a technical option, which was caused by practical reasons, changed the *title page*'s place bringing it from the back to the front of the book. Martin explains the *title pages*'

---

[91] This format of multi-columns is still used today when the page is big and wide, in albums' format, catalogues, and journals, reference books and even on the Internet. Most of the encyclopedias and dictionaries are two columns until today. For instance, most of the encyclopedias that are still printed like: *Encyclopedia of Exploration*, 2004-2006; *Dictionary-of-Environment-Ecology*, Bloomsbury Reference Books, The Oxford Study Dictionary, 1994. See a sample page on: <http://www.elearnaid.com/oxstuddic.html>, 24.7.2016.

birth, after Haebler:

> Since the recto[92] of the first leaf always had a
> tendency to soil, printers conceived the idea of
> starting the text on the verso, leaving the recto blank.
> Then, from a quite natural desire to fill in the blanks,
> they printed a short title on it and this helped to
> identify the book (84).

When the format of the scroll was abandoned for that of the leaf, a need to protect the leafs from becoming soiled and from scattering away, caused readers to bind them; later on, bounded books became the standard and the binding was done by the publishers. Hence, the new medium gave rise to a new flourishing industry of binding, which was not needed in scrolls' times. The binding of the book, in its turn, gave rise to the cover as a new space for writing and/or illustrating. With the growth of book printing, and the need for references in scriptures and commentaries, the book got its pagination, table of content and indexes. (Eisenstein, 64-73)

Scholars recognized that one of the changes, which the electronic medium enables, is a typographical revolution, and expressed much hope for its happening in hypertext (detailed in Chapter 2). I could not find any research that actually compares

---

[92] Recto and verso are two technical terms in printing and publishing industry that denote front and back, respectively, of a leaf of paper, a page.

between print and hypertext's typography, and no wonder. Landow (1997) observes that "Despite the considerable presence of visual elements in print text, they tend to go unnoticed when writers contemplate the nature of text in electronic age" (91), which is in opposition to McLuhan's forecast and prediction. Therefore, in the following pages I will examine two textual norms of the electronic-setting: the cover page and title page in order to find out whether the expectation for a typographic revolution and a change in theses textual norms came about with hypertext. The cover of the book, which distinguishes one work from another will be examined versus the claim[93] that hypertext, being a digital intangible medium, does not have any. The *title page*, together with the cover page and the first page, has a dual importance. From the sociological point of view it serves as the book's public relations agent that provides the works' initial information, and tries to catch the eye of the potential reader and purchaser. From the poetic point it has a crucial influence on the reader's expectations of the work in the long run, and especially at the beginning of the reading as it has to retain the reader's interest so much so that she will not discard the book after the first page. I will try to decide if the same objects exist in hypertext, and if so, do they have the same functions as in print?

---

[93] Landow (1997, 3), Lanham (1994, 7, 125, 129), Bolter (1991, 86-87, 143, 162-63).

3.1.1 The Cover

The cover differentiates the book as a physical tangible object from other similar or disparate objects and establishes firmly the book's boundaries as a single, autonomous, distinct and whole literary work. Yet it was not always so. Understanding the importance of the cover or its lack requires an explanation of some of the main points of the evolution of printed books.

The incunabula were treated as luxury and were bound in the same format as manuscripts.[94] Martin (1999) states that: "They [craftsmen who bound manuscripts] continued to cover the back and the boards, made of solid wood, with precious fabrics like velvet, silk, cloth of gold, if binding luxury editions destined for important people" (104-105), thus, granting the cover a cultural and sociological-economical meaning. However, he adds that "books were not bound as part of the normal publishing process as they are now"; books were sold as unbound sheets and bound later by the owner, according to his individual taste, or not bound at all (105). Hence, only with the growth in book production there arose the need for cheap and light bindings, which can be produced rapidly and inexpensively. Thus, the *cardboard* as the books' cover main material replaced wooden boards and calfskin. Nowadays the book is treated

---

[94] "At the time a manuscript or its successor Incunabula, a printed book, was so comparatively rare and costly an item of merchandise that it merited care in its preservation and adornment." (Martin, 104).

as merchandise, as a commodity, and the cover is used conventionally as a marketing device.[95] The cover-front is adorned with some graphical object: a picture, a lithograph, a painting, or an illustration of some other sort, which serve as an enticement for the reader to acquire it but also as a mark of aesthetic excellence, expertise, and artistic beauty.[96] On its backside there's usually some data about the author, his/her previous books, a summary of the books subject, and newspapers clippings and blurbs praising the work and its merits, though in previous centuries it complemented the esthetics and design of the front-cover.

Hyper-literature on the web does not have a cover, because it is a part of a larger electronic text, the Internet, however it has a *title page*, as I will show in the next section. Stand-alone hypertexts usually come on some sort of digital media: diskettes, CD-ROM etc. These are usually encased in an encasing or envelope, which can be regarded as a substitute for the printed-book cover. Their cover is a physical cardboard box or a plastic caddie, in which the diskette, diskettes or CD-ROM are packaged. Moulthrop's work, *Victory Garden,* came on one diskette, encased in a cardboard folder holding

---

[95] Matthews, Nicole and Nickianne Moody, Eds. Judging a Book by Its Cover: Fans, Publishers, Designers, and the Marketing of Fiction. Aldershot/Burlington: Ashgate, 2007.

[96] Altitude Associates. *The Best of Cover Design: Books, Magazines, Catalogs, and More.* Massachusetts: Rockport Publishers, 2011.

the diskette on one side and on the other one a printed manual, which includes directions for installing the "book" and for navigating through it, and even two articles written by hypertext's specialists: the first is an introduction to the book by Michael Joyce, and the other is a paper about hypertext as a new medium, written by Jan Yellowlees Douglas. While the first article is common in academic literature the second one is unique to this hypertext work – and it indicates the necessity of introducing the new format to the reader.

Placing *Victory Garden*'s encasing next to a printed-book cover, like that of Nabokov's *Lolita*,[97] or Franzen's *Corrections: A Novel* illustrates clearly that there is no discernible difference between the three covers (See Figure 10). Although Moulthrop's cover is a cardboard folder and Nabokov and Franzen's covers are paper ones, which is the regular soft-cover in print-literature, the same elements can be observed on all. All covers display the author's name, the work title, and an illustration: *Victory Garden* shows a black and white photo of mountains, probably referring to Tara's landscape, the town in which the plot is enacted. *Lolita*'s illustration[98] is a colored butterfly on a white background, a photocopy of ink and colored-

---

[97] This work was published in many editions and by many publishers. The cover page in Figure 10 is of *The Annotated Lolita* (Penguin books, 1995). It was chosen quite in random, as it had the same elements of Moulthrop's work.

[98] The drawing is by Nabokov, dedicated to his wife, Vera and dated 5 January 1971. This information is written on the back cover of the book in very small letters.

pencil drawing by Nabokov himself, which was dedicated to Vera Nabokov. The butterfly is a symbol for Nabokov's second pursuit, Lepidoptera,[99] on the one hand, and on the other hand, it serves as a rich and multi-faceted metaphor to Humbert Humbert. He is attracted to young girls as a butterfly to honeydew and moreover the butterfly serves as a metaphor to Lolita herself being so beautiful, gentle, delicate, fluttering and so ethereal, being chased by a butterfly hunter. This metaphor creates identification between Nabokov and Humbert Humbert (who is the butterfly hunter and who is the butterfly?), and thus enhances the ambiguity and significance of the illustration, which participates in the interpretation. Franzen's (2001) cover is divided into two main parts and in between there is a separator, which is a citation of praise. The upper part of the cover holds the name of the author in huge fonts and is addressed to his fans audience that read his previous books. The other part shows a photographed scene of a family's Christmas dinner, which is one of the motivational events in the book.

The difference between the covers lies in the informational data that each publisher chose to display. As *Lolita* is quite a famous work, published in various editions, the publisher wants to stress this edition's uniqueness – it being edited, prefaced and annotated by one of Nabokov's prominent experts, Alfred Appel Jr. Some of this

---

[99] Boyd, Brian. *Stalking Nabokov*, New York: Columbia University Press, 2011.

information appears on the front-cover, albeit in small letters: "Edited with a preface, introduction and notes by Alfred Apple Jr." But the book's back cover provides further details:

> Alfred Apple Jr. also provides fresh observations on the novel's artifice, games and verbal patternings, and a delightful biographical vignette of Nabokov. The annotations themselves were prepared in consultation with Nabokov while newly identified allusions were confirmed by him during the final years of his life.

Since *Victory Garden*'s uniqueness lies in its being an innovative literature-work in hypertext format, the publisher has to introduce the idea of hypertext and fiction. Hence, on the front-cover there is a citation from the *New York Times Book Review*, which praises the work as a hypertext:

> ...indispensible [sic] No one has taken on the hard questions about hypertext and fiction or played so intransigently with the myriad possibilities and obstacles of this new art form as has Stuart Moulthrop.

These praises are written by Robert Coover who was the New York Times Book Reviewer at the time and writes from a literary view. In print literature, such reference is mostly located on the books' back-cover. However, as can be seen in the third cover, that of Franzen's *The Corrections*, it also carries a recommendation that appeared in the *New York Review of Books* on the cover page and it announces itself as being *A Novel*. This announcement is unexpected in light of the novel's seniority as a genre but comprehensible in view of the new media.

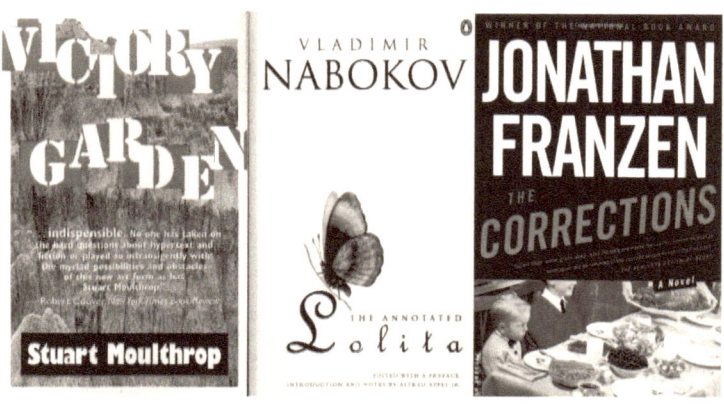

Figure 10 – *Cover pages*

Print literature sanctified, with time, the front-cover by use of special letters, visual metaphors done by artists and designers (as in *Lolita*'s front-cover butterfly and in the thriving art of graphic design). Though the front-cover tries to entice the reader by its look and not by long praising texts, the declaration that Jonathan Franzen is a Winner of the National Book Award is at the upper part of the cover (sometimes there are stickers adhered to the cover saying that the book won an award or other marketing information).

The hypertext front-cover is regarded as a bulletin board open to marketing and publishing, as in print literature. This is continued on *Victory Garden's* back-cover as well and provides the reader with more praises regarding the work as "hyperfiction" and a small summary of the fiction's subject. The same format is found on the *afternoon, a story* front-cover where the encasing shows a picture of the author, his name, the work's title and underneath another praising citation, written by the same book reviewer, Robert Coover, of the *New York Times Book Review*.

In print, books praise and some brief synopsis are mostly kept for the back cover. However, hypertext lost this need for enticing its readers and its encasing became more and more like print norms. Larsen's *Samplers*, which was written well into the peak of hypertext (1997) has no praising words on the front-cover. It holds the author's name, the work's title and a picture, that turns out to be the stories' content table, and the simple announcement: "Nine Vicious Little Hypertexts." *Califia* comes on a C.D. thus it has a caddy that holds a picture on which the work's title is stressed in hand-written fonts and at the bottom – the author's name. Since *Califia* was published as late as 2000 its front-cover resembles that of a pocket book and on its back there are no praises, only publisher's information and the disk's computational requirements. Thus, we see that hypertext literature covers that started with what looked like new norms and a conscious effort to be user/reader friendly, lose their "feeling" of uniqueness with time and resemble print books more and more.

Hypertext literature on the Internet, on the other hand, has no cover at all. On the Internet some hypertext literature compensates for the loss of the cover with a very long and detailed *title page*, although not material, which contains all the data that the cover on both sides usually holds in print-literature as can be observed in Ryman's (1996) *253,*[100] which will be described in detail in the following section. The same is true for Moulthrop's *Hegirascope*, where publications' data, the proclamation of the work as hypertext, the works version, the work's title and the author's name are presented on the homepage/front-cover and other stuff like introduction and direction are announced on the "cover page" yet linked from it.

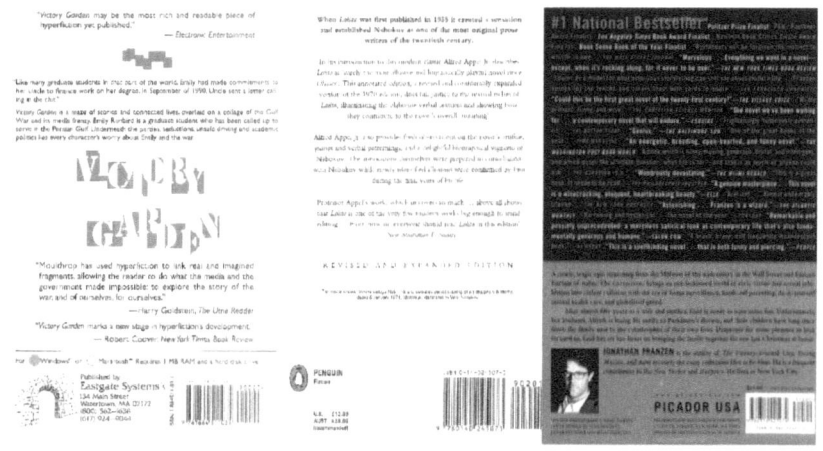

Figure 11 - Back covers: *Victory Garden, Lolita, The Corrections*

---

[100] The work was published in print two years later in London by Flamingo Publishing House.

3.1.2 Title page

All hypertexts have a *title page*, a digital one that can be viewed only on a computer screen. The early works, *afternoon, a story* and *Victory Garden* covers are different from their *title pages*. But with time, with the change of the cover, the digital *title page* turned to be the same as the cover presenting the same picture or illustration and conveying the same information, hence increasing the similarity between print literature and hypertext. If there is a lack of some sort on the cover of hypertext, like the name of the publisher or publication date, usually there are additions and compensations for it on the *title page* as in *Samplers* and *Califia*.

It is quite easy to show that each hypertext, on the net or as a stand-alone application has a digital *title page*. Joyce's *afternoon, a story* title page states the author's copy-rights and publisher's name and address, thus holding information that is traditionally written on the *title page*'s back, and simple guidelines: "for directions click *yes* (y) -- to start press Return" (Figure 12).

Moulthrop's *Victory Garden's* first page (Figure 13) states the work's title and the author's name, as in any printed book; but the last two lines, at the bottom of the page, and the generic label "a fiction", make the difference. They distinguish the work as a hypertext book.

for directions click yes (y)-- to start press Return
©1987,93 by Michael Joyce. All Rights Reserved
Eastgate Press 3rd Edition 1992   1 2 3 4 5...
Eastgate Systems, Inc.
PO Box 1307
Cambridge, MA 02238 USA
(617) 924-9044

Figure 12 - *afternoon, a story* - *front-cover* vs. *title page*.

The description of the work as "a fiction" brings to mind the age of the rise of the novel, in the 18th century, when authors used to declare that what they write is a "history" or at least as "life" and they turned the declaration into a part of the work's title. These declarations are an attempt for a historical-like authenticity by using historical documentary notes of time and place. Thus in Defoe's work *The Life and Adventures of Robinson Crusoe* the *title page* states:

> THE|[101] LIFE| AND| STRANGE SURPRIZING| ADVENTURES| OF|ROBINSON CRUSOE,| Of YORK, MARINER:| Who lived Eight and Twenty Years,| all alone in an un-inhabited Island

---

[101] Vertical line marks the end of the line.

on the| Coast of AMERICA, near the Mouth of| the Great River of OROONOQUE;| Having been cast on Shore by Shipwreck, where-|in all the Men perished but himself.| WITH| An Account how he was at last as strangely deli-|ver'd by PYRATES. | [rule]| Written by Himself.| [rule]| LONDON:| Printed for W. TAYLOR at the Ship in Pater-Noster-|Row. MDCCXIX.

Figure 13 - *Victory* Garden *title page* vs. its *front-cover*

Many of Defoe's colleagues did the same, authorizing authenticity on fiction, though not to that length: Samuel Richardson named his book "Clarissa: or, the history of a young lady. Comprehending the most important concerns of private life; and particularly shewing the distresses that may attend the misconduct both of parents and children, in relation to marriage."

Fielding titled his famous novel *The History of the Adventures of Joseph Andrews and of His Friend Mr. Abraham Adams*, and on the title page, underneath the title stated "Written in Imitation of The Manner of Cervantes, author of Don Quixote." Novelists' tendency to ascribe historical traits to their works is explained by Scholes and Kellog (1968) as a way to solve the problem of "the authority of the narrator. In mythic or traditional narrative, the events being narrated are always well back in the past and the tradition itself carries its own authority" (242). Since the 18th century with the advent of realism in fictional literature novelists avoided mythical or other traditional subjects, and they needed to establish their authority, which they did by adopting the pose of the historical author,

> Since Herodotus and Thucydides the histor has been concerned to establish himself with the reader as a repository of fact, a tireless investigator and sorter, a sober and impartial judge - a man, in short, of authority, who is entitled not only to present the facts as he has established them but to comment on them, to draw parallels, to moralize, to generalize, to tell the reader what to think and even to suggest what he should do (266).

Thus, following Cervantes, who called himself a historian and biographer, 18th century authors set their work apart from their predecessors in proclaiming their work as a "history" and gaining, at the same time, the authority the novel lacked in those early days.

Nowadays the novel is securely established as a genre of fiction. It stresses its fictionality by proclaiming that there is no connection between the narrated events and characters to any real events or characters: "Any resemblance to actual persons living or dead is coincidental" (*Introduction*). Fiction has a distinct place in art and does not need a patronage like history or truth anymore.

Figure 14 - *Samplers front-cover* vs. *title page*

In modern hyper-literature, we are witnessing the same evolutional phenomena. Since the hypertext format was new as a literary genre in the eighties, it announced in a conspicuous manner its fictionality and relation to literature. This declaration is unusual in print fiction today. Hypertext was introduced as a non-literary format for reading and writing and is still more widespread in non-literary and non-fictive hypertext format. In order to differentiate hyper-literature (the less common) from non-literary writings (the more common), hypertext authors needed to declare their work as "hypertext fiction" as Moulthrop declares in *Hegirascope*, adding the words "a story" as is found in *afternoon, a story* title or "a novel for the internet" as in Ryman states in his *253*. However, as the genre became more common it lost its need to declare its fictionality and became more like print literature as is seen in Larsen's Samplers, where the front-cover is pretty much like the title page and neither announces the work's genre or any other attributes. (Figure 14)

Two intriguing lines reside at the bottom of the *Victory Garden's title page* (See Figure 13). No author or editor of a printed book will ask the reader to "Press Return[102] to begin;" or to click on "help" for help, because there's no "Return" to press and there's nothing to click on or to click with in the printed book. These instructions clearly belong to another medium. The reader, on the other hand, does not require any guidance to the conventions of reading a printed work. For instance, there is no need to tell the reader to turn the pages or to read from top to bottom. She knows her options by a long practice of reading printed materials. It has already been mentioned that with manuscripts, that preceded the format of the book, there were other practices. The practice of printed bounded books' reading is only as old as the product's existence, and if the printed bounded book were to disappear we might need instructions for the reading of such an object, but its cultural assimilation turned it

---

[102] At the time when Moulthrop's work was written and published (1991), the *Enter* key in Apple's Macintosh computers was called the *Return* key, after the typewriter.

into transparent and self-understood, thus taken for granted. Nowadays hypertext is the standard for reading and writing on the internet and the hypertext reader does not require any instructions, though not for reading literature. However, at the time, authors and editors alike thought that some assistance was called for.

In *Victory Garden* on clicking on the word "help" the reader is transferred to a node titled *Welcome*. Although, there are other links branching from this node (*Welcome*), the node's title implies that the author expects the reader to click on the word "help," hence the greeting. The node (*Welcome*) describes the work as a hypertext, as the author conceives it: "*Victory Garden* is a hypertext – a story, or a web of stories, whose contours can change every time you read it," and provides a brief explanation for navigating hypertext.

If the reader does not require help, she can hit the *Enter* key from the *title page* node and be transferred to the beginning of the story (a pre-programed linear reading), to the starting point that was programmed by the author, namely, the *properties* node. This node combines what usually, in the printed book, is called *Preface* or *Acknowledgements* and the back cover-page, which contains documentation such as copyright information, date of publication, a disclaimer of any resemblance to "actual people" because the story is "a work of fiction." Another hit on the *Enter* key takes the reader to the node titled *Come In*, a label that speaks for itself and is pre-programed by the author.

It is interesting to note that, with the change in medium, publishers feel the need to advertise themselves on the *title page*. In the age of incunabula, printers and publishers used to publicize themselves and their address on the cover, as Martin says, "Publishers also, in their desire for publicity, quickly adopted the habit of printing their name and address at the foot of the [title] page" (85). Nevertheless, we must bear in mind that in those days the author was usually unknown and did not receive any attention or preserve any copyright, because most of the early printed publications were liturgical or academic. Though hypertexts bear authors names, as in print literature, some of hypertext literature is still available only through its publishers.[103] Returning to the issue at hand, when the *afternoon* reader presses the *Enter* key from node *start* she is transferred to the node labeled *begin*, which is the appointed starting point of the story as the label attests, moreover it is the default from node *start*. The slight difference, between Moulthrop's node label and Joyce's, stems from a difference in hypertext conceptions between the two authors. While Joyce's node label looks upon his work as "a story", as claimed in the hyper-book title, and thus invites the reader to "*begin*" reading, Moulthrop regards his work as a maze, as a "web of stories (as can be seen in his maps). He invites his reader to enter the maze, hence the node's title "*Come In*".

---

[103] Though hypertext works are available from on-line stores like Amazon, these books are still not available from regular book dealers or shops.

In Coverley's *Califia*, published some ten years after *Victory Garden*, the *title page* labeled, *The Island*, 2,[104] takes for granted the reader's mastering of hypertext ways so there are no preliminary "directions." The story starts *in medias res*[105] and each node carries the link "Follow Me," which is textual as well as visual (the silhouette of foot prints) that guides the reader until, quite soon actually (6th node), it reverts to the "old" patterns, providing a detailed "help" file that explains the structure of the book and navigation possibilities. Some of the data that is usually presented on the title page is found on the back of the caddie encasing the C.D., the work's title, author's name, the C.D. compatibility and the publisher details. Hence, we see that within ten years the genre became common and popular that there was no pressing need for help or reading directions.

The same observations apply to hypertexts on the Internet. Looking at Moulthrop's *Hegirascope* we see that the *title page* holds the work's name, the author's name, publication data (version and date), three links ("Introduction," "Copyright" and "Begin"), and the work's status: "a hypertext fiction" (Figure 15). As the work is published on the Internet, there is no need for the author to tell the reader "click here," when referring to the work's links, because that

---

[104] Although *Califia* has page numbering, I will continue to use their labels as well for compatibility's sake. Thus, node's title will be in italics, accompanied with node's page number: *The Island*, 2.

[105] Latin: "in the midst of things."

is the convention of reading pages on the Internet. The reader can see the linked words (words that are linkage signifiers) since the cursor turns into a hand-shaped pointer when passing over them. Moulthrop's *title page* differs, from other *title pages* that have been discussed thus far, in its illustration. The illustration is animated, constructed out of changing image fragments of the nodes that make up the story. Meaning, there is here a digital development that is used in hypertext works.

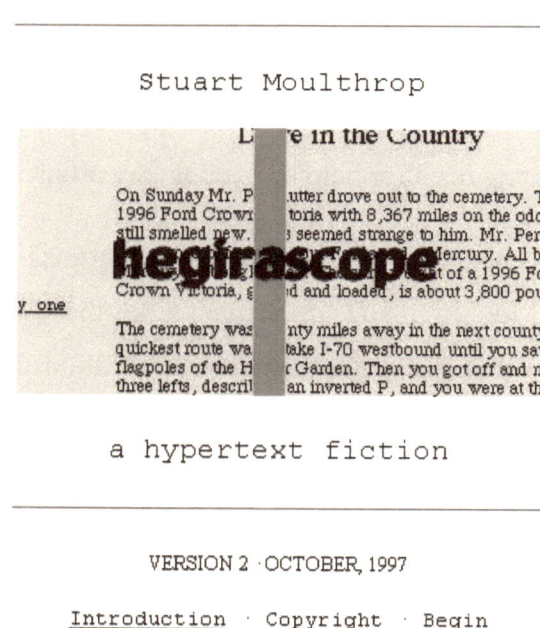

Figure 15 - *Hegirascope title page*

The same observations apply to hypertexts on the Internet. Looking at Moulthrop's *Hegirascope* we see that the *title page* holds the work's name, the author's name, publication data (version and date), three links ("Introduction," "Copyright" and "Begin"), and the work's status: "a hypertext fiction" (Figure 15). As the work is published on the Internet, there is no need for the author to tell the reader "click here," when referring to the work's links, because that is the convention of reading pages on the Internet. The reader can see the linked words (words that are linkage signifiers) since the cursor turns into a hand-shaped pointer when passing over them. Moulthrop's *title page* differs, from other *title pages* that have been discussed thus far, in its illustration. The illustration is animated, constructed out of changing image fragments of the nodes that make up the story. Meaning, there is here a digital development that is used in hypertext works.

Hegirascope's *title page*, although residing on the Internet, is still similar in style to stand-alone digital *title pages* that have been reviewed above. However, the Internet has its own standard for *title pages*. Each Internet site can be quantitatively regarded as a small book (sometimes even a large one), containing various sorts of information. Each site has a gateway, which functions as the *title page* in a book, presenting various diversified information: technological, commercial, advertising, academic, artistic etc. according to each site's subject and publishers (which can be commercial companies as well). Although there is no written standard for the design of the gateway, there seems to be a de-facto standard as most sites contain some preset and recurrent elements that are supposed to facilitate the reader's navigation and orientation on the site on the one hand, and to publicize it as a serious, reliable, and interesting source, on the other hand.

Usually the gateways present some information about the site, such as owner's name and e-mail, the site's fields of interest and the like. This first node holds a menu or some links that, in their turn, serve as a gateway to the site's content. Sometimes a search device, which enables the reader to search for a specific subject, is available. Each site is proud to present rewards and recommendations that it has earned, thus establishing its authority and reliability – a real problem in an uncensored space, where anyone can publish anything. At the bottom of the page there are usually links to a copyright notice stating the legal conditions of use, for contact information, site map etc. Most sites have some graphic elements, like the illustrative object on a books' cover page.

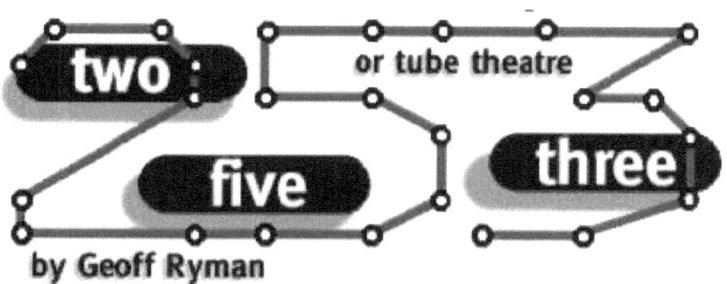

a novel for the Internet about London Underground in seven cars and a crash

Figure 16 – *two five three* **- upper part of node** *title node*

As an example, for the de-facto standard of hypertext on the internet at the time of hypertext's flourishing, I will analyze Geoff Ryman's hypertext "*two five three*," published on the internet in 1996. The work has its own site; hence the *title page* is the gateway to the site, its Home page. The head of the node presents the work's title "*two five three*," the author's name, a declaration that the work is "a novel," which is similar to print, and a two-line abstract: "a novel for the Internet about London Underground in seven cars and a crash." The graphic element is quite sophisticated, constructed out of the standard symbols of London's tube map, but arranged into the numbers 2, 5, 3, thus forming graphically as well as literally the work's title, which refers to one tube-line passengers (253). Within the graphical element of the title are written the words "or tube theater." Thus, while it looks like the work has two alternative names, both referring to London's tube, the title "tube theater" is not an alternative name but specifies the genre as in Franzen's *Corrections*: a novel, Moulthrop's *Hegirascope*: a story etc. At the same time this second title creates interest as it introduces the scene of action (the tube as theatre).

This first node is quite long and the reader has to scroll down to read, it cannot be viewed on its entirety on the screen. At the top of the gateway there is an annotated textual menu holding seven propositions (Figure 17).

253 ? Why 253 ? describes the ground rules of the novel.

The Journey Planner provides links to the first four cars and individual passengers.

About this Site tells you a bit more about 253 and the author.

Select The End of the Line to read about the end of each carriage's voyage.

Another One along in a Minute describes the sequel you are invited to help write.

On each car section, advertisements appear. These are deeply serious and should be read with great attention.

Simply click on the option of your choice. Relax! It's so easy, travelling with 253.

Figure 17 - 253 annotated textual menu

The first one, *253? Why 253?* links the reader to detailed and humorous directions, like the origin of the novel's name, why it is important to read this novel etc. The second proposition links the reader to information about the site and the author. The third transfers the reader to a "Journey planner," a graphical linking device, simulating the small tube maps called "journey planner." The fourth is an invitation for the reader "to read about the end of each carriage's voyage," transferring the reader to a menu that links the reader to each car's end of story. Hence, there is a prescribed end to this novel.

The fifth line is a call for readers to contribute a 300-words story, which will be published as a continuum to the original story, and will be called "Another One along in a Minute." The idea of readers becoming writers is a way for interactivity on one hand, it is a way to by-pass the fixed end, which is counterproductive since the reader, in order to write, has to wait for the end of the story, and at the same time it gives the story a realistic trait: "Immediately behind this train is another."[106] The request of a 300-words story derives from the 5 minutes' wait between trains, which is 300 seconds. The fifth proposition refers the reader to advertisements found in each car of the train and cautions the reader to read them carefully. The seventh proposition does not hold any links, and is a calming advice: "Simply click on the option of your choice. Relax! It's so easy, travelling with 253." The continuum of the node, after this menu, in bold letters, there is a motto "In cyberspace, people become places" (title page), referring to the combination that is presented in the work of tube stations and people. This kind of annotated "content page" is rare in print and is mostly found in avant-garde literature, like John Barth's Table of Contents in *The Tidewater Tales* (1987).

Still on the same node, scrolling down some more, the reader finds quite a large list of on-line reviews, segregated by rulers, written about the novel, and the awards that the site (novel) has won. This feature is found in print literature too, yet this list is linked directly to the reviews' sources and to the sites that grant these awards and the reader can reach it with a mouse click, which of course is impossible in print literature. At the bottom of this title node resides another menu, which is really a table of contents, (Figure 18) for all the train's cars, which allows a quick access to all other sub-menus: the passengers seating scheme in each car.

---

[106] Node titled "Another One along in a Minute," <http://www.ryman-novel.com/info/one.htm>, 24.7.2016.

253 ? Why 253 ?
About this Site
Journey Planner
Car 1 passengers
Car 2 passengers
Car 3 passengers
Car 4 passengers
Car 5 passengers
Car 6 passengers
Car 7 passengers
The End of the Line
Another One Along in a Minute

Figure 18 - 253 quick menu

The structure and content of Ryman's electronic title node demonstrates clearly that the function of the cover and the *title page* is so customary that when the cover page is missing the *title page* compensates for it and vice versa. There were no new electronic conventions for the cover and *title node* thus authors and publishers turned to the old ones. They wanted to wrap the new work in a familiar package thus to communicate the generic relations that the new work has with its predecessors and its framework – books and literature. They gained a side benefit since print norms offered the reader a sense of familiarity and reduced the cognitive dissonance that the new hypertext fiction held for its readers.

In conclusion, information presented on books' covers and title pages is found in hypertexts as well and it is available to the reader by "turning" the nodes (an action that is done in hypertext by clicking with the mouse) according to instructions and a universal intuition. Moreover, these examples show that there is a distinct contact point, where the reader meets the hypertext work. In the printed book the reader holds in her hand the bounded volume, leafs through the *title page* or pages, turns the book and reads its back-cover and critic blurbs – all that as a way of creating a contact with the work. In hypertext as well, though there is no material volume to hold (stand-alone works that are sold in an encasement do not fulfill that function), there is a contact point, the various substitutes of the cover, title pages etc.: the encasement cover, the title node, the gateway, menus etc. And yet, when there is an innovative genre the reader should be guided as to how to read/use it. Thus hypertext desired quite a vast amount of explanations and encouragement for the reader to try and explore the text in order to fulfill its potential. In this respect hypertext resembled board games or a "Do it yourself" objects that come with a huge brochure of directions, or computer games, that although not so innovative nowadays (2016) are still published with directions, explanations etc. It is interesting to note, however, that history does repeat itself. In times of technological transitions, people tend to hold on to the old concepts, which were proper to the old technologies. Looking back to the Gutenberg transition from scribe to print, we find that,

> The early printers tried to make their books identical
> to fine manuscripts: they used the same thick letter
> forms, the same ligatures and abbreviations, the
> same layout on the page. It took a few generations

for printers to realize that their new technology
made possible a different writing space, that the
page could be more readable with thinner letters,
fewer abbreviations, and less ink (Bolter 1991, 3).

Bolter expects that hypertext will follow previous phenomenon
of transition from one technology to another, those of imitating with
the new technology the norms and conventions of the old one, though
with time hypertext will develop its own norms. However, as this
research shows, after the end of hyper-literature flourishing period no
uniform hyper-literature norms were founded and the similarity to
print literature still holds water albeit with some additional
instructions unique to the hypertext platform.

3.1.3 Directions

Almost every *title page* of hypertext literature written with
Storyspace software offers the reader "directions" or "help" about
reading possibilities. There is no difference between the two terms;
both links transfer the reader to nodes that explain these possibilities.
However, the change in link signifier is interesting since it attests to
the lack of electronic binding standards on the one hand, and on the
other hand, it might be premeditated, a response to readers'
contentions over difficulties in reading *afternoon*.

Michael Joyce's *title page* of *afternoon, a story* offers two possibilities: "For directions click yes (y) -- to start press Return."[107] (See Figure 12 – on the right) Almost the same words, although in reverse order, can be seen on Moulthrop's *Victory Garden title page*: "Press Return to begin; for help click on 'help'." (Figure 13)

Deena Larsen's *Samplers*, a later work in the *Storyspace* collection, dates from 1997. She, as well, considers it essential to direct the reader, albeit briefly. The colorful *title node* specifies the work's name, the author's name and the publisher's name in alternating green and blue. (See Figure 14 – on the right) Underneath, in red color, the reader is given two options for reading the collection of stories: "Click on any image for a story… or you can always press ENTER." The reader can choose between one of the nine patterns making up the *title node* graphic, one for each story, by hitting the Enter key. In previous works the enter key transferred the reader to a prefixed first node, in this work it opens the Links window,[108] where the reader has to choose, what she wants to read. This work forces the

---

[107] Although the "(y)" window is not available in the P.C. edition, clicking on the word 'yes' with the mouse can activate this possibility. The Return key of the Macintosh is the Enter key of the P.C.

[108] The Links window is a small window, ten lines long, in which the reader can view all the links that are available at this specific place (See Chapter 3.2.2). This trait is specific to the *Storyspace* software, the *ToolBook* software and Microsoft's typical Internet Explorer does not allow it, however there are some add-ons that make this view possible in Internet Explorer.

reader to choose as there is no prefixed node and there is no other way to start reading but to choose while the other stand-alone hypertext that has been examined has a default starting node (not taking into account the maps that will be discussed later in this chapter.)

Coverley's *Califia* (2000) title page, though published in the *ToolBook* software, does not hold any directions. It consists of a colored picture, on which the work's title and author's name are written and underneath it, a copyrights notice. As *Califia* was published some nine years after Moulthrop's work we can understand the lack of directions; hypertext had been around already for ten years. *Califia*'s *title page* does not respond to the Enter key, here there is only one option – to click with the mouse on the graphical element that will transfer the reader to the first node of the narrative or to click on the copyrights notice, which will transfer the reader to the traditional publishing information. Namely, the information is available to the intuitive user without the known words of code (help, credits, directions, enter etc.)

All the hypertext works that I have cited, published in the *Storyspace* software, have two possibilities of reading; The first one is the pre-ordered sequential one: by clicking the Enter key as Joyce's explains: "You move through the text by pressing the Return key to go from one section to another (i.e., "turn pages")" (*afternoon, a hypertext*). This can be achieved also by clicking with the mouse on the margins or the blanks of the node. Complementing the move between nodes is the possibility of retracing the reading path.[109] This can be done by four ways: by clicking the mouse's right button, or by hitting the *Backspace* key on the keyboard, or clicking on the back-arrow icon on the toolbar or clicking on the "history button" and choosing the "previous node." In Moulthrop's words, "Click the right mouse button or strike Backspace to review the previous moment, or to move back through the story as you've seen it so far" (*Victory Garden, Welcome*).

The second possibility of reading a hypertext work is the interactive one, by activating the linkage device - clicking on hyper-words,[110] words that are linked or, in Joyce's terminology, "words that yield." The reader – so the directions state – can identify these words either by hitting the Ctrl key or by activating the Links window: "If you choose Show Text Links (by pressing the CTRL key), the words that yield will be identified. You can also call up a list of all possible links leading out of a given moment by choosing Browse Links from the *Storyspace* Menu or pressing the Links button." (*Victory Garden, Enigma[111]*) The Links button opens up the Links window, which is actually a Table of contents of all the links available from the active node. Hence the second possibility is the interactive reading. This sort

---

[109] The software "remembers" the reading's history so the reader can go back to choose different links.

[110] Hyper-words are words that are linkage signifiers.

[111] Citing from Storyspace works the reference is by node's label.

of reading can be retraced too by the same devices. This possibility does not have to follow a pre-ordered reading path and the reader can explore the text, thus disturbing the linear order of the text.

In summary, though there was no established tradition of readings' possibilities, publishing information and written directions, *Storyspace* applications keep to similar lines. Each holds two options of reading, the linear one, where the reader is following the author's paths by hitting the Enter key and not choosing for herself, and an interactive one, where the reader is realizing the text's links and chooses between them.

On the Internet, there are usually no written directions. The author reckons that a reader, who has got thus far and found the work, must know some of the Internet norms of reading. Only if the work deviates from these basic norms will directions be made explicit. Since Stewart Moulthrop's *Hegirascope* illustrates such a departure from standard reading he presents the reader with the option of an "Introduction." The introduction explains the special reading mode,

> Most of these pages carry instructions that cause the browser to refresh the active window with a new page after 30 seconds. You can circumvent this by following a hypertext link, though in most cases this will just start a new half-minute timer on a fresh page (HGSAbout.html).

This automatic change of pages is uncharacteristic of hypertext fiction, quite unique actually, and it turns the reading into a chase - will I finish reading the page before it changes? A reader cannot contemplate the narrative twice, and sometimes not even once, as she is in a ceaseless perpetual race against the timer. The author takes advantage of an internet property and prevents the leafing back and forth in the work, thus taking hypertext out of written literature and turns it to an oral story telling-reading session – if the readers/audience lose concentration they may miss the story. This trait introduces a playful quality – the time limitation that is characteristic of games, like the clock in chess, scrabble and other games.

In the continuum of the *Hegirascope* Introduction, the author offers some general directions:

> The best way to encounter this work is simply to dive in, though some may prefer a more stable reference point. For these readers, there is an index to particularly interesting places in the text. You may want to go to that page and bookmark it.

The author directs the reader to "interesting places" thus becoming authoritative and forestalls here the reader's potential reaction. He explains the two ways to 'encounter' the work: one is to read from the "official" beginning and the other is to enter through other possibilities that are listed in the index. The first option is "to dive in." These underlined metaphorical words signify a link leading the reader to the work's first node of the narrative, where the author greets the reader: "Hi, There" (HGS0A1.html). Most hypertext authors regard hypertext's writing space as a physical space, thus using spatial metaphors like a maze or a garden and referring to reading as touring or following pathways. The new metaphor embodied in 'dive in' gives the hypertext work another dimension of depth, the page is not flat and underneath it there are various layers, more nodes. This metaphor refers not only to a physical place, it is underwater and in order to explore it the reader has to be brave and take a long breath. This advice comes in time, as the automatic changing attribute of the nodes actually leaves the reader breathless. However, as the author knows that some readers will like a 'stable reference point', he provides an option to go to "interesting places in the text" (HGSAbout.html) of *Hegirascope* as well.

Yet, Hegirascope links' 'index' leads the reader to a list of propositions, like a table of contents, which do not provide the reader with any such stable reference point as alleged, because the propositions are quite vague and their relation to the linked nodes is mostly associative. For instance, the index link "Some are worth reading!" leads the reader to a node called *Epigraph*. Only in retrospect can the reader comprehend the connection between the link signifier, the proposition, to the linked node. The index links takes the reader to *in media res* kind of reading, thus presenting the reader with options to choose from and yet, the reader is following the choice of the author in this option as well.

In conclusion, authors felt that readers of the hypertext medium required some 'first directions' no matter under which label. To begin with, hypertext literature was a rather new way of writing and reading and no uniform textual norms for reading or writing were yet established. Second, the medium itself was not fixed yet. Hypertext standards on the Internet were still developing and new authoring tools, which would enable more elaborate authoring possibilities, which may change the look of the node along with its embedded objects, were (and still are) conceived daily. Yet, there are some fixed standards of writing hypertext, especially within the same publishing house. Also, there is a relation between the work's date and the amount of directions that the author feels his reader needs and between the software that is used for writing and the amount of works that have already been written with it. Thus the earliest work, *afternoon, a story*, (1987) has intensive directions that are conspicuous on the title page, while Larsen's work (1997) doesn't offer any visible directions and they can be found with some effort. *Califia*, though being the newest of the works, (2000) has intensive directions since it is the first hypertext written with the *Toolbook* software so the author feels obliged to provide the reader with instructions about all the tools that are available for her. Print literature does not need reading instruction, yet there is an artistic device where the author addresses his reader and tells her what to expect, thus laying bare the device (see Kahn, 1980).

3.2 Orientation Tools

The *orientation problem*, distinctive of hypertext texts, was taken into account at the developmental stages of hypertext-software and systems. Ted Nelson recognized this problem as early as 1980. In a paragraph titled "The problem of orientation," he acknowledges:

> There are tricky problems here. One of the greatest is how to make the reader feel comfortable and oriented. In books and magazines there are lots of ways the reader can see where he is (and recognize what he has read before): the thickness of a book, the recalled position of a paragraph on the left or right page, and whether it was at the bottom or the top. These incidental cues are important to knowing what you are doing. New ones must be created to take their place. How these will relate to the visuals of tomorrow's hot screens is anybody's guess, but it is imperative to create now a system on which they may be built (1/18).

Nelson is concerned with the reader's comfort and orientation meaning the three-facets of hypertext reading: how to navigate through the text, how to know where you are in the text, and how to search the text. In printed texts, navigation means leafing in the order prescribed by binding and pagination. The reader knows where she is in relativeness to the number of pages she has read and the amount that is left. Searching the text is available mostly through table of contents and indexes and a quick manual search by leafing through the text aided by the stability of the print on the pages, their pagination and the reader's memory.

Regular electronic texts are the same as print texts; they have a beginning, middle, and an end, they may have page numbering, table of contents, footnotes, and indexes, though they can be link signifiers, thus they can be reached by a mouse click. In a single document the reader can navigate by searching for a specific word, or by scrolling up and down[112] through the document, or by looking at navigational meters that are generic to the software, be it a word processor or any other text reader[113] or editor. In a sense, the regular electronic text is

---

[112] The verb 'scrolling' refers to the fact that there is no limit, except for the computer's memory, as to the electronic text's length; hence, the reader has to scroll up and down in order to read the whole text. Although researchers compared between the electronic text and previous methods of text publishing, i.e. oral literature, interestingly, nobody, to my knowledge, compared it to scrolls, which has many traits similar to the electronic text, one of them is the need to scroll the text.

[113] When word-processing software was first developed, there was no binding format for electronic-texts. Thus, each software company developed its own electronic-text standards. This created a linkage between the text and the application with which it was created. A reader could not read a text unless he had the editing application. In time, text readers or viewers were developed. They enable reading an electronic document even if the reader does not have the text-editing software with which the document was composed. These applications are reading utilities solely, without the option of changing the text, i.e. of editing, adding notes or saving the document.

a "one node" object. Electronic navigational meters simulate print editing and reading aids. They are numerous and diversified: page numbers, line numbers, measurements-bars, scroll-bars, and various other display possibilities such as: thumbnail display, outline display, document map etc. These mechanisms improve navigation and orientation in contrast to the printed book, yet they are merely a compensational device for memory and time, and bring print qualities and possibilities to the electronic text.

Hypertext, however, is different. By definition, it is constructed out of nodes and links, meaning that there is one node (document, page) that is connected to others and that there are relationships of some sort between those nodes. Nevertheless, on the screen, the reader sees "one page" (node) at a time and cannot see its relative position in the network or to the text's beginning or ending, to former nodes etc. Even if the reader can open more than one window, namely – more than one node on the screen, she still cannot see the structural relations between those windows or between those windows and the work as a whole. Thus the lack of a sense of a predetermined, fixed and stable structure that can be memorized causes many readers to "get lost" in the text. This is what is called the problem of disorientation.

The feeling of disorientation is relative to the fixed sequential structure of print texts. The looseness of hypertext is found in the autonomy of nodes as they are presented on screen, as they reside in the work, and in the different optional relations among themselves when the work is performed since each node can be reached from different various nodes. The meaning of the work is conditioned by the reader's performance of it, by the order in which she chooses nodes. The printed book does not have such flexibility – though the reader can decide for herself of other, diverse and unconventional reading practices. The bounded book is stable where each section, be it a chapter, a paragraph, a block, a sentence, has one fixed and unmovable place and it cannot be reached from varied and different places, not in the first reading nor in any other. Actually, reading in a bounded book is a "performance" that repeats itself each time the text is read again and again,[114] while in "reading" hypertext there is a different performance each time (namely, there is a possibility for a changed performance and a variety of potential performances) along with the sequential reading that the Enter key allows.

The orientation problem was already raised, though indirectly, in print literature, in what we would call a "post-modernistic" framework. Post modernistic authors questioned transparent print norms by testing them and exposing them, and by that caused various sorts of poetic disorientation. Borges story *The Garden of Forking Paths* (1999) that belongs to the detective story tradition and researchers tend to compare it with Poe's writings and other detective

---

[114] The reader's response (interpretive reading) can change in each reading but the text as an object is stable.

writers[115] influenced literature with its descriptions of an infinite book:

> In all fictions, each time a man meets diverse alternatives, he chooses one and eliminates the others; in the work of the virtually impossible-to-disentangle Ts'ui Pen, the character chooses – simultaneously – all of them. He creates, thereby, 'several futures,' several times, which themselves proliferate and fork (Borges 1999, 125).

Borges concept of literature as forking paths is considered to have started the genre of "Choose Your Own Adventure" books (McMillan, 2013). The story gave rise to other narrative formats such as the cyclic book, a volume whose last page would be identical to the first, which was adopted by Nabokov in *Pale Fire*; the chaotic novel, "a contradictory jumble of irresolute drafts. […] in the third chapter the hero dies, yet in the fourth he is alive again" (124). which was adopted by Robbe-Grillet; and "heredity sort of work, passed down from father to son, in which each new individual would add a chapter or with reverent care correct his elders' pages" (125), which started joint authorship. These experiments of print literature tried to probe the basic narrative norms and the fixed sequence. Borges examined

---

[115] Bennett, Maurice J. "The Detective Fiction of Poe and Borges." *Comparative Literature*, Vol. 35:3 (Summer, 1983), Oregon: Duke University Press, 262-275. Also: <http://www.jstor.org/stable/1770621>, 24.7.2016.

the plot and hero, Robbe-Grillet tested the one-way causality, Nabokov investigated the one-way linearity and the joint authorship questioned the status and unity of the author. However, while print literature questioned orientation and theorized about it, it was nonetheless based on a fixed structure of the text. Hypertext has no such fixity, and the disorientation problem is built-in the medium. In fact, the reference of print authors to variations of orientations is by laying bare the one-way linearity and fixedness of the text, but there is a difficulty to actualize those variations thus it is rarely found and mostly in avant-garde and bizarre works.

In order to solve the problem of disorientation or maybe as a result of perceiving hypertext as the embodiment of Ts'ui Pen's garden of forking paths, researchers tried to deduce from methods of navigation and orientation in physical space ways of electronic textual-orientation. Turning to psychology and other disciplines like geography, mapping, urban-planning and maze architecture, researchers found, surprisingly, few studies till 1990 of this activity, which is "routinely performed by all of us."[116] McKnight (1991)

---

[116] McKnight, Cliff, et al., 1991. Since the book was written, in 1991, many studies have been conducted in this area because of its relevance for computer networks, for reading, and for the newly arrived graphical Internet. Computer science was concerned with solving a specific problem – the disorientation problem since in hypertext the reader is orienting by the links until she becomes disoriented. Geography, in producing maps, had a need to guide, to become familiar with and to

summarizes the three most popular theories in the psychology of navigation. The first is schemata: "It seems obvious, for example, that we have a schema or model of the physical environment in which we find ourselves. This is acquired from experience and affords us a basic orienting frame of reference for navigatory purposes" (67). This theory is limited as "They [schemata] do not reflect specific instances of any one environment and provide no knowledge of what exists outside of our field of vision" (68). The second theory is based on Tolman's (1948) cognitive maps,[117] which was founded on a "number of studies on rats travelling through mazes" (68). This theory's implications for human cognition postulate "the existence of a cognitive map, internalized in the human mind, which is the analogue to the physical lay-out of the environment." Tolman's work is regarded as seminal for the third theory, the developmental model (69), which is engaged with the question how such maps are formed and manipulated. The developmental model consists of three sequential stages. The first is landmark knowledge, i.e., orienting in relation to known landmarks. The second stage is acquisition of route knowledge, namely, "the ability to navigate from A to B, using

---

orient people from place to place. However, there is no difference between the two needs.

[117] Jeanne Sholl (1987) in her article "Cognitive maps as orienting schemata." says that "According to Neisser, cognitive maps are orienting schemata, cognitive structures specialized to direct both perceptual and motor exploration of the environment" (616). Thus cognitive maps are a particular type of schemata.

whatever landmark knowledge we have acquired." The third is the survey knowledge based on a world frame of reference, which allows us to plan journeys along routes we have never traveled before and is the equivalent to Tolman's cognitive map or orienting schemata. However, there is a difference between navigation in a physical space and in a textual space. The textual navigation is mostly not pure "but an instantiation of several schemata such as domain knowledge of the subject matter, interpretation of the author's argument, and a sense of how this knowledge is organized that come into play now" (74). Hypertext as a textual space is different both from print and from geographical space, but combines some of their properties, so that a new theory of orientation called to be invented.

Landow (1992, 114) regards Jeff Conklin as the author who termed the problem as the *disorientation problem* in 1987. The term assumes that the reader is puzzled, not that there might be a genuine problem in the medium. There is no difference between Nelson's *orientation* problem and Conklin's *disorientation problem*. While Nelson is trying to understand how readers orient in a text, or a book, thus assuming there may be orientation problems, Conklin is trying to solve a specific problem that had crystalized 7 years later.[118] Thus,

---

[118] Kim, Hanhwe and Hirtle Stephen C. "Spatial Mmetaphors and Disorientation in Hypertext Browsing." In *Behaviour and Information Technology*, Vol.14:4, 1995, 239-250. The problem of orientation and disorientation still engage computer science even though the focus has shifted from hypertext to mobile phones: Bay, Susanne. and Ziefle, Martina. "Landmarks or Surveys? The Impact of Different

disorientation problem denotes the mystification of the reader caused by certain loss of bearings, (i.e. "where am I?") and not incomprehension. Indeed, Landow (1997) argues, "We all know that readers often experience confusion and disorientation simply because they fail to grasp the logic or even the meaning of a particular arguments" (116). Namely, disorientation may be caused by misunderstanding the text, which may happen in print literature as well, but will happen more often and typically in hyper-literature because of its segmented and linked nature ("network").[119]

The third facet of the *orientation* problem, after navigation and direction, is that of searching, and has to do with the question of "where was it?" or "where is it?" as the reader is trying to find some text, which she has already read or wants to read. In print literature she can rely on optical spatial memory, if she is searching for something she read, and make use of organizational structures such as: table of contents, chapter headings, indexes, pagination etc. or leave "signs" like bookmarks and notes, which provide a partial solution for searching after something she has read and wants to read

---

Instructions on Children's Performance in Hierarchical Menu Structures." *Computers in Human Behavior*, Vol. 24:3, May 2008, 1246-1274.

[119] Though Derrida claims that a standard literary text will cause the good reader to experience disorientation and disrupt a peaceful and calm reading as that reproduces present repressing forces. He regards each text as a network quite like the later Barthes.

again. Hypertext has certain organizational tools which are derivative from print tradition, and a special one: a quick search for a word or a number of words through their built-in function "search." This function takes advantage of the fact that hypertext as an electronic text is stored as a binary code that permits quick and easy processing. Thus, the search problem is solved in hypertext by various mechanisms and practices. All the same, print literature solved this problem as well, by indexes, though hypertext tools for search are more sophisticated, effortless and effective.

Storyspace software and *Internet Explorer* provide readers with two kinds of built-in orientation tools: navigation tools and searching tools. *Storyspace* developers do not distinguish between the two different orientation tools, which will be discussed in this chapter. The *Navigate* menu holds both options, of navigating and searching, i.e. command "Find text…," which is a searching tool, and command "Previous page…," which is a navigation tool.

In *Internet Explorer,* there is a distinction between these two orientation possibilities and they reside under two different menus, though these menus' titles do not provide more information as to what commands they hold than those of the *Storyspace* software. Under the *Edit* menu we find the command *Find (on this page)* that functions as a searching tool, and under the *View* menu resides the navigational command "Go to," which has three sub-commands: 'Back', 'Forward' and 'Home Page', which are navigation tools.

Since the *Storyspace* software was designed especially as a literary hypertext-authoring tool, its developers took into account readers' need for relational and structural navigation possibilities, which will enable a sense of "where am I" in the text and what is the relation between nodes and between each node and the work as a whole. Thus, they created special graphical tools, which are a collection of map-views, reached through some interactive buttons residing at the bottom of the screen, which enable the reader to obtain a schematic view of the text,[120] its nodes, its connections, hence its narrative structure. *Internet Explorer* however, does not offer any built-in graphical maps. Thus, as a result of the wide spread awareness of the *dis/orientation* problem, some of the web-sites on the Internet provide the reader with a "site map," which is actually lists of the sites' nodes. Though "site map" seems like the equivalent of some of Storyspace map-views, it does not show the reader's place in the work and does not show the relations between the nodes.

The next section will present the complexity (and complication) of navigational, orientation and searching tools that hypertext provides, and point out that there is no such complicated and perplexing equivalent while reading print literature. We have entrenched habits of reading print literature (leaves marking, writing within the book, bookmarks etc.) but all in all the "search" after a specific text that we have read or the creation of a general scheme of

---

[120] The specific text that is being produced and its wider context.

the story – all those rely primarily on mnemonic and cognitive personal and universal techniques. The computational mechanism functions as the ultimate mnemotechnics that frees the human memory. Moreover, it allows the reader to search the text that wasn't yet read, thus providing the reader with a reading overview or with a "foresight."

3.2.1 Searching Tools

Print literature mnemotechnics is based on author-prepared supports like synopsis, paragraphs and paragraphs names, indexes, notes and the like and reader-made aids like bookmarks, lines marking, marginalia and memorization of places within the text. Most of these tools are present and can be used in electronic literature as well, yet the digital medium allows for a quick and effortless way of searching and finding that turns most of those tools redundant.

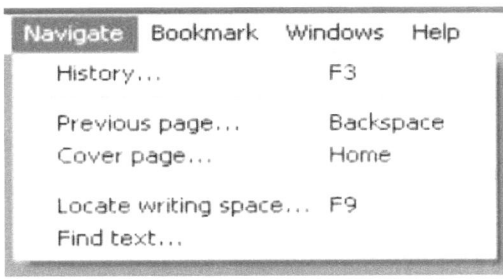

Figure 19 - *Storyspace* **Navigate menu**

In *Storyspace*, the *Navigate* menu (See Figure 19) contains five commands: History, Previous page, cover page, Locate writing space, and Find text. These commands are built-in the software; hence they are present in all the works that are written in the *Storyspace* software. Only the two last commands are proper searching aids, the others are navigational aids.

Storyspace software command *Locate writing space* is one of the two tools that allow the reader to search the work by nodes. It shows a list of all nodes' labels, arranged alphabetically, and requires the reader to remember a node's label in order to locate it. The other one, *Find text* command, allows for a free text-search, be it one word, a phrase or a whole sentence and the result is a list of nodes' labels, in which the sought for text can be found. These two tools take advantage of one of the electronic text's most convenient traits - the ease with which text can be traced and "found." These two methods are based on the nodes labels that the reader has to remember, yet if she doesn't remember she can by trial and error check all the nodes that appear in the list, pretty much like in print.

Internet Explorer, because of the difference in the networks, offers two kinds of searching methods. The first is *Find (on this page)*, which allows the user to find a specific text, again the size is not relevant – it can be one word or even part of a word up to whole sentences – on the active page. This function is an open-text search, similar to the *Find text* command in *Storyspace*. However, in *Storyspace* the nodes are short, thus, the command relates to all the nodes, as though they make up a single document. On the Internet, by contrast, a single node can be very long. When the reader activates the

Find (on this page) ... function, all the occurrences of the sought for text in the document or node are presented one by one for the reader to leaf through and find what she is looking for. The second command *Search* is a much wider one and can be performed all over the Internet. Actually, the *Search* function is assisted by specialized search sites on the Internet. Print literature requires the reader to read or/and re-read the text in order to find a specific text.

Another searching aid is the *Bookmark* function which can be found in the *Storyspace* as well as in *Internet Explorer* and all other internet browsers. In *Storyspace* the command resides on the "menus toolbar" at the top of the application. The first time the reader uses this function and opens this menu there is only one command available *Mark this page*. When the reader activates this command by choosing it, the command changes to *Unmark this page* and the name of the marked node is listed beneath the command. Thus, the reader may create a personal search-results list, though it is limited to ten entries. This command has a shortcut button on the toolbar, which resides on the bottom of the application, in the tool ruler, but apart from being a convenient shortcut, it has another function - that of indicating to the reader that there's a bookmark attached to the page.[121] The *Bookmark* menu, like the *Cover page* command, is a

---

[121] This is done by a change in button's face. The inactive button face looks like this: , while the active button looks like this: .

remnant of print culture, where material bookmarks are used to markup interesting pages.[122] However, in view of the huge number of nodes the reader encounters,[123] the *Bookmark* is an essential tool for an attentive reading, a reading that goes back and forth, as it allows the reader to mark points, which she finds crucial, and locate them for further reference with ease.

In *Internet Explorer* the *Favorites* command is compatible to the *Storyspace Bookmarks*. (See Figure 20) The users can "bookmark" Internet sites and specific nodes in order to locate them later. Yet, unlike *Storyspace* software, the *Favorites* command is not limited in any way and can be categorized and sub-divided, so that the reader can have folders, which may include sub-folders and so on, thus classifying the bookmarks according to her personal interests.

Clicking on the *Favorites* opens a menu, on top of the browser's window, presenting all available "bookmarks," yet concealing the screen. Activating the *Favorites* command from the *View* menu, sub-

---

[122] The bookmark was introduced with medieval bookbinding and with time turned to be an art object and collectable thing. For a history of the bookmarks see site: <http://www.miragebookmark.ch/wb_history.htm>, 24.7.2016. See also Hartong Georg. *On the History of the Bookmark*. A web document: <http://www.duisburg.de/stadtbib/medien/bindata/bookmarkh istory.pdf>, 24.7.2016.

[123] *Samplers*, Deena Lasen's work, is the smallest holding only 239 nodes; *afternoon*, Joyce's hypertext is 539 nodes long and Moulthrop's is the biggest, holding 993 nodes.

menu *Explorer Bar*, opens inside the browser a window[124] (See Figure 20), which can be kept open as long as the reader needs it along the main browsing window, thus allowing the reader to check on her bookmarks, edit them, add and delete and organize by activating the various commands that reside at the top of the favorites window. Thus, the reader can use saved places from previous readings.

Although the *Bookmark* and the *Favorites* tools thus described are searching assistances, it will be more appropriate to call them memory aids because they help the reader or user to search for sites or pages that she has already visited. The proper searching tools, like the *Find* and *Search* commands, can find new pages or nodes, even if they have not yet been visited before. Hence the first two have parallel utilities in print literature while the other two - hardly.

Another memory assistance that facilitates searches is the *History* window that is found in *Storyspace*, *ToolBook* and in *Internet Explorer* alike. The *History* command in *Storyspace* opens a window that exhibits the labels of the nodes the reader has already visited even though she didn't mark them. The *History* allows the reader four actions: Rewind, Visit, Clear, and *Windows'* inherent close sign (x). The *Rewind* allows a partial clearance of the history list so that the reader can retrace her steps and go onto a different path, or reading.

---

[124] The three commands residing under the *View* menu, sub-menu *Explorer Bar*, that is, *Search, Favorites,* and *History*, cannot be opened simultaneously, as they use the same space in the *Internet Explorer* window.

The *Visit* command takes the reader to the node she chooses from the list. The *Clear* command clears the history list, allowing the reader to start a fresh one, a new reading. The *close* option lets the reader close the window without choosing any of the above and return to the node from which the *History* window was opened. The *History* option can be activated not only from the *Navigate* menu, but also from a shortcut button in the toolbar.

The *History* command that is found in *ToolBook* is a constant icon on the screen, which behaves rather similarly to the *Storyspace* software *History* button and no wonder. Though the authoring software is different, it is published by the same people who developed the *Storyspace* software. In *Internet Explorer*, the *History* command resides in the *View* menu, under the *Explorer toolbar* sub-menu. The *History* window lists past visited pages. However, the *Internet Explorer History* window (Figure 21) is more elaborate than its *Storyspace* equivalent. While the *Storyspace History list* presents the reader with pages visited only during the present reading, the *Internet Explorer* "remembers" sites visited over the fortnight before. The different ways in which this function works in *Storyspace* and in *Internet Explorer* derive from the difference in the networks for which each is designed and their different purposes. The Internet is so vast and has so many other uses, beside the literary one, that the user needs a long-range history list. While the *Storyspace* software serves as a reader to specific literary works, the *Internet Explorer* serves not only as a reader to Internet sites, but as a gateway to the Internet and its various application in general.

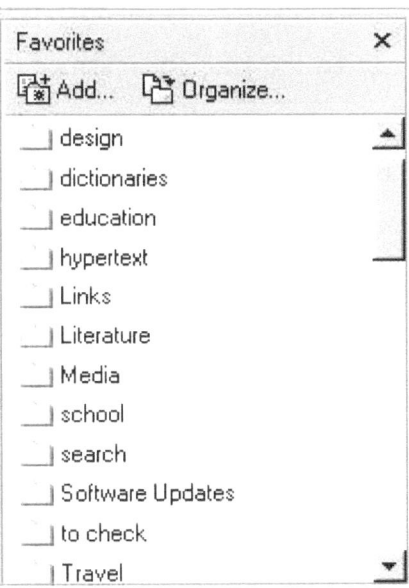

Figure 20 - Favorites window inside the browser – an example

In the *Storyspace* software, some of the menu bar commands can be activated through the short cut tool bar at the bottom of the node's window. However, out of the *navigate* menu only two commands have shortcut buttons: *History* and *Previous page*, which implies that the software's developers regarded these two actions as most imperative to the reading process. Their basic assumption is that reading literature is a short-term pursuit. In print literature history is all the pages the reader had read – thus it cannot have an efficient memory or organization support – and the previous page is just that –

the page read before – which is reached by the reader without any difficulties.

The importance of the *History* function is two faceted. It enables the reader to crisscross the text, for instance to recheck a node and revise its interpretation according to the new information just received, which is the standard way of reading in print tradition. Secondly, it allows the reader to see how much she has read so far, comparable to the feeling generated by holding the printed book and measuring the thickness of the already-read portion vis-à-vis that of the so-far-unread portion, thus it is also somewhat navigational, oriental, nevertheless it does not convey how much more there is to read. Thus, the history list is an orientation tool and an aide for comprehension.

While the *History* command in the *Storyspace* software presents all visited nodes, the *Cover-page* command allows the reader to find one specific node, which is the default node when the work is opened. Thus, the reader can start her reading all over again or choose other paths of reading by activating links which were not activated before. This command is a remnant from the printed book - where the starting point for reading is the cover page, and the reader can start afresh whenever she wishes to do so. However, it more closely resembles a game, where starting afresh "from the beginning" is routine for every performance, and where each new performance will differ in content and sequentiality from previous "takes."

Figure 21 - *Internet Explorer* History window – an example

Internet Explorer has a built-in similar function for instantly reaching the *cover page* though with a different label, the command *Go to Home page*. The term is a combination of the concept of the Internet as a space, hence the *home* part, and the fact that in the internet's beginning it presented only text, hence the *page*. As the Internet is built of many smaller networks and each network has its own individual *home page*, which functions as the gateway to the site, there is no one specific *cover page* to turn to, thus rendering this function useless, unless the reader defined one special page to function as a "home page."

The fact that the *home page* function is found in both applications shows that it is regarded as a stable point in the network, from which the readers start surfing and return to, in order to choose other paths, exactly like the function of the *cover page* in the printed book. Other print culture remnants are the electronic *bookmarks* and margin-notes. The electronic text allows for all sorts of searching assistances, some – *Favorites*, *History*, *Locate writing space*, *Cover page* – refer to finding text that has already been read, and some – *Find text*, *Search* – let the reader locate text she has never saw before, which is unique to electronic texts. Those searching functions are also mnemotechnics and some are navigational tools as well.

3.2.2 Navigation tools

As I mentioned at the beginning of the chapter, *Internet Explorer* has only three generic navigation tools: Forward, Backward, and Home. Big sites, containing thousands of pages, usually take into account the *orientation problem* and used to provide special navigation facilities like short-cut menus, and site maps.[125] Some sites used a spatial metaphor like a village or town, which helped the reader navigate and even locate the information sought. When such a metaphor is used all the conventional establishments found in a "real" town or village, function as sub-menus. A school icon signifies educational content, pharmacy - health topics, shop - a virtual mall, etc. Some sites, in exchange or in addition, provide a map view that allows the user to look for the relevant material directly.

---

[125] Nowadays this tool is replaced by site's menus and toolbars and/or a "search" option.

navigation

Figure 22 - Navigation short-cut menu

Storyspace software offers four types of map view, which are available from the main window via a small toolbar that resides on the bottom tool bar, as a distinct group to the left: a Tree Map, a Chart Map, an Outline Map and a *Storyspace* Map view. Maps' aliases are shown in the status bar when the mouse hoovers over them. All four maps have in common two functions, that of opening another map view from their tool bar and that of "Automatically show text window." These functions conveniently give the reader access to a chosen node or another map view right from the present map view. Other manipulation options, such as "Show text," "Show links," "Scale" etc., are specific to each map characteristics.

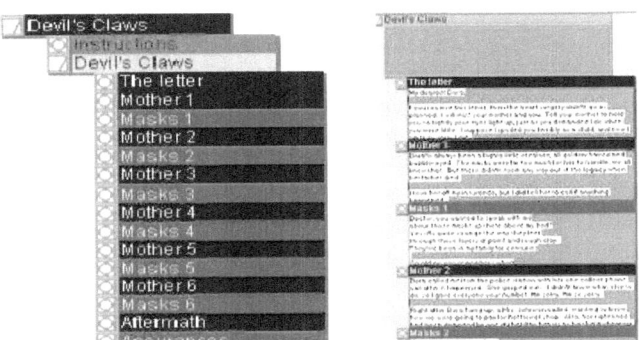

Figure 23 - Full *Outline Map* – on the left and with text – on the right

The *Outline Map*, like a site's map, presents hierarchically all the nodes that compose Larsen's *Devil's Claws* short-story, thus allowing for a direct access to a particular chosen node. As can be seen in Figure 23, the story has three hierarchical levels: level one is called in computer science's jargon the 'father' node, *Devils Claws*, which is the story's title. It has two 'sons', *Instructions* and *Devil's Claws*, at level two. The second *Devil's Claws* has fifteen 'sons', which make up the third level, the nodes that compose the story. The *Outline Map* allows a change in view: a tree map, a chart view, an outline and *Storyspace* map that shows nodes and their connections with each other. For instance, the *Outline Map* (Figure 23) has one command "show text" that shows node's text within the node's frame. Another example is the option of expansion and shrinkage of detail levels, so that level one can be viewed without its subordinates, as can be seen in Figure 24 on the right, merely level one and two as can be seen in Figure 24 on the left or all nodes within the work as is shown in Figure 23 on the right.

Figure 24 – *Devil's Claws* - *Outline Maps*

[Level one (on the right side), level one & two (on the left)]

The *Chart Map* presents the same hierarchical structure as the *Outline Map,* in a graphical deployment of the work as a whole.

Samplers is a collection of stories thus the *Chart Map* will show all the stories and not merely one. The only manipulation allowed here is in scale, resizing text and graphics relatively. There are four fixed scales, out of which the reader can choose the one he wants, 'Tiny' (See Figure 25), 'small', 'Normal', and 'Large' (Figure 26).

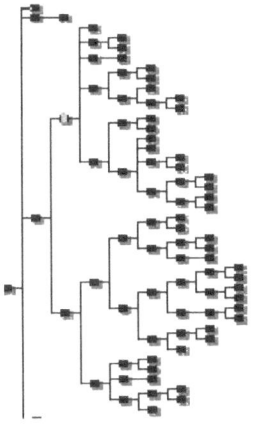

Figure 25 – *Devil's Claws* **- Tiny scaling of** *Chart Map*

Figure 26 – *Devil's Claws* **- Large scaling of** *Chart Map*

The 'father' level, the upper *Devil's Claws*, accommodates the two "sons" nodes, *Instructions* that stands alone and the second *Devil's Claws*, which holds fifteen nodes. This map enables four optical manipulations, by which the visual layout of the nodes and their relative sizes change. The layout can be landscape (Wide)[126] as in Figure 26 – Devil's *Claws* - Large scaling of Chart *Map* or portrait (Tall). The size can be large, as is presented in Figure 26 or small.

This is indeed a complex system for print literature that has no analogical maps to the ones shown above. Hypertext special trait of links caused its developers and authors to look for ways that will ease the reader's navigation in the text and maybe relieve the reader's feeling of disorientation. The closest orientation tool in print is the content page,[127] which shows the overall organization of the book. Print literature is based on some obscurity or ambiguity and does not expose its components as can be seen in Figure 27. The reader can see that there are 6 nodes called *Mother* and 6 nodes called *Masks*, two nodes at the beginning, *Devil's Claws* and *The letter* and two more

---

[126] The *Tree map* is presented in its own window so Figure 26 shows the window resized, thus it is not so "wide."

[127] There are books of fiction that attach genealogical tree of the characters; a map of the region or place; architectural diagram of the house, etc. These are different types of visual and historic information that is designed to relieve orientation in the work and as a mnemotechnics function.

nodes at the end: *Aftermath* and *Assurances* This is used in hypertext to help the reader on her orientation in the text.

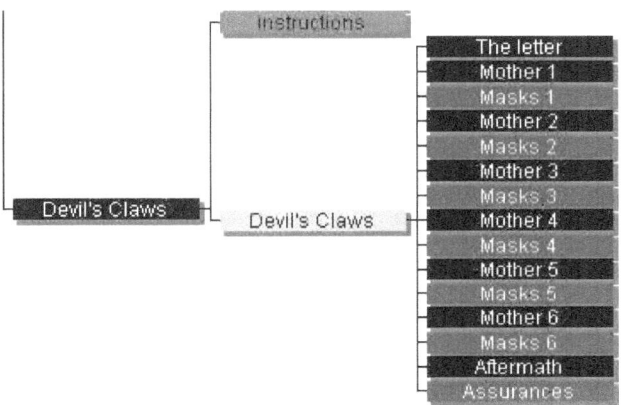

Figure 27 - Devil's Claws - Tree Map

All the maps discussed formerly present the reader with the structure of the network; however, only one map portrays the relations between the nodes, the *Storyspace Map*. This map, like a flow chart, presents the nodes and their labels, and the relations between nodes are revealed through the connecting arrows (See Figure 28). The manipulation options in this map let the reader see inner relations (father-son), by broadening the focus as in the *Tree Map*, (See Figure 29) and another option enables a simultaneous presentation of the text within the node, as in the *Outline Map*. The special trait of the map is the option of presenting the links and their paths – another option of reading given for the reader to choose.

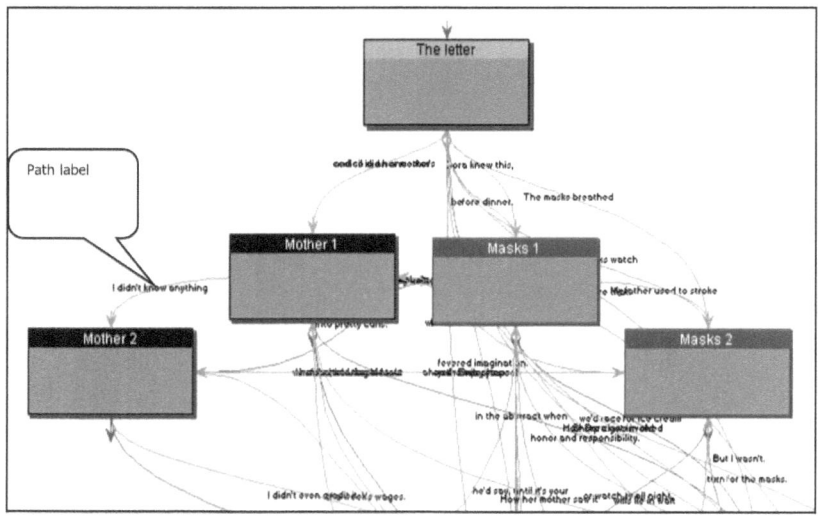

Figure 28 – *A Storyspace Map*

Hypertext literature that is written with *Storyspace* has a unique structural feature, not found in print or on the net, which is the *path*. The *path* is an orientation aid to both writing and reading. It helps the author in creating a narrative sequence of nodes and provides the reader with a default way of reading that does not follow links but an author pre-planned path. Hence, the path can be likened to an episode in print literature. Each path has a label, as can be seen in the *Storyspace Map*, next to the path's connecting arrows (See Figure 28). Figure 30 presents the *Harley*[128] path in *Victory Garden*, in a graphical

---

[128] Each path has a unique name, like path *Harley* that is presented in Figure 30. The name of the path usually refers to the characters, events of place that the narrative of the path is about. Path *Harley* presents Harley and Urquhart share breakfast and a personal conversation.

layout, and Figure 31 presents the same path textually, in a window of its own, which is present to the left of the node's main window throughout the reading process. The reader can follow the path by double clicking the node's label in that window or by the Enter key. Hence, nodes' labels function as a replacement for page numbering and the order is indicated by the path's arrow.

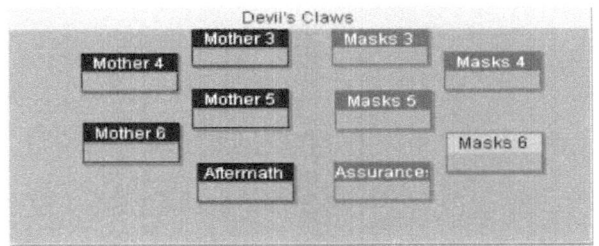

Figure 29 - *Devils Claws Storyspace Map* **presenting father-son**

relationship

While the *Chart Map* and the *Outline Map*, both have, on the toolbar, a compass like navigation button[129] that allows the reader a spatial-like navigation, the *Tree Map* and the *Storyspace Map* has an *up arrow*,[130] which offers a one-way option of broadening the view, zooming out. There is also, a *zoom at* button which lets the reader choose one node among those presented in the map.

---

[129] A compass like navigation button

[130] The up arrow

All the numerous sophisticated and complicated mechanisms that were reviewed in this chapter as navigation and orientation help, like graphical maps in various options, show that the authors, or the software's developers, were very inventive in expecting difficulties in reading. They provided numerous tools for overcoming a long list of difficulties stemming from the problem of orientation. This attests to the central problem: the lack of a physical tangibility and the lack of linearity. While the lack of the physical tangibility disorients the reader as to where she is in the text (how much she has read and what is still left to read), the lack of linearity, which in print literature is the mechanism that ensures the reader's orientation, causes the reader to lose connections between characters, episodes etc.

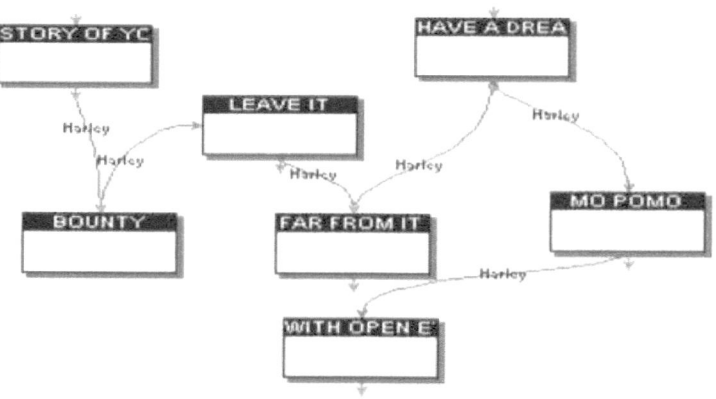

Figure 30 - *Harley* path in *Victory Garden*

In print literature though the social novel, for instance, holds scores of characters there is seldom any characters' list, not to mention an index of their appearance's page or a list of fictive events and their page numbers. Print authors have no concerns about their reader's going astray while reading. Hence print literature seldom holds mnemonic tools, it leans heavily on the reader's memory and on the reader's willingness to concentrate and try to remember throughout the reading process.

The hypertext structure (actually no prescribed structure) is what causes the difficulties in reading for which the assistance tools were built. The concern was so big that an abundance of tools were created, so much so that this plentitude added to the complication of reading.

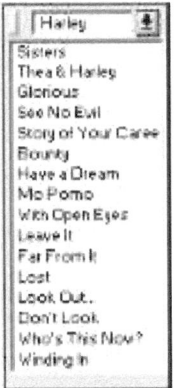

Figure 31 - Path window

What is quite different between print and hypertext literature is the amount of pre-knowledge and assisted guidance that the hypertext reader needs to have as opposed to the measured amount of information that the print writer releases. And yet this is not the "expected revolution" that was envisioned by researchers. The mnemonic tools are technical helpers that are sometimes much needed in print literature too.

While the print reader does not need any directions, maps and other mnemotechnics as she is quite passive, the hypertext reader, the active reader, needs to learn how to read and how to use all those mnemotechnics that is given to her. This difference dictates different ways of writing and reading, which will be discussed in the coming chapters. One major issue is the segmentation and fragmentation which are needed in order to create hypertext multi-paths.

4   Segmentation & Fragmentation

The previous chapter dealt with orientation in the hypertext format in comparison with the relative simplicity of orientation in the printed text and presented a complex, developed, sometimes complicated system of tools that were created to solve, or at least mitigate, the problem. This chapter will look into the main aspect that makes it difficult to orient in hypertext, namely its fragmentary nature.

Hypertext is perceived as fragmented text, as Vandendorpe (2009) sums: "In hypertext [...] the text no longer exists as a whole or in a single flow but is parceled out in segments or fragments" (143). He based his summation on the main definitions of hypertext starting with Bolter (1991) who describes hypertext as a segmented, or fragmented, text without actually using these terms:

> A hypertext is like a printed book that the author has attacked with a pair of scissors and cut into convenient verbal sizes. The difference is that the electronic hypertext does not simply dissolve into a disordered bundle of slips, as the printed book must. For the author also defines a scheme of electronic connections to indicate relationships among the slips (24).

Ryan (2001) in her book *Narratives as Virtual reality* refers to former definitions and says: "In a hypertextual system, text is broken into fragments – "lexias," for George Landow; "textons," for Espen Aarseth – and stored in a network whose nodes are connected by electronic links" (206). That does not mean that there is no fragmentation or segmentation in printed literature, but that in hyper-literature it is not merely an artistic or typological device, chosen by the author in order to achieve an effect, but it stems from the medium's format, thus it forms its conventions of reading and writing. Whereas printed literature, even when using devices named 'segmentation' or 'fragmentation', is finally presented to the reader as a "whole," an intact and linear "whole," hyper-literature is not. While in printed literature segmentation and fragmentation are effects, in hypertext they are material aspects of the text.

In the following pages, I will define segmentation and fragmentation. In light of those definitions I'll inspect their place in literature, printed and hypertext alike, in order to determine whether the segmentation and fragmentation found in hypertext is a new device in literature, or is it an old one? If it is a deep-rooted poetic expedient, does it receive "new wings" in hypertext?

The etymology of the word 'segmentation' is from Latin *segmentum*, which means to cut off; thus, segmentation is the process of cutting off, of dividing into parts, of separating pieces of something. Each segment is a piece, a component of the whole, one of the constituent parts into which a body, entity, or quantity is divided or marked off by or as if by natural boundaries.[131] Segments of a whole may be partial "wholes" in themselves, and do not necessarily bear the marks of their being broken off. The etymology of the word 'fragmentation' is from Latin *fragmentum*, which means to break; thus, fragmentation means the process of breaking, of interrupting, disintegrating. Each fragment is a part broken of some kind of a whole, detached, and incomplete. Unlike the segment, a fragment bears the marks of its incompleteness and disruptiveness.

Though I tried to define a severe and strict difference between these two terms, in practicality they are quite exchangeable and interchangeable, as is reflected in the quote from Vandendorpe "segments or fragments." Asking native speakers about the difference amounted to the distinction that fragmentation has a disintegration flavor in it. Thus, I differentiate these two terms where it may help differentiate between print literature and hypertext. Segmentation will refer to segments as ordered units, as a methodical way of cutting a whole into parts in such a way that the segments can be restored into a complete whole without leaving any marks of ever being segmented, like in a necklace or the segmentation into chapters in a book or a novel; or a TV series in which each episode is independent, yet there is also continuity. Fragmentation is breaking, disintegrating like smashing a china dish or a puzzle, which results in many tiny and

---

[131] Both definitions "Segmentation" and "Fragmentation" are from *Oxford English Dictionary*.

irregular bits, each bearing the mark of having been torn or cut off from a whole.

This distinction is somewhat arbitrary as there might be times when even the fragments can be reconstructed into a complete whole and when segments may bear signs of incompleteness. However, these terms are important to literature poetics because they can serve as distinctive terms between two literary phenomena. The first phenomenon, segmentation, is the partitioning of a literary work into volumes, books, chapters, and paragraphs labeled or unlabeled, as in most of the 18 - 19th century novels, to which I refer as segmentation. As has already been said, the segments can be combined and are actually combined in printed literature to create a whole. The second phenomenon, fragmentation, is the disintegration, where the reordering of the parts is not clear and the restoration process may result in an incomplete whole or at least an ambiguous one, uncertain, unclear as is found in the *Nouveau Roman*.[132]

---

[132] *Nouveau Roman* is a literary movement in France during the 1950s. Its representative authors, among others, are Robbe-Grillet Alain, Sarraute Nathalie, and Simon Claude, who experimented with style instead of focusing on plot, idea, action, and narrative, as was traditional in the "old-fashioned" novel. The *nouveau roman* is also referred to (more broadly) as 'antinovel,' avant-garde novel of the mid-20th century. "New Novel," *Encyclopædia Britannica Online*. Encyclopædia Britannica Inc., 2012. See also Jefferson, Ann. *The Nouveau Roman and the Poetics of Fiction*. Cambridge: Cambridge University Press, 1985. The critics received the new unintelligible genre by pronouncing it as non-fiction since it has no narrative sequence and the lack of connectivity

Modernistic and Post-modernistic literature[133] used segmentation from artistic ideological motives. At the end of the 19th century and the beginning of the 20th century, many groups of artists were seeking ways to break-up the traditional mimetic way of art that ruled since the Renaissance. They turned to foregrounding and de-familiarization techniques, which, while breaking the mimetic tradition, break the spectators' expectations as well, one of which was fragmentation. For example, the Cubist school reduced and fragmented natural forms into abstract, mainly geometric structures that usually rendered the painting as a set of discrete objects, which the viewer had to mentally re-assemble into mimetic objects. This visual artistic concept reached literary poetics some thirty years later with Robbe-Grillet and the *nouveau roman* school (Jaffé-Freem, 1966).

The *nouveau roman* used the segmentation device in two complementary ways: first, to convey through structural means a thematic concept, the idea of an unstable, fallacious, alienated, and

---

between the novel's parts caused it to be indecipherable and obscure. As Jefferson says: "The conservative critics hostile to the nouveau roman condemned the new fiction as inhuman and 'formalist', and the responses of the new novelists themselves had little or no effect in altering his point of view" (58).

[133] McHale (1992) disputes the meaning of the terms *Modernistic* and *Post-modernistic* literature and asks if they have a "fixed essence" as there is an ongoing debate as to what does it really mean and since one of the *Modernistic* and *Post-modernistic* literature beliefs is in the non-fixedness of things.

changing world, which the fragmentation device demonstrated artistically, conveying to the reader the feeling of a torn-up, insecure world, where the only truth and meaning are the subjective ones. The second way was to cause the de-automation of the reading process thus foregrounding the discourse itself. The *nouveau roman* authors fragmented traditional structural segments, like paragraphs, chapters, and typological structures consequently turning the narrative sequence into a typographic, structural, and thematic collage.[134]

When our expectations come true our perception becomes automatic, as Shklovsky (1965) observes, "We do not see them [the objects] in their entirety but rather recognize them by their main characteristics" (12). Shklovsky coined the term *de-familiarization* as a device for turning the beholder's attention to the artistic, artificial and stylized in a work of art. To quote from his *Art* as *Technique*,

> The purpose of art is to impart the sensation of things as they are perceived and not as they are known. The technique of art is to make objects "unfamiliar", to make forms difficult, to increase the difficulty and length of perception because the process of perception is an aesthetic end in itself and must be prolonged. Art is a way of experiencing the

---

[134] See for instance Sherzer, Dina. "Serial Constructs in the Nouveau Roman," *Poetics Today*, Vol. 1:3, 1980, 87-106. <http://www.jstor.org/stable/1772413>, 24.7.2016.

artfulness of an object; the object is not important.
(12)

The de-familiarization of the text is an artistic technique, which serves Jakobson's (1960) 'poetic function' by focusing the reader's attention on the representation itself as a result of breaking the automation of perception. De-familiarization has long been the slogan of the modernistic movements in the visual arts. The Cubists, Futurists, Dadaists, and other schools raised the banner of breaking from old conventions and traditions and causing the viewer to look "at" not "through" the presented objects, as Lanham says when referring to Roy Lichtenstein's works,

> This AT/THROUGH reversal appears in twentieth-century art in various guises, from the Italian Futurists onward. It is a favorite Lichtenstein motif. In his brushstroke paintings, for example, when he makes monumentality out of artistic means, the AT/THROUGH oscillation fairly jumps at you (43).

Although Lanham sees the "looking AT [...] the most powerful aesthetic attribute of electronic text" (Ibid), hypertext does not carry any artistic torch and it was not invented because of an artistic need. The medium was devised in order to provide an answer to a pragmatic need, as stated by Bush, for connecting documents. Literary scholars saw the medium as a realization of artistic theories contemplated by Structuralist and Post-Structuralist philosophers as Aarseth observes:

It is a common strategy among theorists in the field to combine the literary hypertexts (or, skipping those, a direct invocation of hypertext itself) with well-known literary-critical theories by Barthes, Bakhtin, Deleuze-Guattari, Derrida, Foucault, Iser, Lacan and others" (76).

Marie-Laure Ryan (2001) finds quite a surprising reason for this phenomenon,

These analogies between postmodern aesthetics and the idea of interactivity have been systematically developed by the early theorists of hypertext, such as George Landow, Jay David Bolter, Michael Joyce, and Stuart Moulthrop. These authors were not only literary scholars they, had also contributed to the development of hypertext through the production of either software, instructional databases, or literary works and they had a stack in the promotion of the new mode of writing. They chose to sell hypertext to the academic community – an audience generally hostile to technology but also generally open to postmodern theory – by hyping their brainchild as the fulfillment of the ideas of the most influential French theorists of the day, such as Barthes, Derrida, Foucault, Kristeva, Deleuze, Guattari, and Bakhtin – the latter an adopted ancestor. Many of those who came to electronic textuality from literary theory happily joined in the chorus (6).

Undeniably, hypertext has many features that support the modernist and postmodernist approaches, for instance, the actualization of inter-textuality; questioning the relations between reader and writer and their roles; the boundaries of the single work and the closure of narrative structures.

Segmentation breaks readers' expectations in a way that creates suspension, retardation, and confusion accompanied by a need for reconstruction. For example, the reader expects, out of her previous experience of reading and prior knowledge of literary conventions, to find continuity from one sentence to the next, from one paragraph to the next and a reasonable narrative line from one chapter to another. For instance, in Trollope's *Barchester Towers* the bishop's chaplain is introduced towards the end of the third chapter and Trollope remarks: "Mr. Slope, however, on his first introduction must not be brought before the public at the tail of a chapter." Thus he creates continuity between the chapters, a continuity that is reinforced as the next chapter is titled "The Bishop's Chaplain," and holds the history of that gentleman. Thus, the continuity is not merely kept, but is marked out to the reader. The author highlights the segmentation of the text by referring to it: he states at the end of the chapter what is coming in the next one. Thus segmentation becomes present, holding a dimension in discourse, and at the same time it does not disrupt the narrative flow. In comparison, Robbe-Grillet's reader finds in *The*

Labyrinth a real labyrinth of time, place and characters, as Yellowlees Douglas (2000) describes,

> All these expectations, all this readerly patience seems profoundly misplaced. I discover the soldier is wounded without having learned just how or when, and, in the end, I am not sure that he existed at all, leaving me perhaps less certain about the status of characters and events than I was even at the outset (95).

Katheryn Hayles (2004) finds nine points that can be made about the specificities of electronic hypertext, of which the third is labeled "Electronic Hypertexts Are Generated Through Fragmentation and Recombination" (76). Hayles is aware that fragmentation can be found in printed texts as well, however, "With digital texts, the fragmentation is deeper, more pervasive, and more extreme than with alphanumeric characters of print" (77). She does not differentiate between segmentation and fragmentation and uses, in the article, only the term 'fragmentation.' Thus, in light of the great similarity between segmentation and fragmentation and the fact that most researchers use them interchangeably, the decision to distinguish between the two is mostly interpretive, hence subjective and does not contribute to my analysis. I will connect the two into a joint discussion and call the shared phenomenon 'seg\frag.' Only in places where analysis and interpretation raise matters of difference between segmentation and fragmentation will I stress the variance.

Seg\frag can affect three strata of the literary work: typography, namely: layout on the page; text, namely the sequence of letters, words, sentences, paragraphs etc.; and narrative, namely the action's sequence. Seg\frag can be a poetical effect residing solely in the reader's realm of making meaning and having no bearing on the characters or on the action within the fictional world. Nevertheless, seg\frag can be also a mimetic or quasi-mimetic narrative device, which has the same effect in the fictional world as in the reader's domain.

Modern typography is segmented in essence by the measures of the page and by norms and conventions of print era like paragraphs, the direct representation of speech etc. The page dimensions dictate line's length, the number of lines it contains, and the number of letters. While early manuscripts were written without spaces between words and with various spaces between lines, print literature fixed firmly the convention of spaces between letters (kerning), words (tracking), sentences, and lines (leading), thus conventionalizing typographical segmentation.

The constraint of typography, via its lucid and fixed segmentation conventions that regulate and order the semiotic system, causes a further segmentation by breaking up sentences, which are longer or shorter than the measure of a line. Since the measurements of the book and its pages are fixed, thus holding a certain number of letters[135] and spaces, sentences do not end at the end of the line, nor do words for that matter. Thus, when a sentence is longer than a line, it slides typographically into the next one. Seg\frag occurs also when the writer does not exploit the whole line's length, for instance in case of a shopping list, a poem, a menu, an advertisement. A quasi-mimetic presentation of such objects will follow the very short lines, which people usually use to write down lists or announcements. Another such quasi-mimetic example is the case of calculations, as is found in Federman's *Double or Nothing*, which aims to give the impression of authenticity (Figure 32). The same typographical seg\frag is used heavily by poetry for poetic aims. For instance, by shortening the measure of a line, poets can create enjambment, thus creating surprise, stressing a point, rhyming, or attaining a certain rhythm.

Though typography is segmented immanently, its conventions are so old and well established that they have become over time transparent to the reader. Only when the work deviates from the "natural" typographical seg\frag is the reader alerted to its segmented nature, for instance - in a prose written poem or a rhymed novel.

---

[135] There is the difference between "fixed letters," which hold a certain fixed space on the page without regard to their actual size, and "proportional letters," which present the real dimensions of the letter in proportion to all other letters. Thus, an "i" will take less space on the page and will allow the line to have more letters than other lines that have less "i's" events. However, no matter what format of letters is used, the line's length is still constrained and a word, or a sentence, which will be longer than a line will slide to the next.

```
8 bucks a week for a room
6            that's what it should be
             that's what it was the last time          No! 9

52 times 6 makes only 312
                      312 for a room almost half almost
                      human              not quite
```

Figure 32 - Federman's calculations (2)

Manners of deviation from typography's conventions causes the seg\frag of the text (words, lines), as in Apollinaire's *Calligrammes* (Figure 33 on the right) that "draw" with words, in e. e cummings unusual typography and renunciation of capital letters and in Raymond Federman's works which make use of the typographical layer to heighten the meaning of the text by styling it in visual patterns (Figure 33 on the left): the text is about jail, where the outside is viewed by prisoners through the key-hole.[136] Another example is Toni Morrison's *The Bluest Eyes*'s beginning with a "Dick and Jane" story, which was common in books that were used to teach children to read. The same story repeats itself three times with typographical changes; the first time the story is written clearly in a standard form. In the second telling it loses its capitalization and punctuation. By the third time it loses also words' spacing. The typographical changes can be interpreted as a concretization of the learning process to read, where the first reading is hesitant, the second one is better and the third one

---

[136] Segmentation of words and phrases to concretize poems' subjects are characteristic of Dadaist Poets. For instance, cummings' *r-p-o-p-h-e-s-s-a-g-r* (1991, 396).

is fluent. These changes can be explained in other ways as well, for instance as the deterioration of a mind. Never the less as a rule, typographical segmentation is mostly not a poetic phenomenon but a semiotic convention, though it can be exploited for poetic effects.

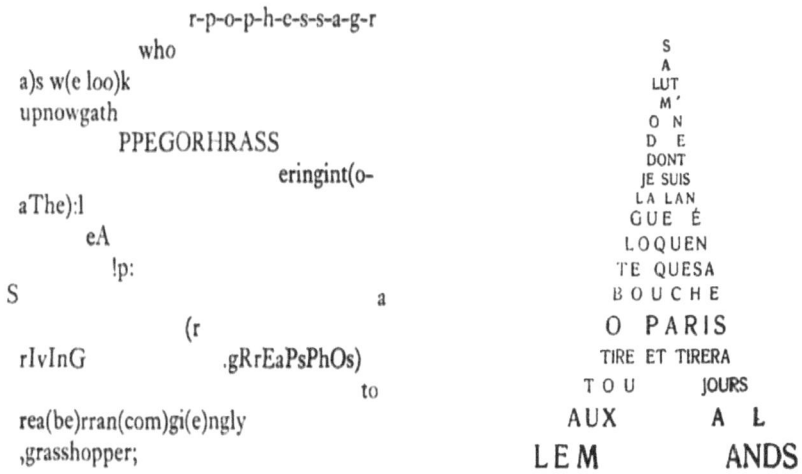

Figure 33 - cummings' r-p-o-p-h-e-s-s-a-g-r and Apollinaire's

Eiffel Tower[137]

Textual seg\frag is the partitioning of the text into units or blocks of text like volumes or books, chapters and paragraphs.

---

[137] cummings e. e. *Complete Poems*: 1904-1962. Ed. George J. Firmage, New York: Liverlight Publishing Corporation, 1991, 396. Apollinaire, Guillaume. *Calligrammes: poems of peace and war (1913-1916).* Trans. by Greet Anne Hyde, Introduction by Lockerbie S.I., Los Angeles, London: University of California Press Berkeley, 1980, 126.

Textual seg\frag does not stem from any immanent traits of the text, but is the result of early print economics,[138] and consumers' needs in view of the cognitive processes of the human mind.

The book turned to be a common and cheap commodity when many of print limitations were overcome at the end of the 18th century; however, nothing had changed in the way in which the mind operates except for conventions. For instance, early print technology caused the segmentation into volumes, which is quite rare nowadays and is still found in "heavy" books, while the cognitive process of reading caused the segmentation into chapters and paragraphs, as we still know them.

Authors took advantage of textual segmentation to serve narrative segments, thus creating a correspondence between textual segments and narrative ones, and at the same time turning each segment, be it a volume a chapter or a paragraph, into one cohesive structural and thematic unit. Thus, typically, segmentation, which divides the whole into segments, creates many small wholes – contained in the total "whole" of the work. This is quite similar to

---

[138] For instance, the revival of the installments as a result of the renewal of the Stamp Act. The British tax influenced the publishing industry since it was calculated by paper sheets. Since the cost of paper turned premium publishers tended to make larger paper-sheets and fill the added columns with installments that were regarded as a way to attract and retain customers. See in Wiles 1957.

computer games, where the segments are also small "wholes" or episodes that differ from each other by time, place, characters etc.

The multiplicity of narrative elements is created through segments, thus the correlation between the textual seg\frag and the narrative seg\frag is quite understandable. The only consistent narrative components are time and space, which are continuous external objective entities. However, mankind has segmented them into small units in order to denote specific and different places and to mark the passing of time: seconds, minutes, hours, days, months, years, and centuries. The segmentation of time has become so transparent that it is regarded as "segmented by nature" – "natural and objective"

Because of the correspondence between the two different levels of seg\frag, the textual and the narrative, it is difficult to discuss textual seg\frag without referring to narrative seg\frag as well. Thus, in the following section I will try to separate them as much as possible, but there cannot be an absolute division between the two.

4.1 *Typographical segmentation and fragmentation*

The conventions of print typography follow the mode of the Gutenberg's biblical setting. Johanna Drucker, in her book about modern art (1994), describes typography as a "single grey block of undisturbed text, seeming, in the graphic sense, to have appeared whole and complete." (95). Hence, a different typography of the page, segmented or fragmented, to quote Jan Tschichold, (1995) will result,

> Asymmetry is the rhythmic expression of functional design. In addition to being more logical, asymmetry has the advantage that its complete appearance is far more optically effective than symmetry (68).

Tschichold regarded the standard text's layout on the page, justified lines and centered pages in title, as the "symmetrical" style of typography. She saw the asymmetric typography, which does not align in predefined order or abide other fixed typographical norms, as "more optically effective." Yet, it was rarely used in literature except for title pages.

An example of the typographic possibilities of seg\frag in literature is Raymond Federman's "real fictitious discourse" *Double or Nothing* printed book. The story turns around a young author, whose creative procedures, preparations, and thoughts about his hero, a Holocaust refugee, are documented by a second person, who, in his turn, is described by the author. Thus, the novel presents a four-level perspective or prism,[139] or as McHale (1987) labels this structure, a Chinese Box. He refers to Chinese-box as the Russian babushka dolls – one within the other – multilevel texts (112).

Federman uses this multilevel structure to segment not only subject-units, but also every possible typographic, narrative and literary convention, including syntax and punctuation, thus, his work deserves close attention. Punctuation rules require capital letters in the beginning of a new sentence, commas in the middle of the sentence, and dots at sentences' close; those punctuation marks are signals that define the sentence as a textual segment. Federman's novel does not follow these rules; quite the opposite, there is a notable effort to break them up, hiding beyond a realistic motivation, "trying to be as faithful and as precise as possible in his recording of the second person's activities, however screwed up, chaotic" (000).[140]

---

[139] These multi-perspectives take us back to Lewis Carroll's *Alice*. Alice, "the dream-child," dreamt by the author (according to the framing poems), is dreaming about Wonderland. This multi-perspective device is developed even further in *Through the Looking-Glass,* where she finds herself dreaming about the king (Chapter IV, Tweedledum and Tweedledee), who is dreaming about her.

[140] Since Federman's book is structured as a Chinese Box its beginning is numbered by zeroes, pretty much like Morrison's beginning which is unnumbered.

Hence, for pages on end, there are no dots or commas[141] and the reader has to figure out where a sentence begins and where it ends. This device is extended to absurdity on page 91, where he cites, in tiny letters, a dream he had after winning some money in Vegas; he omits not only punctuation but also the use of spaces between words and capital letters, thus the reader has to figure out not only where sentences start, but where do words begin and end exactly as in Morrison's example,

> iwasswimminginbeangreenwaterhugeoceanandthe
> waveshadnumbersonthemfromonetotwelveimaginet
> hatbignumberinblackanditwastryingtodrownmeandi
> wastryingtoswimasfastasicouldatthesametimearabb
> ingasmanyofthenumbersaspossiblehandsfullofthem
> butifeltm (91)

Thus, presenting in a textually realistic-like way a dream, which is a collage of floating pictures without a beginning or an end. Similarly, Lewis Carroll uses typology to illustrate meaning, see *Through the Looking Glass*, Chapter III, where the small insect's voice is concretized by tiny letters. The endless flow of tiny letters without any obvious break conveys to the reader the dream's qualities

---

[141] Yaakov Shabtai in his book *Past Continuous* use mainly commas and very few full stops, which causes the reader to feel out of breath. Shabtai, Yaakov. *Past Continuous*. Trans. Dalya Bilu, London: Duckworth & Co, 1985 (1977).

and texture as in the *Stream of Consciousness*[142] style and creates the floating characteristic of dreams, its endlessness and clutter.

Looking at the above example, we instinctively feel that it is not segmented, but continuous, as the text is clumped into a block of streaming letters. Nevertheless, the conventions of English print typography ask for capital letters in the beginning of a line, spaces between words and punctuation between, within, and at the end of sentences. Seg\frag, or actually non-seg\frag, in this example is actually reversed, the result of subtraction of spaces, punctuation, and capital letters, which creates a de-familiarization of the reading process, as does seg\frag of typography, thus it turns readers' attention to the text's textuality by breaking automatic reading. And at the same

---

[142] The term *Stream of Consciousness* was coined by the American psychologist William James and taken into the realm of literature to label a type of fiction that has as its essential subject matter the consciousness of one or more characters. Thus, everything narrated is presented to the reader through the characters' mind and point of view without it being spoken; hence it's an inner thought process of a character with itself and to itself. Its main technique is the monologue which is a direct quote of the flow of thoughts without any filtering on the one hand and without any unnecessary explanations as is common when we talk to someone on the other hand. The inner-monologue is characterized by associative leaps in syntax and punctuation and much use of deixis. See Humphrey, Robert. *Stream of Consciousness in the Modern Novel*, Berkeley: University of California Press, 1954. Cohn, Dorrit. *Transparent Minds: Narrative Modes for Presenting Consciousness in Fiction.* Princeton, N. J.: Princeton University Press, 1978.

time it sends the reader to segment the text in the conventional way to enable the meaningful reading of the text.

Thus, it seems that accepted and established seg\frag does not inconvenience the reader and does not create a feeling of disruption of the whole as can be seen in the examples that are from print literature. On the contrary, it looks "complete" and normative. The notion of dismantling is caused by unexpected and uncommon modes (typographical). On the other hand, the relinquishment of seg\frag where it is accepted and well-established creates foregrounding and causes typography to be present.

 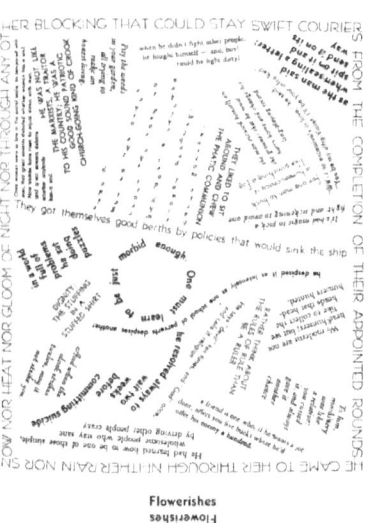

Figure 34 - Federman - page 1 and Burke - *Flowerishes*

Most common than not seg\frag is achieved by the addition of spaces, capital letters, spatial dimensions, and the use of different styles of letters as can be found in Federman's novel, thus fragmenting the conventional and regular one-letter-type typography by using a mélange of letters and capitals letters together (as in Figure 34).

14

It's like a guy in jail or on an island carving the days on the wall or on a piece of wood with a knife with anything a fork with his teeth *Robinson Crusoe of the Noodles* but in this case it's different it's backwards diminishing rather than augmenting the boxes that is not the days when there'll be no more boxes you'll know then it's the end *end* of the year The guy in jail he's stuck unless of course he knows when he's coming out but if he's serving for life if he's a murderer or a sex maniac then in his case it's hopeless Don't un   derstand why he goes on carving the days   on the wall unless he's just faking it Didn't   think of that But if he's a thief a petty thief   serving only for a few months then he has a   right to go on carving on the wall unless of   course he doesn't have anything with which   to carve except his fin gernails or else unless   he doesn't want to carve That's his business   Nobody is forcing him But the other guy on   the island he can't give up For him it's a dif   ferent matter than for the guy in jail There's   always a boat in the back of his carving or   something like a boat a submarine a seaplane a destroyer unless that's quite possible he decides instinctively to carve a boat a canoe in a tree instead of carving days on a crummy piece of wood Though the guy may very well decide to do both There are guys like that *idiots* who always do everything the hard way But it's his decision Nobody is telling him what to do on his deserted island unless of course there are cannibals on his ass then the carving serves a double purpose on the one hand to save his life on the other to escape alive It may be double work but eventually it pays

Figure 35 – Illustrative use in pages 14 - 15

In many cases, the main motivation for the breaking up of the typography's conventions is the poetic one, a foregrounding of the text as sign. Nevertheless, sometimes the motivation is illustrative; description of the text as can be found on pages 14 – 15 (Figure 35)

which presents the feeling of trepidation the writer feels in light of his future stay in a closed room for over 365 days. He conveys his feeling of apprehension and says, "It's like a guy in jail or on an island carving the days on the wall or on a piece of wood with a knife." The content of the text produces an image of solitude in the reader's mind, but the typography, which forms a keyhole image through which a person in jail sees the world, conveys more expressively the feeling of detention, of trepidation and isolation by creating a "hole" in the block of text.

Federman announces the work's Futuristic typography by the setup of the first page, the "real beginning," page number 1 (Figure 34 on the left). This page holds mutually exclusive calculations of the room's costs, scattered in such a way that it brings to mind the works of Filippo Tommaso Marinetti and Kenneth Burke who use words not only for their denotative function, but also for their illustrative function, as symbols presented on the paper's space (See Burke's *Flowerishes* – Figure 33 on the right). Jan Tschichold describes the "new" Futuristic typography as a way for gaining a better expressiveness, one that combines the visual presentation with the content: "The New Typography is distinguished from the old by the fact that its first objective is to develop its visible form out of the functions of the text" (66). All that fragmentation is found in print literature, which is supposed to be coherent and complete.

The two pages, Federman's first page and Burke's *Flowerishes*, (Figure 33) are enclosed by text, written in capital letters as a frame, circling the page clockwise, and causing the reader to turn the book around and around in order to read it on the one hand, and on the other hand blurs the text's beginning point and end. Looking at Burke's composition, the reader gets a feeling of dynamics and movement, which can be explained by its being a collection of sayings, "a series of comic apothegms" (35), as Lanham claims, words that are whirling around in the air. Lanham explains this playful typography as questioning the tradition of the literary canon in its function as transmitting "the canonical wisdom found quintessentially in the proverb" (37). By introducing "visual patterns and typographical allegories," the work suggests "that proverbial wisdom never comes into the world purely transparent and disembodied, totally serious, unconditioned by game and plat, by the gross physicality of its display" (37). Federman's page which looks as a draft, a note, made for personal use concretizes the process of calculating.

The concretization of meaning by the text, by its typographical layout, is intensified when Federman illustrates the meaning of single words by distorting the straight customary line of print breaking up of the word as a fixed and conventionalized visual object. Figure 36 shows the word "fall" actually falling down a slope and the word "climb" literally climbing up steps. The words serve two different functions at the same time: the referential function, where letters are transparent linguistic signs that when combined together denote a meaning, and the iconic function, where letters are arbitrary symbols that can be used to present an image, resulting in an integration between a pictorial element and the visual shape of a literary work.

Following Marshal McLuhan, who presented in his book *The Medium is the Massage* other possibilities than the orthodox lines written from left to right, from top to bottom, Federman's text is aligned and written in all directions, even from bottom to top and backwards. On Page 182 the reader is requested, "go to the bottom of the page," and at the bottom he is ordered, "start here and work your way up." The same phenomenon that was found in hypertext, the reading directions, is seen here – where the order of reading deviates from the norm. On the top of page 183 the reader is sent, yet again, to the bottom of the page, but there the instructions are, "work your way up from right to left this time." Thus, the reader has to read words and sentences backwards. On page 196 the words are written backwards and some even presented from top to bottom.

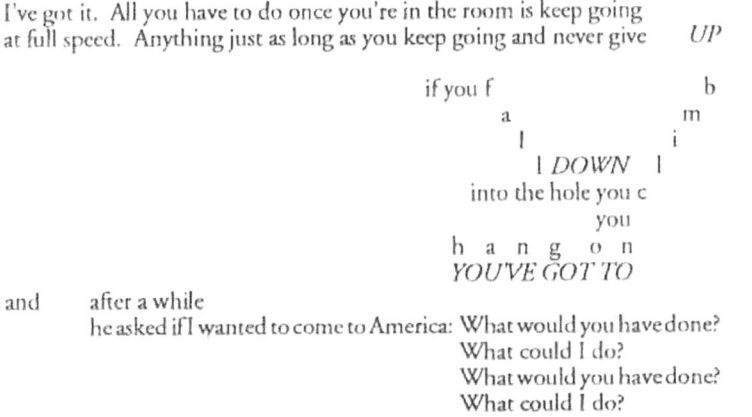

Figure 36 - Detail of Federman, page 24

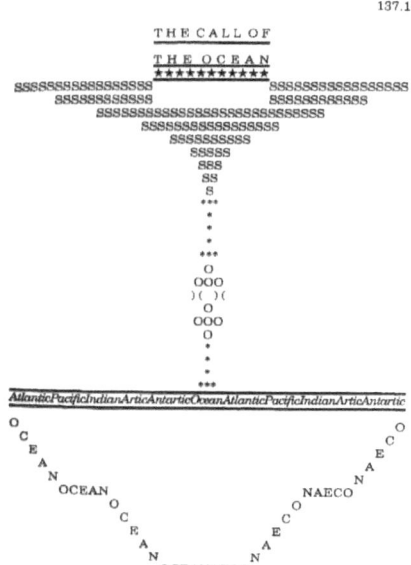

Figure 37 – The Call of the Ocean (p. 137)

Federman exploits the typographical fragmentation not only to fragment print conventions in order to de-automate the reading process, but also to illustrate his text and convey a more concrete meaning. The oscillation between the two functions is developed until the iconic function of the letters takes over the referential one, as in page 137 (Figure 37) where letters of the word "ocean" along with oceans' names and the letters s, o, and brackets construct an image of a boat. The text is transferred from the semantic system, where letters function as arbitrary symbols, which the reader has to "convert" into a meaningful object, a referent, into the iconic system, where they receive their meaning by combining their visual properties in order to create a visual resemblance to the object they present. The transformation in letters' functions corresponds to the thematic transformation that the fictive author and his fictional hero go through in the course of the story, thus reinforcing each other. The imaginary hero will be turned from a Polish citizen into an American, and the fictive author turns out to be the imaginary hero. Their distinct identities blend throughout the novel until it is quite impossible to distinguish between them, thus raising the question of the relationship between authors and their fictional heroes.

All the fascinating and radical examples are from one book only, Raymond Federman's *Double or Nothing*, which has a rare collection of every possible typographic device, but a modest dose of such schemes appear in other literary texts: Sterne's *Tristam Shandy*, Apollinaire's *Calligrammes*, Mark Z. Danielewski's *House of Leaves*, to mention only a few.

Lanham predicts that one of the outcomes of the text's transition from "page to screen" is that the "fixed, authoritative, canonical text, simply explodes into the ether" (31). However, there were no hypertext examples like Federman's avant-garde typology. Print literature was looking for techniques to override its conventions, to de-familiarize the reader with the common typography thus printed typography received more importance and consideration than hypertext typography. Hypertext's main concern, in its beginning, was centered on the linking device and little attention was given to typography, due to two reasons; the first is the limitations of the writing application, and the second is writers' fascination with the new linking device. However, some examples for the use of typography in hypertext beginning can be found, albeit they are scarce.[143]

Notwithstanding Lanham predictions, or aspirations, the most common typographical phenomenon in hypertext is the almost "vacant" node, holding from one word to few sentences, like in *afternoon*, node *Giulia*, which holds only one sentence: "< You could call me Giulia. > She says." Forty percent of *afternoon's* nodes hold only one word (220 out of 540), residing under a "chapter" called *Fragmentation*, located within a volume called *Begin*. Together all the one-word-nodes compose the text of the first node called *begin*, though in a jumbled order. This word play gives the reader the feeling of fragmentation, because there is so little text in those nodes, they are merely a collection of words. The "chapter" is reached from node *begin*, the first node of *afternoon*. It is anchored on the word "fragments" in the sentence: "This was the essence of wood, the fragments say." Instead of an explanation or an elaboration over the word "fragments" and what it means, the reader gets an illustration of what are fragments. The same word play is found in *Victory Garden*, though with some significant changes. The default linkage from

---

[143] The absence of complex typography designs is not surprising since most of hypertext literature is written with unfriendly tools for complex textual and typographical designs. Only lately, with the emergent of *Macromedia*'s tools, typographical design was becoming easier, though it is a time-consuming task and is mostly applied in poetry, which is shorter than a novel, thus easier to design.

Victory Garden's cover-page, not counting the *properties* node, is to node *Come In*, whose first link (word "IN") is to node *Come Often*.

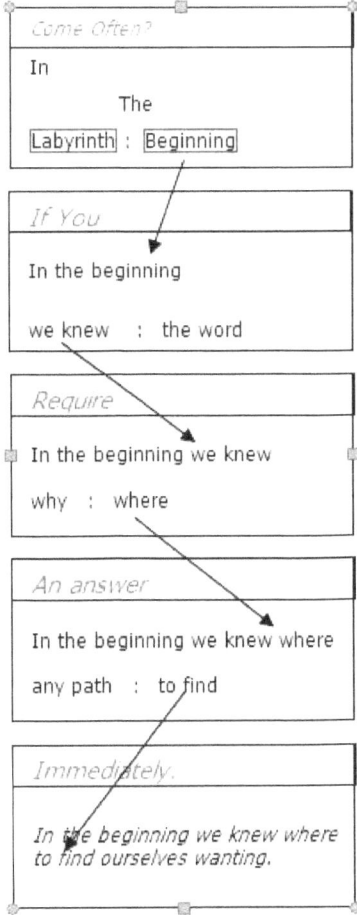

Figure 38 – *Victory Garden* "word play"

Typographically and textually, those two nodes (*Come In* and Come *often?*) are identical. The typography of the nodes (Figure 38) tips the reader that the two words separated by the colon at the bottom line are optional and she has to choose one of them. Node *Come often?* starts an additive "word game." Each consequent node adds the word, or words, chosen by the reader to the first line, the proposition, and offers a new couple of alternatives. Thus, though more than one word is presented on screen, only one word is added in each node (only the 'end node' receives unexpected words that create a meaningful proposition.)

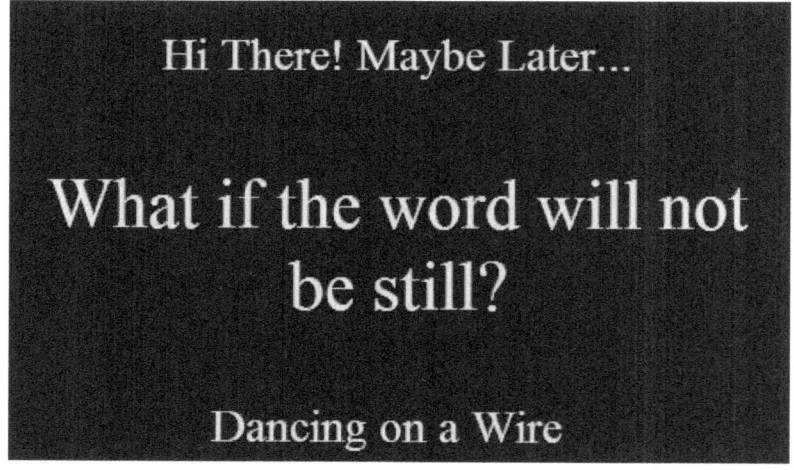

Figure 39 – *Hegirascope* "beginning" node

Elaborate typographical attention, not merely the reduction of the page into a game of words, is found in Moulthrop's *Hegirascope*, which starts with eight auto-changing nodes, each containing three unfinished and centered propositions. The upper one and the lower one are written in regular-size fonts and the middle line in big bold fonts, thus visually and textually holding the reader's attention (Figure 39). The nodes change after three seconds; hence, the reader can hardly catch even the central bold line and is missing most of the other text. The unfinished quality of the propositions, accentuated by the three dots at the end of the first proposition, emphasizes its segmented nature, and confers the notion of cut slips.

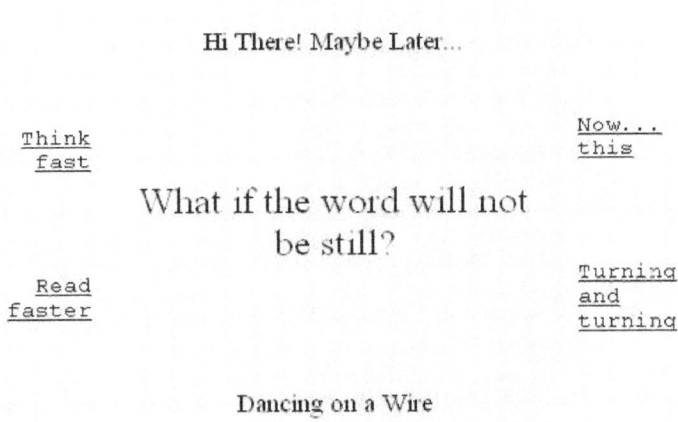

Figure 40 – The first node of the second phase of *Hegirascope*

This structure demonstrates what Bolter (1991) sees as the process of writing hypertext, a process of cutting and pasting, cutting into segments and pasting segments, by linkage, into coherent story lines: "A hypertext is like a printed book that the author has attacked with a pair of scissors and cut into convenient verbal sizes" (24). This is the reverse of the original intention for hypertext: the original motivation was to link discrete un-attached texts, thus viewing them as segments, so to speak, of a larger complete "whole," which has no author save the person or device which links them. Now the device is turned around to initially (as if) dissect and segment a whole text and consequently to offer re-sequencing options.

Moulthrop's nodes keep changing continuously through eight nodes, without allowing the reader to intervene, as they do not carry any links, and because of the short presentation time. After this phase comes a phase of another eight nodes holding the same text, but in reversed colors, the fonts are black and the background is yellow. There are four links (Figure 40) that are fragments of propositions placed in the text's margins, encircling the middle proposition from four directions: one at the upper left corner of the line, the other at the bottom left and the other two correspondingly on the right side.

Here the presentation time is prolonged a little, to eight seconds (and in the 2nd version prolonged to 30 seconds), and the reader can interrupt the flow of nodes by choosing one of its links. The links are not merely an anchor to other nodes; they are fragmented propositions in their own right, having diversified relations with the main propositions. The fragmentation and parsimoniousness of the propositions opens a wide range for possible interpretations. The two-left links-anchors can be understood as advice to the reader in response to the question posed in the main proposition: if the word will not be still, the reader should think faster or read faster. Alternatively, they can be interpreted as though the author is mocking the reader, exhausted by the struggle to read as much as she can in the quick changing nodes of the first phase. The upper link instructs her to think faster and the lower one tells her to read faster, as though she is an incompetent reader, as though she is to blame for not keeping track of the text and not keeping time with it.

The two links on the right margin (*Now… this* and *Turning and turning*) seem to belong to the second (What if the word will not be still?) and third propositions (dancing on a wire) in the middle. The upper one, "Now… this," though having similar typographical traits of fragmentation (…), stands in opposition to the upper proposition "Hi There! Maybe Later..." While the proposition is about "later," the link is about the present, "now." The lower link qualifies the third proposition; "dancing on a wire" is like "turning and turning." Of course, there may be other interpretations and the links destinations should be taken into account as well. However, the seg\frag typography allows for multi-interpretations and multi-ways of reading. Thus again, creating multiple possibilities of linking by way of segmenting and fragmenting and at the same time foregrounding words and sentences and leaving the reader to find her way through the text and through its meanings. Meaning, the reading takes a performative dimension and leaves behind the standard passive reading.

To sum up the typographical aspect of the literary work in print and in the hypertext medium according to the above examples, it seems that print literature is conscious of typography and tries to overcome its "neat" and formal nature. Some print authors, in order to achieve effects of defamiliarization, questioned the "transparent" typographical norms of writing and reading, by trying various different ways like: from top to bottom and from right to left, backwards, by breaking lines, by eliminating punctuation marks and words spacing etc. until the words and letters became just graphical signs that can be used for drawing. Though hypertext was busy with the innovative nature of linking of the medium, it scarcely used typography, mostly to foreground the linking trait of hypertext. Joyce use of one word nodes, Moulthrop's word-game which is built on the typographical layout of the node, and in *Hegirascope* where the typographical layout takes seg\frag to the point of disintegrating because of its incompleteness and at the same device itself, foregrounds the options of linking.

4.2 *Textual*

Most of the novels published in the 17 - 19th centuries, were published in several volumes, due to technological limitations and high costs of production (Payne, 2005. Ihara, 2007.). Fielding's *Tom Jones* (1749) first appeared in six volumes, though it is segmented into eighteen "books; (Stevick, 1970, 175)" Sterne's *Tristram Shandy* (1760) was published in nine volumes over a period of eight years; most of the 19th century novels were published in three-volume editions. Since this multiple-volume structure was a given form, it turned to be one of the considerations taken into account by authors when planning and writing their novels.

Hence, each volume is not only a textual material entity, but turned into an autonomous and cohesive narrative unit as well, like the first volume of Dickens's *Great Expectations*, which revolves entirely about Pip's life in the country as an orphaned child. The volume ends with his departure for London and the author's declaration: "This is the end of the first stage of Pip's expectations." Consequently, the volume is a cohesive narrative unit on the one hand, but, on the other hand, its ending raises the reader's curiosity as to what will befall the hero in his new status and new urban life, hence - a hint to the beginning of the next segment. The same structure is found in the second volume, which holds the description of Pip's new way of life and new friends in London, ending with the revelation of his benefactor. Again, each segment holds one overall theme, yet the last paragraph opens many possibilities and expectations, to be fulfilled or to be found groundless in the next volume. The volume is the biggest textual and narrative segment in a book while the smallest is the sentence. In either case it is complete and stable.

The partitioning into volumes is not common nowadays, as novels tend to be thinner than they used to be in the 17 - 19th centuries, thus they do not desire so many sub-divisions so I will not discuss this issue. However, the same phenomenon of a segment becoming a whole is found in sentences, in paragraphs and in chapters.

The sentence is the smallest narrative unit to be found in prose poetics. The structure of the sentence – the collocation of words and the syntactical order create the overall meaning. Each sentence has a meaning and the placing of one sentence next to the other creates the narrative. Hypertext sentences keep to syntactic rules and are mostly proper. In order that one node will fit with many others there is extensive use of deixis that causes a feeling of seg\frag though the sentence is a full grammatical unit. For instance, in *afternoon, a story* node *begin* starts with the propositions:

> I try to recall winter. < As if it were yesterday? > she
> says but I do not signify one way or another.

Though the sentences in the above citation have proper grammatical structure the reader is left with many questions and a need to find a connection between the three. This phenomenon, the lack of hypotaxic statements that brings about the need to "make sense," was termed by Ron Silliman (1987) as "the new sentence." In his article, named "The New Sentence," he states: "I am going to make an argument, that there is such a thing as a new sentence and that it occurs thus far more or less exclusively in the prose of the Bay Area[144]" (63). Yet at the end of the article as he lists its qualities the reference is to the sentence as part of a paragraph and not as standing

---

[144] The Bay Area refers to San Francisco, California, where the culture of the Beat generation flourished at the time. See Lawlor, 2005.

alone by its self, as Bob Perelman (1993) explains in his analytical article:

> A new sentence is more or less ordinary itself but gains its effect by being placed next to another sentence to which it has tangential relevance. New sentences are not subordinated to a larger narrative frame nor are they thrown together at random. Parataxis is crucial: the internal, autono-mous meaning of a new sentence is heightened, questioned, and changed by the degree of separation or connection that the reader perceives with regard to the surrounding sentences (313).

Thus, though the sentence may make sense by itself, in narrative the sentence is a part of the whole, be it the work, its chapter or even its paragraph. The paragraph is the smallest seg\frag unit from a typographic point of view. The first line of the paragraph, which is usually indented, distinguishes the paragraph typographically, and its last line might be shorter than all the others, thus becoming a typographical unit as well.

The paragraph is constructed out of one or more sentences, usually conveying one idea or referring to one event, one topic etc. The unity and coherence of the paragraph is an accepted standard: the reader accepts as a given the continuous relationship between sentences in the paragraph and the change of subject in transition between one paragraph to another. The relations between paragraphs and among them to the work as a whole can be divergent; they can be analogous, inverted, continuous, particularized, explanatory, and the like. At any rate they are linear and the reader expects linearity, fixed and given.

Chapter II of Dickens's *Great Expectations* Vol. I starts with Pip's description of his sister. This description is three paragraphs long. The first paragraph tells the reader about his sister's, Mrs. Joe Gargery, great reputation for bringing him up "by hand." The second paragraph is a description of her husband, who was already mentioned in the previous paragraph. To tighten the bonds between these two paragraphs and at the same time to convey the impression that the narrator is a child, who is able to recount only in a personal and associative way, the transition from the sister to her husband is anchored on the idiom 'by hand', although the narrator does not really understand its meaning; "She was not a good-looking woman, my sister; and I had a general impression that she must have made Joe marry her by hand" (8). The continuum of the paragraph is the description of Joe's inner and outer figure. The third paragraph is the outer description of "My sister, Mrs. Joe," thus creating an analogy between the characters and between the paragraphs. The relations between the first and second paragraphs are continuous and the relations between the second paragraph and the third are analogous, yet each one of them is a textual block and an autonomous subject-unit.

Hypertext did not bring any innovation to the paragraph, to its typological structure or to its place as a structure of meaning, either. For example, let's examine a node out of Joyce's *afternoon, a story*. The node's label is *Die*, in which the narrator describes what he saw on his way to work:

> I felt certain it was them, I recognized her car from that distance, not more than a hundred yards off along the road to the left where she would turn if she were taking him to the Country Day School.

> Two men stood near the rear of the grey buick and a woman in a white dress sprawled on the wide lawn before them, two other men crouching near her. Another, smaller body beyond.

> In the distance, coming toward them and the road along which I passed, there were the insistent blue lights of a sheriff's cruiser and a glimpse of what I thought to be the synchronized red lights of the emergency wagon.

> It was like something from a film: Blowup or the Red Desert. [Die]

The description is segmented into four paragraphs. The first is an explanation of why the narrator thinks that the accident has anything to do with him, namely -recognition. The second one is a description of the scene and the bodies, expanding on the deixises that are mentioned in the first paragraph. The deixis "she" is detailed somewhat more, "a woman in a white dress" and the deixis "him" is enlarged upon by the epithet "smaller body beyond," which would be the child taken to school that was mentioned in the first paragraph. The use of deixises signifies that the narrator thinks that he knows the people, so he does not need to call them by their names. However, the mystery about the casualties' identity remains because he is not sure. The third paragraph is about the emergency forces, which would be called to an accident scene, thus there is continuity, and the fourth is a simile, an attempt to convey to the reader the narrator's feeling of unreality, dismay, and hopelessness. Thus, each paragraph has its own subject and all of them together make up a scene of an accident while conveying the narrator's personal experience (or if you will - fantasy), around which the whole story evolves. The relations between the paragraphs are continuous, each adding some more details in order to sketch a whole scene. Although this is only an example it is characteristic of hypertexts and the paragraph is still one of the story's building blocks and they may be any size – holding one word or a whole story.

Wittgenstein, while trying to write his book *Philosophical Investigations*, found out that the linear form of print does not satisfy his needs. His thoughts were "written down […] as *remarks*, short paragraphs, of which there is sometimes a fairly long chain about the same subject, while I sometimes make a sudden change, jumping from one topic to another" (vii). Thus he could not make them "proceed from one subject to another in a natural order and without breaks" as is requested from contemporary academic conventions. Liestøl (1994) referring to Wittgenstein's praxis says,

> The quest for continuity and linear, successive order gave way to a form in which something analogous to a hypertext lexia,[145] the paragraph, became the largest textual unit, since it provided a form flexible enough to accommodate the complexity and multidirectness of the subject matter (88-89).

The paragraph functions as the largest thematic-unit in Wittgenstein's writings because he is not bound to continuity; on the contrary, he is looking for a form that will enable discontinuity. Nevertheless, the narrative literary work's main task is the presentation of an imitation of an action (or if you will, a process), to use Aristotle's words or, according to Sternberg (2001), the generating of "the three universal narrative effects/interests/dynamics of prospection, retrospection, and recognition – suspense, curiosity, and surprise, for short" (117). Thus, in fictional literature, although the paragraph is a narrative unit, it is only one unit in an additive, or causal chain that creates continuity – the chapter (or the work as a whole).

Chains of paragraphs may make up the chapter, which has the

---

[145] Liestøl refers to a hypertext node as if it was a *lexia*.

same autonomous structure that is characteristic of the volume and of the paragraph, thus setting it as an intermediate textual unit. Chapters are discerned typographically by various elements like their beginning point that is usually on a new page, or at least by a separation of a double space between them, by their title and by their narrative coherence, which may be governed by the subject, the time, the place etc.

It is this autonomy of the chapter, as a narrative unit, which allows for the titling of chapters. Sometimes the chapters are labeled only by their ordinal number, as in Fielding's *Joseph Andrews*, and sometimes they have a meaningful label. According to Stevick (1970) chapters' name usually suggests the chapters' topic, theme, or an abstract "from the totality of the words on the page" (186). The first chapter of Carroll's *Alice's Adventures in Wonderland* describes how Alice gets to Wonderland, thus it is labeled "Down the Rabbit-Hole," the second, describing Alice's frustration, and the outcome of her weeping is labeled "The Pool of Tears."

The use of chapters' titles as conveying the gist of the chapter is very common. The theme of Fielding's *Joseph Andrews* first chapter, as is attested by the author, is "Of writing lives in general, and particularly of Pamela;[146] with a word by the bye of Colley Cibber and others." The second chapter's topic is "Of Mr. Joseph Andrews,

---

[146] Meaning, Richardson, Samuel. *Pamela; or, Virtue rewarded.* Manchester: Russell and Allen, 1811.

his birth, parentage, education, and great endowments; with a word or two concerning ancestors." Dickens labels the first chapter of *A Tale of Two Cities* "The Period" because it holds a comparative description of the relevant time in England and France. The second chapter, which is called "The Mail," describes the route of the mail-coach to Dover that is the transportation or communication device between those two countries. Trollop, as well, uses chapters as a device for narrative segmentation. His third chapter of *Barchester Towers* is titled "Dr. and Mrs. Proudie," describing the new bishop and his wife. In the conclusion of the chapter Trollop introduces Mr. Slope, the bishop's chaplain, and says in a new paragraph, which holds only this line, "Mr. Slope, however, on his first introduction must not be brought before the public at the tail of a chapter." Consequently, chapter four is about the chaplain and is labeled "The Bishop's Chaplain." Although Stern's *Tristram Shandy* chapters do not carry any author's notes or any meaningful title, there is a clear-cut theme to each chapter. The first chapter is about Shandy's opinions of what determines "the figure" of the human being. The second is about the "Homunculus" and the dangers that await him, etc. However, authors can use the chapter's label in order to say something on a poetic level. John Barth in his work *The End of the Road*, labeled each chapter with the first few words from the text of the chapter itself. Thus, Chapter 4 begins: "I got up, stiff from sleeping in the chair, showered, changed my clothes, and went out for breakfast." The title of the chapter is "I Got Up, Stiff from Sleeping in the Chair." Stevick analyses this unorthodox labeling and says:

It is a slight mannerism, odd and amusing, but in its own way a little shocking. What Barth's title implies is that Chapter 4 is not simply "Chapter 4", which would be to designate it abstractly as the fourth block of a developmental whole; it is not "At Wicomico" or "Two Difficult Days" or "A New Job and an Intriguing Friendship," which would be to locate the chapter spatially, temporally, or substantively; it is not even a block of material designation altogether. The implication of Barth's title is that to state the theme or the subject of the chapter would be to repeat the words of the chapter, since the chapter has in no sense of the word a theme, no subject, and is about nothing which can be abstracted from the totality of the words on the page (186).

This analysis gains weight as Barth goes to extremes in his novel *The Tidewater Tales*, where he labels his first chapter:

Katherine Sheritt Sagamore, 39 Years Old and 8½ Months Pregnant, Becalmed in our Engineless Small Sailboat at the End of a Sticky June Chesapeake Afternoon amid Every Sign of Thunderstorms Approaching from Across the Bay,

and Speaking As She Sometimes Does in Verse,
Sets Her Husband a Task (CONTENTS)[147]

This "label" is the first paragraph of the chapter. Other chapters carry a more conventional title, yet Chapter 34's (my count, chapters are unnumbered) label holds the whole content of the chapter.

Stevick, while trying to locate the origin of chapters as a segmentation device, claims that there were three pre-novelistic segmentation traditions "which influenced the great originators of the eighteenth century and which continue, directly or indirectly, to shape narrative organization to the present time. They are the Homeric example, the biblical example, and the conventions of rhetoric" (162). In an attempt to understand why this tradition was not defied, Stevick turns to the formulations of Gestalt psychology and claims that chapters are the byproducts of the perception process. He argues that the mind is "accustomed to respond to experience in certain ways, and thus predisposed to respond in certain analogous ways to works of art. Of these analogous responses perhaps none is more important – in experience, in art, and in the relation between the two – than the impulse to shape materials into intelligible and satisfying forms" (9-10). He calls this impulse "gestalt formation" and regards it as the cause for the division into chapters, "Consequently, the shaping of narratives into patterns is simply the ineluctable result of the universal

---

[147] This label is taken from the book's Table of Contents, which is un-numbered pages.

human perceptual modes that lie at the basis of that shaping act" (10). It is even harder to make gestalts when the narrative is a novel, "an extended narrative" in Stevick's terms. The short story can be read in one sitting, while the reading of a novel is longer, and is usually interrupted.[148] Hence Stevick's observation:

> If art in general, then, demands in creator and observer a heightening of the gestalt perception which organizes experience itself, then the writer of extended narrative is obliged to make his work out of subordinate, distinguishable parts, each of which can be seen as a form in itself. Thus the writer induces anticipations which can be fulfilled at different levels: days which begin and end, alliances which are made and broken, locations which are visited temporarily, antagonists who are vanquished. [...] Or, to put it another way, one responds to the form of an epic by responding to the successive form of its books; one responds to the form of a novel by responding to its chapters (15-16).

Though authors were not oblivious to the issue of the chapter as a partitioning device, as I have shown above, not many referred to it

---

[148] The length of the narrative work is undoubtedly taken into account by authors, as is attested in Poe's (1850) description of the compositional process of his poem *The Raven*.

in their works or other writings. Fielding referred to this issue in a special chapter, in *Joseph Andrews*, where he perceives segmentation as one of the secrets of the trade,

> There are certain mysteries or secrets in all trades, from the highest to the lowest, from that of prime-ministering to this of authoring [...]. Among those used by us gentlemen of the latter occupation, I take this of dividing our works into books and chapters to be none of the least considerable. Now, for want of being truly acquainted with this secret, common readers imagine, that by this art of dividing we mean only to swell our works to a much larger bulk than they would otherwise be extended to. (Book II, Chap. I)

Regarding the "dividing" of the literary work as one of the "secrets" of his trade, Fielding feels obliged to dispute the general opinion that the significance of chapters and books is merely to "swell" the book, and explains to his readers their functions. He refers to segmentation from a practical point of view. Firstly, as one of the author's duties to his readers, since the vacant pages between books and spaces between chapters or paragraphs are "places" for physical (the eyes) and spiritual rest and a time for reflection (this is a bit humorous). Secondly, the partitioning into chapters provides the author with an opportunity for inscribing at the beginning of a chapter what is to come – namely it is a pre-figured ordering device – prospection in Sternberg's words. Thirdly, it prevents the dog-earing of the book (humor), and last, but not least, chapters have the sanction of antiquity, which corresponds with Stevick's claims about the origin of chapters, thus giving the whole work a seal of dignity.

The origin of the segmentation phenomena together with Fielding's reasoning (despite its somewhat humorous nature) and the poetical possibilities that it offers to authors may be the reason why the chapter as a partitioning device did not vanish in hypertext; it is still alive and kicking. In Ryman's *Two Five Three* or *Tube Theatre*, each train on the line has seven carriages, each holding 36 seats. "A train in which every passenger has a seat will carry 252 people. With the driver, that makes 253." (Why.htm) This concept explains the novel's structure and its title.

253 ? Why 253 ?
About this Site
Journey Planner
Car 1 passengers
Car 2 passengers
Car 3 passengers
Car 4 passengers
Car 5 passengers
Car 6 passengers
Car 7 passengers
The End of the Line
Another One Along in a Minute

Figure 41 - *253* Table of Contents

The cover-page shows a table of contents that lists, as in a printed book, the work's "volumes", seven in number as the number of the cars, and an introduction titled *Don't miss this important* 253 *announcement*, a prelude titled *Journey Planner*, an ending - *The End of the Line* and a finale - *Another One Along in a Minute* (see Figure 41). Each volume has its own table of contents, which is the car's seating plan (including the accurate position of the doors), which enables the reader to navigate between the 37 nodes, "chapters," that each volume holds, like the number of passengers that a whole car holds. Each chapter is built out of an unfixed number of paragraphs, which are actually a scrollable web page, each containing an identity card-like information of one passenger, under three labeled categories: *Outward appearance, inside information*, and *what he is doing or thinking*. The realistic motivation for this table of contents derives out of London's transportation-system.

Hypertext works, placed and written for the web do not have any fixed textual and navigational elements, like a Table of Contents, except those provided by the author (as in Figure 23) and some primitive options (like the "Back" command) provided by the viewing application.[149] Hypertext stand-alone novels, which are written with

---

[149] Hypertext pages on the Internet are built in a special programming language called HTML, which enables the writer to define not only the content of the work but the look and structure of each page, of the work as a whole, and what navigation tools will be available to the reader. However,

Storyspace software, have fixed textual elements and navigational tools yet not a formal table of contents like the one that was described in the aforementioned example. However, a closer look will reveal that the *Storyspace* application too has textual segments equal to the printed chapters, though presented through graphical maps that the software provides.

The table of contents of short stories' collection in print presents the stories' titles, while a novel's table of contents presents volumes or chapters' labels. I will take advantage of this traditional format of a stories' collection table of contents to examine Deena Larsen's story collection *Samplers* (1997), in order to find in hypertext the equivalent of the printed "Table of Contents" and see what format it has, and where is it located in *Storyspace* hypertext narratives. The *Storyspace reader* provides four graphical views, one of which is the "Outline view." As the name of the view implies the outline sketches out the work's structure and can be viewed in different levels of detail.

Sampler's outline-view, Figure 42, presents the upper level of Larsen's work, which is actually a conventional table of contents, listing all nine available stories, the traditional cover-page (the second rectangular, marked by -), directions' page, and a dedication page. Thus, the outline view in the *Storyspace* application is the replacement of the traditional print "Table of Contents."

---

these pages are viewed through an application, a reader that has its own navigation tools.

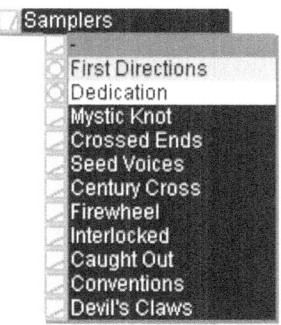

Figure 42 – *Sampler's* Outline

Looking at the outline-view of Joyce's *afternoon, a story*, (Figure 43) shows the division between the proper fictive work and acknowledgements, dedication, directions, publisher information, copyright etc., which is usually found in literary works and placed at the beginning of the work, before the beginning of the story. These pre-narrative objects are assembled under the title "*start*" while all the segments of the fictive work are assembled under the title "*structure*," which actually presents the work's "chapters," hence the work's structural partitioning, which shows that hypertext did not abandon print partitioning devices. In fact, partitioning (segmenting) is mandatory, given that the main device of the work is its linking options.

The same Table of Contents is found in Moulthrop's *Victory Garden* outline view as well. However, a closer look at the work's structure reveals that these are not chapters, but volumes. This double segmentation, into volumes and chapters, can be explained by the work's length as in print literature. While *afternoon, a story* holds "only" 539 nodes, which are called "writing spaces," and 956 links, *Victory Garden* holds 993 nodes and 2,804 links, hence the need for the double partitioned, into volumes and chapters.[150]

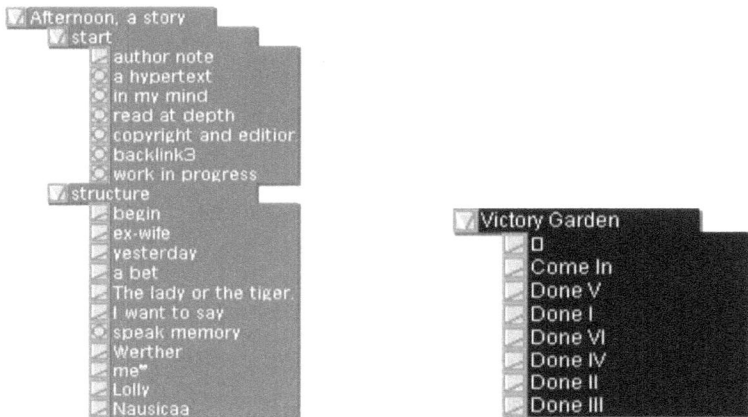

Figure 43 - Outline views of Joyce's *afternoon, a story* (left) and Moulthrop's *Victory Garden* (right)

The examples shown above demonstrate hypertext's segmentation into similar or equivalent parts, or segments, that print literature has. The last example, Moulthrop's *Victory Garden* shows not only that the literary work's partitioning still exists in hypertext, but that there is a return to the volumes structure that has become scarce in modernistic and post-modernistic literature, though so common in the novel's early days. Thus, there is no significant difference in textual partitioning between print literature and

---

[150] Each of Moulthrop's volume holds six chapters as can be seen in Appendix A.

hypertext literature. They both use a segmentation mechanism – which goes to show that the reasons for partitioning are quite deeply rooted in cognitive and psychological foundations of the reading process, as well as in conventions.

Hypertext was created, in the first place, as a connecting device that will link together distributed and unassociated units. Thus, segments are embedded in the format's universal concept of textuality. Nelson's *chunk style hypertext* starts with a chunk and branches to connect other chunks and Engelbart's concept of hypertext as a group communication tool that brings together single items. Hence hypertext is based on devices of separation, isolation, segmentation that in order to create the text uses devices of connections and linkage.

4.3 Narrative

A story is usually and conventionally composed out of chains of events, actions in Aristotle words, which are characterized by a unity of occurrence, and/or narrator, and/or time, and/or place or any combination between them, and are connected by one out of many possible relationships: additive, associative, analogous or metaphorical, metonymical, causal etc. Thus, many authors create a correspondence between the medium size textual unit, the chapter, and narrative units.

Normative fiction has numerous norms and devices to overpower its segmented, fragmented, full of gaps and un-given information nature. Thus, literary norms do not hold meaningful segmentation and fragmentation; on the contrary, a lot of attention is given to unity and sequentiality. And yet, on the other hand, there are lots of devices that foreground segmentation and fragmentation starting with the 'twisted end' stories, detective stories, reverse chronology, and a lot of other ways of cutting, dividing, tearing off etc. of segments and fragments of text, and creating effects that are dependent on these.

While the use of textual units as segments for multiplicity of points of view, or characters, or events, which will be discussed later on, is apparent to the reader, there are other segmentation options and devices which are hardly felt by the reader. For instance, the work may hold an informational gap,[151] the concealment of vital information, that though disrupting the chronological sequence, maybe unfelt by the reader. Only at a later time, when the gap is fulfilled, does the reader realize the disruption in sequence.

---

[151] See also Žižek who refers to the gap as "the missing link": Žižek, Slavoj. *For They Know Not What They Do: Enjoyment As a Political Factor*. London: Verso, 1991.

Perry and Sternberg (1986) explain this prevention of information:

> The world of situations and events constructed by the reader - causal sequence and all - is far from identical with what is explicitly stated in the text. From the viewpoint of what is directly given in the language, the literary work is composed of fragments that must be linked and pieced together during the reading process: it establishes a system of gaps that must be filled in (276).

The closing of gaps should be done by hypothesizes that "must be legitimized by the text" (277). Sternberg (1987) refers to the ways in which gaps are closed:

> This gap-filling ranges from simple linkages of elements, which the reader performs automatically, to intricate networks that are figured out consciously, laboriously, hesitantly, and with constant modifications in the light of additional information disclosed in later stages of the reading (186).

Iser sees the gap as inevitable in narrative:

> Even in the simplest story there is bound to be some kind of blockage, if only for the fact that no tale can ever be told in its entirety. Indeed, it is only through inevitable omissions that a story will gain its

> dynamism. Thus whenever the flow is interrupted
> and we are led off in unexpected directions the
> opportunity is given to us to bring into play our own
> faculty for establishing connections--for filling in
> the gaps left by the text itself (284-285).

As Iser discerns, no tale is told in its entirety, but the question is what is omitted. Is it regular, everyday actions and obvious details, like teeth brushing or a house having a door? These details are quite taken for granted and won't be missed by the reader. Or is it vital information about the value of things, the identity of a person or his origin, like the question "how many children had Lady Macbeth?" etc.[152] The omission of crucial information has a poetical justification, the creation of suspense and surprise. The reference, when talking about 'gaps,' is to the second kind, which play a role in shaping readers expectations and the forming of gestalts.

Between strict unity and chaotic fragmentation stretches a graded range of segmentation orders. While the following example of

---

[152] The essay "How Many Children Had Lady Macbeth" was composed in the thirties by L. C. Knights and originally appeared in 1946. The particular question as to the number of Lady Macbeth's children had arisen in nineteenth century Shakespearean criticism because Lady Macbeth talks of having "given suck," yet there is no mention of any living male child who might follow Macbeth onto the throne of Scotland. However, Knights never really addresses this particular question in his article but refers to the question of characters and their makings.

Robbe-Grillet's fragmentation method illustrates one end of the unity vs. fragmentation pole, the narrative gap (for instance - Tom Jones origin) presents the other extreme, the opposite pole. While reading Robbe-Grillet, readers cannot ignore its fragmented nature since the reading turns into a quest through the text due to its high level of fragmentation; the ordinary gap, however, may be utterly unfelt thus not producing a sense of fragmentation. One of the most notorious examples of an unfelt gap is found in Agatha Christie's detective story *The Murder of Roger Ackroyd* (1927).[153]

Gaps as a poetical device are found in the twisted-endings stories since ancient times as can be seen in Perry and Sternberg elaborated article about the system of gaps in the Bible. Greek literature used this device as well, for instance *Oedipus Rex* that finds at the plot twist that he actually killed his father and married his

---

[153] In chapter 5, when Dr. Sheppard finds Ackroyd murdered in his study he says: "I did what little had to be done. I was careful not to disturb the position of the body, and not to handle the dagger at all. No object was to be attained by moving it." This statement is vague and hides more than it reveals. What did the Dr. do? Only at the end of the narrative, in chapter 27 *Apologia*, the doctor says: "Then later, when the body was discovered, and I sent Parker to telephone for the police, what a judicious use of words: 'I did what little had to be done!'" Genette refers to this technique of omission and vagueness and says: "The trick here lies in the paralipsis – that is, in the omission of essential information that focalization through the murderer ought to include." Genette, Gérard. *Narrative Discourse Revisited*. Trans.by Jane E. Lewin, Ithaca: Cornell University Press, 1988, 67.

mother. Many of Guy de Maupassant's short stories and his followers, like O. Henry and later on the classical detective story, are all based on the early textual omission of crucial narrative information. The omission is intended and, in order to have its effect, will be revealed eventually, mostly at the end of the story, thus causing the readers, and sometimes the characters, to rethink and reconstruct the fictional world in light of the new-found information. For instance, in Maupassant's story *The Necklace* the value of the borrowed necklace is not doubted and not even raised until the final lines of the story, where Madame Loisel meets her friend, Madame Forestier, who had lent her the necklace. Finding the real value of the necklace turns the fatal mistake around – for most of the story the reader and the heroine think that losing the necklace or even borrowing it was the fatal mistake, but at the plot twist the reader and the heroine find that the fatal mistake was not telling the truth (on part of both women).

Significant gaps that are filled and closed are mostly unfelt at the point of their creation and by thus the feeling of seg\frag is withheld for the effect of sequentiality, streaming of narrative information and coherence. Nevertheless, the device of omission and procrastination always involves fragmentation, cutting, tearing and separation of a text snippet from its natural sequential position, thus it can be put on one axis with other instances where the seg\frag of the sequence causes the reader to become so disoriented that she can hardly reconstruct the story like Robbe-Grillet's works.

A bewildering example is Robbe-Grillet's novella *In the Labyrinth* (1959), which is an extreme example of textual and narrative fragmentation. Robbe-Grillet's story is segmented into chapters, albeit their only distinctive feature is blank lines that separate them from each other. The chapters do not carry a meaningful label or a numeric one, nor do they necessarily start on a new page. The story holds fourteen such chapters, each segmented into paragraphs, which are discernible by their indentation. These structural segments, chapters and paragraphs alike, are not coherent and have no unity and they give the impression of having been cut off from some larger inclusive text, without attention to their fragmented nature.

The story begins with the statement, "I am alone here now, under cover." This statement raises the reader's curiosity as to who is "I," why am I alone or why is it so important to declare it? What does the narrator mean exactly by the word "cover?" From what kind of threat is he sheltering? Moreover, what was before "now"? The second sentence shades some light on the referent 'cover,' "Outside it is raining," which somewhat limits the range of threat to the weather, and explains somewhat what 'cover' may be, hence satisfying one of the reader's perplexities. The continuance of the sentence is a description of the hardship of walking in the rain. This seems quite a regular description familiar to the reader from other literary works and her own experiences. However, what seemed to be a classic exposition is disrupted in the third sentence. When the reader reaches the end of the second sentence, which is quite long, seven and a half lines long and broken in the middle by a semi-colon, she finds another long sentence, which ends the paragraph, that starts with the same words, yet presents an antonymous situation, "Outside the sun is shining," telling, in analogous details the hardship of walking in the sun.

The paragraph is thus segmented into three propositions, which create narrative fragmentation. The first one presents the subject/narrator that can be ascribed to either of the two following sentences but not to both - by laws of nature, if it is raining so hard that you have to walk "with your head down," then the sun is not shining. The paragraph can be read as a statement concerning two different times: the first is a time of fierce winter where the rain is so dense that you can stare ahead only "a few yards ahead" (141), and the wind blows through the trees and makes their shadows dance. The second is the exact opposite: the sun shines; there are no bushes so there are no shadows. The single resemblance between the two rough weather conditions is that the one to walk outside has to shield his eyes and see "only a few yards in front of you" (141). That kind of narrative fragmentation causes the disintegration of the paragraph's unity and coherence. It attacks the reader's most basic instincts and norms of reading and making sense of narrative, namely that a paragraph has one coherent subject and not two mutually exclusive ones.

The same method of fragmentation, of quick changes of topic, heroes, time, and space, which was described within a paragraph, can also be found between paragraphs as well, yet this fragmentation is less shattering to the reader since she is used to the passage of time between paragraphs that may cause changes from paragraph to paragraph. In the first chapter, close to its end (paragraph 24, 148), there is a description of the soldier on the sidewalk and his package. In the next paragraph the package is on the chest inside the room, "The box wrapped in brown paper is now on the chest." Due to the use of deictic means of language, there is no doubt that the reference is to the same object that was described in the previous paragraph. The definitive article "the," which is one of language's means to make a noun definite, acquaints the package. The time deixis "now" denotes a passage of time since the box was under the soldier's arm, in the previous paragraph, and its location in this paragraph, though we cannot estimate how much time elapsed since the first paragraph and the second one. The two paragraphs are brought in sequence, as though they are segments of the same subject or event and as subsequent time units, which, as the reader finds out, they are not. They are two fragments sewn together.

Narrative fragmentation then can be an unfelt gap on the one hand and on the other hand, can break up the coherence of a structural thematic-unit, which causes the reader to become puzzled and confused, and to quote Douglas, "What are readers to make of Robbe-Grillet's *In the Labyrinth*, which continually reverses our expectations from sequence to sequence, and from paragraph to paragraph – and even, occasionally, from sentence to sentence" (94)? Robbe-Grillet creates fragmentation by putting side by side unconnected objects, events and persons. Print literature, as well, has extreme patterns of seg\frag and the phenomenon is not unique to the digital format.

While gaps, juxtaposition and other fragmentation devices break the coherence of the structural segments, techniques of multiple voices, points of view, highlight the correlation between chapters and episodes. Point of view is the presentation of a concept, or an event, or an object, or a person, or an episode, via a specific prism. The presentations from various points of view usually take advantage of chapters as containers, thus presenting each viewpoint in a separate segment. In print, one of the famous multi points of view works was written by Akutagawa and found in his short story-collection named *Rashomon,* published in 1952. *Rashomon*'s first story, *In a Grove*, is constructed out of seven narrative and textual segments (chapters), each presenting one persona telling her/his version of the same past incident, thus creating seven points of view of the same event. The realistic motivation for this segmentation is the police-investigation conducted in order to determine who killed Takejiro: all the characters testify to what they think they saw at the murder scene and the last to testify is the murdered-man himself, as conveyed through a Medium. Thus, seven segments, which could not be considered as proper narrative sequence, are ordered by the device of the investigation to create a whole.

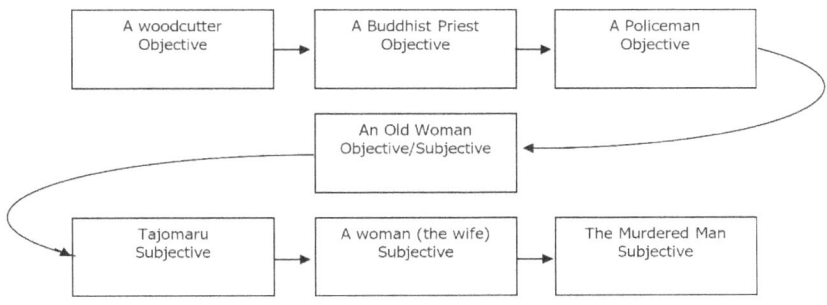

```
A woodcutter          A Buddhist Priest          A Policeman
Objective             Objective                  Objective

                      An Old Woman
                      Objective/Subjective

Tajomaru              A woman (the wife)          The Murdered Man
Subjective            Subjective                  Subjective
```

Figure 44 – *Rashomon*'s narrative-line

Each narrative segment is a chapter, carrying a unique label, e.g. "Testimony of a Woodcutter before a High Police Commissioner," thus dividing also the typographic writing space into seven segments. The characters can be classified into two symmetrical groups. The first is the "objective" one, people that do not know the murdered man, who happened to meet him randomly and for a short while, like the Buddhist Priest. Or else, they have some professional role, which caused them to be involved in the story, like the Policeman, who represents the law, or the Woodcutter, whose work-place turns to be the arena of the crime. These appear first in the text. The second group is the characters that are involved directly in the murder: the attacker, the murdered man's wife, and of course the murdered man. An additional "witness" is an old woman, that seems to be a stranger to the murdered man, hence "objective," but she turns out to be his mother-in-law thus turning into a "subjective" witness. She is the fourth witness in the linear sequence, hence in the middle of the investigation – three witnesses precede her testimony and three witnesses follow it, hence becoming a junction between the "objective" and the "subjective," though her main worry is for her daughter. The graded transition from the impersonal or objective to the personal or subjective forms a textual symmetrical pattern that depends on the pre-fixed linear order of the narrative as can be seen in Figure 44.

Since the story presents multiple versions of the "same" event the author takes advantage of segmentation to clear-cut each point of view, or version, and dedicate a chapter to each. This structure in its closed and mutually exclusive segments allows separate reading of each, and resembles the nodes system quite closely. The multiplicity of voices calls for an additive structure, which the author exploits to raise the reader's curiosity and expectation with each additional voice reaches its peak with the murdered-man's story. The author makes use of the linear order of print and the segmentation into chapters to create a progressive personalization, which intensifies the reader's curiosity as to what really happened and at the end, creates surprise and indecision. The murdered man's story raises the reader anticipation for the unraveling of the mystery and the unfolding of the truth. However, his surprising 'testimony' does not resolve the mutually exclusive multiple voices into one coherent and authorized solution regarding who the murderer is and what really happened there.

The story is a sample of multiple mutually exclusive voices, while its subject is the quest for one "objective" truth. The quest has a narrative structure: a variety and number of obstacles which eventually lead to the desired object. When the same basic story is repeated from various points of view, versions of the same story are naturally created. However, these versions are mutually exclusive; if the rapist committed the murder as is told by the rapist himself it could not have been the wife as she testifies and vice versa. As the story's effect rests on linearity, if it had been written in hypertext the author should have conditioned the access to the last segment, to the murdered man's story, with reading all the other segments beforehand even if in a variety of sequences, otherwise the effect of surprise would be lost and multiple conditions should be made so that the graded effect that progressively raises the reader's curiosity would be kept. So, we have here a node system which, barring the last one, could have been entered from any entry point even if by losing the gradual heightening of tension.

The same device of multiple voices, separated into nodes, is found in modern literature[154] like David Coover's (1973) story *The Door*, in his story-collection *Pricksongs & Descants*. The reader gets an insight into the minds of three persons, a father, his mother, and

---

[154] The multiple points of view reached TV as well. An Australian TV mini-series by the name of "The slap" was produced by Matchbox Pictures and broadcasted in the ABC Australian network. Each episode presents the personal point of view of one of the witnesses to the slapping event. See Hale Mike. "Drama at a Barbecue Leads Relationships to Fizzle." In New York Times, Television Review, 15.2.2012. Also: <http://tv.nytimes.com/2012/02/15/arts/television/the-slap-on-directv.html>, 24.7.2016.

his daughter. Each "retrospective monologue" is separated by a blank line from its formers and has a different style, thus characterizing the person to whom it belongs. The monologues are short, thus creating the feeling of segmentation or fragmentation. However, the story is narrated in the 'consciousness-stream' style, which by definition is fragmented, as its composition rule is the character's stream of thoughts, which makes sense to the character, though it might not make sense to the reader. The effect of the story depends on the order of narration. The first two persons, the father and his mother appear first and they are thinking about the third character, which is the daughter or the grand-daughter respectively, thus preparing the reader for the last monologue. The tension that is built gradually, depends on the sequence of reading; starting with the father who is thinking about folklore's tales, ogres, wolves, witches, and terror, continuing with the grandmother that focuses the terror on sex. When the granddaughter's thoughts are presented, on her way to enter her grandmother's house, we are looking for the lurking wolf as in Little Red Riding Hood. In this case, the three stories are not mutually exclusive but complementary. However, each is textually separated like a chapter in a book and the specific order is necessary for achieving the effect of rising tension.

Hypertext authors employ the multiple-points-of-view as a poetic device in much the same way as print-literature authors do. As can be seen in Figure 45, (a screen-capture) Larsen's (*Samplers*, 1997) hypertext short story *Crossed Ends* can be described as having five chapters: Patty, Charles, Diane, Cherry, and Retirement, which is the focal event of the story (in the middle).

The same type of multiple points of view that was described in *Rashomon* is found in *Crossed Ends*. The story presents four family members and their life-story as is conceived through each person's eyes, creating a mosaic. The story is constructed out of four parallel story lines. However, unlike *Rashomon*, the four points of view are not mutually exclusive and they stand side by side, each adding information, thoughts, and feelings to the narrated family's relations, resembling Coover's *The Door*. In the *Links window* that opens from node *Retirement*[155] the author states that "Every story has at least four sides: what you see as truth and what they see." The *Links window* provides four beginning points, one for each character. By choosing a character's name and following the default linkage the reader can read in sequence that character's whole story-line as is narrated by it, each is like a chapter in *Rashomon*. Each "chapter" is seven nodes long. Through those monologues, a web of relationships is spread out before the reader, filled with hate, feelings of betrayals and contempt.

---

[155] The author declares that the starting point of the story is node *Retirement*. Hitting the Enter key from the story's cover-page opens-ups the *Links window*, which presents four possible ways for reading and directs the reader to the node that will start her on her way:
"Where it ends - to node *Crossed Ends*.
Where it starts - to node *Retirement*.
Give up now - to the work's cover-page.
Or try to understand - to the directions node."

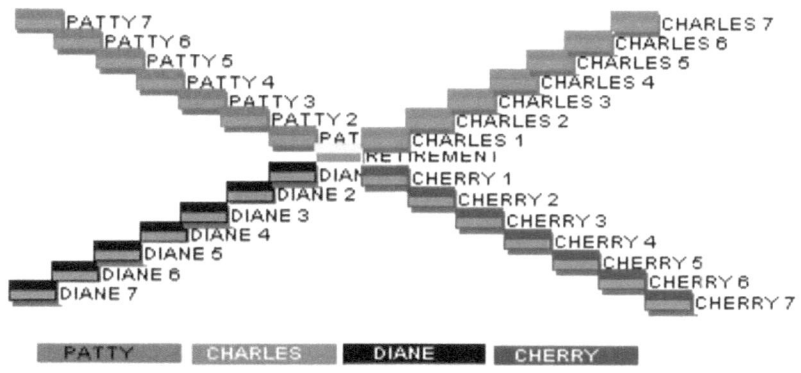

Figure 45 - *Crossed Ends* story line

Though the monologues are interior monologues, having no outward presentations, as though the narrator is strolling from one consciousness to another, they are analogous since they are all associations triggered by the same external events that are taking place throughout the retirement dinner, in which all four characters participate. The retirement party is hurriedly arranged for Charles, the head of the small family, as the other option was him being fired due to a buy-out. Each person is pondering his life through the years and Charles announces his plan for the future, which is sailing. Patty, Charles's socially incapable, religious and old-fashioned wife, is very upset about this announcement, which is news to her. She was thinking about her success with arranging the party and her hopes that through the good things and congratulations that Charles receives from his co-workers their value will rise in the eyes of her daughter and granddaughters. After her hysterical flight to the toilettes room, Charles starts calculating the options of going without her.

The *Links window*, when opened from the *Retirement* node, shows all four parallel nodes (and paths): *Charles1*, *Patty1*, *Diane1*, and *Cherry1*. The outline of the retirement dinner party holds a scant description of the place and its decorations, the traditional farewell toasts made by the employers, describing the worker's contribution to his work place, the endowment of gifts, the employee's farewell words, a toast and thanking for the gifts and the time spent together. This sequence is not described directly but is narrated through the eyes of each member of the family, thus creating four points of view towards each event. These attitudes mirror the different characters and the relations between them by way of analogy.

On hearing the traditional farewell greetings Charles concludes that his colleagues thought him a decent solid fellow. Patty, who admires her husband, is very proud to hear his praises and hopes that they will raise her esteem too in the eyes of her daughter and grandchild. Dianne, their eldest daughter, thinks that all the praises are "crap," and Cherry, the younger one, thinks that her father cannot see that the guys are roasting him. The same analogy is created by the characters' attitudes towards the dinner's place and decoration. Charles likes the place, Pete's Landing, yet he finds the pink room a little too fussy. Patty thinks that the dinner's place is a little silly, yet she is very happy with her choice of the pink room and the overall effect of the pink table clothes and the "gold and rose-rimmed plate ware." (*Patty1*) Diane is fingering the pink cloth not noticing it much.

Cherry is not noticing the decoration of room, but "grabbing the last piece of bread from smurky pink-cloth basket." (*Cherry1*)

Though there is an obvious connection between the characters' thoughts and actions, there are no textual links, between the four personal stories, except the default, which can be activated by clicking anywhere in the text or by hitting the Enter key. The default linkage causes a sequential reading of each character's life-story. If the reader opens the *Links window* she can find other links there, to the analogous nodes of the other three characters, but there are no textual links. This story is written in hypertext, a technique that allows for linking between the characters' nodes, unlike *Rashomon*'s print format, and yet there are no links between the four family members. The same lack of communication that characterizes their 'real' life is presented in the story by the lack of direct links. The last node of each story-line, no. 7, holds no links at all, as though the reader has reached the end of the story, but the only end he has really reached is the end of this character's monologue. In order to continue reading the reader has to use the built-in tools of the software, such as "previous page ...", "cover page", "History" etc.

This story is an example of how an author enlists his chosen medium, hypertext in this case, for conveying his meaning of alienation precisely by not using its most unique traits – the linkage device, though it uses linearity within each character's story. The story conveys the idea of estrangement in the tightest social-cell of society, the family. The family in this story though gathered in the same room around the same table for the retirement party, which is the realistic motivation, is as far apart as can be imagined. The subject, the idea of alienation, is emphasized by the story's structure - the lack of linkage between nodes though in this story it is available to the author, unlike in print. Thus, the story does not use seg\frag though it allows the reader a couple of ways of reading, like reading sequentially or going from one conscious to the other thus it can be presented in print with very little loss of its narrativity, showing again that hypertext does not necessarily bring any novelty.

Crossed Ends, unlike *Rashomon*, shows another problematic point in narrative literature, that of simultaneity, which denotes two or more occurrences that happen at the same time though it might be in different places or to different people. Temporally speaking, simultaneity is two events that run, as Sternberg (1990) defines it, "side by side, rather than early before late" (941). Where in the fictive world events and actions happen at the same time, albeit in different places or to different people etc. As much as they happen in real life, they cannot be presented in the same way in the printed media as it goes against the grain of textual communication which is linear. In painting and sculpture, the viewer receives the "whole picture" at the same time, hence simultaneously. In literature however, actions unfold before the reader throughout the reading process one after the other because of the linearity of the text. Literature and storytelling in general present one thing after another thus it had to find ways to bypass its linearity in order to present simultaneity. One of the techniques authors employ to convey simultaneity is through the textual segmentation, which could take the form of division into paragraphs, or chapters, or "directions" etc.

For instance, Trollop's solution in *Barchester Towers* for the simultaneous occurrences, which follow the return from the party at Ullathorne, is to dedicate one chapter to each occurrence. Chapter 44 is labeled: "Mrs. Bold at Home" and starts with the statement that "Mrs. Bold, when she got home from Ullathorne on the evening of Miss Thorne's party, was very unhappy, and moreover very tired." Chapter 45 is labeled: "The Stanhopes at Home" and start with the author's declaration "We must now return to the Stanhopes, and see how they behaved themselves on their return from Ullathorne." Hence, those two chapters describe simultaneous occurrences in time, though in different places and to different characters. The knowledge regarding their simultaneity is conveyed by putting it in words in the text. This technique is quite common and modern and post-modern literature use it and additional techniques, which take advantage of other textual traits.

In print literature that tends toward the unusual, modernistic and post modernistic ends we may find additional devices for effecting simultaneity. One of these innovative ways is taking advantage of the book's format as a two-sided object, having a front cover and a back cover. For instance, Carol Shields (1994) *Happenstance* (Figure 46) has no conventional back-cover, but two frontals turned upside down. Both sides of the cover have the same design, a tiled background, two thick black lines carrying the book's details and a small-framed photo. On one side, the tiled background is in shades of pink and the framed photo of a woman's body, presented from chin to hips, dressed in a heavy coat. On the other side, the tiles are in shades of blue and present man's legs, half covered by a tweed mantle. Unconventionally and against reader's expectation, the pink side of the book is named "The Husband's Story," and the bluish side is labeled "The Wife's Story," telling his spouse's story. Both covers state: "two novels in one about a marriage in transition." Originally, each "novel" was published separately. In 1980, "*The Husband's Story*" was published under the title *Happenstance*, and two years later "*The Wife's Story*" appeared under the title "*A Fairly Conventional Woman.*" Only in 1991, the two novels were joined into one book. However, no one could ignore the fact that the two characters are related in matrimony, thus creating a connection between the two separate novels.

The story is about Jack and Brenda Bowman separated for five days due to Brenda's participation in a quilting convention. This situation causes a reversal in their "normal" life; actually, Brenda's going away for a convention is already a reversal of their common order of life, since usually Jack is the one to go on conventions due to his academic occupation. Now Jack has to handle all the housework and deal with the kids. This unfamiliar situation causes Jack to review his life, and so does Brenda, who finds herself, for the first time in her life, on her own, free to do whatever she chooses (or chooses not to do), including having an affair. All this happens in temporal simultaneity though in two different places and to two different characters.

Figure 46 - *Happenstance* **two cover pages**

This example in fact forces the reader to choose her reading sequence, which is similar to hypertext. The reader has to select between the two official "entering" points – that of the wife or that of the husband, thus she is an active reader no less than the hypertext's one. The fact that the characters are related and that the time frame of the stories are parallel creates a two threaded story. Hence, print literature allows the use of the book format to be segmented into two parallel books at the same time and present double reading options. Other multiple reading devices in print are: the use of different fonts or different font's colors, dividing the two sides of the page to present two sequences etc. The reader's decision about the order of reading segmentation device in order to create small and coherent units such

(choosing her point of entry as "first reading") may have an effect on the meaning creation process, and in a variety of aspects as was demonstrated previously in print and hypertext works.

To sum the issue of segmentation thus far, we have seen that authors, print and hypertext literature alike, take advantage of the segmentation device in order to create small and coherent units such as paragraphs or chapters that are narrative units as well. These units are used for various different artistic and narrative effects, for instance, the presentation of multiple and/or simultaneous and sometimes mutually exclusive voices or points of view. Print literature uses the correspondence between textual and narrative units and their labels to create different orders of sequentiality, multiple entering points and in general, overriding the medium's limitations, as we saw in the above examples. Hypertext literature, contrary to researchers' expectations, keeps this correspondence and the general partitioning into paragraphs and chapters and does not use it in any different way; on the contrary, it is used in the most traditional print-like ways. Hence seg\frag without linkage is not special to hypertext.

Hypertext literature adheres mostly to the coherence of paragraphs. The node, or page, or "lexia," holds a variable number of paragraphs presented in logical, temporal, and spatial sequence. For example, in *afternoon*, node *4 what I see*,

> A J-shaped skidmark extends perhaps fifty feet of
> the westbound or--from her perspective --

oncoming, lane, the curve of the J slanting across the single yellow line. Another shorter skidmark, something like a roostertail, stops short of the first. They seem to have taken care to sweep the street, and yet I am able to find a scattering of glass, here and there, glinting like raindrops in the late afternoon light in the space between the skidmarks. There is neither blood nor oil on the road.

I have halfway expected to find the remnants of a chalk outline of a body, the kind of thing one sees on television. I do however find the place where the bodies have lain. It is relatively easy to locate them on this manicured grass. The wheelmarks of a gurney lead up to each of them.

Each of the three paragraphs is a cohesive thematic unit, describing the location of an accident scene, starting from the external and the discernible skid marks on the road, through the clearing actions, which wiped away the evidence, to the observer's thoughts and feelings. All these make up one coherent, logical sequence that looks and is read like a standard and typical part of print literature. Another example for that coherency from Moulthrop's *Hegirascope*, node *Without Staples*:

At the invitation of Wired magazine, defrosted death-of-print prophet Marshall McLuhan flies to New York for a demonstration of the World Wide Web.

McLuhan's hosts offer a guided tour of various Web wonders, but the well-preserved professor keeps backtracking to the Penthouse site. After downloading a couple of skin shots, McLuhan shakes his head in disgust. "They're not the same without the staples."

He spends the rest of his visit reading the interviews.

The flow from one paragraph to another is time-based sequence of events: McLuhan flies, his behavior at the *Wired* magazine and what he does in the rest of his visit. Though these are only two examples, they represent the state of affairs in hypertext works at its beginning.

Many authors take advantage of fragmentation in a minor way for poetic or rhetoric purposes, so much so that fragmentation is found in all the elements that construct a story, like space, time, events or episodes, and points of view. Out of those, time is a foremost issue in poetics since literature is considered a temporal art in contrast to the visual arts which are spatial. The temporality of literature stems from its linear medium, which unfolds actions one after the other. Lessing's *Laocoon* is an attempt to explain the "limits of painting and poetry," meaning the difference between literature and the visual arts. For instance, what is more suitable for painting than for literature? Lessing compares between two *Iliad* scenes, both in the fourth book, that of Pandarus shooting his bow and that of the assembly of gods drinking in council. While the scene of the gods is short and sketchy it was recommended by Caylus as a subject for painting, yet the description of Pandarus, which is narrated in great detail, was not considered as fit for painting. Lessing observes that "in the one case [Pandarus] the action is visible and progressive, its different parts occurring one after the other in a sequence of time, and in the other [the assembly] the action is stationary, its different parts developing in co-existence in space." (Chapter 15, 77) Thus, literature is better fit to present actions while painting describes one moment in a space. Sternberg (1978), following Lessing, defines the nature of narrative, "Narrative presents characters in action during a certain fictive period of time" (14), in contrast to painting or sculpture that present one specific moment which holds forever. Lessing finds the reason for this difference in the artistic medium,

> If it is true that in its imitations painting uses completely different means or signs than does poetry. Namely figures and colors in space rather than articulated sounds in time, and if these signs must indisputably bear a suitable relation to the thing signified, then signs existing in space can express only objects whose wholes or parts coexist, while signs that follow one another can express only objects whose wholes or parts are consecutive. (Chapter 16, 78)

Thus, time is an inherent trait of the literary medium, and creates a basic twofold-layer of unity in the literary work, that of fictive time and its events' order and that of communication time and its order of reading – one page after another. The fictive time is always in the past in relation to communication time.

The two aspects of time, fictive time and communication time, have two types of relations that may be exploited for segmentation. The first is the ratio between represented time and the time an episode really lasts; meaning, the amount of textual space an episode holds in relation to its duration in the fictive world. One moment may be described so elaborately that it will expand for many pages,[156] creating an overflow of information, while years may be summarized into one sentence. Each literary work has its own temporal rhythm so much so that a long and detailed description in an otherwise flowing narrative will create retardation and fragment the natural stream of events, likewise an extremely concise paragraph will disrupt the rhythm.

The second relation between fictive time and communication time is between the chronological order of fictive events and their distribution order in the communication act. The sequence of a fictive action or event is always chronological as in real life; meaning, it follows from early to late, from cause to result. However, communication order can break up the causal-chronological order by

---

[156] For instance, *The Mezzanine*, (1988) which is Nicholson Baker's first novel about what goes through a man's mind during a modern lunch break, in which he is riding an escalator along 140 pages.

gaps, as has been already discussed above, and digressions.[157] For instance, the narrative can start in the middle of the action, (*in medias res*) and after a while provide past events (in terms of narrative time), expositional events, thus turning to digressions, which provide the narrative's past and again, create segmentation of the flow of events.

These multiple relations have been a major topic in poetics for a long time as the breaking up of the chronological order is one of the most widely used segmentation devices. The Russian Formalists coined the chronological "natural" order as *fabula* and the non-chronological one as *sujét*.[158] Those two temporal terms, *fabula* and *sujêt*, are based on the arrangement of motifs, a term coined by Tomashevsky (1965). He defines motif as "the smallest particles of thematic material," which are the building blocks of the literary work. These building blocks can be arranged in two orders, a sequential order or a non-sequential order. The sequential order is that which follows the chronological-causal sequence of events like that found in

---

[157] Rimmon-Kenan (1983) defined digression as "In order to increase the reader's interest and prolong itself, the text will delay the narration of the next event in the story, or of the event which will temporarily or permanently close off the sequence in question" (130). Thus digression is a delay that the author introduces into the story in order to prolong the reader's curiosity.

[158] These terms were compared with other terms like "story" and "plot" or "story" and "discourse" and the subject is much discussed in poetics. See for instance Walsh, Richard. *The Rhetoric of Fictionality: Narrative Theory and the Idea of Fiction.* Columbus: The Ohio State University, 2007.

Fielding's *Joseph Andrews*, beginning with the hero's birth, the "deepest" past, and following the sequential events of his life. Nevertheless, there are works that although starting with the fictive past and unfolding forward, after a while abandon sequential unfolding for the sake of digressions and regressions. For instance, Stern's novel *Tristram Shandy* starts its time-sequence not only *ab ovo*[159] but before the time of the hero's birth, at the time of his being conceived. However, after a short while, already in the second chapter, the author abandons the straightforward unfolding of time and starts his notorious digressions. Sternberg (1978) amends and develops these terms:

> The fabula involves what happens in the work as (re)arranged in the "objective" order of occurrence, while the sujét involves what happens in the order, angle, and patterns of presentation actually encountered by the reader (8 - 9).

In works that follow the chronological order, presenting the events in the order that they have taken place these two terms are united, while other works utilize the discrepancy between the *fabula* and the *sujét* as a segmentation device that creates the "three master functions of narrative," suspense / curiosity / surprise.[160] Hence, the

---

[159] Latin: "literally, from the egg," namely: from the beginning.

[160] Sternberg, (1992): "Our suspense/curiosity/surprise trio constitutes three master functions of narrative, as one process both disclosed and developing in time, hence the arch-

literary work can be described as a system of digressions and gaps, which both create segmentation of the fabula. While the function of digressions is to suspend the flow of the actions by the provision of expositional materials, thematic analogies, redundancy etc., the function of gaps is to advance the development of the story while at the same time to hold back some information for rhetorical and emotional effects. Thus, digression is the provision of information, even though belatedly, while the gap is its negative, the prevention of information, even if temporarily.

Chronological interceptions reside within the two facets of time in the literary work. Interceptions that are located within the fictive world and affect the characters no less than the reader, and rhetorical interceptions, which are located only in the communication time of the work, having no bearing on the characters. These time multi-facets and multi-orders call for an investigation, which will compare the way both facets of time are presented in hypertext and in print literature.

Seg\frag as an outcome of interceptive occurrences in the fictive world is quite common in literature due to interruption's mimetic nature. In life too, events are interrupted by other different occurrences. For instance, the disturbance caused by the appearance

---

regulators of its assorted forms of ordering, disordering, and reordering. Whatever the appearances to the contrary, all other roles and effects operating in narrative are either actually subsumed under them or shared by discourse (compo-nents, genres, arts, media) outside the duality of time."

of another character, the call for dinner, or a request issued urgently, as happens in *Barchester Towers* (Chapter 21), when the whole party, consisting of the archdeacon, Mr. Arabin, Mrs. Grantly, Mr Harding, and Eleanor, drive over to inspect the parsonage at St. Ewold, which would be Mr. Arabin's new parish. Eleanor has quite a long conversation with Mr. Arabin about the place of the church in the life of its parish. They are so immersed in their conversation that they fail to notice that the others have continued their tour of the house and are no longer with them in the room. The reader expects that this will be Mr. Arabin opportunity to propose marriage, however, "Here they were interrupted by the archdeacon, whose voice was heard from the cellar shouting to the vicar." The conversation is broken off, along with the reader's expectations, and Mr. Arabin runs downstairs to the cellar where the archdeacon is. These interceptions are found in hypertext as well and due to cultural and technological changes, they might be caused by technological objects, for instance - the phone, "On the very twitch of midnight Thea's telephone began to ring." [*Victory Garden, Telephone*] While in literature it segments the flow of action in hypertext it can also be an occasion for linkage.

A story within a story can produce the same fragmentation effect as is achieved by Fielding's history of the man of the hill in *Tom Jones*, which lasts four chapters, thus partitioning the text into 'before' and 'after' and heightens curiosity, suspense, and expectation. This sort of retardation is located in the fictive world as well as in the reader's sphere.

Narrative fragmentation, located in the communication level, is quite common as suspense and curiosity devices. A rambling narrator, found mostly when the narrator is a character in the fictive world, is a famous narrative fragmentation technique. For instance, in *Tristram Shandy* (Vol. VI, Chap. 11): "I am so impatient to return to my own story, that what remains of young Le Fever's, that is, from this turn of his fortune, to the time my uncle Toby recommended him for my preceptor, shall be told in a very few words in the next chapter."

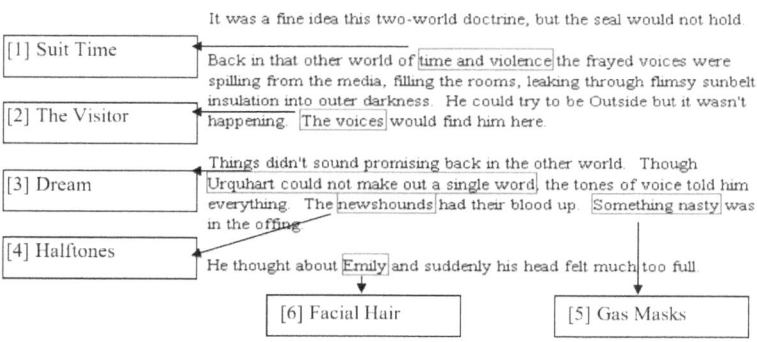

Figure 47 – node *Worlds Collide – Victory Garden*

Although Sterne is notorious for his digressions, he does not regard it as a delaying device, as he himself bears witness in Vol. I, Chap. XXII that deals with regressions and their merits, "In a word, my work is digressive, and it is progressive too, — and at the same time" (52). Sterne has at his disposal the fixed sequence of pages that turns the readers into a captivated audience; Hyper-literature however, as it is based on the linkage device, does not have even this fixed order. The linkage device enables multi-sequences and multi-paths. Some of which will create retarding digressions, some will create prophetic digressions, and some will keep to the chronological order.

In order to demonstrate the multi-sequences property of hypertext I shall look minutely at node *Worlds Collide* from *Victory Garden*, which holds six visible textual links, a default link and two conditional ones, thus turning into a major crossroad in the story as can be seen in Figure 47. The first link [1] takes the reader to path *T&V*, which compares between the folks at home and the folks at war, where node *Suit Time* illustrates "time and violence" by presenting an episode from the soldiers' barracks in Saudi Arabia at the beginning of the war, meaning January 1991. The second linkage [2] is to node *The Visitor*, the first node in path *visit*, which describes Urquhart's decision to "Do something." Temporally speaking, this episode is much later than the one described in the previous link, though there is no specific date or time deixis. The third linkage [3] takes the reader to path *unintelligible*, node *Dream*, which holds a terrifying experience from Urquhart's childhood, where he "could not make out a single word," pretty much as he is feeling right now. The fourth link [4], anchored on the word "newshounds," leads the reader to *newshounds* path (the same as the anchor word), and to node *Halftones* that belongs also to path *H&V*, which describes Harley and Veronica's relationship. This episode takes place on January 15, the day the war started. The next link [5] is simultaneous to the last one; it refers to the media, bringing into every home the news on the first day of the war, presenting "something nasty." The link takes the reader to path *nasty*, node *Gas Mask*, which brings the reports from the media. This node shows another angle to the same time that is presented in path *H&V*, the previous link. The sixth link *Emily* takes the reader to node *Facial Hair*. The node belongs to path *Emily*, which portrays the relationships between Urquhart and Emily;[161] hence it is before August 1990, when Emily enlisted.

The default link from node *Worlds Collide* continues path *U.* to which the node belongs. This path presents Urquhart's feelings and thoughts when the war starts and he understands that Emily is in a life-threatening situation. Hence, it is simultaneous to the time phase that is presented by links 1, 4, and 5.

Thus, the sequence depends not only on the writer but on the reader as well, as she can choose from a diversified collection of links, which will take her to different phases of time. Some of it causes retardatory digressions, for instance Urquharts' childhood experience, some will keep to the chronological line, and others are simultaneous happenings, as Borges states in his story *The Garden of Forking Paths*, "he (Ts'ui Pen) believed in an infinite series of times, a growing, dizzing web of divergent, convergent, and parallel times"

---

[161] Urquhart and Emily are two of the characters inhabiting Multhrop's *Victory Garden*. Emily is Thea's student and friend, Urquhart's girlfriend and Veronica's sister. She enlisted and is, during the narrative present, part of the First Gulf War in Saudi Arabia.

(1999, 127). This phenomenon, the dependence of sequentiality on the reader's choices is unheard of in print literature and is special and unique to hypertext. This is probably the most prominent element of novelty that came true out of researchers' expectation of hypertext: there is little control over the order of "reading," as far as there are more links. Of course, they are planned by the author, and yet his control is limited.

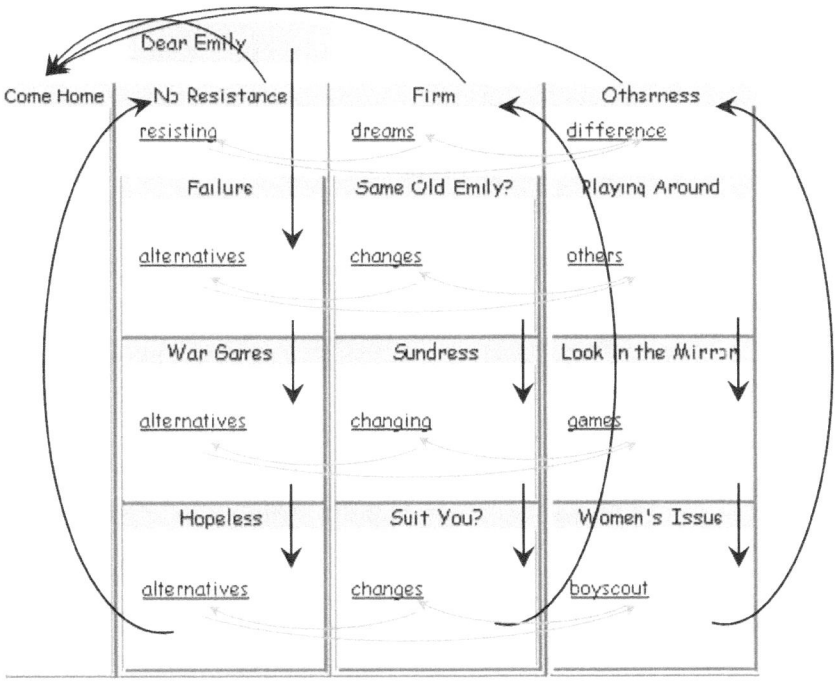

Figure 48 - Thea's letter to Emily, versions – *Victory Garden*

The multi-digressions are used in hypertext to introduce multiplicity, not just of voices, but also of a single voice, even though internal. In contrast to the *Crossed End* example, where four characters, though connected by time, space and blood-relations, have no links between them, though the reader is looking for them. Thea's letter to Emily, in *Victory Garden*, does not create any expectations for links and yet it is heavily linked to present four versions of the same letter (Figure 48), thus actually presenting the creation process of a letter with its drafts and corrections.

The first node of the "letter episode" is labeled after the classical beginning of a letter, *Dear Emily*. Thea is writing to Emily who is staying, as a soldier, in Saudi Arabia. Thea starts her letter by apologizing for not having written earlier. She excuses the tardiness by saying that at first, she was scared, and then she blamed Emily for going, as though if all the soldiers refused to go there would not be a war. Nevertheless, on that night, as the war started and she realized that Emily is in the midst of it, she cannot hold back any more "as she cares about her deeply."

Node *Dear Emily* has only a default link that takes the reader to the second column in Figure 48. The first column labeled *Come Home* is the last node, which is common to all versions. The other three columns are the three parts of the letter. Each part holds 4 versions. For instance, part "*No Resistance*"[162] is parallel to nodes *Failure*, *War Games*, *Hopeless*. They are reached by default (the black arrow). To reach the continuum of the letter (see the gray arrows) the reader has

---

[162] I will refer to the parts by its first node's label in order to distinguish between them.

to activate one of the links (the underlined words). The links keep the reader within one version while the default takes the reader to the parallel versions, hence the reader cannot miss the multi-versions.

A comparison between the versions of the second node of Thea's letter[163] reveals changes that can be attributed to rhetoric, as that is Thea's expertise as a university professor, or to a retrospective contemplation. For instance, the first line of the first draft states Thea's position quite brusquely, "You were wrong to go, Emily, though I never asked if you'd considered alternatives." [*Failure*] In the second draft the proposition is moderated, though the content does not change, "I thought you were wrong to go, Emily, and I still do, though I never asked if you'd considered alternatives." [*War Games*] The blunt accusation, "you were wrong" turns into the more restrained "I thought you were wrong," though without a change in her standpoint, "and I still do." The third draft continues the mitigating tone and shows a growing degree of self-reflection. Finally the first line of the first version turns into a fully developed paragraph in the fourth version and by that it concretizes the process of re-writing, reflects an inner musing and presents Thea's struggles to express herself. Though there is no textual way to know which version was sent, the comparison between the drafts can help to determine that the fourth draft is the one that Thea sent to Emily, as it is a fuller version

---

[163] For a full transcript of the four nodes see Appendix B. - Thea's letter – multiple versions.

than all the others are, and it does not contain unfinished propositions.

This multi-version presentation serves many contextual and poetic goals. First, it characterizes Thea as a professor of rhetoric as she is writing and re-writing to achieve the effect she wants. At the same time, the multi-drafts show the difference between the ways we speak and the way we write. While speaking we are more concentrated on the content of what we say, and less on the way we say it. Writing enables a moment for reflection over the 'how' and causes us to soften blunt words, as Thea does in most drafts.

From the point of the narrative flow, this 'episode' is a retardatory structure no less than is the "Story of the Man of the Hill" in Fielding. Fielding uses the story as an analogy thus supplementing the story with another angle. Moulthrop, on the other hand, is experimenting with mutually exclusive versions, thus the reader has to subtract the irrelevant drafts, the ones that were thrown away, in order to decide what the real letter was. In doing so, the reader can feel Thea's anguish on the one side, and on the other side, see the process of self-enlightenment that Thea is going through the writing course. In print literature it is possible to present all the versions and drafts of the letter but in a certain fixed order.

Thea's letter causes a merging of 'communication time' with the fictive time, by causing the reader to spend a lot of time, like Thea, to sort these drafts. The term 'communication time' refers to the time spent by the reader in reading the literary work. This issue never got much attention in itself, as it depends on many reader's environmental variables such as the duration of one session of reading, reading pace, favorite reading places etc. There is no difference between hypertext and print literature communication time but there may be a difference in presentation time.

While the printed text is visible at all times, digital text can 'vanish' from the screen as in *Hegirascope* and by that creates a seg\frag of the reading process. Ryan (2001) explains,

> Reading a print book takes time, but the book form assumes that time is unlimited. Deadlines come from teachers and library policies, not from the book itself. In the electronic medium the temporal allowance can be restricted and the passing of time be made significant (216-217).

The printed book has accustomed readers to an encounter that combines certain duties with certain liberties and guarantees like the duty to turn pages in sequential order, alongside the freedom to dwell leisurely on each page and easily return to earlier passages, and to the security of always knowing how much remains to be read.

This print tradition and reading norms is so deeply rooted that the reader does not expect the words to flow of their own accord even in hypertext-works, as John Tolva and David Balcom point out in their review of Moulthrop's *Hegirascope*,

> Of course we expect printed words to stay still while we read at our own pace. More striking is that this assumption persists (at least with these readers) even while reading hypertext. We expect the text to be fluid only to the extent that our clicking makes it so.

Moulthrop's *Hegirascope* denies the reader that leisurely reading, taking the meaning of communication time into an unknown level in print literature (and the first in hypertext). *Hegirascope*'s nodes keep changing after a fixed amount of predefined time, predefined by the author.[164] "What if the word will not be still?" the reader is asked in the opening node of *Hegirascope* and the whole work turns into an opportunity for the reader to find out the answer. The effect on the reader is usually annoyance and irritation, while he races with the text, with the ever-changing nodes. Thus, the author is mastering not only fictive or quasi-fictive time, but the reader's reading time as well. This trait of the work attracted much attention by hypertext researchers because of the innovative way in which the work is utilizing the digital medium and because of the temporal questions, the work raises. *Hegirascope* centers on "time" thematically as well as technically. Tolva and Balcom define its technique as "a temporal hypertext link, disturbing our ideas of what a link is and does." This is indeed a special link, since the reader has

---

[164] In the introduction to the revised edition of *Hegirascope*, Moulthrop details the "Changes and improvements to the initial version." One of which is "The delay on most pages has been increased from 18 seconds to 30."

no control over it, she cannot "click" it, thus activate it, nor can she deactivate it. What is more, this link occupies no space in the text, as other kinds of links do. It is embedded in the code-level of the narrative and yet it is a link since it transfers the reader to other nodes. This ability, to master communication time is unique to hypertext, though most authors do not take advantage of this trait. This unique trait was not used much probably because it does not have literary qualities since it deals with perceptions and cognition, as the clock in a chess game or other games allotted time. *Hegirascope* is like a game since the reader cannot concentrate on reading, especially in the beginning, and is close to computer allotted time games, where the reader/user is playing against the computer.

All the examples that were discussed above show that there is no difference in the ways that, print literature and hypertext literature handle seg\frag, and in principle there is no more fragmentation or segmentation in hypertext than there is in print literature. On the contrary, print literature shows more daringness in seg\frag than hypertext. Print literature is on the one side, bounded by norms and conventions of linearity and on the other side it uses this linearity for multiple effects. For instance, the 'twisted story,' where the end causes surprise so that the reader has to re-consider her interpretation, or other devices, which rely on the prevention of information in order to create curiosity and suspense. And yet there are numerous examples that break that linearity and thus foregrounding print literature sequentiality as is opposed to painting as Lessing explains.

The treatment of typographical segments and textual ones like time, space, characters and events are not different in the two media, though, as Thea's letter and Moulthrop's *Hegirascope* show, hypertext has the potential to raise narrative, poetic and thematic questions in innovative ways, yet this potential was little realized in practice.

The difference between print literature and hyper-literature is located in the conventions of reading and writing. While print literature is presented to the reader as a whole work, hypertext presents its reader with segments, nodes, chunks of text in Nelson's termination, lexias in Landow's termination, though the term is borrowed from Barthes, or "textons" for Aarseth. The reader is the one to gather the segments, thus having some control over the work. This is similar to computer games where the player is assembling the episodes and controls the "hero's" paths, interactions and actions.

Since the other side of segmentation is combination, in the next chapter I will examine the way hypertext combinatory-techniques merge all the segments into a whole, the one that is given to the print reader in the first place, in comparison with print customary techniques.

5   The structure of hypertext narrative

Aristotle's basic requirement of a mythos/narrative is it being a whole, "A whole is that which has a beginning, middle, and an end." (*Poetics*, Chapter VII) In other words, a whole narrative should hold all these parts. It should be pointed out that Aristotle refers mostly to tragedy not as a written narrative, but as a play performed on a stage, in which all partaking elements are perceived spatially. The live performance enriches the text with additional levels of reference and information not available in the written text, of which the most obvious is the mimics, the sound and the décor. The performance itself is an interpretation, by the director and the actors, presented through the aid of non-textual elements such as pantomime, gesticulation and movement, sound and music, décor, etc., as the director and the actors perceive them. The non-textual elements call to mind the ancient bard, who himself was a performer in time. The written narrative however, is perceived textually linearly without any aides, besides the reader's own imagination.

As has already been said it is customary to discern two (at least) major beginnings in literature, namely the point of entry: that of the fabula and that of the *sujêt*. The *sujêt* equals the beginning of the book or story and the *fabula* is the earliest event that is found throughout the narrative, which is really the chronologic beginning of the story. Literary works are notorious for beginning *in medias res*. This is based on the difference between the communication time, time of reading, and the time of the narrated events, which is always in the past in relation to the communication time. Every narrative has a *fabula* since it is a construct that the reader reconstructs as she finishes the reading. Thus, I'll question the *sujét* – the beginning of the material book.

Jorge Luis Borges describes an example of the concept of a book without a beginning and an end, an infinite book, in his story *The Book of Sand*.[165] The story is about a sacred book offered to the narrator by a Bible-peddler, "I examined it; the unusual heft of it surprised me. On the spine was printed *Holy Writ*, and then *Bombay*" (481). He finds that the book's pages are always changing, so that each time that the reader opens the book she finds there another "first page," thus the reader cannot see the same page twice. The narrator opens the book and looks at one of its pages. The peddler tells the narrator, "Look at it well. You will never see it again." Not only the page cannot be found again, but also the book seems to have no beginning and no end,

> He suggested I try to find the first page.
> I took the cover in my left hand and opened the
> book, my thumb and my forefinger almost
> touching. It was impossible: several pages always
> lay between the cover and my hand. It was as
> though they grew from the very book.

---

[165] Borges. Jorge Luis, *Collected Fictions*. Trans. Andrew Hurley, New York: Penguin Books, 1998, 480-483.

"Now try to find the end."

I failed there as well.

"This can't be," I stammered, my voice hardly

recognizable as my own.

"It can't be, yet it is," the Bible peddler said, his

voice little more than a whisper. "The number of

pages in this book is literally infinite. No page is

the first page; no page is the last" (481-482).

This possibility of a text which is fluid, dynamic and living organism is feasible only in fantastic fiction. It can be written about, as Borges did, but it cannot be conceived as a material object.[166]

Researchers characterize hypertext as a text without a beginning and an end. This attribute of hypertext has been mentioned already in previous chapters, yet in light of the momentous importance that is attached to narrative beginnings and endings,[167] there is a definite necessity of looking into this issue in profundity in an attempt to answer what does a text without a beginning and an end mean exactly? Does it mean that there are no symbols of a beginning to the work itself, such as cover-page or title page? Or else, does it mean that there

---

[166] There are such toys, kinetic objects etc. but not a normative book.

[167] Said (1975), in his book *Beginnings: Intention and Method* says: "*The beginning, then, is the first step in the intentional production of meaning*" (5). (Italics is in the original) For beginnings see also Sternberg (1978), Richardson (2009). For endings see Herrnstein Smith (1970), Kermode (1966).

is no fixed "first page," alias page one, chapter one etc. Is there no fixed beginning-point for the reading process, so that each time the reader opens the work the "first page" changes and she finds another node (page) functioning as the starting-point of the reading? And the same goes for endings: is there no end at all? Or at every time does the reader reach another end?

The issue of the structure of the hypertext works raises other issues like the place of the exposition or the method in which the reader is introduced into the fictive world. On the other hand, it questions the way the work ends; the issue of closure and how is the reader to know that she has finished reading the work?

In the following chapter, I will describe in detail the concept of beginning in print and at the advent of hypertext literature. Though the beginning is mostly not solely one specific node I'll first tackle scholars' claim that there is no beginning in hypertext due to the disappearance of its container – the book and show that there is one specific entry point to each hypertext in the corpus. Then I will examine how hypertext works begin, in the broadest sense where does the 'first node' take the reader and what are her reading options. What happens after the reader has passed the entrance, the beginning node, what comes between the beginning and the end? Is there one constant *Fabula* or the reader arranges the narrative into different paths at each reading? Then I'll examine the end of the works which should be a final node, from where there is nowhere to go. Moreover, I will look at the issue of closure and find whether the reader is the one to decide where to stop her reading as some scholars claim.

5.1 The Beginning

The beginning might be anyone of the three common terms in literature; the beginning of the book, the physical container of the story (though Aristotle did not refer to that), the *sujêt* which is the beginning of the narrative as narrated, or the *fabula* which is the beginning of the chronologic reconstruction of the *sujêt*.

First, there is the cover-page, the tangible object, which distinguishes one book, or literary work, from other literary and non-literary objects in print or on the computer screen. This structural element has already been discussed in Chapter 3 above, where I have shown that even though hypertext is a digital medium, it still preserves print conventions such as the cover-page and a title page that holds the work's informative data. The existence of the cover-page is explained by Marie-Laure Ryan (2001) who says, "Every hypertext has a fixed entry point – there must be an address to reach first before the system of links can be motivated" (226). Hence the beginning, in the narrow sense of the word, is the entry point to the work.

Then, there is the actual beginning of the narrative fictive work; "page one," chapter one or what comes after acknowledgements and introduction (in hypertext - the first node making-up the story), the starting-point of the narrative reading process. This point has a crucial rhetorical function in the reading process for the creation of high narrative interest that will cause the reader to continue her reading as Dr. Johnson (1820) observes, "Works of imagination excel by their allurement and delight; by their power of attracting and detaining the attention. That book is good in vain, which the reader throws away" (418). Two hundred years later this advice is still valuable as can be found on Books & Such Literary Agency's web site, where blogger Mary Keeley[168] tells their potential authors:

> With the growing number of electronic and social media diversions competing for people's attention, the hook on the first page of your book is proportionately more important to grab readers' attention, make them hungry for more—and eventually to recommend your book to friends.

This special function of the first page/node of obtaining the reader's attention, which in print literature received a great deal of

---

[168] <http://www.booksandsuch.biz/blog/8-tips-for-writing-a-powerful-hook-for-your-book-proposal/>, 24.7.2016. See also Jakobson, Roman and Pomorska, Krystyna and Rudy Stephen. *Verbal Art, Verbal Sign, Verbal Time*. Minneapolis: University of Minnesota Press, 1985, 173.

attention, should be looked at in relation to hypertext. Did hypertext authors choose a particular node as the "first" or is the first node changeable – randomal, optional or selectable?

Figure 49 - Coverley's *Califia* first node

The reader/user arrives at the starting node through a link that is embedded on the cover-page, be it a textual link, a graphical link or the default. As I have already shown in chapter 3, Moulthrop's cover-page of *Victory* Garden directs the reader "Press Return to begin," Joyce's cover-page of *afternoon, a* story tells the reader "to start press Return." One of the three options that Moulthrop's web story *Hegirascope* offers the reader on its title page is "Begin." All the textual links are bounded to one specific, fixed node that is the first that is encountered by the reader. Even Coverley's *Califia*, which was published towards the end of hypertext's boom time (2000), though not stating explicitly "start here," has one preprogrammed entrance point: clicking on the cover-page illustration the reader will always be transferred to node *The Island* (Figure 49). Consequently, it is quite safe to conclude that there is a fixed textual beginning for the narrative in hypertext as in print literature which forks off the title page. Hypertext has a cover/case, which carries authoritative and identification details, such as author's and publisher's names, and there is a stable, fixed unavoidable and linear entering point for the reading process to begin.

The above statement is true for a stories-collection as well, with the modifications needed because of the different format. For instance, Larsen's *Samplers* nine-story collection title has a starting story as default though it is concealed. Print technology does not allow this kind of concealment, and in this instant the fact that it is concealed does not change the fact that there is a fixed beginning point. In her *First Directions*, she tells her reader "Press <enter> throughout the work for an "orderly tour through most of the pages." Larsen refers to the default reading as an "orderly tour." The word "orderly" implies that there is a pre-determined sequence in the default reading, where the hypertext author, as in the printed work that is always read by the default, directs the reading sequence. The work's title page is a graphical quilt constructed out of nine small sewn patterns, which is actually a visual Table of Content, where each pattern is linked to a certain story (Figure 50).

Figure 50 – *Samplers's* Cover page

Clicking on any of the nine small patterns that make up the graphical pattern is similar to choosing a story out of a book's Table of Contents though with a difference. While a book's Table of Contents provides the reader with an indication as to the story's subject by its name or by the chapter's label, choosing a pattern from the quilted image does not give the reader any idea about the stories' topic. In principle, it is possible to substitute stories' names with a visual imagery and chapters' names with numbers, but it is not acceptable. In addition to the graphical object Larsen's cover-page offers the reader some preliminary navigation directions, "Click on any image for a story ... or you can always press ENTER." If the reader chooses to hit the Enter key, in expectation of getting to the "first" story by default, like in the aforementioned hypertexts, she is in for a surprise. The Enter key opens the Links window, which functions as a textual Table of Content, showing all the stories' titles so that the reader can choose which story she would like to read first as is in print stories-collections where any story can be the reading starting point. However, if the reader chooses not to hit the Enter key but to click with the mouse anywhere in the node but on the graphics, she is transferred to the story *Century Cross*, a beginning-point set by the author. Hence, this stories-collection, as well, offers the reader a pre-programmed starting point, though it's not really needed.

The 'first node' usually carries a "tell-tale" label: Joyce's first node is called "begin"; Moulthrop's starting-point of the reading process is called *Come In.* Coverley's first node, solely, holds the title *The Island,* which breaks the tradition of welcoming and is different from all other beginnings. She compensates for this breach of "convention" with visual data and use of poetical pattern. The first page presents a picture of footprints rising from the sea and leading onto dry land. The text, which is written on the picture, invites the traveler, "Come ashore." At the head of the node, there is a proposition that says: "Once there was an Island called Califia where dreams came true…" which is the traditional beginning of fairytales. However, if we inspect the following nodes, all arrived at sequentially without any other option, we will find that "the beginning" stretches over six nodes, and their labels make up the proposition: "The island of Califia awaits and welcomes you to read with delight." Thus, although hypertext was born out of the concept of infiniteness, endlessness, in hyper-literature the number of nodes is final and the author retains some of his control over the sequence of reading.

The studied hypertext works[169] show clearly that even if the story is in hypertext format it does have an inherent beginning-point chosen not by the reader, as is claimed by hypertext researchers, but by the writer, as is evident by nodes' labels or by the actual process (*Califia*). Landow (1997), trying to reason why this "begin here" instruction is the common case, calls it "the start here approach" (189). He discerns "several technological, rhetorical and other reasons" for this phenomenon. The first reason he offers is the technological one. He says that writers that use stand-alone applications feel that their work is "self-contained, in a traditional manner," thus they keep the traditional structural element of a beginning. The second and third reasons, that Landow suggests, are rhetorical and have to do with authors' concepts,

> Some writers' obvious reluctance to disorient readers upon their initial contact with a narrative, and some writers also believe that hypertext fiction should necessarily change our experience of the middle but not the beginnings of narrative fiction (190).

Hence, the second reason concerns the problem of orientation, or disorientation, which has already been discussed above and has to

---

[169] To remind of the studied corpus: Joyce's *afternoon, a story* (1986), Moulthrop's *Victory Garden* (1991), Ryman's "*two five three*" (1996), Larsen's *Samplers* (1997), Moulthrop's *Hegirascope*, 1997 and Coverley's *Califia* (2000).

do with users' dexterity level of practice in the hypertext medium. It leans on the innovation of the medium, yet it doesn't hold water in 1996, which is the publication date of Larsen's work *Samplers* or in 1997 when Moulthrop's *Hegirascope* was heavily revised, as he himself attests: "This is an extensive revision of a Web fiction originally released in 1995" not to mention Coverley's Califia that was published in 2000. Hence, although we could suppose that as hypertext will become more familiar authors will abandon this "start here" approach and take advantage of hypertext's other options for beginnings, it seems that the beginning point is so important that authors did not feel like changing this norm.

The third issue raised by Landow is about hypertext poetics. According to Landow some hypertext authors think that only the experience of the middle of a literary work should be distinct from traditional printed literature. Landow does not enlarge on the poetic reasons that authors have for this belief but offers a different approach, the "randomize" approach. Landow quotes William Dickey (1991) who refers to the requirements that this approach poses upon the writer:

> The effect of this central metaphor of HyperCard
> [stack of cards] is to abolish the concept of the poem
> as having a single linear authority, the authority of
> consecutive plot-governed narrative, the authority of
> succession on a fixed immutable page. The poem
> may begin with any one of its parts, stanzas, images,

to which any other part of the poem represented on any one card[170] must be a sufficiently independent statement to be able to generate a sense of poetic meaning as it follows or is followed by any other statement the poem contains (147).

According to Dickey the beginning in one reading can turn into the end in another. To phrase it in other words, Dickey describes the possibility of any card in a stack to become the first one, the "beginning." There is no fixed order, no "single linear authority." The only limitation this approach has is that any card/node has to "generate a sense of poetic meaning as it follows or is followed." Landow is well aware that Dickey is referring to poetry and not prose, yet he says: "Dickey, who is writing about poetic rather than fictional structure, nonetheless offers organizational principles that apply to both" (190).

The poetic explanation stresses the momentous[171] double function that the "first page" has: to raise curiosity and suspense and to capture the readers' attention and to retain it. This obliges the author to choose the most "suitable" and "eye catching" moment in

---

[170] Dickey is a poet who wrote his poems in Apple's HyperCard, which is a hypertext-software, where each node is a card. This difference is solely terminological.

[171] This gave rise to all kinds of narrative devices. The most popular of all is the use of the *in medias res* device, which was shown above in hypertext and will be dealt with in the continuum.

which to begin the narrative. If the reader decides, after reading the first page, that there is nothing of interest in the story and she leaves the book without reading it, the author has lost his chance of communicating (be it an aesthetical, a philosophical, a political, or a rhetorical communication). Thus, the requirement that the first page, the beginning of the work as a reading process, should create such an interest that the reader will be intrigued into continuing her reading through the book is vital. Brian Richardson (2009) states: "The beginning is a foundational element of any narrative, fictional or nonfictional, public or private, official or subversive" (1). He provides as proof for that importance a long list of salient opening sentences that readers remember for decades.

Though technically speaking it is possible to use a random command and to create multiple different beginnings, all of them raising the reader's curiosity and presenting crucial moments, it was never done at the advent of hypertext. An explanation for that reluctance of authors to create multiple beginning points, may be found in Said's (1975) words: "Every writer knows that the choice of a beginning for what he will write is crucial not only because it determines much of what follows but also because a work's beginning is, practically speaking, the main entrance to what it offers."

The beginning point, which is always an author's prerogative, may be responsible for the need to determine and control one's work, its' "entrance" and where it leads the reader, what "follows," thus causing authors to stick to one entering point and only then loosen their control and let the reader roam on her own. At that same time, it answers the realistic need of an address for the reading process as Ryan discerns, and the cognitive concern of the beginning of reading, which creates the effect of separation and distinction of the specific work and differentiates it from other writing and even the "world."

Hence, hypertext authors choose to adhere to print norms and create one decisive beginning point and not take advantage of the fact that getting the reader's attention in the first node is easy in relation to print literature since the node is short and the reader is "fresh" as well as assumed to be eager to challenge the new "hype" format.

After establishing a fixed and predetermined beginning-point in all the works examined, it is time to examine in depth how long the default reading lasts and how the beginnings continue.

In Coverley's *Califia* the first node, *The Island*, states, "Once there was an island called Califia where dreams come true…" The node is accompanied by calm yet mysterious music. The fairy tale like beginning combined with the mysterious music raise the reader's curiosity as to where Califia is exactly, (is it a real or fictive land?) why is there such a similarity in the island's name to California, what dreams did this island fulfill etc.? The next node, like Joyce's *afternoon*, presents the subject of death, which is an emotional subject raising curiosity. The death of the narrator's father is the dynamic event that starts the story, creating "an emergency," in an attempt to intensify curiosity. Gradually the narrator reveals that she is looking for a gold treasure, "the treasure of Califia" and the reader is invited to join and assist in a search that previous generations have conducted with no success.

Only after the reader has read the first six consecutive nodes, which carry no links, can the reader choose at last: to read the help file, which describes the tools and options that are available to her, or to start the actual treasure hunt along with the fictive characters. If the reader decides to start the search (another beginning point, that was not available before) she has to choose "To set off NOW click here," which is the "the start here approach." The link takes the reader to one specific fixed node, which name states its "start here" quality, *Califia – The Roadhead* and to one specific path: *South: The Comets in the Yard*. Only after another click, in a node stating: *Califia – South: The Comets in the Yard*, can the reader choose her way and decide if she wants to continue this journey south or if she prefers some other path as there are three possible links on the left margin: "View Landmarks in the South," "Follow paths of Augusta, Kaye and Calvin" and "Compass & KitBag." Hence, the narrative turns to hypertextuality only after a long orderly beginning, expositional mainly. The reader learns about the time and place, about the characters and about the main task to be achieved along the narrative – finding the gold. At the same time the reader can see what tools are available for her to guide her in her reading. As a typical quest narrative, the exposition is similar to stories of its kind in print literature, and the genre is a most conventional one.[172] Thus, along with technological innovations (due to hypertext format), this work leans heavily on generic literary conventions, which serve as "fixed" points of reference even if they are not stated. However, once the reader receives choices she moves into a gaming mode like a Treasure Hunt etc.

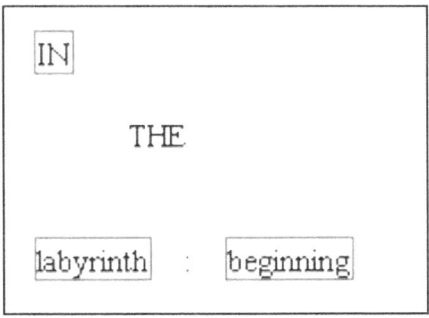

Figure 51 - node *Come In* – The three textual links

Unlike *Califia*, which does not allow the reader any choice even after the first node, node *Come In*, which is the first narrative node that the reader encounters while following the default linkage in *Victory Garden*, offers the reader three optional links and a default (Figure 51). The first option, which is not presented in the image, is the default and is arrived at just by hitting the Enter key or on any blank space of the node with the mouse, is the default linkage that

---

[172] Propp in his morphological analysis of folktale says that there is and initial situation that begins the story. Propp, Vladimir. *Morphology of the Folktale*. Ed. Louis A. Wagner, Austin: University of Texas Press, 1968, 26.

transfers the reader to *North Garden* node, which is a graphical multi-linkages plan simulating a garden's touring map. The author's choice of a map as the default linkage device indicates that the author prefers his reader to choose one course out of a number of options, which the map enables in a visual, familiar, and realistic-like way. At the same time, the fact that a multi-choice map is the default may attest that the author does not trust his reader to look for "hidden" links thus, foreseeing that his reader's choice will be the default, he is forestalling her and turns the Map into the default, thus emphasizing the numerous options.

Hence, in *Victory Garden* the reader is forced to select an option in order to continue her reading after the fixed entry, nevertheless the selection options are not random but carefully pre-constructed by the author. On the cover-page the reader is called to "press Return to begin." This transfers the reader to node *Come In*, which is the works definitive starting-point. The content of the node, "In the beginning" or "In the Labyrinth," affirms it as the beginning of the story if only by the resemblance to the first verse of Genesis: "In the beginning God created the heaven and the earth." and of The Gospel of John: "In the beginning was the Word, and the Word was with God, and the Word was God." The three red rectangles shown in Figure 51 signify the three textual links the reader can choose from in order to continue her reading. If the reader chooses not to pursue these links, she can hit the Enter (aka Return) key, thus following the default, namely the map.

The default takes the reader to node *Properties*, which functions as a preface. Another hit on the Enter key brings the reader back to the cover-page. Hitting the Enter key once more transfers the reader to node *Come In*. If the reader insists upon this mode of reading, she is transferred to node *North Garden* map, the garden plan that provides multiple linking options. Should the reader still decide to follow the default she will be transferred to *Map Overview*, containing the plan of the whole garden, not just the northern part. Continuing with the default will lead her sequentially to nodes *Welcome*, *Enigma*, *The Place of Big Wind* and then back again to *Come In* and to the *North Garden*. Hence, even when the reader chooses what looks like random choices, there is a tight control of the author where every link is leading to.

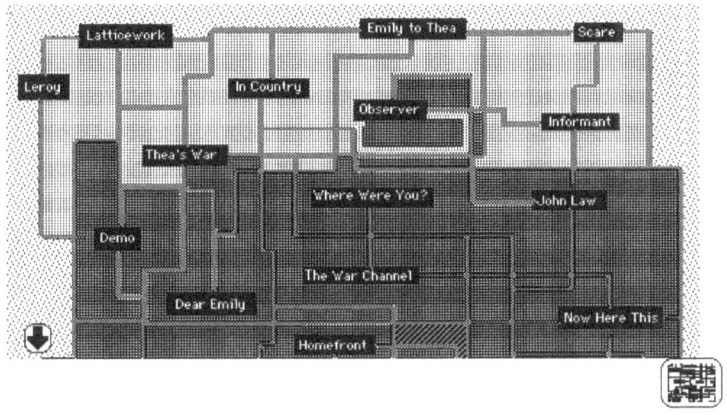

Figure 52 - *Victory Garden's* **North Garden**

Persisting on this mode of reading the reader of *Victory Garden* is transferred again, to the *Map overview*, then to *Paths to Explore* that is an explicit list of paths, as implied by the node's title. The list includes illuminating notes in order to whet the reader's appetite and to arouse her curiosity. If the reader decides not to choose a path and continue by the default once more, she arrives at node *Paths to Deplore*, which is another list of illuminated links.

The names of the two last nodes demonstrate the communicative function between reader and author. Trying to seduce the reader to choose a link by providing appetizing notes and failing to do so, the author is trying to make the reader choose a path by use of negation (a psychological approach - those links you'd better not choose). If the reader continues to refuse and hits the default key again, she will find herself in a loop through the last three nodes: *Map Overview, Paths to Explore* and *Paths to Deplore*. As though the author says to his reader, I asked you nicely in all the ways available to me to choose; if you decided to ignore me, I must force you to select. Now the reader realizes that without activating a link she is stuck, and she will be cycling among those three nodes until she makes a choice. That is as far as (five nodes) the author allows his reader to go without committing herself, namely, without making any choices, without using the linkage device. Thus, though the reader is the one to choose links, the author retains control of the reading sequence in his hands and the reader's control is just an illusion, and yet he wants his reader to activate links and is determined to cause her to choose. Meaning, the choice is a way to create an effect (suspense/curiosity/surprise). As can be seen in Figure 53, the reader encounters a loop leading from the *Map overview* to node *Paths to Explore* and node *Paths to deplore* sequentially and repeatedly. The only way to get out of this loop, without the help of any navigation tool, is to choose a link out of any of the nodes. All in all there are 26 links in those three nodes; *Paths to Explore* and *Paths to deplore* hold 20 links and node *Map overview* holds another 6.

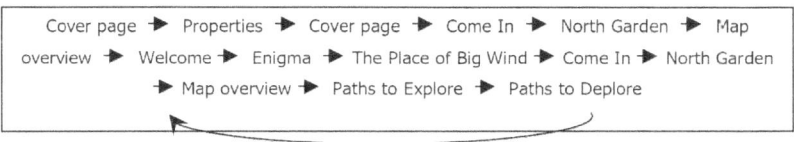

Figure 53 - *Victory Garden* Enter path

Besides the default linkage the *Come In* node in *Victory Garden* has three links, one for each word (Figure 51). The link from the word "IN" leads to node *Come Often?* which holds the same content and almost identical links as node *Come In*, thus not seeming to make narrative progress. Nevertheless, the node's label implies that the node's function is rhetorical and communicative; it is a simulation of the communication function. The label is the author's response to the reader's choice. The reader did as the medium's conventions dictate her; she chooses a word, a link, in order to continue her reading. What she receives in return is the same content with a different label. Thus, the author's question "Come Often?" is mocking the reader, as though she intentionally wanted to re-visit the same node. However, in this node the word "IN" is not a link any longer, thus the author shows his control over the links and signals to the reader that she had already exhausted this possibility. Consequently, although the content of the node is the same as the previous one, the reader feels that she is making progress in the reading process. Here, as well, an interactive experience is created which is in fact an illusion since the reader's choices are limited by the author's control even if he conceals and hides that control. Now the reader has to choose only between the other two textual links that are left: *Labyrinth* and *Beginning* (See Figure 54).

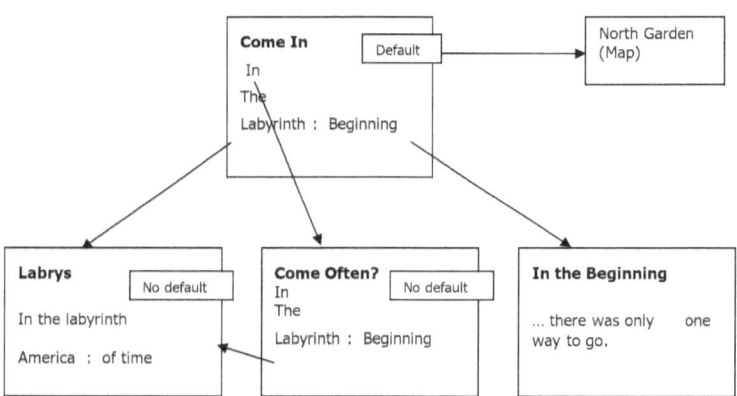

Figure 54 – Node's *Come In* branching in *Victory Garden*

Choosing the word, "Labyrinth" leads the reader to node *Labrys*, which opens a narrative line where each node starts with the words "In the labyrinth." The word "Beginning" leads the reader to node *In the beginning*, which opens a narrative line where each node starts with the words "In the beginning."

Node *If You* is the first node of the narrative additive-line "In the beginning." Each node has only two links, without a default, thus coercing the reader to choose. The linked words reside on a separate line which emphasizes their importance; they are separated by a colon that signifies their mutually exclusive relations - one or the other (As can be seen in each square, which signifies a node, Figure 55).

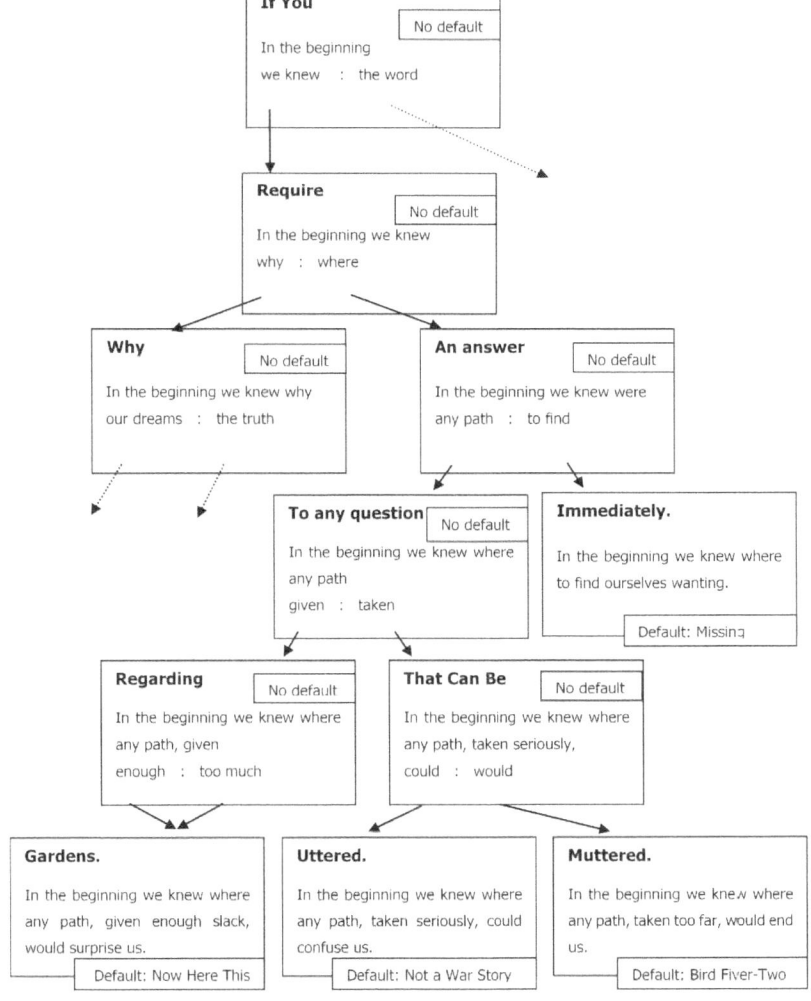

Figure 55 - Partial Branching of Node *If You* in Moulthrop's

Victory Garden

Each time the reader chooses one linked word out of the two, she is transferred to the next node where she finds that the chosen word is added to the first line of the node, therefore creating an effect of selection and interactivity.

By clicking on a chosen word, the reader actually activates the traversal function, defined by Aarseth as "the mechanism by which scriptons are revealed or generated from textons and presented to the user of the text" (62). These scriptons are static, pre-embedded, thus after the reader has read two or three nodes, she can see the recurring pattern and her choices become meaningful. It is no longer a "blind" choice, the reader knows that she is choosing the next words that will be added to the main proposition, and hence she can be regarded as a co-author as some of hypertext scholars claim (Slatin and Landow (1997). Yet that is not the situation. We must keep in mind that the author placed the additive words there for the reader to uncover and he is responsible for the two choices laid before her. This word game achieves the desired effect on the reader, her inquisitiveness is aroused, she is curious to reveal the next two optional words awaiting her choice on the one hand, and on the other hand, to see where all this is leading, and yet there is no real creative freedom as everything is pre-determined by the author.

If the pattern shown in Figure 55 is scrutinized closely it will show that all the nodes between node *If You*, as far as the final nodes, *Gardens.*, *Uttered.*, *Muttered.*, which have no branching, no links and only defaults, are contextually unimportant, though they serve as a selection and revelation path, since the three end-points are fixed ahead. By selecting the next words to be added to the proposition between node *If You* through the final nodes, the reader uncovers the next selection that is awaiting her up to the full proposition, hence the revelation. The only meaningful nodes in those strings are the last ones, the three presets by the author and containing a full, general yet intelligible sentence. These nodes have a full stop in their label, like *Gardens.* or *Muttered.* The full stop is a grammatical visual author-derived sign, informing the reader that she reached the end of the line, the full sentence, which was started so many nodes ago.

The discussion above shows quite clearly that although the reader performs some additional activity while interacting with the text by choosing between choices, this interactivity is limited, illusory, since the author is the one to pre-arrange and to anticipate the outcome (all outcomes in fact) of the reader's available choices. The reader cannot really change the text by adding or subtracting to the work. The presentation of mutually exclusive optional words, grants the reader a feeling of a meaningful selection and a sensation of co-authorship. This playful mode of spreading out the sentences before the reader allows for the playfulness that is special to the digital medium and provides the reader with a sense of participating in the formation of the proposition. This device is what generated critics and scholars' expectation that hyper-literature will yield a new active reader. Indeed, the reader has a feeling of partnership with the author, as her choice is added to the text in the next node. As can be seen in

Appendix C. - Branching of path In the beginning" the selections the reader is making are composing the final propositions. Thus, there are many 'last' sentences, each created by the reader's interactivity on the one hand, and on the other one, it is all written in advance by the author and him alone. Thus, unlike print literature, there are many alternate sentences and yet, like print literature the author is the one to control and allow these alternatives.

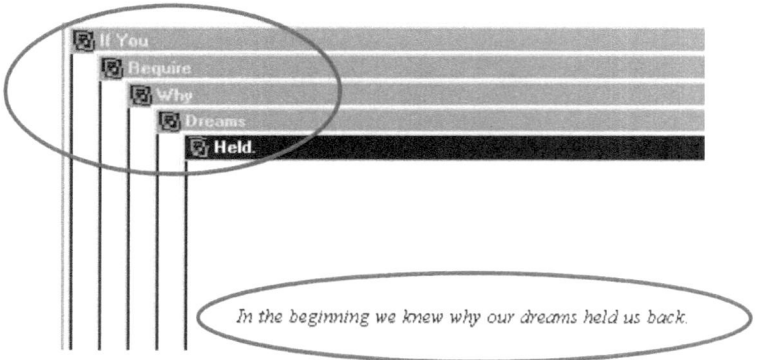

Figure 56 - cascading windows in Moulthrop's *Victory Garden*

The digital format of the *Storyspace* software allows other writing spaces then the node's space. Since in *Storyspace* a node is actually a window it has a frame and at its head a "title bar." Choosing a link opens a new window which is a little lower than the one holding the link and somewhat to its right, thus on the screen there's a 'cascading' of multi-windows. This grants the author the use of the title bar, where nodes' labels reside, in such a way that although the reader encounters one node at a time, she can see the nodes' labels sequentially (Figure 56). In *Victory Garden* for example, the reader following the path stemming from the word *beginning* in node *Come Often?* until its end point, node *Held*, will see two propositions, the first is the final node's proposition, "*In the beginning we knew why our dreams held us back.*" and the second is created by the node's labels when viewed in cascading position and read sequentially: "*If You Require Why Dreams Held.*" In this example, we see that the proposition composed by the labels holds an unfinished question; the proposition which is written in the node supplements it, though it does not answer the direct question. It endows dreams a negative epithet, dreams can hold us back.

The cascading labels create a virtual writing space and the reader can perceive that despite the mutually exclusive effect caused by words' selection, all the last sentences, the full propositions, can reside side by side, forming a poem-like structure. For example, the last four propositions starting from node *Desire*:

> In the beginning the word turned meanings upside down. [*More.*]

> In the beginning the world turned much more slowly.
> [*No more.*]

> In the beginning the word sounded so high above us that we really didn't notice. [*Better.*]

In the beginning the word sounded strange to our ears. [*Returning.*][173]

Not only are these lines not mutually exclusive, they can be read sequentially as one contextual unit, even though open to debate as to the relations among its components as the sentences are fragmented, which fits the "new sentence" concept that discussed above. Thus, "In the beginning" will be the abstract starting-point of the statements, and everything else will describe this state of beginning. The first statement declares that at this abstract point in time and space (the beginning) 'the' word inverted meanings. The second statement could be placed in a causal relationship: because of this inversion of meaning, the world seemed to turn "much more slowly," or in an oppositional relationship: although the meaning of words was inverted, the world turned more slowly. The third statement refers to the word, the one that inverted meaning, or any other word or words, which was so detached from us that we did not pay attention to them. This might explain why it (the word) sounded so strange to us, or maybe, because the word sounded strange we did not pay attention.

This broken collection of propositions in *Victory Garden*

---

[173] The propositions are ordered from left to right. The first two propositions are the ones the reader reaches when she follows the left link in node *Desire*, and then the left link in node *To see*. The third and fourth propositions are reached when following the branching out of the right link in node *Desire* (See Appendix C. - Branching of path *In the beginning*).

alludes to T. S. Eliot's poem *Mr. Eliot's Sunday Morning Service* (59), which is one of the connotations of the above sequence of propositions. The first and most obvious connotation is to the opening sentence of the Bible, "In the beginning God created the heaven and the earth" (Genesis 1:1) and the second and even more similar, is to (The Gospel of John 1:1) "In the beginning was the Word, and the Word was with God, and the Word was God." Those two connotations link the world with the word. In Eliot's poem exactly the same "phrase" appears twice, in two successive lines, one closes a stanza and the other opens it "In the beginning was the Word:"

> Polyphiloprogenitive
> The sapient sutlers of the Lord
> Drift across the window-panes.
> In the beginning was the Word.
>
> In the beginning was the Word.
> Superfetation of τὸ ἕν,
> And at the mensual turn of time
> Produced enervate Origen.

This poem is constructed, as is characteristic of Eliot, of fragmented lines, between which the reader has to reconstruct the relations in order to understand the meaning of the poem. If we combine the three connotations, we receive, in *Victory Garden*, a declaration about the nature of the text that we are examining: the word is the world, yet in order to understand it we have to reconstruct the fragments that words create.

Only a thorough and learned reader studying the text in depth can make out this pattern, described above. The regular reader, most probably, does not see these propositions one next to the other, although the software allows this positioning of nodes and the possibility to go back and into a new path is always available. In the process of reading, the reader encounters one node at a time, thus, she can grasp the additive pattern of both, nodes and labels, but on arrival at the final node, she is left with an indefinite sentence. The vague sentences arouse the reader's curiosity (what does the author mean exactly) thus coaxing her to go on reading or to examine it minutely.

Since hypertext with all its innovations and new technological abilities does not use the freedom of a random opening the beginning functions are not different in hypertext then in print, thus its poetic devices are also the same, mainly providing a one sequence introduction or enlisting the ancient device of the *in medias res*. The term in medias res is based on the assumption that in literature at least two time lines reside side by side throughout the whole reading process. The first is the communicative time, the unique time in which the reader is reading the work while establishing an interaction with the author as he is exposed through his work (for instance, the author's mocking question that was described in *victory Garden's* node *Come Often?*) The communicative time is our present, anchored in the reader's reality and in the sequence in which the story unfolds before her eyes. The second time, the fictive time of the work, is the time in which the characters are living and is represented in the narrative. In both cases time has one distinct property, its sequentiality. Time is based on three phases, of which the only constant, precise, and attainable is the present. The other two, past and future are relative to the present; past is what comes previous to this moment, and future is what will come after this moment. World time unfolds to us only in one direction, from past to future. However, mimetic time, represented time, does not have to follow this sequence. Indeed, many authors prefer not to start their work *ab ovo*, from the moment the hero is conceived so to speak, but to create a dissonance between natural time and represented time. These two-time lines are known in poetics also as "story" and "plot,"[174] where story is the natural time of events that sometimes has to be reconstructed out of the plot, which is the mimetic time that has no commitment to any time order and can be distorted for rhetoric and poetic purposes.

The two different beginnings, that of the reading process, the plot, versus the beginning of the story, are one of literature's important temporal devices. In opposition to the *ab ovo* mode of beginning a narrative, there is the *in medias res* mode of beginning. Hyper-literature narrative starting point is mainly of the *in medias res* mode along with certain backwards details, as there is a need for starting the narrative with some dramatic action, which is more interesting, and not with prolonged descriptions and other background details thus there is almost no exposition in the traditional meaning of

---

[174] Forster, Chapter V. See also Richardson (2002), Scholes.

the word. The exposition's role is to present before the reader the fictive world (milieu) as is defined by Sternberg (1978), "It is the function of the exposition to introduce the reader into an unfamiliar world, the fictive world of the story, by providing him with the general and specific antecedents indispensable to the understanding of what happens in it" (1). This definition does not bind exposition with the beginning of narrative, yet the "unfamiliar world" is unfamiliar at its first introduction to the reader.

I try to recall winter. < As if it were yesterday? > she says, but I do not signify one way or another.

By five the sun sets and the afternoon melt freezes again across the blacktop into crystal octopi and palms of ice-- rivers and continents beset by fear, and we walk out to the car, the snow moaning beneath our boots and the oaks exploding in series along the fenceline on the horizon, the shrapnel settling like relics, the echoing thundering off far ice. This was the essence of wood, these fragments say. And this darkness is air.

< Poetry > she says, without emotion, one way or another.

Do you want to hear about it?

Figure 57 - Node *begin* of Joyce's *afternoon, a story*

Joyce's *afternoon, a story* is another example of a hypertext that starts *in medias res*, yet his first node *begin* starts in the midst of a conversation between the narrator and an unknown "she." The node holds 15 visible links (Figure 57), and several conditioned ones. Most of the nodes lead the reader to nodes by the name of their linked word. For instance link word "she" takes the reader to node labeled *she*. These nodes have some conditioned links and one default that is activated if the reader clicks on a word or somewhere on the node, which turns the reading, at this stage, to one sequence reading like that of *Califia*. Only after two to three nodes the author lets his reader start choosing on her own and the narrative starts it forking.

Hypertext option for the beginning, which is too new to be called tradition, is to present the reader with multiple choices from which she has to create her own sequence, yet she is being led, sometimes without her knowledge, by pre-written sequences that the author made available for her in the first place. This sort of beginning was not used as a conventional exposition, but as a kind of "game" that enabled the reader to get used to hypertext's ways and give her a feeling of activeness and control and ensure the stimulation of curiosity. Even Joyce multi-links *begin* node sends the reader to something that looks like a game – multi-nodes that holds only one word. This quest has a demonstrative motivation: the word 'shrapnel' starts a long one-sequence and one word nodes line. Yet, there is only a default from those nodes; the reader does not have any choices.

Hence, we see that hypertext authors use beginnings in pretty much the same conventional ways that print authors do: by providing the reader with an exposition (Coverley's *Califia*) or by starting *in medias res* (Moulthrop's *Victory Garden*). The *in medias res* sort of beginning is more common in hypertext because it is more dramatic and authors needed something dramatic that will bypass the apprehension caused by the new format.

After getting to hold the reader's attention so that they finish reading the beginning, authors have to tackle the problem of retaining the reader's attention until she grasps the layout of this new media and the unique fictive world of the work, into which she is stepping, so that she becomes immersed in the story.

5.2 In between

After establishing a fixed and predetermined beginning-point and finding two sorts of beginnings in all the works examined, it is time to examine where the fixed beginning leads. In Moulthrop's *Victory Garden* when the beginning selection process, which is game-like, is over the reader starts her exploration of the narrative that branches from the final nodes, the ones holding the complete proposition. The final nodes do not have any links except of the default linkage, which throws the reader into the narrative. For instance the default and the only link anchored on the proposition, "In the beginning the word sounded so high above us that we didn't really notice" (See node *Better.* In Appendix C. - Branching of path In the beginning") leads to node *Something Happens* that is the first node after the selection game is over. The node describes the events that happen in Whitman's Creek when Miles, Harley, Thea and Veronica go swimming together. They see a TV crew, hovering in a helicopter, covering a demonstration against a construction plan and the destruction of the Creek as a park. The connection between the proposition that ended the game-like selection process and its linked node is associative; the "sound" of the word "high above us" turns in the linked node into "the whip beat of rotor blades," the sound of a helicopter in the narrative's world.

The reader does not know what Whitman's Creek is nor does she know who the characters, the participants in the scene are, thus she is thrown to the story *in medias res*. Without knowing, the reader has met the two subjects of the work: the academic world at the time of the First Gulf War and the media, communication in the wide sense of the word. This node too has only a default link[175] to node *Well In Hand*, which reveals what all the fuss is about and provides expositional materials. By default, the reader reaches node *Timely* that describes Urquhart, who is Emily's boyfriend and Thea's colleague, and an important character that wasn't presented in the previous scene. This node has six links (Figure 58); three of them hold parts of Urquhart's characterization (*U Turns*, *8088*, *Showtime*) and the other

---

[175] Though the node has four links, at this time only the default is active as the other three are conditional links, which will be available only after the reader completes a certain amount of reading.

three present the main issues that the work deals with. Two of the linked nodes (*War Zones*, *Bad Timing*) throw the reader into the midst of the First Gulf War by presenting two discussions among the soldiers who are in Saudi Arabia, in the war: one is between Emily and her Sergeant and the other is some musing of the soldiers over the effects the war has over them and over the people back home. The first issue is presented by the participating character and by Urquhart and the second issue, communication, is brought in by a citation of Yu Tsung's words from Borges' *The Garden of Forking Paths*, which is regarded as a description of hypertext, of a work that is like a labyrinth, a maze[176] (*Observer*).

Better. → Something Happens → Well In Hand → Timely

Observer   *War Zones*
Bad
Showtime
U Turns   *8088*

Figure 58 – Default links from final node *Better.* in Moulthrop's *Victory Garden*

Another example from Moulthrop's *Victory Garden* is the proposition "In the beginning the word sounded strange to our ears" [*Returning.*], to which the reader arrives if she chooses the word "strange" in the word play of node *to know* (see Appendix C.). This

---

[176] The experience of reading hypertext is regarded by researchers like walking through a maze. For instance, Yellowlees Douglas, 63-82.

proposition sends the reader to node *Wadi*, which is a citation from Barthes's (1979) *From Work to Text*. The strange sounding of the word is exemplified by Barthes' strange analogue of text to what a person perceives while strolling by a wadi. Unlike the previous example that dragged the reader for three nodes until she was presented with any choices, node *Wadi* holds eight links and a default; hence it is a major narrative junction. The default sends the reader to node *come again*, which is similar to node *Come Often* that started the *In the beginning* additive line (See Figure 54) and if the reader will make the same choices she will arrive at the same nodes. She can, of course, choose different links, the ones that she did not choose before, and arrive at a different word play. However, the word "Labyrinth" in this new node is linked to a different node than in the original. While the 'original' node takes the reader to node *Labrys*, which starts the *Labyrinth* additive narrative, in this node it is linked to node *Labyr innit*. This node holds only one fragment of a line, "… *things are very seldom simple.*" This node has one textual link and a default link. The default throws the reader back to node *Wadi* and the other link, anchored on the word "simple" takes the reader to node *Come Often?* which is the second node in the beginning of the additive line. Thus, the default creates a cyclic linkage yet again, which goes to show that the author desires his reader not to keep activating the default, but to choose for herself from the eight links that the *Wadi* node holds and by that he is ready to pass the authorial control onto his reader.

These examples represent the conventional pattern of Moulthrop's *Victory Garden* sequence structure, in between the beginning and the end. After the word play of the beginning is finished in the last proposition, the reader is introduced *in medias res*, by a default link, into the narrative. These default nodes function as junctions for the reader. For example, node *Observer* holds 4 textual links, one conditioned link and one default link, node *Watch My Back* holds 7 textual links, 4 conditioned and one default, thus it is a major junction. Some of the nodes have a conditioned default that is conditioned by first reading the default, then if the reader retraces her steps or gets to this node again the default shifts and the feeling is of randomness, dynamics and interactivity as is generated by all conditional links. These nodes allow the reader to choose for herself her own sequence of reading out of the multi-sequential options that the hypertext author prepared for her. Thus he loosens a little his tight authorial control and allows his reader to choose a sequence, even if formed by him in advance. Once again, we face the tension between control and freedom that hypertext holds: the freedom of the reader has in reading (the notion of freedom anyway) against the control of the author who decides where are the points of freedom, to where will the points of freedom lead the reader and the concrete content of each node that is conditioned by the link. Meaning, the author has to compose some different "stories" (to some extent) in order to present a work that has some freedoms.

Since the hypertext author cannot be sure where his reader has already been through the text and as there is use of the *in media res* technique the author has to enable the access to expositional materials throughout the work. This is one of the methods with which the author "overcomes" the randomness of the free choice and directs the reader to a controlled choice activity. Hypertext uses two common devices for introducing expositional materials: the *encyclopedic link* and some "tools," which substitute digressions. Such are *Califia*'s various "tools" – diaries, picture albums, letters, maps, manuscripts, geological data, legends, and memories – which are all devices that allow the reader to call on expositional materials, which cover a hundred and seventy years before the beginning of the story. The encyclopedic link, on the other hand, is similar to the scattering of expositional materials throughout the literary work, which is as old as literature itself. And yet, there is a great difference between the way the print reader finds the expositional materials and the way the hypertext reader gets at it. In print literature the author is the one to scatter the materials where he thinks fit in order to create and control effects of suspense/curiosity/surprise. In hypertext the author can create an expositional material node and make it available to the reader in one out of two ways: it can be available anywhere and everywhere or it can be conditioned so as not to ruin those three effects. Each author can choose according to his aims and poetic beliefs. Joyce is quite reluctant to give up his poetic control over the story's sequence and effects, and therefore there are few choices and many conditioned links. Moulthrop, on the other hand, gives his reader more freedom, while giving up some of his authorial control.

Hypertext's writers allow for some well 'planned,' freedom of choice that will promise the attraction of the reader and the continuation of the reading by the creation of suspense, curiosity, and surprise while engaging the reader in an activity that creates a feeling of interaction. After the author has ensured his reader's curiosity, and attracted her to continue her reading, she is led into the forking paths that were discussed before, the various narrative lines. Does the author pre-plan the ending point of the work? And if so, does he keep printing norms of closure?

5.3 The end

Hypertext produces a sensation of an endless quest, as though there is no end to the book, since the reader cannot see how much she has read and how much is still left to be read as she can in the printed book. This fact brought Bolter (1991) and others to regard the hypertext work as a "network" that "can extend indefinitely, as a printed text cannot" (24). Unlike the printed book the reader cannot usually jump, go directly, to the end to see if she likes it. First, she has to find it, as there is no one definite place for the end in the revealing and unfolding work as there is in the printed book, unless the author declares that this is the last node.

Bolter likens hypertext endlessness to oral literature, "there is nothing in storytelling that quite corresponds to the reader's sense that in turning the pages he or she is coming to the end of the book" (109). He refers to the mutual feeling that a listener and the hypertext reader has of not knowing how long a time the story is going to last, unless there is an external time limit as in a theater play or a movie. The ending of hypertext has no time limit and is much more complicated than it is in print literature where there is a physical place for the ending, a tangible, stable, last page, or even in the oral storytelling, where the narrator ends the story - a session of a performance, or a slot of time in a program (theater).

There is no arguing that we cannot see the end of the hyper-work, because it is not a tangible object as the book, and there is no last page one can sneak a peek at to see if the heroine really marries the guy or who is actually the murderer. However, this does not resolve the question – is there no ending to hypertext narrative? Is it truly indefinite?

Aristotle considers as an end that which "has nothing following it," (Chapter VII) which is similar to Herrnstein Smith's distinction of 'end' in the sense of stopping, ceasing or of the tangible pages being totally consumed. However, Herrnstein Smith finds another sense to 'end', that of closure. She says, "The ringing of a telephone, the blowing of the wind, the babbling of an infant in its crib: these stop. A poem or a piece of music concludes" (1). Namely, the term 'end' is not merely stopping but also concluding,

> We tend to speak of conclusions when a sequence of events has a relatively high degree of structure, when, in other words, we can perceive these events as related to one another by some principle of organization or design that implies the existence of a definite termination point. Under these circumstances, the occurrence of the terminal events is a confirmation of expectations that have been established by the structure of the sequence, and is usually distinctly gratifying (2).

Thus, Herrnstein Smith sees closure as "a confirmation of expectations." In this meaning, closure is not merely time dependent but has to gratify the reader's expectations: "Closure, then, may be regarded as a modification of structure that makes stasis, or the absence of further continuation, the most probable succeeding event" (34). While Herrnstein Smith refers mainly to poetry, Kermode, (1966) who deals mostly with narrative, sees conclusion as a two-way option. The first is the confirmation of expectations, and the other is by negating them, in Aristotle's terms by peripeteia,[177] "The interest

---

[177] Peripeteia is a sudden or unexpected reversal of circumstances or situation especially in a literary work. "Peripeteia, n."

of having our expectations falsified is obviously related to our wish to reach the discovery or recognition by an unexpected and instructive route" (18). Kermode finds closure even in fragmented texts as Robbe-Grillet's, where the closure is entirely reader oriented, meaning the reader has to create the coherency at the end of the work. Namely, closure is the intention and aspiration of the reader because of psychological and cognitive reasons, and it finds substantiations in the work.

Perry (1979) seconds this concept of closure as one of the effects that is created by the dynamics of the reading process,

> The nature of a literary work, and even the sum total of its meanings, do not rest entirely on the conclusions reached by the reader at the end-point of the text-continuum. They are not a "sifted," "balanced," and static sum-total constituted once the reading is over, when all the relevant material has been laid out before the reader. The effects of the entire reading process all contribute to the meaning of the work: its surprises; the changes along the way; the process of a gradual, zig-zag-like build-up of meanings, their reinforcement, development, revision and replacement; the relations between expectations aroused at one stage of the text and

---

Merriam-Webster dictionary, 2012. <http://www.merriam-webster.com/dictionary/peripeteia>, 24.7.2016

discoveries actually made in subsequent stages; the process of retrospective re-patterning and even the peculiar survival of meanings which were first constructed and then rejected (41).

For Perry too, the rearrangement of the components, alternatives and potential expectations throughout the reading process create the dynamics of the work, its meaning and perception of closure. They are built-up through the adjustments and readjustments made by the reader during the course of reading.

Hence, closure is the fulfillment or negating the reader's expectation, in other words, resolving the suspense, curiosity, and surprise. Thus, I will regard as 'end' where most of the obvious gaps, which raise the reader's curiosity, are satisfyingly closed, and the unfelt gaps, questions that were raised during the reading session, which create the surprise, are answered.

Keep and McLaughlin see several possible "ending options" in hypertext:

> The reading path **terminates** at a node which announces "the end" and does not allow further readings. Of course, there may be more than one such node. This is the method used by most interactive fictions.
>
> The path never ends, but eventually begins **recycling** nodes. After a time, the reader will tire of

the repetition. This option is put to effective use in such hyperfictions as Victory Garden.

The path returns to the first node, completing an obviously **cyclic** narrative.

The path concludes by oscillating between two nodes (as in Hopscotch or cycling among an obviously finite number of nodes. Borrowing the language of chaos theory, we will call this the **strange attractor** method. (hfl0130.html)

They describe two main techniques: the first technique is similar to print literature, where the end of the book denotes the end of the work and the narrative, the announcement of "the end." The second technique is multifaceted: cycling possibilities which will eventually cause the reader to tire and give up the work with or without feeling that she has reached the end, thus not always reaching the notion of conclusion. Keep and McLaughlin provide some detailed description of the second option: the cycling among nodes that had already been read, reaching the beginning for the second time, which means the recycling of the whole work and the cycling among a certain number of nodes, for which they use a term taken from the chaos theory and refers to a dynamic situation: "the strange attractor". These possibilities are available only to hypertext's authors/readers and present one of hypertext innovations. They are based on the structure of nodes, which have no binding direction of reading and each node can appear endless times again and again, where in print literature the reader can of course re-read, but she is reading in a conventional direction that is directed towards the material end of the book.

All the options are possible in hypertext; they are new techniques that were enabled by the new technology, the computer, and the new format, hypertext. These techniques subvert the meaning of stability and finality that are the characteristics of the conventional literary work. However, not all Keep and McLaughlin's techniques were characteristic of hypertext's endings or closure at hypertext flourishing time. For instance – the cycling between nodes, their "strange attractor" method, which is found in Moulthrop's *Victory Garden* where the author wants to force the reader to choose a reading path other than reading by default and not as an ending device.

"The end" approach (Keep and McLaughlin's first option) is equal to the physical ending of the printed book though in print the author does not need to announce its ending. In print it is the result of the lack of pages, or the encounter with the book's cover, which is an avowal of its end. This approach has in hypertext two variants; the first is the closing of the application when the words "The End" or "Exit" are clicked, and the other is by the prevention of links, the creation of a dead end, thus the reader has nowhere to go.

An example of "the end" option of shutting down the application is found in Coverley's *Califia* (Figure 59). Its main structural concept is the compass as the story is built out of four journeys, one for each celestial direction. Each "journey" starts with a node that is labeled with an ordinal number. For instance, the second journey, to the East, starts with a node whose heading is: "To the Reader – Part II" and ends with a node labeled by the name of the direction, like *East*.

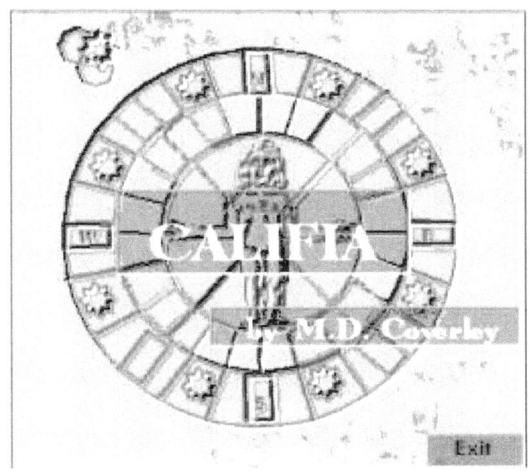

Figure 59 – *End node 29*

The last node carries two buttons: "switchback" and "Home" (See Figure 60 – Califia: *Node South*) and some links: one allows the reader to re-read the text she just finished: "return to any section," another takes her forward: "Califia will continue to the east, with Wind, Sand, and Stars." The last option is "exit" that actually closes the application and causes the stopping that Herrnstein Smith was talking about since the reader might want to continue reading – to the east. Thus the "exit" option causes the physical closing of the work.

The "Home" button has the same function of stopping. By clicking the "Home" button the reader does not reach the first node as was to be expected, but to a node that carries the same label and the same picture of the Solar Table that can be seen in Figure 59, yet this time it is colored blue and instead of the "Exit" button, there's a button labeled "Return to Shore." When the "Return to shore" button is activated it takes the reader to page No. 28, labeled *On the Shore Again*, which background is a picture of footsteps starting at the seashore and heading to land, which is the same picture as the one on the first node of the reading. Hence, the work answers two of Keep and McLaughlin's options: "the end" technique that of the cyclic effect, which takes the reader back to the first page.

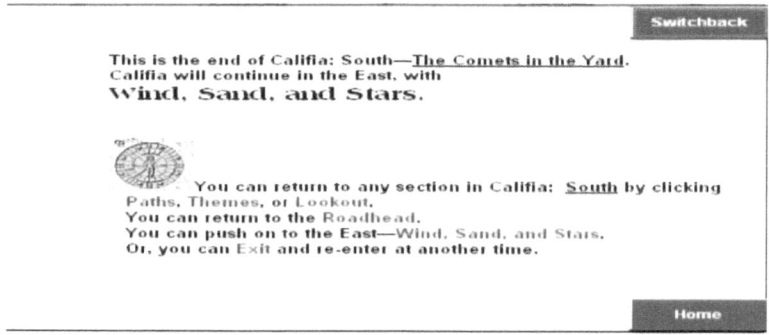

Figure 60 - Califia: Node *South*

The *On the Shore Again* node says,

Here we arrive at the shore, facing westward. As you can see Three Forking Paths, Four Compass Directions, Seven Stars of the Dipper, the Land of

Promise, and the Constellations of Forever have been explored. The eighth, the Polar Star, belongs to you.

Abide t/here.

This node is a summation of the work's structure and the proclamation that all the nodes "have been explored." Hence, telling the reader that she has investigated all the available texts therefore her reading is finished. However, if the reader did not read all four "directions" she did not finish the reading but left after one, or more, parts of it as "The Solar Table," which is one of the special tools for navigation, shows clearly that there are four parts to the story.

The single and last line of node *On the Shore Again* has an unusual style. Two antonyms are combined into one word by the aid of a slash, leaving the reader to choose what she will; "abiding here" means that she arrived at the end, or she can choose to "abide there." Whatever the reader's choice is, this link leads to the next node, No. 29, which holds the "Exit" button (Figure 59) that closes the application, hence terminating the reading session. This, once again, is a "built-in" end, which brings no more pages/nodes to turn.

The forth option of an ending, the endless cycling, which is called by Keep and McLaughlin the "strange attractor" is in wide use when the author wants to force the reader into choosing a link, otherwise she won't go anywhere let alone reach the end, yet not as a sign, or a replacement of the end.

In print literature, the closing of the book and the declaration of the author that his reader reached the end are the same. In hypertext, as there is no tangible object like the book, the end can be defined as the closing of the "book," the application, which is a direct way to denote "end," or in an indirect way, as we saw in Larsen's *Crossed Ends*, where there are no more links, textual or default, therefore the reader is brought to a stop. Another example for the "dead end" method is, node *And Now...* in Moulthrop's *Victory Garden*, which has only one word, "— peace —," and no links branching from it. The only possibility to continue is through one of the tools that are built in the software. However, that is not a narrative sequence, but a new reading.

Except for the material aspect/sense of the work's end that was discussed above, there is the question of closure. A close inspection of hypertext will show that hypertext complies with Herrnstein Smith and Kermode's rules of closure and there is a sense of closure as in print literature whether the reader is stopped because of lack of links, or because of the closing of the application or if the text begins cycle between nodes.

Victory Garden, the same as *Califia*, has some ending points. The first one that the reader encounters is node "."[178] The node has no verbal elements but a big graphical black rectangle, similar to the one

---

[178] The node's name is the dot, which denotes an ending, though usually denoting the end of a sentence.

that is found in *Tristram Shandy* denoting death when the narrator mourns over "Alas, poor YORICK!" (23)

The node is reachable through several paths. The first path that takes the reader to this node is path *praecox*, which starts at node *Paths to Deplore*, one of the two nodes, which look like a Table of Content and were already described in my analysis of the fixed beginning. Choosing the last option in this node, "PRAECOX *jumping to conclusions*" takes the reader to node *No More*. This node holds one of the last sentences in the narrative line *In the beginning*, and has no textual links but a default. The default leads the reader to node *...and finally:* that has only two graphical elements, a big white rectangle, and a tiny black one. This node too has no textual links but a default, which brings the reader to node "." The default takes the reader to node "..." that holds only a small contour line of dotes. From there, by default, the reader gets to node *and now* ... The node has only the word " – peace – " and no links, not even in default. There are other links which were not part of the default and are available to the reader only after she has read certain pre-desired nodes (conditioned links). This sequence does not make sense; hence it seems that the reader arrived at this node too early in her reading. The path's label, which means in Latin 'premature,' supports that conclusion and the comment attached to this path in node *Paths to Deplore*: "*jumping to conclusions*" strengthens this deduction. The reader has to retract her steps or go to the beginning and start again, this time choosing other paths, which goes to show that the author created some "dead ends" to create a feeling of freedom, of reader-control reading.

However, if this node is reached through path *darkness* that describes the soldiers in the barracks under a missile attack, the "." node denotes Emily's death. Nodes *Down in the Dark, Waste Not Want Not*, and *Shortly* in sequence, present a discussion the soldiers are having in the barracks under a missile attack. The conversation is about what they are going to do when they will be back at home. They wonder why the war is still going on as they have freed Kuwait, which was the cause for this war. The default is node *Time* where a flash of light and heat breaks up the chat as they get to the subject of how soon they will be back at home. The typology of the node, scattered unfinished sentences, concretizes the disorientation caused by the Scud missile that hits them. (See Appendix D. - Typography of node Time) The default linkage takes the reader to a long node that presents Emily's thoughts, as she is lying wounded, until she loses consciousness [...*and*...]. Again, the default linkage and the only one available is to node ...*and*... that holds only a picture of the previous node, which explains its identical labels, yet it is almost unreadable as it is presented through a broken glass (see Figure 61). The node holds only a default link that takes the reader to node "." Through this path the reader understands that the black rectangle is the author's comment and reaction to Emily's death, or his way to tell his reader about it, by way of allusion. The full path gives the node its meaning while the premature arriving at this node will leave the reader astonished and perplexed. Hence, Moulthrop allows the reader to arrive at nodes prematurely and is not afraid that the reader will become frustrated by indecipherable nodes. Thus the reader will feel the freedom of choice. For him it is part of the reading, exploring process, otherwise he would have blocked the reader's premature arrival at it by conditioning rules.

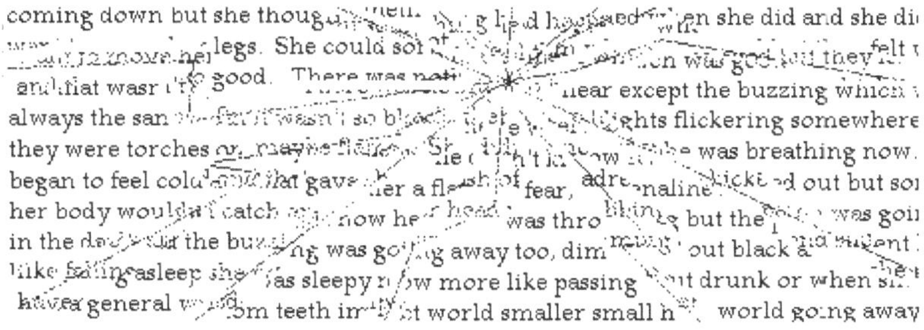

coming down but she thoug... ... ... g lip d h... ... en she did and she di... ... ... legs. She could so... ... ... n w... g... ... they... and that wasr... good. There was n... ... ... ear except the buzzing which... always the san... ... wasr... so b... ... ... hts flickering somewhere they were torches or... maybe... ... ... le ... ... was breathing now. began to feel cold... that gave... er a fle... of fear, adr... naline... out but so... her body would... catch... now he... head was thro... ... but the... was goi... in the da... the bu... ... ng was go... g away too, dim... ... out black a... ... ent... like falling asleep sh... as sleepy now more like passing... ... t drunk or when s... have a general w... m teeth in... ... t world smaller small h... world going away

Figure 61 - *Emily's thoughts*

The hero's death is a common and forceful way in literature to denote the end of a story because of its mimetic qualities; there is nothing more final than death. As the node does not have any textual links, it emphasizes the "stopping" quality of this node not only by its structure, but by its content as well. Emily's death is a possible event and the reader cannot disregard it as she is a soldier in a war zone and her friends worry about the possibility of her getting hurt. Then they get used to her being in danger and as the war continues everyone goes about his/her daily life and each time a worry over Emily is raised it is discarded aside and the characters think about her home coming, which causes the reader to feel too that Emily is secure. This expectation, of Emily's safe return, gains momentum in light of the worthy cause that has motivated this war – the rescue of Kuwait. By narrative standards of folktales and fairy tales and narratology in general, the good cause of the fighting associates the story with the tradition of the happy end of the hero. Thus, the reader is looking forward to Emily's safe return home. The nodes "showing" her death produce closure, as Kermode defines closure, by the negation of expectations along with the presentation of a "no more links," a "dead end" which forms a feeling of closure.

Another theme that is emphasized through the work is the unreality of the war that students and teachers alike watch through screens. (For instance, nodes *Unreal* and *War zones*) The unreality is strengthened if the reader chooses to activate the textual link "Home home home," (in node S*hortly*), she will find, (in node *Because because because* to which she reaches), that Emily did not die, "Because she did come home." This node is part of path *happy*. The path starts with node *Reality-Based* that states the banal greeting on TV, "Hi, honey – I'm home!" The second node is *Because because because* and the third is *All Right*, describing Emily entering the townhouse to find there a huge bed. In the next node, *Greenback*, all the rest, Thea, Veronica, Harley, Leroy and Jude come out of the kitchen like a surprise party, and Miles is congratulating her via satellite and they all drink for her return. The last node, *West End*, says,

... and the day is fine

the birds are singing

and the sun goes down gently

in the

west

Ithaca-Austin-Dallas-Atlanta [179]

This "happy-ending" concludes the *happy* path and parodies the American film industry that was quoted in the first node, *Reality-Based*. This is the version of the optimistic ending, which also has a strong sense of closure. This version has a supplement describing Emily's behavior at home after the war. Path *4:00* node *Four O'Clock* says, "Days, weeks, months, almost a year now back in the life, back in the Real World. If that's what you call it. Emily's not so sure." Thus, she not only came back but the reader is told about her life afterward. The following nodes that make-up this path describe her incapability to choose between Boris and Victor, and the suffering that is caused to both men. This line of closure is less dramatic, as it answers the reader's expectation for the safe return of the student that enlisted for the worthy cause.

However, these two possibilities, of Emily coming home or Emily's death, though they are undoubtedly mutually exclusive, and both have a clear dimension of closure, do not carry the same credibility. The author puts more emphasis on the pessimistic option, which has confirmation from two other sources, in the narrative as well as in the real world, as the historical records show. History tells

---

[179] Typography is in the original.

us that "The largest single loss of Coalition forces happened on February 25, 1991 when an Iraqi Scud missile hit an American military barracks in Dhahran, Saudi Arabia killing 28 U.S. Army Reservists from Pennsylvania."[180] Not only history confirms the probable death option, but the end of the narrative as well, namely ".". This extra-narrative knowledge strengthens the feeling of closure of the negation of expectations and Emily's death. When the reader finds that there is another option of Emily coming back from the war, she has to choose for herself what version she prefers. This mutually exclusive end is scarce in print literature and is the "no end" option that critics were hoping for. And yet, despite the novelty of the device, and in spite of the enormous freedom given to the reader to decide what the story is about (by its ending), this device has no added value aesthetically, poetic, literary or other. We just got two stories in one packaging.

The other confirmation of the pessimistic option is in the "afterward," that the story holds, though not stated officially, that describes the whereabouts and doings of all the characters. In a path labeled *post*, which is a telltale name, the first-person narrator describes his or hers life with Thea in California and says, "I don't begrudge Thea her sense of loss, her mourning." [*And Now*] The

---

[180] <http://www.fact-index.com/g/gu/gulf_war.html#Casualties>, 24.7.2016. See also the New York Times original report: <http://www.nytimes.com/1991/02/26/world/war-in-the-gulf-scud-attack-scud-missile-hits-a-us-barracks-killing-27.html>, 24.7.2016.

node's default link is to *And Then Again*, which describes a calendar he finds at the bottom of one of Thea's drawers,

> Only then do I realize that it's last year's calendar, untouched since February, 1991. I start to say something but then my eye catches another detail. Using a razorblade, someone has sliced the square for February 26 out of the page. The cut was deep, taking several other days with it .

The narrator finds a calendar in Thea's desk where Thea, in an attempt to bring Emily to life or to deny her death, cut out Emily's death date probably in a furry as the "cut was deep." These words have a double meaning: the first is the physical deep cut of the calendar and the second is the mental cut caused by the Emily's death. Thus, the tragic option of Emily's death is fortified when the narrator, who is a new character that was not involved in the occurrences of the previous year in Tara, finds by accident the evidence of their being real in the fictive world as well as matching real-world events.

The stress given to the death option is to divert, actually to balance, our natural tendency towards the happy-end as the many films that are produced in Hollywood attest. It does not mean that it is the "right" answer (Pape, 1992). There is closure not only about Emily's destiny, but about all the other characters as well. In a node labeled *Aftermath*, again a telltale title, the reader is told that Heidel resigned and is going to Poland. Thea moved to California, where she met the narrator, Veronica and Harley traveled until they settled at

Camden, New Jersey, where Veronica is back in college and Harley is writing a book about the war. Leroy, whom Veronica and Harley met on their way, realized his dream to "make music" and play in a teen club in Boston; Miles Finished his film about apocalyptic Christians and Boris lost his sanity, as Emily feared, yet he will be O.K. This information creates a feeling of "and they lived happily ever after," on the one hand, and on the other hand it closes each story line. For example the theme of Leroy that is left open after his sudden visit to Thea, raised our curiosity and disappeared until this node where we find what happened to him. The effort to create closure even in the smallest detail (as Leroy's story) is a kind of compensation for the segmented nature of the work.

Thus, one of the differences between print literature and hypertext stems from the book as an object, its container that signals to the reader – "it ain't over till it's over." This lack of signals in hypertext causes a feeling of uncertainty, the feeling that we missed or are missing something, that there is more to read and more lines/paths to travel, and maybe there all our expectations and temporary closures will be turned inside out. And yet we saw that hypertext, as well, leads in different ways to choosing an end that is closure too. In this respect the author is bounded to the narratological norms as much as he is freed by the digital norms.

Hypertext does not dismiss closure but endows it with a new twist. It can present two mutually exclusive ends that are not hinted at as in James's *The Turn of the Screw*, but are fully developed paths presented side by side, even if he enlists history to support one of the options that the reader may like less. This multi-ending is similar to Fowles' *The French Lieutenant Woman*,[181] which is an exceptional example.

Nevertheless, the author chooses his medium out of the available ones, hence the feeling of uncertainty, vagueness, or ambiguity, is one of the effects that he wishes to create. The feeling of mutually exclusive ending options in hypertext is one of its goals. This fuelling of uncertainty is found in Joyce's *afternoon, a story*, as well, where the main suspenseful question, "I want to say I may have seen my son die this morning." [*I want to say*] does not have a definite answer. Herrnstein Smith says, "The sense of closure is a function of the perception of structure" (4). In hypertext the perception of structure is intentionally problematized but not to the point of destruction or annihilation. The author practices his control over the possible sequences and creates concatenations, causes the reader to cycle through nodes and paths, throws her back to choose a different link, creates mutually exclusive narrative lines and even creates dead-

---

[181] See in Douglas (2000): "Fowles' *The French Lieutenant's Woman*, for example, features three endings: a parody of the tidy-but-breathless tying up of loose ends so characteristic of the Victorian novel; a happy but conventional resolution of the tortured relationship between Charles and Sarah; and a more complex, "modern" resolution that serves to deconstruct the paternalistic perspective of the traditional Victorian novel of love and marriage. Not surprisingly, none of the three endings is compatible with another" (59).

ends paths to give the other the feeling of free choice. Hypertext authors pre-determine not one ending-point but several. Though this is found in print narrative as well, it is the exception there, while in hypertext it is common.

And yet, in the early days of hypertext, authors did not abandon the concept of closure and invested much effort in keeping closure in their hypertext narratives as has been demonstrated by the *aftermath* node in Moulthrop's *Victory Garden* and as can be seen in Coverley's *Califia*, node *West/Agusta's Path* that is a summation of the quest's adventures and findings. There is a general cognitive need for closure, which is defined in psychology by Kruglanski & Webster (1996) as: "The need for cognitive closure refers to individuals' desire for a firm answer to a question and an aversion toward ambiguity." Although the need for closure varies from person to person it is still a basic need accordingly the cognitive importance of closure might explain authors desire to maintain this print norm in hypertext as well.

6   Combination – Order & Disorder

All systems, from linguistics to society, are a convergence of two dimensions: units, and combinatorial principles that connect them together. Hypertext's basic unit is the node. Although hypertext literary research defines the node as a segment, a lexia, an object, a block of text or image, hypertext has no artistic-ideological background that requires fragmentation or segmentation as can be found in modern and post-modern literature or in visual art along the ages, as I have already argued in previous chapters. On the contrary, hypertext as a technological device was conceived as a connecting medium. Nelson explains that hypertext, "simply connects chunks of text by alternative choices" (1/15), or as Yankelovich, the developer of the *Intermedia* hypertext system, defines its purpose, "to link information together" (81). Neither Nelson nor Yankelovich refer to linking of fragments or segments. Their information, or "chunks of texts," was fully developed papers, which authors or readers could link together by the linkage device, provided by hypertext systems, thus turning it into a bigger, global if you will, object. Hypertext literature, however, has put the 'node' as its basic segment owing to the multiple, or alternative, story lines it enables and thereby hypertext refers to segments of texts and not to whole blocks, and it pays attention to the nature of texts as segments of a whole and not as wholes which requires segmenting.

The main innovation of hypertext is in its combinatorial patterns, which allow the linking of nodes, be it a segment, a fully developed story or any other partial or wholly developed object, into multiple potential sequences. The author, while creating the work, and the reader, while navigating through or generating the story, both create sequences of nodes, which is commonly called a *path*, to cite Bolter (1991), "In general, the connections of a hypertext are organized into paths that make operational sense to author and reader" (24). The path corresponds to Vannevar Bush's concept of a "trail," which he developed by analogy to the human brain.

The rise of the metaphorical description of hypertext as a "network" was the result of the linking of nodes into paths, and the linking of paths into each other. Thus it is necessary to look at the linkage device and examine the three main different varieties that I found: the default, the encyclopedic and the analogous. Then I'll sketch the mode by which the links and nodes create paths of narrative. The next issue will be the *network* term that all researchers use, though their referents differ greatly. Thus, a close inspection of the term and its implications are called for, though it might lead to the conclusion that despite the fact that the concept of network is applicable to hypertext, it might confuse more than help when we come to analyze hypertext narratives.

382

6.1 The Link

Hypertext's theorists unite in defining the main structural property of hypertext as the link, which is a connecting device. The link may be a word, some words, a multimedia object like graphics, sound etc., or the whole node itself, which transfers the reader to another node, when activated. There is no such phenomenon in the printed tradition. Texts that can be regarded as having a linked construction in print are usually reference and encyclopedic books, where footnotes are regarded as the linked node. This is a format that is rarely found in printed literary works.[182] Although in print, the reader cannot click or point at the text in order to reach another page, footnotes numbers or endnotes numbering function in much the same way.

Media theorist John Slatin (1991), referring to hypertext as a 'system,' a new medium for conceiving text, argues,

> Everything in hypertext depends on linkage, upon connectivity between and among the various elements in the system. Linkage, in hypertext, plays

---

[182] There are some notorious exceptions like Nabokov's *Pale fire* that is a one thousand lines poem and commentary, hence the reader has to crisscross between the poem and its commentary; Pavic's *Dictionary of the Khazars* that is structured as a dictionary by alphabetic order; Perec's *Life, a user's manual* that is a network of stories whose connecting factor is primarily their living in the same building in Paris.

a role corresponding to that of sequence in conventional text. A hypertext link is the electronic representation of a perceived relationship between two pieces of material (161).

Thus, he perceives the link as an electronic connecting device that creates the sequence of text. This seems to be the basic and main difference between print literature and hypertext. While print literature, by its existence as a bound volume of pre-printed text, has a single pre-established order of reading, where the story evolves "according to the law of probability or necessity" (Aristotle, Poetics, Part VII) hypertext has no unique and predefined sequence but many possible ones.

Hypertext, by having many sequences may not adhere to Aristotle's condition of sequentiality as a "necessary or probable result of the preceding action."

> Of all plots and actions the episodic are the worst. I call a plot 'episodic' in which the episodes or acts succeed one another without probable or necessary sequence. (Aristotle, Poetics, Part IX)

Thus, hypertext may tend toward the episodic, which Aristotle regards as inferior since it may "break the natural continuity."

As a mechanism for connectivity, the link can be explicit or implicit. The link gains its blatancy by a typographical sign, accepted by the computer users' community, which is mostly visual. For instance, on the Internet the change of color, the underlining of words, the change of letters' style, and the change of the cursor's form, serves as the agreed marks, which denote the link. However, the Internet norms for formatting links are changing with time, or if you will, developing. In its beginning, the link was marked mostly by a change of fonts' color to blue and an underlining of the words. At the beginning of the second decade of the 21th century the tendency is to drop the underlining of the words, but to hold on to the change of color, although the blue color is vanishing too.

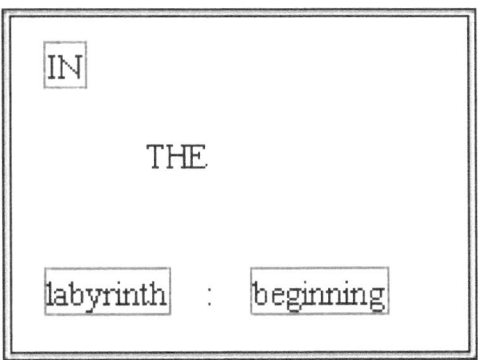

Figure 62 - Marked links - Storyspace software (*Victory Garden*)

The Internet browser is built to identify links by their special HTML tags,[183] thus changing the shape of the cursor into the shape of

---

[183] Hypertext on the Internet is composed in HTML – Hyper Text Markup Language, which is a designers' language constructed of tags, which defines the way in which the text or other objects will be displayed. The browser, the application that

a hand. The *StoryBook* software (*Califia*) works in much the same manner, by a change of letter's color and the cursor's form. The *Storyspace* software, on the other hand, indicates the links, "words that yield" to use Joyce's expression in his directions to the reader of *afternoon, a story*, by encompassing them with a red rectangle when the user hits the Control key. After the reader has seen which words function as links' signifiers, she is free to click on any of them (Figure 62).

An implicit link, on the contrary, will not be visually conspicuous, thus, the reader has to click wherever she feels like, in the hope of finding a link. Even then, she cannot be certain that what she clicked on is a link signifier, as the transfer might be the cause of the default linkage mechanism and not of a particular link signifier. Jane Yellowlees Douglas was teaching a writing workshop in the Macintosh Writing Lab of the Expository Writing Program at New York University in 1987, when she decided to test her students' reaction to electronic reading. She gave one-half of her students Borges's short story *The Garden of Forking Paths*; the others were asked to read a copy of Stuart Moulthrop's electronic *Forking Paths*[184] loaded from diskettes to their Macintosh. She gave her students a brief introduction as to what hypertext is and then they

---

enables us to view the media, "knows" how to demodulate these tags into styles format.

[184] Former title and version of Moulthrope's hypertext work *Victory Garden*, which was based on Borges' story.

began their reading. Their assignment was "to *tell* the story back in several paragraphs." Moulthrop's hypertext version had implicit links. Her documentation of the "test" describes their confusion,

> The students facing the electronic Forking Paths began by attempting to move through the narrative by clicking on words in the text, testing their choices to see if these triggered links with other segments. When, however, the students' original choices failed to connect them to new segments, they took to first clicking on words in the text in a nearly random fashion, in an attempt to see which words in the text might prove to be linked to another node (74).

Hence, the linkage device is important not only as the connecting device that creates the sequences, but it is the means by which the reader can go on reading, as Douglas found in her electronic test. Moulthrop's electronic *Forking Paths* didn't show any linked words and didn't have any navigational tools as the software with which it was read was in developmental stage (beta version).

Landow (1997) observes three variables that characterize the link: its size, its direction, and its structural relations. Link's size refers to both the node and the link signifier. The node is theoretically[185] unlimited, though in the beginning of hypertext the

---

[185] Theoretical because there might be technical constraints though not textual, this should be taken into consideration

preferred size of the node was one-screen size. With time, as the size of screens varies greatly, authors take more liberty with the node's size. The link signifier, however, can be the entire node or only parts of it - one word or a phrase, there is no preferred size for the link in hypertext and it comes in all sizes.

Landow sees two optional linking directions: the unidirectional and bidirectional. While the unidirectional is the basic one, he thinks that a long document with that kind of link disorients its reader. The bidirectional link allows the reader to retrace her steps hence "Its advantage lies in the fact that, by permitting readers to retrace their steps, it creates a simple but effective means of orientation" (11). All the hypertext in this corpus are of the "simple" unidirectional, and yet the software, be it *Storyspace* or any web browser, have a "back" options, thus turning any unidirectional linking into a bidirectional one.

The *structural* relations of the link cover three possibilities: one-to-one, many-to-one, and one-to-many, all common in hypertext. The one-to-one relations mean that one node, or parts of it, is linked exclusively to another node. The second relationship is the many-to-one sort, whereby many nodes, or parts of them, are connected to the same one node, which enables the writer to refer the reader to a single text from multiple other contexts. The one-to-many relation occurs

---

when the author decides on nodes' size, such as available computer's memory, or loading time on the Internet etc.

when one node, or parts of it, is linked to many nodes. This is the case where the node has more than one link signifier, but there is also a possibility that the same link signifier will lead to various different nodes according to pre-defined (by the author) conditions. The one-to-many relation of one particular link signifier requires some programming; hypertext applications, by concept, allow the linking of only one link signifier to one node. In order that the reader will be transferred to different nodes, according to the author's preset conditions, although she is activating the same link signifier, some mechanism, that will record the reader's steps and refer her to "new" nodes according to what she has already read, is called for. Such relations are found in the *Storyspace* software where it is a result of a "conditioned" link, which acts according to preset conditions. In hypertext applications, the author can limit readers' access to nodes by conditioning links availability according to predefined requirements. For example, no links will be displayed if it is the first time the reader reaches this node, but by activating the *Link* button, she can see those other links that are not shown in the text when hitting the Control key, and follow them. For instance, *Victory Garden's* node *Your Generation* has two default links; the one is the regular sequential link leading to node *Resistance?* and the second is a conditioned link to node *Futility*. Thus, the reader can activate the default link twice and each time she is transferred to a different node, which is unprecedented in print literature and impossible to implement, like the beginning and the end of Borges's *Book of Sand*. While node *Your Generation* is part of a path that describes Thea and

Veronica's watching the news of the outbreak of war in Thea's house, and the sequential default node continues the scene there, node *Futility* describes Veronica, still in Thea's house, showing Thea her physical bruises, which she got a few hours ago in the bar where she was working. The scene in the bar is described in another path labeled *Veronica*. The author decided that his reader won't understand the scene at Thea's house without first reading this path and understanding what happened in the bar; hence he created a conditioned linkage that will be available to the reader only after reading the episode in the bar. The conditioned link is found in all the links, the default and the encyclopedic, thus it will be discussed in each sub-section.

The reader needs some clues in order to decide which link to choose if there is more than one. Landow (1987) has recognized this need as early as the first Hypertext convention in 1987, where he talked about what is known in computer science as the "rhetoric of arrival and the rhetoric of departure." Designers of hypertext and hypermedia materials confront two related problems, the first of which is how to indicate the destination of links and the second, how to welcome the user on arrival at that destination. Drawing upon the simile of travel, we can say that the first problem concerns exit or departure information and the second arrival or entrance information. In both cases, the designer/author must decide what users need to know at each end of a hypertext link in order to make an educated choice. The general issue here is one of interpretation, namely, how much interpretation must the designer/author attach (1) to link pathways and (2) to nodes at the links' end to permit them to function efficiently in a multi-user system.

Landow, referring to hypertext systems' designers, does not mean the literary text in particular; on the contrary, he presents conclusions gained by the use of a specific system (*Context32*), which was developed for educational purposes. However, this problem, raised by the link technique, is crucial to literary hypertext poetics as it questions the reader's ability to make an intelligent choice without knowing what exactly she is choosing on the one hand, and on the other hand it questions the ability to regard the reader as a partner of the creative process, hence questioning the concept of the reader as an author.

Slatin (163-165) describes some hypertext systems that inherently allow for different marking of each kind of relations or, alternatively, for a brief explanation to be attached to each link signifier, so that the reader can have a notion of the linked node's relevance and content. This shortage of the linking mechanism, the lack of information where each link leads to, though much discussed in computer science,[186] was only partially remedied by adding to the

---

[186] See Carter, Locke M. "Arguments in Hypertext: A Rhetorical Approach." In *HYPERTEXT '00 Proceedings of the eleventh ACM on Hypertext and hypermedia*, 2000, 85 – 91. Brooke, Collin Gifford. "Revisiting the Matter and Manner of Linking in New Media," in *Small Tech: The Culture of Digital Tools*.

text some scripting. However, it was not applied in most systems that were used for literary works. Thus, usually the selection of links was actually a blind plunge into the unknown.

Though it looks as though the reader has many available options open to her in order to create the sequence of the story by choosing the next nodes which turns her into a co-author, the one that really has all the options is the author. He can link, he can condition accessibility, he can direct the reader by using only default, etc. The reader follows blindly in the footsteps set for her and actually activates her author's pre-set links and has no part in the planning of the work as a co-author should. Furthermore, the trial and error process that this blindness creates, as was observed in Douglass's test, has the qualities of a game and not of a work of art.

In the *Storyspace* software there are no inherent marking options of the relations between nodes, and the reader has to blindly guess where each node signifier will lead. Nevertheless, there is a possibility of bypassing this problem as Moulthrop did with his 'word play' in *Victory Garden*, which was discussed in the previous chapter. The consistent adding of a chosen word to the next node's proposition allows the reader to anticipate what the next node will hold because of cognitive conventions. Another way to allow the reader an insight, or some intelligent selection, is by using the *Link Window* to supply

---

Eds. Byron Hawk, David M. Rieder and Ollie Oviedo, University of Minnesota Press, 2008, 69 - 79.

the reader with clues as to the node's content or function. I found only one writer that utilized this window, for a usage different from technical details and links' names: Deena Larsen in her work *Samplers* exploits it as another writing space. In the *ToolBox* software there is no inherent descriptive attachments to the links as well, though in *Califia* the author tried to circumvent this problem by using long and descriptive link anchors that hold some information about the optional choices. Though this information should have given the reader a better feeling of being part of the creative process, the work is so structured that the reader's collaboration is restricted to only a few fixed options.

Although the technology has come a long way since Slatin's article was published in 1991, there are still no binding conventions at present (2016) for marking hypertext links and allowing the reader an intelligent, clever, selection. Slatin's statements of hypertext's state as a medium still apply today,

> Because the technology isn't mature enough yet to support a single set of conventions, each hypertext system has to develop it's own conventions. [...] thus one element of the hyperdocument will be an ongoing critique of its own procedures (165).

This state of hypertext will last until one prominent company will be powerful enough to dictate its conventions as a binding standard, as has happened in other applications.[187] The general tendency in the field is towards the conventional standards of the Internet, where the "rhetoric of arrival and the rhetoric of departure" are not attended to yet[188]. Thus while the reader of print literature has to find out as she reads the text's inner patterns and paradigms as well as the deviations from narrative conventions, which the text as a literary work employs, the reader of the hypertext work has a double task. She has to uncover the text's modus operandi like a regular print reader, and at the same time to ascertain the hyper-textual conventions, as in the examples cited above, where the link has a major role.

Links can be, and are, classified in many different ways, according to their context, their purpose, or their behavior and so forth. Computer science is engaged with the link phenomena since the format was first conceived and is still seeking for a proper

---

[187] Nowadays (2016) the state of the art is HTML5, a code for structuring and presenting content for the World Wide Web, originally proposed by Opera Software, and adopted by many other companies. Opera is a Norwegian software company that proposed the code to the World Wide Web Consortium (W3C,) which is the main international standards organization Founded by Tim Berners-Lee at MIT and currently headed by him.

[188] The large number of Java scripts and other programming languages' scripts that try to remedy this deficiency confirm a real need for links enlightenment. For instance, see: <http://www.javascriptsource.com/navigation/pop-up-link-with-description.html>, 24.7.2016.

typography. Most of the classifications are binary: implicit/explicit, potential/actual, static/dynamic, strong/weak etc. The most innovative pair is the static/dynamic dichotomy. Static hypertext is mostly combined with strong authoring as Bonder and Chignell (1991) say,

> In a completely static hypertext, links, once authored, do not change over time. [Sic.] A "strong authoring" model of hypertext assumes that the author "knows best." Authors express their vision of relationships within and between texts (nodes), and readers must then discern this structure and respond appropriately when navigating the resulting hypertext (2).

Thus, the static hypertext allows for browsing only, as in print texts, and the reader is the one merely to actualize it, or not. The link replaces the turning of the pages. In this case, the reader cannot be considered as an author since she does not contribute anything, she does not "author" but implement what was authored for her. Computer science regards hypertext static links as having some limitations: "Unfortunately, a number of problems arise during the use of static hypertext technology, namely: disorientation; cognitive overload; inflexibility; higher authoring effort; organization for retrieval: poor and confusing structure; localizing the user" (Tam, 5). Some of these problems are actually hypertext properties that attracted authors to that format: the disorientation that causes the reader to invest more time and cognitive work over the narrative on the one hand, and on the other the inflexibility that leaves the author in control.

Dynamic hypertext, on the other hand, is where links are "created at run-time rather than being generated earlier (pre-computed links) or through modification of or selection from existing sets of links (adaptive links)." (Bonder and Chignell, 3) This mode is called "query-based dynamic linking," where the dynamism is the outcome of a query, thus turning the hypertext system into an effective text retrieval system rather than simply a navigation system and as a hypertext for browsing and might create a personal version of a story like in computer adventure games.

Computer science was and still is much occupied with links' categorization since the link is one of the basic building blocks of hypertext. The literary world, authors and scholars alike, were engaged in the changes that the link will bring to literature, as has been shown throughout this work. The computational category that is most appropriate to apply to the early days of hyper-literature is the static versus the dynamic. While the dynamic link, which is "created at run-time," is the one that researchers hoped for, where each reading will provide a different story, it is rarely found in hyper-literature. The regular links found in hyper-literature are of the static model, which is author pre-designed, necessitates strong authoring, takes a high degree of authoring effort, and actually leaves the author in control.

The author control issue, the concept that the "the author 'knows best'," is not a trivial one but rooted in the base of art and literature. The artist with his genius and exceptional talents is the creator of the unique work of art. Dynamic hypertext is a threat to this absolute status and together with the growing acceptance of different theories of reader response, and of critical interpretation etc. allows for a new concept, the space of the reader. In print literature the reader's space is outside the fictive world. She does not redesign the work anew, but offers interpretations and commentaries. In hypertext the reader's space was placed inside the work and widened into an active part, "real" or imaginary, hence technology people regard static links as rigid and too confined. They want to strengthen this reader's space for more autonomy and freedom. However, they don't hold the artistic point of departure of the author's autonomy and creativity process. In light of the concept of author's control which is held by the static links, the dynamic hypertext creates something that is more similar to a game then to a literary work of art.

Harrison sums the popular classifications in the field and presents another one, based on two principles of linking, "links are semantic by nature and rhetorical in purpose." Hence, she finds seven types of links: authorizing, commenting, enhancing, exemplifying, mode changing, referencing/citing, and self-selecting. Though Harrison is analyzing commercial sites on the net, and consequently their purpose differs from that of literature, her categories are applicable to poetics as well though they should be modified.[189] However the multiplicities of classifications attest to the centrality of the link in hypertext.

One of literature's a-temporal connecting devices is based on analogical and metaphorical relationships that develop wherever characters, events, threads of narrative etc. are placed side by side. Metaphor is a spatial pattern which is not necessarily causal. Hence, linking of two nodes necessarily creates comparison and juxtaposition at the same time which generates a relationship between and among objects, people, actions and reactions, events or occurrences, thoughts, ideas and places. The points of similarity can range from the corresponding or synonymous, a resemblance based on general associations, conventions, and understandings, to the associative, which may be quite private or personal.

Hyper-literature realizes these spatial relationships that in print literature are scattered throughout the narrative as, for instance, is found in *Victory Garden*, when Veronica looks for the bean dip in a party that she is having. She finds it at "the drummer's feet and spent an interesting minute or two slathering it over his facial parts." [*Public*

---

[189] Some of the categories are external to the literary work, for example, the authoring type that "Describes an organization's legal, formal policies, contact information, etc. that authenticate the site and its content." This information is irrelevant for the literary narrative as it refers to the publishing house, copyright materials and other information about the book and is considered external to the work.

Opinion] The "bean dip" is a link signifier, which transports the reader to Thea's house, where she is looking for some food for the hungry Leroy, her son that suddenly appeared in the middle of the night at her doorstep. All she can find is "some stale tortillas and bean dip." [*Into the Country*] The connection, generated by the linkage between the two nodes, creates an analogy between the two different situations in which the words "bean dip" appear. While in the party the bean dip is fresh and edible, though Veronica uses it as paint, at Thea's house the bean dip is stale, although Thea is trying to use it as food, (a dissimilarity point.) The juxtaposing of those two nodes causes the reader to look for an analogy and infer, for instance, that the state of the bean dip alludes to Leroy's looks and situation, and to Thea's marriage. At the same time, Veronica's use of it illuminates the high mood of the party; "The mood was running high even though one of the titular hostesses has just trooped off to the oilfields to defend our western way of life." [*Public Opinion*]

This study, which is specifically about hyper-literature, will focus on the semantic-textual relationship, of which the link in hypertext "is the electronic representation," to use Slatin's words. The interactions are between the base node – the one that allows the transportation of the reader, its label, and its link signifier – and the end node, its content and label. There are two main types of relations between those links: temporal and explanatory. The temporal relations are presented mainly through the default link, where the sequence follows time order, cause and effect etc.;[190] the explanatory relations resemble the relations between a title and its encyclopedic entry, providing expositional data.

6.1.1 The default link

The default link presents the temporal order, which hypertext did not abandon, in spite of countless expectations and hopes for non-linearity or a-linearity. Default is defined in computer science as "A choice made by a program when the user does not specify an alternative. Defaults are built into a program when a value or option needs to be assumed for the program to function."[191] Hence, the default linkage is the one that will be activated if the reader did not choose any other type of linkage and simply clicks anywhere in the node (but obviously not on links) or hits the Enter key. This kind of reading is similar to reading a printed work and the links substitutes the leafing.

On the Internet, in narrative works and even in other texts there is no default reading unless it is specially pre-programmed by the author; the reader must choose a link in order to continue reading. And yet, a default linkage can be achieved by programming, though

---

[190] As hypertext is segmented, in most situations it is hard to discern time simultaneity or co-existence.

[191] "Default." *Bookshelf 2000*, Computer and Internet Dictionary, Microsoft Press, ed. 1997.

it is quite rare yet. For instance, Moulthrop's *Hegiroscope* is programmed to present a preset document every 30 seconds if the reader did not choose a link. Thus the default reading will cause the work to run pretty much like a screensaver, wherein the documents, nodes or pages will change after an interval of 30 seconds if the reader is there to read it or not. The only way to bypass this default is to select a link, though this does not circumvent the time restriction of a 30 seconds presentation in the chosen node, only starts a new count. This is a unique occurrence in hypertext's early stages.

The default in the Storyspace software is activated through the Enter key or by clicking with the pointer on an empty space on the node. If the reader does not want to choose a link, she can also hit the Enter key in order to continue reading, to cross from one node to another, without realizing any of the other links available from that specific node. Deena Larsen, in her *First Directions* (*Samplers*), tells the reader: "Press <enter> throughout the work for an orderly tour through most of the pages." By referring to the default reading (Press <enter>) as an "orderly tour" Larsen implies that there is a preset sequence in the default reading. The author, as in the printed book, has designed and is suggesting the sequence of reading. Hence, activating the default link is similar to turning pages by print readers. Nevertheless, while the reader of the printed book has no other option, but to turn pages, if she is a regular normative reader of course, the reader of hypertext can choose between three ways of readings: reading by default, following links, or any combination of the two.

The book reader can do the equivalent (more or less) but it is unusual and goes against her instincts and certainly against conventions of reading a narrative work.[192]

Thus, the author of a hypertext work has to take into account not only planning the links that branch out from each node, but also the option of a default link. Therefore, the default linkage should be treated and examined as any other kind of link, as it is not an element dictated by the software, but one of the elements that the author creates and is responsible for, moreover: it is intentional from a narrative point of view.

Moulthrop sees the default reading as movement in time, as he states in *Victory Garden* "from one moment to another" [*Welcome*], thus creating a temporal sequence. In *Victory Garden*, *Whitman's Creek* is the first node of path *creek*, declaring Whitman's Creek as one of Tara's attractions. The default link is to node *Meet the Creek*, where Thea is introducing Miles to the Creek. The next node by default is *Anomaly* describing the creek's characteristics. Next in the

---

[192] The default is similar to watching a movie in the cinema – everything is fixed. But if you have a movie on an electronic disk you can skip at any moment to a different place, run forward and backward, retrace etc. Ben Shaul (2012, 2008) created Turbulence, a movie which new format provides smooth interaction and transition between scenes as audience members watch and determine the plot of a movie by choosing on their hand-held tablets one out of two optional points.

default sequence is *Miles in nature*, where we find two additional participants to this expedition, Harley and Veronica. They jump into the water, except for Miles that stays on shore. The next node by default is a description of their pleading with him to come in [*Coming In?*] and in the next default node, we find Miles surrendering and diving in [*Splashdown*]. One of the swimmers tells them about a developer that bought some of the land up stream [*While You Can*]. Harley does not understand what the problem with that is [*Fertile Subject*]. They get out and, while settling under a tree, explain to him the danger of pollution that might be caused by the new development [*Up the Creek*]. Veronica declares that something has to be done [*With a Bullet*]. Suddenly there is a helicopter in the air [*Et Vila*]. The local TV crew has arrived [*Something Happens*]. They videotape, up stream, a small protestation against the proposed developments [*Well in Hand*].

All fourteen nodes are accessible through the default linkage in the above sequence, and the sequence creates a temporal order, as can be seen in figure 63, where the labeled arrows mark the default linkage. Hence, the long temporal sequence is created by the default link that was pre-fixed by the author and is one of the reading options.

Another example of the default link is the narrative path *Thea's War*, reachable via link from the north map of *Victory Garden*. The first node [*Thea's War*] describes Thea and Veronica, at Thea's place, watching the news on the first evening of *Desert Storm*, the Gulf war. While watching, they hold a conversation striving to understand the meaning of this war for America as a nation, and for the world in general. In between this dialogue, the node presents Thea's feelings toward the war.

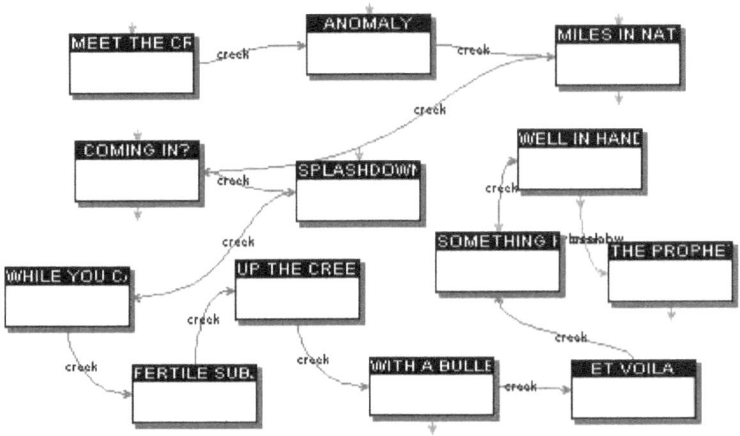

Figure 63 – *Creek* **path and default linkage**

The second node, by default, presents Veronica's feelings and disbelief, while Tea is trying to console her, pointing out that they should have been ready for this war [*Unreal*]. Thea's words serve as a pretext for a summation of the preparations, political and military, which proceeded this night, thus providing the reader with expositional materials without disrupting the temporal sequence [*Buildup*]. Veronica finds it hard to believe that this war is a kind of "plot" [*Games*], but then Thea bursts into a heated lecture about the war, the state of women in the world, and the connections between them [*Big Games*]. Thea notices a necklace on Veronica's neck and refers to it. Veronica tells her that it is an heirloom, which reminds Veronica of her mother [*Heirloom*]. This association is another pretext for providing information about Veronica and her childhood and a way to introduce Emily, her sister, into the story [*Our Mother*]. Thea feels disoriented and uncertain as to her own identity when Emily and Lucy, their mother, are introduced. Tea distinguishes herself from Veronica's generation and says that she's probably older even than their mother, and casually, trying to cause Veronica to open up, asks if she thinks that there will be resistance to the war, thus leading the conversation back to it [*Your Generation*]. Veronica does not answer but have two flashbacks [*Resistance?*]. One is a vision of people's reaction to the news of the breaking of the war, in the *No* this evening, and the other is of her sister, Emily, leaving on her way to the Gulf, where she is serving in the mail squad. All the transitions that are described above are by the default linking.

While the second flashback is fully developed and the reader gets another segment of exposition materials, the first is only partially developed as it belongs to another path. The reader can understand from the flashback people's stunned reaction to the war, but she cannot conceive what is the *No* and what was Veronica doing there. While providing exposition materials and thus closing previous unfelt informational gaps, the story opens new gaps, which the reader cannot overlook and is left unsatisfied, unless she activates a "non-default" link. The phenomenon of gaps in the text is well known in print literature. Yet, if the print reader felt the gap, she has no alternative but to be patient until the narrator chooses to close it. Hypertext allows the reader the option of looking for the "missing information" herself at the "place" of its going amiss. She can activate the non-default link from the word *NO* and see if she can find more information about it, or she can do what the print reader does, wait and see while continuing the default path.

In the next default node, Veronica finally speaks her mind about the war [*Resistance Begins*]. She says that she does not support war and she does not agree with her sister's decision to enlist, but she respects Emily's decision because she respects her. The reader is waiting to hear what Thea has to say to that, only to find out that Veronica is not talking to Thea anymore, but to "the man leaning on the refrigerator," of whose identity Veronica is uncertain. The reader was transferred by the default to another time, another scene. Thea is gone and Veronica is looking for the bean dip, while the subject of the previous conversation, the war in the Gulf, keeps on, though the participants are her contemporaries, her own generation. This node transfers the reader, again by default, to a new episode - the party, and to another time sequence - the middle of the war.

Thus, reading by default keeps a temporal continuity, as the author promised, until the reader is transferred, by the default link, to another path, a new episode, a new temporal order. Using the default link is like reading in the printed book.

The use of the default as a means for creating temporal sequence is not unique to *Victory Garden*, and it is found in other *Storyspace* hypertext narratives as well. In Larsen's *Samplers*, in story *Crossed*

Ends, the labels of the nodes carry the character's name and an ordinal number – Charles 1, Charles 2 etc. Starting with node *Charles 1,* the reader can strike the Enter key, which is like the default, and the story keeps moving from one node to another until she reaches node *Charles 7.* There is no default from this node; it is a dead end, which signifies the end of Charles' story. The closure is stressed even more as there are no other links either at that point. Going back to the beginning of the story, by the aid of the software's tools, like the back arrow or one of the maps, and selecting node *Patty 1* and striking the Enter key continuously, the reader is acquainted with all of Patty's thoughts and feelings in a temporal default sequence. This path ends too when node *Patty 7* is reached, as in Charles' story. Hence, after the reader chooses the initial node, the default linkage keeps her along the character's story and stream of thoughts, until completed. Reading these nodes by the default thus confirms that the numbering is not accidental or playful; they make up each character's story in a temporal sequentiality of its private thoughts. Though the thoughts may be flashbacks to childhood memories, their sequentiality follows the external events in the story, which triggers them. There is no interaction between the characters in the default reading, as the story is constructed out of four monologues (Charles, Patty, Diane and Cherry), keeping a temporal sequence in the literary tradition of the Stream of Consciousness and placing each interior monologue next to the others. There are examples of simultaneous interior monologues in print literature too (Faulkner's *Light in August,* Yehoshua's *A Late Divorce*), yet in print literature the order of the reading is dictated and fixed and does not change from one reading to another. Thus the author commands the narrative effects, while in hypertext Larsen allows her reader to read in any order that she will choose to, thus giving up some of her control over the narrative effects.

Hypertexts that are created in other applications also have a sequential linkage, for instance the "next" anchor link or the "continue," which resembles the "the start here approach." Hence the temporal order is not extinct in hypertext, but the fact that there is a temporal order and a default option is not self-understood in light of the "great expectations" that were discussed in Chapter 2. The argument that has been raised repeatedly throughout this work for hypertext's tendency to retain print conventions can be applied here as well, namely that its novelty lies in the technology but not in poetics. Each reading by default will show that authors keep print conventions.

The power of the chronological order stems from the fact that it is the only order that is latent in reality and not in poetic norms and as such, it is the most familiar order and cognitively it is the most compelling and naturalized one. In real life we perceive actions and events as happening in a temporal order, where one event follows another, cause comes before the consequence, and effect comes after the act. The temporal order is one of the commonest orders of narrative, mostly because of its mimetic force, and yet not much valued as Sternberg (1990) explains:

> Chronological ordering has long suffered from a bad name as an inferior method of arrangement, if artistic or viable at all. Backed by the prestigious practice of Homer and Greek tragedy, Aristotle's Poetics already ranks the "simple" plot, plodding from beginning through middle to end, below the "complex" plot with its unexpected reversals and discoveries (902).

Chronology, as a natural order, is the most legible sequence of reading and of making meaning, and hypertext authors use it to facilitate the comprehension of the text and gain more readers that will explore other ways of reading as well. Authors base the artistic/literary dimension of their work on the foundations of the conventional poetics and utilize the skills of the print accustomed reader. Disturbing the chronological order might disturb the possibility of understanding, unless the disturbance is fairly shallow and there are enough signs, or landmarks, that will lead the reader and help her to find, or eventually reconstruct, that mimetic order. This is similar in print literature and in hyper-literature. Hypertext-literature tries to take advantage of the technological innovations that the medium offers and disturbs the chronological order, at the same time it keeps a path of default (at least in the early works).

But the temporal order can be multi-temporal orders that will create multi possible chronological sequences. Moulthrop states in node *welcome*, "*Victory Garden* is a hypertext - a story, or a web of stories, whose contours can change every time you read it." He refers to the option of the reader choosing different links than those chosen in the first reading and to the option that conditioned links will be available in the second reading by previous read nodes; hence the story will change according to the links activated or ignored. Thus the author can create multiple chronological paths that can replace each other according to preset conditions; therefore, the default link can be also a conditional link. The conditional default link is a unique property of hypertext that cannot be utilized in print literature.

Figure 64 - Two different readings by the default in *Victory Garden*

To illustrate this possibility, the continuum will deal with a second reading that activates the default links of the path beginning with node *Thea's War* in *Victory Garden*, which was discussed above. In the second default reading, the sequence of nodes is different, and some nodes that were read before are not reached at all as is presented in Figure 64. Hence, the second reading activates a conditioned default, conditioned by a first reading.

The first two nodes, *Thea's war* and *Unreal*, are common to both readings in content and in sequence, as they sketch the plot's background, the time, the place, and the general atmosphere in the U.S.A. on the first day of the Gulf War. The main theme of these nodes is the unreality of the situation; the filmy quality of it aggravated by TV reports. The third node reached through the default is different in the second reading from the one reached in the first one. In the first reading, the reader is transferred to node *Buildup*, which is a factual description of the events that preceded the war, albeit through Thea's point of view that goes on to lecture on war as a political game, and from there to the issue of women's rights. The default of the second reading transfers the reader to node *Face the Wall*, which starts a sequence of four nodes, providing more details about Thea and Veronica and their reactions to the breaking of the war, intercepted by the media's reports. The next nodes elaborate on their personal feelings and attitudes toward the war. Thea and Veronica listen to the TV (the TV is turned to the wall), though both think of their own special soldier – Veronica's sister, Emily. While Veronica is watching the houses down the canyon, Thea is watching her, thus providing the reader with expositional materials about her and Emily, and indirectly about herself as well.

Continuing with the default reading (by hitting the Enter key) the two paths, (the first time reading and the second time) unite in node *Heirloom* and then in *Our Mother*. Node *Heirloom* starts with uncommitted words, which are adequate as a continuation to the two different nodes that lead to it: "'I don't know about this', said Veronica." These nodes provide the reader with some more expositional materials about her childhood, her mother, and her feelings towards her.

The next default separates the two readings for good. The first reading brings the reader to node *Your Generation* in which Thea states that there is a generation gap between Veronica and herself, in an attempt to draw Veronica into the conversation. Node *Resistance?* provides the motivation for Veronica's withdrawal, she is thinking of her sister Emily, remembering her leaving on her way to the Gulf where she is right now, in the middle of the war. The last two sentences of the node mark the end of the conversation, "'I wonder,' she said. 'So do I.'" [*Resistance?*] The sentences have a ring of finality about them, which gives the episode a sense of an ending, though the discussion is so bizarre that the reader catches the change of subject only in retrospect, when she continues reading.

The second reading transfers the reader to node *Lucy Reasons*, which continues the presentation of Veronica's mother for three nodes, presenting her activities nowadays. The last sentence of the node has the same tone of an ending, albeit recognized, here as well, only in retrospect.

In summation, we saw two parallel paths that share some nodes between them. Each one is sequential by itself, though one is previous to the other in chronological sequentiality and each is reached by the default way of reading. The path, which is reached first, emphasizes the war in the Gulf in a global perspective, its filmy, theatrical, and unreal qualities as it is presented through the media. The path arrived second, is not a mandatory path, if the reader does not come this way again she will never know that there was an optional default reading.[193] In order for the reader to read the second path she has to reach node *Unreal* again. This path endows the war with a more personal perspective, providing personal details about Veronica and Thea and their personal interest in the war thus it thickens the expositional material but it is not essential for the reader's understanding. The conditioning of the reader's access to the second path by creating a default conditioned link creates a hierarchy between those two paths and understandably so. Only after setting the general situation which operates as an exposition the reader can

---

[193] Print literature does not have the option to hold text that that the reader does not know about. Of course, a book can be made with "hiding places," like an envelope holding a letter – but that turns it into a toy or a game: a book designed like a chest of drawers, some of them are hidden drawers, and thus the reader can miss it.

appreciate the personal point of view of the characters and receive some more information about them. The author created two sequences, each reached by default, but one is the first reading default and the other is the second reading default. Thus the default link will bring the reader to a different narrative content according to the information that the reader has gathered thus far.

An even bolder example of the conditioned default linkage is the programmed mechanism of node *Last Days* in *Victory Garden* that is part of the path describing Veronica's mother and her exploits in the past and present, which has four different defaults. Hitting the Enter key after the first reading of this node, which describes Lucy and her fellow secretaries' interest in "disaster cinema," the reader is transferred to node *Apocalypaso*. This node describes Macarthur through Urquhart's eyes. Those two men have in common "that nasty taste for apocalypse." There is an associative relation between those two nodes; together they describe three characters (Veronica's mother, Macarthur and Urquhart) that are apocalyptically oriented.

If the reader returns to node *Last Days* for a second reading and reads by default again, pressing the Enter key, the default changes[194]

---

[194] The *Storyspace* software has a "history" list so the reader's reading path is documented. As long as the software is open the history list is available to the software and to the reader by the aide of the History button. If the reader exits the software the list is distinct. However, the reader can keep this list by saving the reading.

and the reader is transferred to node *Timely*. This node is a description of Urquhart's feelings that "Something had been at work in the world, some wave front of rapid change only dimly felt but no less powerful for that." The juxtaposing of these two nodes endows Urquhart's feelings with a negative apocalyptic meaning.

Arriving at node *Last Days* for the third time and hitting the Enter key, takes the reader to node *Bird Fiver-Two*. This node brings some citations concerning the B-52 aircraft and a song from "the last war" declaring that we cannot live without armament and wars, thus referring to evils that will bring on the "Last days." This node provides an example for what may cause the materialization of the apocalypse by allusion to Stanley Kubrick's film *Dr. Strangelove* (1964), which satirizes the nuclear scare.

If the reader gets to node *Last Days* for the fourth time in the same reading, and activates the default linkage she is transferred to node *Where Were You?* This node asks the banal question usually asked in disastrous times when people are all excited and shocked at the same time: where were you when so and so happened. The node describes the news pulsing through cables and satellite lines into Americans' homes. This node demonstrates Lucy and her fellow sectarians' excitement brought on by the war, as an answer to the last line of the previous node, which ended with the sentence, "Needless to say, the Gulf War was made for them."

All four linked nodes provide expansions to the original node *Last Days*. The first linkage answers the question – who? By describing other people that are not members of the sect, but never the less have the same apocalyptic attitude, thus the sect people receive a seal of their being normal people and not weirdoes. The second linkage answers the question – when? by describing Urquhart's feeling that this is the time. The third node answers the question – what will bring on the apocalypse? The answer is armament, and the fourth node describes people's reactions toward it.

If these nodes provide only expansions, why limit and condition the reader's access to them? The answer is that they have an inner hierarchy. Without understanding that the apocalyptic notions are not a special whim of Lucy's sect, the reader will treat it as a caprice. Thus, after establishing the apocalypse as a reasonable possibility, the statement that apocalyptic times are now, alerts the reader and causes a feeling of concern for the characters. Not only the time is ripe, the third conditioned default link adds the description of armament that is at hand thus, the concern is heightened as all the necessary conditions are at hand and may be that is the way the story is heading – the nuclear bomb. Juxtaposing these nodes with people's attitude towards the beginning of the war increases the concern for the characters on the one hand, and on the other hand raises the interest of the reader in the personal and global outcome of the war. The hierarchy causes the intensifying of tension as the feasibility of apocalypse becomes tangible and it replaces the chronological order with expositional materials. In addition, this conditioning creates a hierarchy that requires a certain order of reading, thus the author keeps his control over the sequence of reading. This resembles digressions in print literature and on the one hand and analogical relations on the other.

Unlike the default link, which relations to other nodes are based mainly on sequence of events, the conditioned default does not necessarily follow the chronological order, yet it depends on previous given information, without which the information provided by the linked node will be unintelligible or will lose its credibility and importance.

While default reading is an imitation of the reader's habits of reading a book, the main effect of the conditioned default is that of expansions, temporal or spatial. We have to keep in mind that reading by default is the reader's choice. There are other links that the reader can activates in each node, yet she may choose not to. At the time discussed here (the 90ties) hypertext was a fairly new way of reading and had no well-established tradition, thus the author, after his first initial declaration of hypertextuality, backs off and leaves the reader with an optional reading in the style she is used to. The conditioned default linkage creates the effect of choosing even if the reader did not really choose anything but continued to read by default, yet she arrived to a different default with each reading. The second time she arrives at the same node the default shifts, as in the event of activating a link. This shift is unique to hypertext and cannot be done in print literature. The print reader will find the same sequence of pages every time she is reading the same book.

The default link's reading is identical to the leafing in a printed work. It takes advantage of the fixed connections that were created by the author and leaves him in charge, as the reader is following his guidance and the temporal sequences that he created. However, it is the conditioned default linkage that creates a simulation of choice as it takes the reader to different narrative nodes conditioned by what the reader has read before. This is an innovation of hypertext and is not found in print literature. Print literature is fixed in such a way that each time the reader arrives at a page the next one will be the same as in the previous time she arrived there.

The default linkage allows the reader to read according to her regular habits and guarantees a basic orientation and a notion that the narrative has order, sequence, and a customary literary logic. The default reading creates a basis for more readings and grants a "source" text, or a narrative frame for more readings. The changing defaults illustrate to the reader the options of a changing narrative without frightening her and in an attempt to cause her to choose for herself.

6.1.2 The encyclopedic linkage

People turn to encyclopedic books when they seek data: information about dead or alive people; facts, figures and statistics about places; clarification of terms, explanations of ideas etc.

Encyclopedic books have two structural elements, the subject's title, ordered alphabetically, so that people can quickly search for the required topic, and the article itself, the explanation, or information. The encyclopedic linkage in hypertext has the same structure and mainly the same function; the link's signifier is equivalent to the encyclopedic topic, and the linked node corresponds to the article, which provides the information. The signifier of the encyclopedic link, the link's anchor, is mostly a pronoun or proper noun, as Joyce states in his instructions to his reader, "character names and pronouns." [*read at depth*] the reader is supposed to identify the encyclopedic link by herself, there are no special external signs, except for the reader's need for more information concerning a certain name or noun.

The encyclopedic link communicates basic information: detailed descriptions, historical data, sociological or geographical facts, figures, and dates, which are all expositional materials that lay the background for the narrative, even if they appear late in the text's sequence. All the information could have been brought directly in the node, however the author decided to use the encyclopedic device and by that he is making use of the linkage device. Hence, the compensation for the lack of a regular exposition as is found in the printed book is mostly by the encyclopedic link. For instance, in Moulthrop's *Victory Garden*, link signifier "Tara" will always transfer the reader to node *Tara*. Tara is the name of the fictive college town, in which the characters reside. The node provides information about the town: a scenic description, data about its population, reference to its commerce, etc. Through the encyclopedic linkage, the author serves the reader with "objective" like data, though the name Tara carries an inherent allusion. Tara is the fictive name of Gerald O'Hara's manor house in Mitchell's *Gone with the Wind*, called after *The Hill of Tara*, which was the seat of the high kings of Ireland from ancient times until the 6th century.[195] The name of Gerald's manor in Mitchell's novel is motivated by the Irish origin of the family, thus referring to its original meaning, Moulthrop employs its literary acquired meaning, an allusion to a place of war. In *Victory Garden* Tara is a place of war between generations: Thea against Leroy and Emily, a war between conservative academics versus a liberal one: Heidel against Thea and Boris.

While *Tara* is the name of a town, *Heidel* is the name of a character, functioning as a link signifier in node *Chances*. It transfers the reader to node *Academic*, which holds information about him. As the source of the information is the Secret Service's files, the description has an "objective" flavor,

> SOURCE HEIDEL, Erich K. White male age 44, about six feet, 180 pounds, dark hair going grey. College professor, Classical Literature and Culture.

---

[195] See *Tara* in Monaghan, Patricia. *The Encyclopedia of Celtic Mythology and Folklore*. New York: Infobase Publishing, 2009.

Concerned about erosion of traditional values, tenured radicalism, sapping of the moral fiber, promotion of drug abuse and nihilistic behavior, the whole nine yards of the New Right. He could name names. [Academic]

The paragraph starts with Heidel's physical appearance, and though it has little significance in the story's dynamics, it has a rhetorical function, to authenticate[196] the information source as being the Secret Service file by imitating those files' style. As can be seen in the citation the text conveys three important characteristics of Heidel: his professional life as a Classical Literature and Culture Professor in Tara, his interests, mainly his concern with conserving the "old world" and its culture, and his being an informer. A summation sentence that refers to the long list of Heidel's concerns is "the whole nine yards of the new Right. He could name names." While all that information seems quiet objective and authentic, the continuum of the node, its second paragraph, starts: "Madden found himself puzzled and a bit distracted, suddenly out of concentration. He tried to focus on Heidel, sitting across the room nattering on with the usual mix of rumor, fear, and rank suspicion." [*Academic*] The juxtaposing of the two paragraphs poses the information in the first paragraph that seemed objective, in a more subjective light, as

---

[196] The encyclopedic link takes advantage of the encyclopedic information credibility and uses it as a literary device.

Madden recalls Heidel's file as he is interrogating him.

Unlike the sameness of node's title and link signifier *Tara*, the encyclopedic node about Heidel, *Academic*, and its link signifier, "Heidel," differ, although the encyclopedic mechanism is the same: wherever the name Heidel functions as a link signifier, the reader is transferred to node *Academic*. Node *Academic* however, carries Heidel's "neutral" description, a description of Madden's feelings towards him in the second paragraph and there is a third paragraph saying "Something a little too familiar about the case, perhaps?" The word "familiar" in this sentence is a link signifier that takes the reader on a path that describes Heidel's "other concerns" and his past, before becoming an "academic," before becoming Heidel in fact.

While the encyclopedic linkage keeps its neutral or objective voice, as is found in Tara and Heidel's cases, it may present various styles of information. For instance, link signifier "Urquhart" in node *Audience* transfers the reader to node *Timely* that contains encyclopedic information about Urquhart, a "Scholar and showman." The word "scholar," a link signifier in itself, is a neutral observation about the man's occupation, thus an encyclopedic linkage. By activating it, the reader is transferred to node *8088*, which holds the course description as though taken out of the university's information brochure. Though providing details about his scholarly interests, the description characterizes him by the advertising style used to represent his course, a most unusual mode for this type of publication,

> Do you suffer from frequent headaches? Believe in
> extraterrestrial life? Have you ever had an out-of-
> body experience, with or without the use of drugs?
> Do you watch a lot of television? Are you a
> proficient COBOL programmer? [8088]

Except from satirically criticizing advertising methods in general and the universities' marketing methods in particular, the description characterizes the person himself. The second descriptive, "showman," relates to the character's personality and activities. This word too, is a link signifier transferring the reader to node *ShowTime*, where the reader encounters a broken citation from Borges' story *The Garden of Forking Paths*: "… *an indeterminate heap of contradictory drafts…*" [*Showtime*] This citation provides the characteristics of Urquhart as is revealed throughout the story, thus strengthening our previous impressions stemming from the course description.

While the information's styles described above are neutral, there's a characterization style which is subjective, where a character in the fictive world provides the information as in the description of the Runbird sisters, Veronica and Emily. The name *Veronica Runbird* is a link signifier in node *Thea's War*. This node presents Thea's feelings towards the war, while watching the night news with Veronica. The realization of the link transfers the reader to node *Sisters*. As its name insinuates, the node is a description of the Runbird sisters, two of the main characters in *Victory Garden*. The node contains not only a description of Veronica, through Thea's eyes, but also an indirect portrayal of her sister, who is far away in Saudi Arabia and at the same time characterizes Thea as well, "Sometimes, Thea reflected, looking at Veronica was like watching a projection of herself reeled back from twenty-five years past." [*Sisters*]

Another example for the possible subjectivity of the encyclopedic linkage is found in Leroy's (Thea's son) answers about his father. Leroy's father has little to do with the narrated events; his function is mainly to characterize Thea and her generation through their relationship in the past and in the present. Node *Truant* presents a conversation between Thea and Leroy, mother and son, about Leroy's comings and goings. When Thea hears that Leroy left school she cynically comments, "Maybe if Dr. Parker agrees he'll refund the ten grand your father and I just paid out." Link signifier "your father," transfers the reader to node *Your old man*. The change in style in the labeling of the node, from standard language "your father" to slang "your old man," demonstrates a shift in perspective: "father" in Thea's voice turns into "old man" in Leroy's mind, into whose mind the omniscient narrator enters. The node presents a two faceted expositional material, enlightening the reader of Thea's personal status and her former life on the one hand, and on the other hand informing her and the reader of Leroy's life and his attitude towards his parents, as well as stressing the generation gap. For instance, answering his mother's question about his father's doings Leroy answers: ""Not a whole lot. He was real mellow for a change." [*Your old man*]

While the first examples of Tara and of Heidel are presented by a neutral voice, by the information about Urquhart is by indirect characterization of his course's description and by Borge's citations. The Runbird sisters' description and Leroy's father's and mother's descriptions are mediated through a character's consciousness in the fictive world. The Runbird sisters' encyclopedic information is presented by the "personal" voice of Thea, their friend and tutor, "Thea studied Veronica's face in the glare of a long drag." [*Sisters*] While describing them she indirectly characterizes herself, as Leroy's story describes the whole family. Though the nodes are subjective and the narrative technique is a combined expression where the omniscient narrator enters one character's mind yet he keeps to the third person's voice, the nodes follow the encyclopedic linkage traits, by providing exposition materials about the characters, and its being available from various other nodes as in the other examples aforementioned.

The encyclopedic nodes contain expositional information about names, places and objects, and are available to the reader whenever they appear in the text, hence creating a relation of many-to-one. To mention only a few occurrences, node *Tara* can be reached from nodes *John Law*, *Thea's War* and *Emily to Thea* that hold the name Tara. Hence, the hypertext format makes the encyclopedic information more readily available to the reader than it is in print.

While reading a print book, the reader follows the sequence of the book by its pages, presuming of course, that she obeys the "rules of the game," thus the author controls the order in which the reader encounters expositional materials, and provides this information in accordance with his artistic goals and his imagination of the readers' requirements for understanding present events. Typically in print literature there are no repetitions of information even if it is needed again and again and it is difficult to remember (as in a long novel or a saga). The diligent reader will browse back again and again in search of the needed information that she knows she has already encountered.

Thus, while print literature controls the presentation of information and unfolds it as the author thinks will get him the effect he is looking for, hypertext literature more readily provides information and makes it accessible throughout the work, wherever the name of the character, place or the object is mentioned. Hence it is a mnemonic device that provides an immediate availability of the text

The hyper-literature author has at his disposal three linking options. The first one is the prevention of linkage; by not creating any links in a particular node, but the default, the author can control the reading order even in hypertext. This option cancels hypertext's most special trait, the linkage, and turns it into an electronic print book. The second option is to limit some of the reader's branching options, by conditioning accessibility to links according to previous visited paths and nodes. This option also ensures the order of reading; some nodes will not be visited before others. Yet, there are other links to activate so that the text's hypertextuality is kept, the connectivity by linkage, albeit somewhat restricted. The third option is hypertext's unique one. Although the author can limit accessibility, the special mechanism of hypertext creates insecurity and uncertainty of the reader's realization of unrestricted links. It is still for the reader to decide if she wants to activate a link or not, or to read by default or by any mixture of the two. Thus, the author has to enable access to expositional materials from multiple nodes if he intends to control meaning-making and effects. Hence, the one-to-many and many-to-one structure of the encyclopedic link as the Tara link demonstrates so well. This trait doesn't exist in print literature and is unique to hypertext.[197] Therefore the author's control diminishes and the reader has real freedom to influence the material concrete text, unless all the links converge to one place or one end.

The encyclopedic link is not particular to *Victory Garden*. It is found in Joyce's *afternoon, a story* as well. Joyce too uses the encyclopedic link to provide the reader with expositional materials, albeit the information seems somehow confusing, as the narrative itself. Most of the characters' names are linked to nodes that provide

---

[197] Print book version for an electronic reader might override this limitation as the electronic reader allows for searching the text on the one hand, and on the other hand lets the reader to add bookmarks which can help her find a previously marked text.

"encyclopedic" data, meaning expositional material about them. For instance, in node *ax-player*, the name Desmond is linked to node *Desmond*, which provides details about the man, his looks, his status and occupation, his habits etc. Another example is node *I call*, from which ten links branch out. The first one branches from the name *Nausicaa*, taking the reader to node *she, shyly*, which characterizes her through the eyes of the first-person narrator. Another link that branches from the word "Datacom" takes the reader to node *Datacom* that presents the way the machine welcomes its users.

Coverley's *Califia* too utilizes the encyclopedic link in order to present the reader with expositional information. For instance, in Augusta's path, while she is digging she refers to *Whitley Heights*, which is a link signifier [*Augusta 3*]. Following the link by choosing it opens a pop-up window labeled *Whitley Height* that relates some of the history of the place and presents an image of the place. The continuum of the node holds reference to members of Augusta's family and her ancestry. Each name is a link signifier by itself, which opens a window, labeled after the character it discusses, presenting the reader with the character's biography. The bibliographical data is provided in an encyclopedic fashion, in an attempt to create authenticity. Thus, the encyclopedic linkage is exploited to provide expositional materials, create credibility to the story, raise curiosity and interest, and build the reader's expectation.

While the encyclopedic link is found in all the works that were studied, there is a difference in its referents' ontological status. While encyclopedic books refer to existing places and 'real' people, the encyclopedic link refers mainly, and in the case of *Victory Garden* solely, to the fictional world of the work, turning into the work's private, or inner, encyclopedia. This phenomenon is emphasized considerably in *Victory Garden*, as the work combines 'real' events, places, and people jointly with fictive ones unlike *Califia* and *afternoon, a story*. Names like Dan Rather, Charles Jaco, and Nixon, real flesh and blood people alive or dead are not linked or explained. As these names belong to reality, which was inserted into the fictive world, the author supposes that his reader knows who they are exactly like in print literature.

The hypertext reader can always go backwards, retrace her steps, aided by the *Back* button or the *History* list, and resume her reading from the place it was interrupted or continue reading the new paths that she encountered, or even wander into other paths, without ever coming back. This is not done in print literature in normal reading. When the author decides to hold the narrative back the reader has no choice but to comply with his choice. Though she can jump ahead (and also back and forth) and miss some of the narrative, it will not change the work. The hypertext reader in contrast, can change her reading paths and create multi-versions of the work. As a matter of fact, every unconventional act of the print literature's reader (starting at the end, skipping chapters, marking places in the text, writing notes at the margins etc.) is realized in hypertext whether on a shallow level or a profound one. The difference between print literature and hypertext is found in the presentation of the text: while in print it is fixed and all the reader's acts do not change the text (for the second reading or for another reader), hypertext creates several texts that (in some applications) can be saved and restored or, if not, are ephemeral. This is the result of the combination between seg\frag and the linkage concept. And yet, the author can keep his control over the text in full or in different amounts of partiality. A full waiving of control gets us closer to the game and may eject the work from art's domain.

The author takes advantage of the encyclopedic linkage in order to achieve the informative function, to present expositional materials, as well as other functions like attaining several texts out of the hypertext work by transferring the reader from one narrative path to another thus creating storylines ramification. The multi-storylines are typical to hyper-literature and one of the reasons that authors turned to the format of hypertext in the first place, as an attempt to achieve Borges' *Forking Paths*. The branching of the hypertext work revokes the monolithic author's authority and creates a variety of liberties and creative personal options for the reader, at all levels of the narrative.

In summation, the link is the unique phenomena of hypertext and its main apparatus of connecting and ordering. While in print literature the order of pages and reading-conventions generate the order of reading that allows the author to take advantage of it and produce the effects he desires, hypertext's ordering device is the linkage. The link allows for more than one order thus it is the sign of a possible freedom, a promise for an independent creation of the narrative. And yet the links' signifiers and the connected nodes, the transfer, are all controlled by the author so much so that a minute and intricate planning by the author can create a strong impression of freedom even if the work is totally dictated and controlled by the author. Through the links the nodes are assembled into narrative sequences, to episodes, that are called in hypertext - paths.

6.2 The path

In communication, the path denotes "a link between two nodes in a network,"[198] where one node is the starting point and the other marks its end. In hypertext, each time the reader passes, by default or by activating a link, from one node to another she pursues, or creates, a path. Print literature holds only one single path, there are no alternatives, and the path is controlled by the author who has laid it before his reader.

In hypertext, author and reader alike create paths. The author, as part of the creative process, structures them according to the effects he wants to achieve, thus presenting potential ways of reading and creating meaning. The reader is the one to actualize their potentiality

---

[198] "Network", Microsoft Press® Computer and Internet Dictionary.

by choosing between optional reading courses. Each time the reader follows a default linkage she decides to follow the author exactly as she would have turned a page in print literature. Though paths are latent and predetermined in the work and the reader cannot add to them, the reader, by other methods of reading like using navigational tools that are generic to the reading/writing software, can create, de-facto, new ones ad-hoc, single and unique for the specific time and place of reading and of reader. For instance, reading by nodes-labels' alphabetic order or reading first all the nodes starting with the letter A, she creates her special sequence of path. This reading is not dictated by the author or the software with which the work was written. It's the reader's creative decision and choice, and the author enabled it.

There are two kinds of authorial paths: the episodic[199] path and the traversal one. In the episodic path, nodes are organized in temporal sequential chains, namely chronologically, which create coherent episodes, available to the reader mostly through the default mechanism, reading by hitting the Enter key, or through a lack of any other alternatives as I have shown in the previous chapter. Hence, the path is 'episodic' as it holds mainly one sequential event.

Episodic paths are similar to episodes in print literature; both are segments of what is called in print literature "story lines." For

---

[199] By "episodic path" I mean a hypertext path which is part of a longer story but which is viewed as complete by itself.

instance, Austen's *Pride and Prejudice* has at least four story lines: the story of Elizabeth and Mr. Darcy, the story of Jane and Mr. Bingley, the story of Mr. and Mrs. Bennet and the story of Lydia and Mr. Wickham, each built out of multiple episodes of which some are shared.

Episodes in hypertext follow the well-established structures of print literature. For instance, in *Victory Garden*, the *Harley* path holds (apart from the first node) seven sequential nodes. By hitting the Enter key, the reader can read them consecutively, in the sequence presented by the arrowhead links (see Figure 65), as they unfold an episode in a chronological order, though some nodes hold links to other nodes. The path is predefined by the author and the reader can leave it by activating links. If she chooses to read by the default linkage she will read a whole episode.

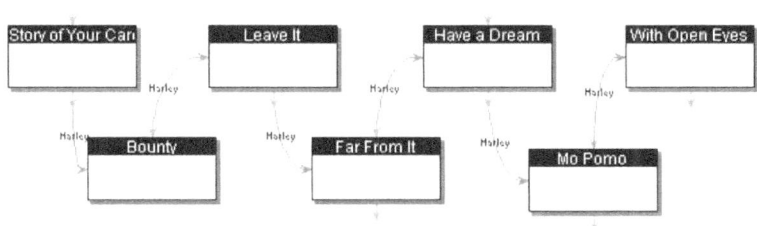

Figure 65 – Harley path map in *Victory Garden*

Harley path episode is about Urquhart and his friend Harley, a week or so after Emily's departure to Fort Benning. Urquhart gets up in the morning to find Harley, a black reporter who is supposed to be in Bahrain, asleep on the floor [*See No Evil*]. They breakfast over a melon on the terrace, and Harley tells him why he is not in Bahrain and that his latest story, "Bounty of Shame," has lost priority to the Desert Storm coverage [*Story of Your Career*]. The next node describes Harley's latest work, "Bounty of shame" [*Bounty*]. Harley says that he took a 'stress leave' as he has strange dreams [*Leave It*]. Urquhart answers that dreams are no excuse to leave a job since everyone has them and asks what does Harley's shrink thinks about it. Harley says to Urquhart that since he is interested in dreams he will tell him one [*Far From It*]. Then he goes on to tell a scary dream he has [*Have a Dream*]. The next node is an expansion of this dream, as it was experienced the night before [*Mo Pomo*]. The conversation and the description of the dream continue into the next node (*With Open Eyes*). Although the conversation is between the two of them, they have a visitor, a grackle that covets their breakfast. His responses to the conversation create a comic relief, until Urquhart tosses over the rail half of the melon and the grackle flies after it. The conversation is over and so is the episode.

While episodic paths make up the core of the work, traversal paths, as is implied by their name, bridge between two paths. In this sense they resemble the linkage device, since they connect two nodes in order to create a passage between two paths. Thus, the traversal path holds only two nodes. One refers to the previous path, the one the reader has just read, and is more often than not its last one. The other refers to the next path and is mostly its beginning point, hence both nodes are members of other episodic paths.

Except for a direct access from the *South Map*, which is one of the navigation aids available in *Victory Garden*, Path *Harley* can be reached from twelve other paths. Two of them are traversal paths: *see no tube* and *postparable*. Each holds only two nodes, and both belong to other paths as well. For instance, path *see no tube* first node is *Daybreak*, which is the last node in path *tubes take,* the second one is node *See No Evil*, which is the first node of path *Harley* (Figure 66).

Tubes take (episodic) –The last node is Daybreak

Path see no tube (traversal) – nodes Daybreak and See No Evil

Path Harley (episodic) – First node is See No Evil

Figure 66 – see no tube – a traversal path in *Victory Garden*

Node *Daybreak* is the last node of path *tubes takes*, which is quite a long path, holding sixteen nodes, describing the media's coverage of the war, in a fragmented style, resembling a TV watcher's zapping between different channels, presenting the starting events of the Golf War in January 1991. Node *See No Evil* is the first sequential node of path *Harley*, which, chronologically speaking, takes place three month before path *tubes takes*, "It was early October, a week or so after Urquhart watched her get on that bus to Fort Benning, a few days into his life of unforeseen solitude." The traversal path is a chronological passage point from later events to previous ones, and creates a gradation from path *tubes take* to path *see no evil*. After the jumpy style of the media, we turn to one specific reporter, to Harley, whose position we cannot understand unless we understand the significance that the media ascribed to the war's coverage three months before it actually took place. The stressing of the chronological position of the two paths creates a feeling of closure in the first path *tubes take*, and a feeling of beginning in the second path, although it is actually a digression.

Another example of the traversal path is path *dressing up*, which holds two nodes, node *Speaking of U...* that is part of path *so on*, and node *Whitman's Creek* that is the beginning of path *creek*. Path *so on* describes the university's Halloween party and its special subject – heroes. In order to understand the traversal we have to look at the whole previous path, which starts with node *Our Heroes* that presents the popular masques, in which the Gulf war is having a considerable presence. The description of the disguises continues in node *Absent Brothers*, with a note of solidarity with the ones gone to war. Node *Going West* describes Harley, Veronica, Macarthur and Tate's disguises. In node *Decline of Man* they are talking about "something on the air" when Thea joins them dressed up like Marilyn Monroe. Her dress has a built-in mechanism that causes it to float up in order to show "Affixed to the front panel of her tap pants was an inverted but very accurate life mask of her colleague, Erich K. Heidel." [*Doubly Incorrect*] Thea explains that Boris has constructed the mechanism and everyone wonders where he is, as "dressing up is sort of his thing." [*Speaking of U...*] The words "dressing up" are the link signifier that takes the reader to path *dressing up*.

When first arriving at node *Witman's Creek*, the reader cannot see the connection between the previous scene and the present one. The node lists Tara's attractions and states that one of the great inducements to visit the city of Tara is Whitman's creek. The default linkage takes the reader to an episode situated at the creek, where Miles is dressed up in Boris's swimsuit,

> "In," Miles repeated. He glanced down at himself. Somehow they had inveigled him into a pair of Urquhart's bathing trunks, these enormous baggies which seemed to be, well, enameled with day-glo images of 747s, ocean liners, stretch limousines, machine pistols, and other tokens of American Affluence as seen by a Chinese pieceworker. Miles wasn't sure he wanted to know what the suit looked like once it got wet. [Coming In?]

His feeling about the Boris bathing trunks is similar to the feelings the others have in the Halloween party.

Traversal paths are found in Joyce's *afternoon* as well. For instance, path *out asks* is constructed out of two nodes; the first belongs to path *wife*, labeled *asks*, and the second, labeled *CT* belongs to path *Connecticut*. The traversal path connects the present discussion, in which his friend asks whether he will mind if he will sleep with his wife (ex-wife actually), to past memories of his life as a married man. The reader follows the narrator into a path of memoirs, the same as in the case where Veronica thinks about her mom, which was discussed before.

Thus, the traversal path is a trail that contains only two nodes, each a member of other fully developed paths, and thus it links those paths. The first node is usually one of the last nodes of the first episodic path and the second node is mostly the first node of the second episodic path, the linked one.

The developers of the *Storyspace* application, bearing in mind the concept of the path and its importance, decided to present it visually through a variety of maps and a *path* window. The *Storyspace* "map view" is a graphical cognitive map, which presents the path: the nodes, the links between them and the order of default linking, as is shown in Figure 65, which presents the *Harley* path, a graphical presentation of the default. This is also a way to lead the reader in both meanings: to lead her through the available links, which denotes the author's control and to help her orient in the text. The map creates a fixed ant stable infrastructure for some of the story's components and constitutes a grid or base, to which the reader refers in her choices. From this point of view the map exposes the skeleton of the relationships between the story's components and thus reveals its devices. In the printed text the reader produces this kind of map (sort of) while reading or after the reading in order to uncover the story's "skeleton."

Figure 67 – The path window[200] in *Victory Garden*

The structure of the path to which the node belongs to is available throughout the reading process in the *Path window*. As can be seen in Figure 67, all the node labels, which make up the path, are listed on the left side of the *Storyspace* main reading window, in the *path window*, which is a concatenated narrow frame within the main window, actually another graphical way of presenting the default, the pre-ordered sequentiality. The frame carries the path's label, in this example – *Harley*. The concatenated window allows the reader to choose her way and override the default textual links' order or

---

[200] "Path window" is my term for the window that resides on the left side of the screen (can be hidden by the reader if it disturbs her) and presents all the nodes that are included in a path.

constrains. Reading these nodes in succession reveals that the path is a coherent episode though not all the nodes are necessarily accessible through the default mechanism, as some of them are conditioned by preliminary reading of other nodes and an untimely reading of them does not make sense to the reader.

Comparing between the nodes that construct the *Harley* path in the cognitive map (Figure 65) and the ones that the path window lists (Figure 67), shows that there are more nodes in this path than the map reveals. This is due to the fact that the map holds only the scene between Boris and Harley, which is contained under node *See No Evil* as can be seen in Figure 68:

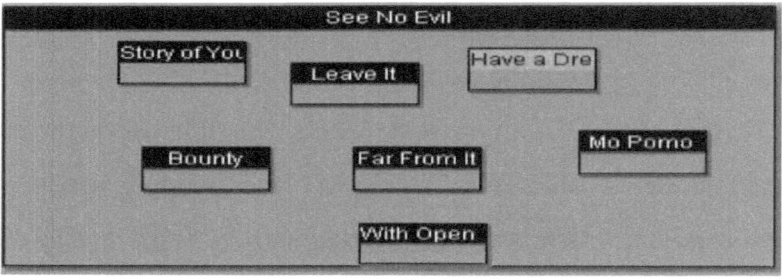

Figure 68 - Node's *See No Evil* contained nodes in *Victory Garden*

The path starts with node *Sisters* that takes place on January 15, late at night, and presents Veronica and Emily through Thea's eyes by private observations and meditations. Node *Thea & Harley* is linked associatively to Thea's thoughts, as Harley, who is at the narrative present Veronica's boyfriend, was once Thea's lover. Node *Glorious* demonstrates Veronica and Harley's relations, thus continuing the associations started by Thea. Chronologically speaking, the temporal position of these nodes is latest. The ones that construct the *Harley* path, according to the map view, occur at the beginning of October, which is the earliest. The last five nodes, which are missing from the map view as well, describe a previous episode, on the same day of Thea's observations. Hence, the *Harley* path holds three temporal lines, which take place in three different places with different people. The earliest that is presented in the cognitive map, is situated at Boris's apartment and only Boris and Harley are present. The second takes place at the *No* Café, where a crowd of students watches the breaking up of the war on the TV news. The latest episode is enacted in Thea's living room, where only Thea and Veronica are present. They watch the war that has just started on TV. While the *Harley* path holds three different moments in time, the map view presents only the default linkage, which presents only one point in time that is also a subject unit and the others are digressive ones that belong to other paths as well.

The path window is a major deviation from regular print literature. In printed literature there are no skeletal maps or lists for reference. The print reader, while reading, constructs hypotheses, which he adjusts throughout the reading. She may make lists of names, places, episodes, dates, she may draw a map or a graphic chart of the flow of the plot (linkage) etc. but usually these aids are not available from the author. Still – they may be there in principle, and some works actually include such aids like the *Laxdæla Saga* that includes a Genealogical Tables, Glossary of Proper Names, Maps etc. A genealogical map is found also in Gabriel Garcia Marquez's *One Hundred Years of Solitude*, treasure maps in westerns and house and ground sketches in detective stories etc. The path window and the graphical maps are generic tools that allow the reader to see the overall plan one the one hand and on the other hand to disregard the plan, choose at will and override any preplanned paths, sequences and conditions.

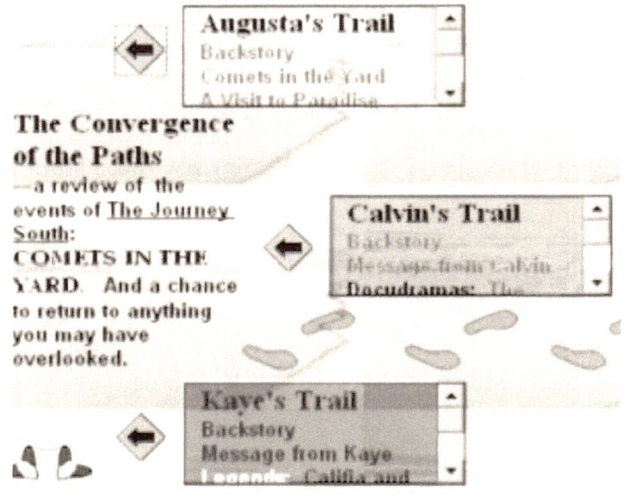

Figure 69 - Califia, node paths

A close look at *Califia*, which was composed with the *ToolBook* software, does not reveal the make-up of the paths as was shown above in the *Storyspace* application. The narrator declares, "Califia is organized into four journeys." [*with delight*, 7] The journeys are four narrative parts; each describes a different expedition, according to the four celestial directions. However, the narrative "trails" are three, one for every character that is taking part in this hunt, as can be seen in Figure 69, which is the main part of a node, labeled *paths*. As the node's name implies the node holds links to each one of the three trails. Thus, the node functions as a Table of Content that allows the reader to reach the starting point of each path. Not only its function is special, its availability is unique too; this node is available to the reader through the entire reading session. Each node in *Califia* has at its left-bottom an icon of a pocket compass that allows the reader to navigate quickly to one of four chosen ways. The right arrow takes the reader back, the left one – forward, the upper one presents a history list and the downward arrow sends the reader to *Paths* node, as the author attests, "The **bottom arrow** takes you to an index at the convergence." [*Pocket Compass Page*, in the Help File] Hence, though the aids are different they are all the same there, ready for the reader in time of need.

The 'index' presents the three trails. Augusta's trail, as the author declares [*Forking Paths*] is "the chronological narrative"; Calvin is the history man, "Calvin's Path – thematic organization, back-yard snooping, and docudramas"; Kaye's path is "legends, family myths, geological certainties", hence she provides solar tables, star maps, geological and typological data, and legends. Thus, in *Califia* the reader is not presented with the spatial connections between the nodes or the paths and the graphical maps are special to the *Storyspace* software.

Web hypertexts, like *Califia*, do not show a *path window*. Thus, the reader cannot see the path visually. However, it employs other devices to denote a path, by exploiting the node's typographical properties like fonts' styles and colors or background colors or other structural and visual devices. A close inspection of Moulthrop's *Hegirascope*, which is written in HTML code and is viewed in any Internet browser, reveals that the work is constructed out of 20 paths, mostly holding eight nodes each (14 of them, the others have a variable number of nodes). Each path, which is characterized by a common background color and in many cases a common label[201] as well, is also a subject unit. For instance, the light-olive path (in HTML code color #999966) labeled "Drivers" is about Gina and Bent setting at dawn on their way from Dallas to Manhattan. The path, holding 10 nodes,[202] is a description of their journey's events. All the nodes, which have a lime colored background[203] (#FFFFCC), compose the story of the retired Mr. Perlmutter and his car, his two wives, and his hobby of flattening out tires. Other typographic devices, except the background colors, may be used too. For instance, Deena Larsen in

---

[201] Not all the nodes that construct a path have the same label, but in cases where all nodes have the same label, we can speak of a path label.

[202] The path contains files HGS012.html, HGS013.html, HGS052.html, HGS096.html, HGS097.html, HGS133.html, HGS134.html, HGS165.html, HGS166.html, HGS168.html.

[203] Files HGS232.html, HGS233.html, HGS234.html, HGS245.html, HGS246.html, HGS252.html, HGS253.html, HGS256.html.

Seed Voices, in Storyspace, one of the stories that make up *Samplers*, differentiates between two paths by attaching different font's colors to each path. The story presents two attitudes toward an accidental pregnancy; the father's attitude, who is surprised and feels trapped, is presented in black fonts, and the mother's feelings towards it are presented in green fonts. Not only do the colors differentiate between the paths, they express the attitude as well. The black color stresses the father's anger and harshness towards the woman, while the green color has a meaning of growth and novelty.

Thus, the episodic path in hypertext is a structural device that denotes a whole scene, episode or a story line. It follows the temporal order, unless it is a traversal path, the function of which is to connect two paths. Although not all applications provide the reader with a view of the path, as the *Storyspace* software does and in several modes, there are other ways in which the path is presented and emphasized to the reader.

The listing of nodes and paths and the graphical distinctions of paths are unique to hypertext literature and are rarely found in non-experimental print literature. This phenomenon seems to be a way of compensating the hypertext's reader for the fragmented nature of hypertext. The reading tools like maps, listing of nodes in the path window, the marking of paths by colors and font's styling of size and color are all intended to help the reader become familiar with hypertext and facilitate her reading in the unknown format. The different tools are great strangers to conventional print literature yet they illustrate the extent of author's control over the reading sequences. The same tools that aid the reader help the author to create the optional paths throughout the work.

6.3 The network

The multi-fitting of one node into many paths caused hypertext theorists to regard hypertext as a network of nodes, as Bolter (1991) observes, "In place of the static pages of the printed book, the electronic book maintains text as a fluid network of verbal elements" (4-5). This network is an optional one, which needs a reader to realize it by choosing between the possible available nodes, a reader that interacts with the text to materialize the network.

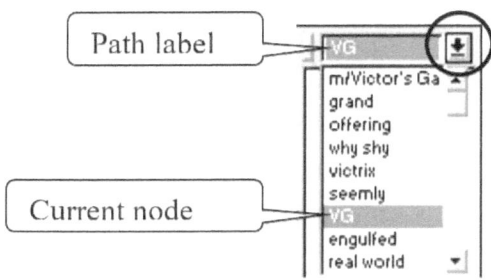

Figure 70 – Open Path window in *Victory Garden*

In the *Storyspace* application, the multi-fitting is presented visually and graphically. The graphical view, which is based on various maps, has already been discussed. However, there is a textual view that is reached by opening the *Storyspace path window*. Next to the path's label there is a small arrow (Figure 70) that allows the reader to open a list of nodes. The list presents the reader's current node (marked in gray) as a "member" in the *VG* path, and all the other memberships in other paths are listed as well, thus every node is an intersection between other nodes, yet there are some nodes that function as huge junctions and are members in many paths.

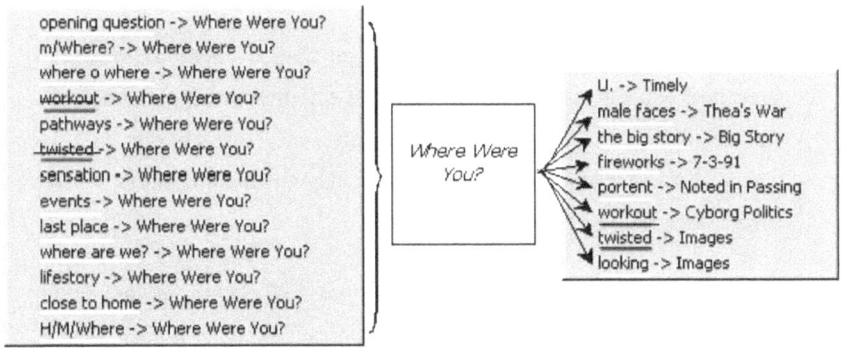

Figure 71 - Links leading to and from node Where Were You?

(*Victoy Garden*)

Node *Where Were You?* in Moulthop's Victory *Garden* is a big crossroads of paths and nodes and therefore is a good example for this multi-fitting of one node into many paths or episodes, the network structure. The node is reachable from thirteen other nodes (See Figure 71) and eight optional links branch away.

The first line of node *Where were you?* poses a formal question (hence its label), "where were you when the news came?" The phrasing of the question,[204] about the breaking out of the news, and not of the event itself, creates a detachment, which suggests two of the subjects of this hypertext work. The first one is the observer, the person who watches the action and does not partake in it, in contrast to the participant.

Where were you when the news came?

You might have been among the half million shipped to Armageddon, in which case it was no news to you.

Or perhaps like the rest of us you got caught looking. Maybe it reached you on the air, down from the satellite, pulsing through the cable, all those male faces taut with excitement, with concern, with the rush of the big story. Did it catch you at your evening meal, a blast from decades past?

How did it make you feel – scared, depressed, elated, unreal? When History unfolded around you, did you see it as a poison flower (fucked, like the man say, down to its eternal root), or did it seem to you a fantastic firework, some gorgeous portent of the skies?

Figure 72 - [node Where were you? Rectangles mark unconditioned links]

---

[204] Node *The Place of Big Winds* is linked to node *Where were you?* via a text link that is anchored on the word "question."

The node poses a dichotomy, between participants in a war and the rest of us, observers. The participating troops are not this node's subject, which is emphasized by the fact that the sentence, which refers to them "the half million shipped," does not hold any links, yet it is needed in order to define the observers. The point of focus of this node is the observers, their reactions toward the event, which unfurls in the next paragraphs, and the optional ways in which the news, as a product of the media, could have reached them.

The node describes in an indirect and metaphorical way the multimedia means through which the news reached the observers, which is the second subject of the work. The news came "down from the satellite, pulsing through the cable, all those male faces taut with excitement, with concern, with the rush of the big story." The reference is to the media's mediating channels: the satellite, the cables, the reporters; yet, we are still in the dark as to what the news is, what is the big story.

The next paragraph refers to the onlookers' feelings, "scared, depressed, elated, unreal?" presenting the possibilities with some elaboration, but leaving them merely as options. Thus the node is a reference to an impressive event, unspecified yet, experienced by most of the world through the TV medium, causing the observers various contradicting sensations. This simplification and generalization enables the integration of this node into so many paths. Node *Where were you?* functions as a junction in thirteen traversal paths (marked in white in Figure 71). The node is part of two long paths (marked in black). The structure of nodes linked by multiple paths to multiple nodes is what caused researchers (Bolter 1991, Landow 1997) to regard the hypertext structure as a 'network.'

The first path shown in Figure 71 is *opening question* where node *Where were you?* is its second and last as it is a traversal path. The path takes the reader from path *help* that holds only three nodes *Welcome*, *Enigma*, and *The Place of Big Winds*, all are reached through the default linkage. Path *help* is one of the optional links branching from the cover-page thus, having an important structural role as one of the first choices available for the beginning of the reading process and, at the same time having a poetic role as it holds reading instructions and a declaration of intents.

Node *Welcome* informs the reader of the reading options available to her in the new medium, hypertext. The default link, and the only one available from this node, leads the reader into node *Enigma*, which is a continuum of the previous explanation, describing the loop-phenomena in hypertext and how the reader can find links that will help her out. By default, and again as the only link available from this node, the reader is transferred to node *The Place of Big Winds*. This node holds the narrator's declaration of intents, and a comparison between the two World Wars and the narrative's present, 1991, "Now we find ourselves living once more through world conflict." There is no clue as to the referred "conflict," neither in the node's label nor in its content, and the reader will have to go on reading in order to find out which conflict the narrator refers to. The narrator distances himself from the events and reflects on the post-modernistic universe, which "looks suspiciously like a Garden of Forking Paths." The author's objective is not to resolve the above-cited issues but "to put some stories in motion." This multiple stories concept is found in Borges short story *The Garden of Forking Paths*, where it is told about but not materialized.

Borges' short story is regarded as the conceptual poetic model of hypertext. The story holds two spy stories. The first is the actual story of Dr. Yu Tsum, former professor of English who became a German spy on English soil, and who is trying to convey to Germany the whereabouts of the new British artillery park on the River Ancre. The second spy story is the story of the search for Ts'ui Pên's novel and his labyrinth "in which all men will become lost" (122). One man holds the solution to both stories, Albert, whose name is identical to the name of the park that Dr. Yu Tsum wishes to convey across the channel and the one to decipher the mystery of the novel and the labyrinth by understanding that they are one, "the garden of forking paths was the chaotic novel" (125). The explanation for that is that

> In all fictions, each time a man meets diverse alternatives, he chooses one and eliminates the others; in the work of the virtually impossible-to-disentangle Ts'ui Pen, the character chooses – simultaneously – all of them. [...] Fang, let us say, has a secret; a stranger knocks at his door; Fang decides to kill him. Naturally, there are various

> possible out-comes – Fang can kill the intruder, the
> intruder can kill Fang, they can both live, they can
> both be killed, and so on. In Ts'ui Pen's novel, all
> the outcomes in fact occur; each is the starting point
> of further bifurcations (125).

The simultaneous occurrences of all things and the choosing of all the options create the concept of an infinite work. This concept is like the concept of an interactive network. All the nodes are present in potential and the reader is interacting with them simultaneously by activating links, even though sequentially. Thus, the node, *The Place of Big Winds* in *Victory Garden*, as a garden of forking paths itself due to its seven links, leading to other nodes that are huge junctions by themselves, takes part in a virtual network of nodes and links which explains how multi-paths are created and how one node can participate in so many different paths without losing its narrative meaningfulness.

This multi-path to and from one node to another creates the concept of hypertext as a network, and its dominant property as a connecting device, virtual or material, is spatiality. Literature, however, is not a spatial art. Unlike sculpture and painting, which present shapes, or objects, in space or in a mimetic space respectively, literature portrays characters and events in words. It tells a story, where the characters and their exploits are presented in words sequentially one after the other. Thus, in literature, spatiality can be conceived as re-construction of sequential words that connect across the text, or texts, as opposed to connections between objects in space.

Such a connection across the work in print is achieved by the motif that bridges over time and place and the reader keep meeting along the reading process. This can be found as a cyclic link in *Victory Garden* where Veronica looks for the bean dip in a party that she is having and was presented in Chapter 6.1 - The Link.

Another example of the spatial connections in a hypertext work, also taken from *Victory Garden*, starts (or continues, as the order is irrelevant) in node *Our Mother* that presents Veronica's thinking about her mother and her relations with her, which caused her to leave home, "The day after her fifteenth birthday she left for good." The words "her fifteenth birthday" are linked to node *Absence of Boris* that presents Boris's students reactions to his recurring absences. The last reactor is Amanda, about whose words the narrator comments and excuses, "You could say things like that when you were a fifteen-year-old Presidential Research Fellow." Amanda's age "fifteen-years-old" is a link signifier to node *Into the Country*, where Thea listens to her son's words thinking "… but this was still pretty impressive for fifteen-and-half."

The three concatenated links create an analogy between these three fifteen-years old youths that appear in different situations and in different contexts; Veronica, who left home due to disagreements with her mother, Amanda who is a university student with a

Presidential scholarship, and Leroy who decides to drop out of school, as he feels ready for life: traveling through America and playing in the streets. The "similarity point" which links these three youths turns the age of fifteen into a turning point in one's life, while at the same time juxtaposing three common youth types without imparting any evaluative judgment. This analogy, or motif, creates spatiality across the text exactly as in print literature.

Aarseth regards reading a hypertext as an activity of "mapping the network,"

> There are certainly narrative elements in the text working to achieve coherence and meaning, but there is also an opposite force, a destabilizing disfiguration that bears down on the reader's patience and sense of progress. To counter this antihermeneutic circle, the reader has to become a metareader, mapping the network and reading the map of her own reading carefully (94).

For him understanding the hypertext work, which he regards as "sabotaged narrative" (94),[205] is by the map that the reader creates while reading as she maps the work's network. And yet, while talking about hypertext structure he attempts to provide a different term for

---

[205] Aarseth is actually talking about Joyce's *afternoon, a story* but he refers to it as an example and prototype for hypertext works.

hypertext then 'network.' Aarseth's rejects Eco's (1986, 80-81) division of labyrinth into three types: linear, the maze and the net. He regards the inclusion of the net along with linear and maze as inappropriate since the net structure has "very different qualities from the other two. Especially as the net's 'every point can be connected with every other point'" (6). Surveying briefly the development of the term, Aarseth accepts the labyrinth metaphor and discerns two different types. The first is the labyrinth as the unicursal structure, which has a single non-branching path yet difficult and winding, and the second is the multicursal, which is "the bewildering chaos of passages that lead in many directions but never directly to our desired goal" (5). While in early times the labyrinth was unicursal or multicursal, had "a harmonic duality" (7), the Renaissance model was pure multicursality and "we now regard *labyrinthine* and *linear* as incompatible terms, and since the labyrinth no longer denotes linear progress and teleology but only their opposites, its status as a model of narrative text has become inapt for most narratives" (7). Therefore, he regards hypertext as "a dense, multicursal labyrinth, and the reader becomes not so much lost as caught, imprisoned by the repeating, circular paths and his impotent choices" (91). Meaning, Aaseth disapproves of researcher's enthusiasm for hypertext's superiority and says about print literature: "But if codex text allows two basic ways – homolinear reading (with the line) and heterolinear reading (tmesis) – the hypertext structure of nodes and links only allows one: hyperlinear reading, the improvised selections of paths across a network structure." Aarseth sees in hypertext the familiarization of the reading process: "in *Hegirascope*, on the other hand, the reader is forced to reflect on the project of reading, the use or futility of it, in the most dramatic way yet invented" (80).

Ryan (2001) likens reading hypertext to playing a game while referring to the labyrinth metaphor:

> Approaching the text as computer game, some readers – here I speak for myself – experience it as an imprisoning maze of secret pathways devilishly designed by the author to make them run in circles. Their goal is to navigate the system with a purpose, thus escaping the tyranny of the labyrinth master, and the means to this goal is the reconstitution of the underlying map of the network. [...] Finding this hidden treasure is the reward for having played long enough with the text – for having conquered the labyrinth (183).

Thus, conceptualizing hypertext as a game where the reader/player has to find the hidden treasure, the key fragments of the text, which become her reward.

The network is the outcome of the multi-options that are laid before the reader together with the reader's input, which causes the realization of the network potential. By choosing a link the reader creates an interaction with the text, thus hypertext is regarded as interactive literature. Ryan (2006) finds a conflict between interactivity, which "involves a nonlinear or multilinear branching structure" whereas narrative meaning "presupposes the linearity and unidirectionality of time, logic, and causality" (99).

Ryan regards these three as the most prominent concerns of interactive narratology: the structures of choice (textual architecture), the modes of user involvement (types of interactivity), and the combination of these parameters that preserve the integrity of narrative meaning. Hence, she distinguishes (2001, 246-258 and 2006 100-125) nine interactive structures of narrativity that are "a function of the architecture of its system of links" (246), which are not limited to the electronic media but can be found also in print literature. *The complete Graph* is a network where "every node is linked to every other node, and the reader has total freedom of navigation," which is like Aarseth's 'net', and can be found in print only in Marc Saporta's *Composition No 1.* that is actually a deck of cards that should be arranged by the reader. This is not print literature proper, it is a game. The second structure is the architecture of *The Network*, where "paths can be uni- or bidirectional." This is "the standard structure of literary hypertext," a structure where "the reader's movements are neither completely free nor limited to a single course." Hence, this is the model where the author may share some of his control over the narrative with his reader. Ryan says that this model may be suited in print literature to "a system of analogical connections or for a Dadaist/surrealist carnival" (248). Again, this "carnival," is actually anarchistic, experimental print "literature" as much as Saporta's, namely hardly literature at all. The third interactive structure is *The Tree* architecture that has one starting point, but many diverse endings and the reader's navigation is limited from top to bottom without any circuits, hence the author does not lose/share his control with the reader. The print example that Ryan proposes is the *Choose Your Own Adventures* children's stories. Again, this genre is not proper narrative fiction. The fourth structure is *The Vector* network, which has defined beginning and ending points, one "determinate story in chronological order," and links, which allow the reader to take "short side trips to roadside attractions." *The Vector* network describes quite accurately the structure of *Tristram Shandy*, but the format of print makes the trips obligatory and not optional, since they are embedded in the text.[206] *The Maze* is the fifth narrative structure, in which "the user tries to find a path from a starting point to an end point." The reader, or player as this structure is common in electronic adventure games, is not confined by links, but by riddles and tasks, which have to be accomplished in order to reach a goal. However, the player may not reach the end but waste his "lives" and die, which will end the interaction. Ryan's *Maze* architecture corresponds to Aarseth's multicursal labyrinth, thus both of them talk about narrative that is found in adventure games and not literature. The sixth interactive structure is *The directed network*, which resembles a flow chart, "horizontal progression corresponds to chronological sequence, while

---

[206] Unless they appear in the text as appendixes, thus they are not an integral part of the linear order.

the branches superposed on the vertical axis represent the choices offered to the user." This architecture has one definite starting point and all nodes and links are directed toward an ending point, followed by hidden other endings. The navigation is by the reader's choices between alternatives. While the reader chooses an alternative, she abandons many others. Though Ryan gives as an example for this model, the story of *The French Lieutenant's Woman*, it resembles the model only in its multiple endings, since it does not allow any choices throughout the reading process, as the model allows. Hence, it is rare narrative literature. The seventh structure is *The Hidden Story* architecture that "consists of two narrative levels: at the bottom, the fixed, unilinear, temporally directed story of the events to be reconstituted; on top, the a-temporal network of choices that determines the reader-detective's investigation of the case." This architecture, unlike the previous ones, does not refer to links and the navigational possibilities they present to the reader, but to the relations between the sequence of reading (the upper level) and the temporally reconstructed narrative (the bottom level). While the upper level is the reader's interaction point with the text, the sujét in formalistic terms, the bottom level is the reconstruction, the fabula, which the reader can reconstruct only after she finishes the reading process. This model is "the fixed, unilinear, temporally directed story" which is the main model of print literature, where the reader has to reconstruct the story. This model does not require any interactivity except that of interpretation and meaning making. *The Braided Plot* is the eighth interactive structure that presents a "multistranded but determinate narrative." This architecture refers to narrative units and their location in terms of fictive time and space. Reading in horizontal axes presents simultaneity and the vertical axes present space. This model is not found in print literature since it allows the reader to choose her way of reading while in print literature this way is fixed and pre-determined by the author.[207] The last architecture, the ninth, is the *Theme park model*, which is called by Ryan "Action Space, Epic Wandering, and Story-World." This model "is an epic structure of semi-autonomous episodes in which the user plays a largely passive role." This model presents narrative free navigation between episodes; however, each episode is constructed out of a number of nodes where the traversal function is preset by the author. Ryan's print literature examples for this model are Gabriel Garcia Márquez, Isabel Allende, Gunter Grass, Patrick Chamoiseau and, of course Boccacio. This model fits likewise any story collection since the reader can choose where to start and which will be the next.

The six foremost architectures in Ryan's typology of interactive narrative structures, The complete Graph, The Network, The Tree, The Vector, The Maze and The Directed Network refer to navigation possibilities between nodes as a combination of two factors, which have several different statuses: links properties (limited or free,

---

[207] And yet there are such works. To cite Ryan's examples: The Lurker Files, a campus-life mystery by Marc Ceratini formerly available on the World Wide Web, or Ayckbourn's play *The Norman Conquests* trilogy, which somewhat resembles this model.

unidirectd or bidirected) and the existence or absence of starting and ending points and modes of closure. The last three architectures, The Hidden Story, The Braided Plot and Theme Park model refer to other factors: the order of reading versus the order of the reconstruction or fabula, the relations between events in terms of fictive time, space and characters, and the relations between nodes and episodes. These modes can exist jointly with each of the other six architectures, because they refer to events and characters, which can be presented by any link with or without a starting and ending points. It is quite expected that a multi-linked architecture will produce a-temporal stories that the reader will have to reconstruct, hence the two levels of the seventh mode. Thus, only the first six architectures can be regarded as networks models by hypertext properties of links and nodes. Ryan mapped these networks since in order to find the interactive texts narrative potential, however as the various designs show, the networks models are not unique to hypertext or to interactive texts. They are present in print literature as well.

Print literature was perceived as a network, in which there are spatial links between events, characters, objects, words etc. even before hypertext was introduced to the literary domain. Literature was already regarded as a complex network of networks, of phonemes, signs, words etc. De Saussure discerned, in his seminal lectures that were documented by his students, between synchronous linguistic relations, which are static in time, and diachronic linguistics relations that refers to the language's historical development,[208] and by that turns language into a network. Hence, the selection from the diachronic repository of possible characters, events, and actions, into a unique synchronous text may create many possible story-lines as Bolter (1991) notes about Homer's oral poetry,

> Established by repetition in the minds of both the poet and the audience, the Homeric network contained all the mythological characters and theirs stories. The poet drew upon that network to tell each tale (113).

Here 'network' denotes the crossing between a reservoir of characters, relationships and events, from which the author recalls his narrative materials into the synchronous and multiple possible narratives.

---

[208] To cite De Saussure: "To synchrony belongs everything called 'general grammar'; for only through linguistic states are the various relations involved in grammar established. [...] In practice, a linguistic state occupies not a point in time, but a period of time of varying length, during which the sum total of changes occurring is minimal. It may be ten years, a generation, a century, or even longer. A language may hardly change at all for a long period, only to undergo considerable changes in the next few years. Of two contemporary languages, one may evolve considerably and the other hardly at all over the same period. In the latter case, any study will necessarily be synchronic, but in the former case, diachronic" (99-100).

Barthes (1974), who regards the ideal text, the writerly text, as a plurality of networks (5-6) dissects the literary text into *lexia*, units of reading, which he categorizes according to his "five codes": hermeneutic, seme, symbolic, proairetic, and cultural. For him "each code is one of the forces that can take over the text (of which the text is the network), one of the voices out of which the text is woven" (21). Barthes sees the text as a network of codes, which structure the single literary text.

Hypertext was defined as a network by its creators and researchers as a result of the structure of nodes, which are simply "chunks" of text as Nelson says, and the links that connect them together. The network structure is created by the author that enables the connections between nodes, through the linkage device. Thus, computer science refers to the network from a structural point of view as there is a visual resemblance between a sketch of hypertext's nodes and their links and that of a network. Poetics' concept of network is mainly abstract and reconstructed as it refers to meaning, as Barthes says: "The five codes create a kind of network, a topos through which the entire text passes (or rather, in passing becomes text)" (20). The network which is created by the five codes is not a structural one but a thematic one, a network of meanings. Hypertext has the power, through its network structure, to concretize the abstract networks of meanings. In this sense it is indeed a "sabotaged narrative."

Hypertext is considered as a medium, which enables the legible presentation, the concretization, of the thematic, poetic, and verbal networks, as Bolter attests,

> The invisible network of associations becomes visible and explicit to an extent never before possible. (The network can never be fully explicit, however, because the verbal ideas of the text will always reach out beyond any given electronic text to all other texts that the writer and reader know) (113).

Hence, the main difference between a reading of hypertext and print literature reading is the structural options that hypertext allows. While hypertext network's architecture enables the author to present his reader with optional choices of sequences, print structure allows a single sequential turning of pages. All the choices have been already made by the author in print literature, while in hypertext they remain to some extent to be made by the reader.

As has been discussed above there may be different modes of links' systems, thus creating various interactive layouts as was shown by Ryan. Yet, not all the different interactive modes that were described by Ryan suit hypertext literature structure. The most common in hypertext at the time is *The Network* mode, where links can be unidirectional or bidirectional. Some of the modes are not suitable to hypertext literature at all like *The Maze* mode, which is characteristic of adventure games.

In conclusion, the combination devices of hypertext are the node and the link, which create the hypertext narrative structure. The link can be a default one, meaning a predefined sequence that the reader will reach if she won't choose a specific link. The link can be an "encyclopedic" one and contain expositional material that is needed so that the reader will be able to understand the background, time, characters, and events. The link can be a combinatory device by creating analogy between time, place, characters, behaviors etc. Links and nodes create paths of reading. Some are sequential reading paths and some are traversal, generate the transition from one episodic path to another.

This structure gives its reader the notion of freedom, or the illusion, to roam the text at her will by activating or ignoring links, and yet the author's tight hand is felt on the "reins," which conditions and directs the reading process according to his objectives. Thus the author uses the combinatory devices of the multicursal network in order to control "the bewildering chaos of passages that lead in many directions." (Aarseth, 5) If the freedom is too much and is real we leave the literary domain and move over into the domain of games, amusement, carnival and anarchism. Indeed, there are authors that reached out to the experimentalism in an attempt to overcome the fixed and stable character of the literary text, but they are the exceptions, that deal mainly in the revealing of the device and with the surprise effect that comes with defamiliarization. Hypertext defamiliarization is manifested in electronic narrative games.

Conclusions

At the end of the 20th century, Information Technology presented the world with a new writing format – hypertext, created by piecing together nodes and links. Literature's scholarly community perceived this format as a way for realizing structuralist and post-structuralist ideas, and as a way for creating a 'new literature.' There were great expectations of the new medium for breaking and exhausting print literary conventions and their problems. To mention only a few: breaking off the linearity of printed narrative and finding new possibilities; turning the reader into an author, hence realizing Roland Barthes' "the death of the author;" erasing the literary work's borders and concepts of closure, unity, and between literature and other texts thus questioning concepts of the text's uniqueness; the integration of the arts, Multi-Media.

In an attempt to prove their concepts and expectations, some literary scholars themselves became hypertext writers; for instance, Joyce, Moulthrop, McLaughlin, Coverley. They aided *Eastgate Systems, Inc* mainly in developing hypertext applications, tested the new format potential by writing hypertext fiction, and researched it, all at the same time.

This study employs a comparative methodology to locate the differences between print literature and hypertext in order to determine whether hypertext created a 'new literature', a new genre, new textual norms, a significant novelty as was expected, or whether it is only an expansion of the experimental printed literary tradition aided by technological tools, namely, a realization of old existing norms.

The work includes a historical description and poetic analysis of hypertext works during the 15 years of intensive preoccupation with the hypertext format by developers, authors and researchers alike. The hypertext corpus was selected to represent the whole spectrum of possibilities in hyper-literature, to cover the hypertext applications common at the time and to present the whole term of hypertext's prosperity, mainly between the years 1985 to 2000.

The first hypertext, Joyce's *afternoon, a story* (1986) was written in *Storyspace*, which was developed by Michael Joyce and Jay David Bolter who met at the Yale Artificial Intelligence Lab (1984). They presented it before Mark Bernstein, the founder of the *Eastgate Systems, Inc*, who decided to adopt and develop it. In 1986 Michael Joyce wrote *afternoon, a story* as (among other things) the "test file" for the *Storyspace* software, and in 1987 *Eastgate* started publishing hypertexts that are claimed to be "serious hypertext, fiction and non-fiction: serious, interactive writing."

In 1987, Apple Computer Inc. released *HyperCard*, a hypertext software, the availability of which, on all Mac computers, turned it into the second most practiced software for hypertext literature (the first was *Storyspace*) even though for a short time. Moulthrop's *Victory Garden* (1991) was first written in *HyperCard* that year as

Moulthrop attests: "My hypertext called "forking paths," which was a sort of low-grade literary pastiche concocted as a laboratory demonstration--or parlor game--for an undergraduate writing class in 1987." In 1991 *Victory Garden* was published in *Storyspace* format as a fully-fledged fiction and replaced the *HyperCard* pastiche. Larsen's *Samplers* (1997) was written with *Storyspace* application and presents a hypertext story collection option. The latest is Coverley's *Califia* (2000), which was written with the *Toolbook* application. The study refers also to two web hypertexts: Geoff Ryman's *253* (1996) and Moulthrop's *Hegirascope* (1997 [1995]). These hypertext works are compared with various print literature works, starting with Stern's *Tristram Shandy* (1759-1767), through, to mention only some, Dickens (1860-61), Apollinaire (1913-1916) Robbe-Grillet (1959) to Morrison's *The Bluest Eye* (2007).

The novelty of the format caused all authors to provide their readers with reading directions, since the new format required various navigation/orientation aids that were not available in the printed book due to five hundred years of print tradition that did not require any. In hypertext though, even after fifteen years of the medium's existence, authors still continue to provide their readers with reading directions. For instance, Stephanie Strickland's *the Ballad of Sand and Harry Soot* (as late as 1999, found randomly on the net) has on its "cover page" a link called "How?" that takes the reader to node *How to read the Ballad*, which sketches three ways of reading: "Random reading", described as "Choose any gray zero from the navigation bar at the bottom of the page in any order you wish;" "the Complete reading," that states "Choose *begin* and click on each image until you return to the beginning of the poem;" and "the Link-Driven reading," which is the hypertextual way of reading. Four years later Milorad Pavic (2003) starts his web hypertext *The Glass Snail* by explaining,

> You can choose yourself which of the two introductory chapters you will read first and with which of the concluding chapters you will end the story. The path you choose will influence the line of the story and its ending. If you wish, of course, you can read the story several times in different orders. The rest is up to the writer (intro.htm).

These explanations are quite similar to the 'directions' that were found in initial hypertexts. However, after fifteen years of hypertext literature's existence there is little excuse for these guide lines unless authors still feel insecure as to their readers' acquaintance with hypertext literature, as the format did not become prevalent and obvious, and since hyper-works on the Internet allow for a great deal of variances in reading methods and options.

Hypertext, as a literary medium, is indisputably quite different from print. While the printed book is a material object that we can touch and hold, hypertext is a digital entity depended on machinery, electricity, and software for its existence. The digital object changed the experience of reading by bounding the reader to a reading site (at the time the only "hypertext machine" was the personal, static computer), by the change of light requirements (the computer does not require light as reading a book, the light comes from the computer itself) and mostly, by the new textual structure and innovative navigational tools.

Still, hypertext did not change most of the typographical structures of print works. Hypertext's typography maintains print typographical conventions: hypertext is a verbal text (printed words), occasionally with visual images (illustrations), the node functions as a page and the text is scattered on page/node, and there's a leafing through pages, though in hypertext it is by links. Hypertext works still keep to print literature main typographical structural characteristic properties as well, such as the title page, and those that come on a CD-ROM and diskettes have a cover page as well (Chapter 3); there is a fixed beginning point similar to print literature (Chapter 5); the main typographical (and structural) change is the alteration of the place of literature work's 'end' though, poetically speaking, hypertext literary works end too where there are no more links or when the application is closed, which imitates the "no more pages" or the closing of the book. *Califia* presents a declaration of an end by the closing of the application, which is similar to the act of closing a book.

Scholars regard hypertext as a fragmented text, since the structure of nodes and links, where the reader is the one to combine into a story, is based on many nodes and links. This subject is discussed in some length in Chapter 4 which reveals that hypertext is much less fragmented typographically than the Futuristic movement writings in printed books in the twenties of the 20th century. Nor is it fragmented in the sense of the 'new novel', where time, places, events and people are juxstapositioned by the linear sequence of the book. Though hypertext is divided into segments they are combined into paths, which keep a temporal flow as opposed, for instance, to Robbe-Grillet's works, which "continually reverses our expectations from sequence to sequence, and from paragraph to paragraph – and even, occasionally, from sentence to sentence" (Yellowlees 2000, 94) The node can be likened to the printed page, while the path is like a chapter or a story line, thus substituting the medium size structural unit found in print literature.

The main innovation of hypertext is its visible combinatorial pattern, the link, which connects the nodes together into multiple potential sequences. The node may be a segment or a fully developed story or any other partial or fully developed object. Thus, hypertext provides its readers with optional or multi-reading paths, though they are carefully premeditated by the author. If the reader follows hypertext's reading norms, namely activating links and interacting with the text, she is actually realizing the options that the author laid before her. And if the reader chooses to follow the default linkage she is following another premeditated story line that mostly follows the chronological sequence. Thus, though the author is the one to lay out all the possibilities, the reader has a feeling of creation, of innovation, involvement and intervention, autonomy and responsibility, participation in the composition of the work in a greater measure than that of the print reader, despite the author's control over most of the hypertext work, which is almost absolute.

The linkage device binds the nodes to each other and creates sequences of narrative. All the links are characterized by their connection function, which is one of the options that the work, actually the author, provides the reader with in order to continue reading. However there are links that have additional functions: the default linkage, which also simulates the temporal sequence as in the printed book; the encyclopedic linkage, which additional function is to compensate for the lack of an exposition, and for the throwing of the reader into the midst of the action, which is inevitable in a multi-choices work. Some analogous linkage simulates the motif device in printed works, by creating inner, outer, antonymous and synonymous connections within the text and between texts.

By choosing links, multi-optional paths of reading are created, so much so that one reader may read quite a different story, meaning different *sujét*, than another (not a different *fabula*), and even the same reader will find in repeating readings - different stories. This creates numerous different effects, since each reading is only one performance out of many possible of the same work. However, this does not change the work as a whole, meaning the reconstructed *fabula*, exactly as multi-readings of Fielding's *Tom Jones* will not change the work, though the second reading will certainly be different from the first one etc. The effects the work will create through the processes of multi-readings will be different, but not because the work itself has undergone any changes. Moreover, all these effects may be claimed to have been planned intentionally by the author.

The binding of nodes by links creates the path that is, from a narrative point of view, a story line. The connection of one node to many others and into multiple story lines caused scholars to use the metaphor of network when referring to hypertext narrative structure in order to explain its distinction from the linear structure of printed texts. However, as hypertext is two-dimensional and a network is a three-dimensional object, some caution should be taken in the practice of this metaphor in relation to hypertext. Even more so, the concepts of the term 'network' in literature and in hypertext theory vary so vastly.

Network in literature can denote a network of voices and codes as Barthes sees it, or a reservoir of characters, episodes, story lines and verbal fragments as Bolter sees it. However, the act of reading is a linear action, and even if a number of nodes are presented simultaneously to the reader she cannot read them all at once, but one at a time because of our cognitive limitations. When the reader interacts with the text by choosing a link she actually chooses the next segment of reading, creating sequentiality, thus flattening the text into a printed text. And yet, hypertext, by the linking of two nodes together, brings the referential and invisible network of associations to the surface of the text, thus it becomes visible and explicit, and hence the reader has to relate to them and cannot ignore or regard them as unimportant. Meaning, there are many stories under one cover, but each one is linear. The innovation is the multi-stories mode.

Hypertext became the hot subject in literature studies between the years 1992 and 1998[209], raising many expectations among scholars and readers alike. However, nowadays, after almost twenty years, it seems that literary scholars abandoned hypertext poetics and embraced the term as a buzz word denoting non-linearity, fragmentation, endlessness, chaos etc. in print literature. Landon Brooks (1993) in a review of the hypertext science fiction *Beyond Cyberpunk*[210] predicted:

> Better add "hypertext" either to the list of words
> you've already heard waaaay too many times or to
> the list you know you'll be hearing waaaay too
> many times in years to come. You know the list;
> top-heavy with "de-" and "post-" prefixes, it has
> recently grown fond of "hyper-" and "cyber-"
> anything. Former nosebleed theory words like
> "deconstruction," "decen-teredness"
> "poststructuralism," "postmodernism,"
> posthumanism," now have to compete in the

---

[209] Judging from the number of articles and books that dealt with the subject.

[210] *Beyond Cyberpunk* is a science fiction that was developed with the HyperCard software in 1991 by Gareth Branwyn, Peter Sugarman, et al. and is available nowadays on the Internet: <http://www.streettech.com/bcp/>, 24.7.2016.

buzzword marketplace with "hypertext," "hyper-media," "cyberarts," "cybercrud," "cyberculture," and, yes, that golden-oldie- "cyberpunk" (449).

In order to check when hypertext lost its place as the hot subject it used to be in the academic literary field I searched the Muse Project® web site. The Muse Project "is the trusted source of complete, full-text versions of scholarly journals from many of the world's leading university presses and scholarly societies, with over 120 publishers currently participating," and covers the fields of literature and criticism, history, the visual and performing arts, cultural studies, education, political science, gender studies, economics, etc. and is one of the academic community's primary electronic journals resources. The search was to find when the interest and curiosity of literary scholars was lost, thus it concentrated around the years 1991-2004.

The search term "literature" in "All Fields w/Text" brought up 32,549 answers, out of which only 395 answered the refinement of the search into "literature AND hypertext" in "All Fields w/Text," namely only 1% of all the articles that use the word 'literature' use the word 'hypertext' as well. Narrowing the search, once again, into "literature AND hypertext" in "All Fields w/Text" and "AND 'criticism' in LC subject," which resulted in 68 articles, meaning 17% of all the articles that have the words 'literature' and 'hypertext' are categorized under criticism.

A check on all 395 articles that were found in the "literature AND hypertext" search was performed to see what they were about (literature or hypertext), and if they were about literature, in what way they refer to hypertext. After filtering notices and indexes there were 295 articles left. Each one was opened and a search for the word 'hypertext' was done to find out in what context it was mentioned and if the article was about hypertext's poetics. As can be seen in Table 1, in the year 1991 only 4 articles answered the criterions of the search, 3 of them were about hypertext's poetics and none about print literature. In the year 2001 19 articles were found, out of which 13 were about the hypertext format and none about hypertext's poetics.

Subject	1991	1992	1993	1994	1995	1996	1997	1998	1999	2000	2001
Hypertext poetics	3	0	2	3	0	12	15	0	1	1	0
In print literature	0	0	0	0	1	1	0	1	1	2	0
The hypertext's format	1	1	1	4	4	12	8	8	15	20	13
In education	0	0	0	0	2	2	0	0	7	1	4
Reference to books about	0	0	0	0	1	1	2	2	1	3	2
Total Sum of articles	4	1	3	7	8	28	25	11	25	27	19
Hypertext's percentage	75%	0%	67%	43%	0%	43%	60%	0%	4%	4%	0%

Table 1 – Divergence of articles by years

As can be seen in Table 1 and in Table 2, in the year 1991 75% of the articles that were about literature and hypertext discuss hypertext's poetics, none were about print literature. While the number of articles that indicate the interest of computer science and hypertext's researchers reached its peak in the years 1995-1996 (15 articles dealt with hypertext poetics and 8 with computer science line of interest – the hypertext's format) only sporadic reference to the format is found in literature's poetics. However, these years mark an inversion of tendency, as hypertext's poetics articles are running out and print literary are embracing hypertext as a metaphoric term.

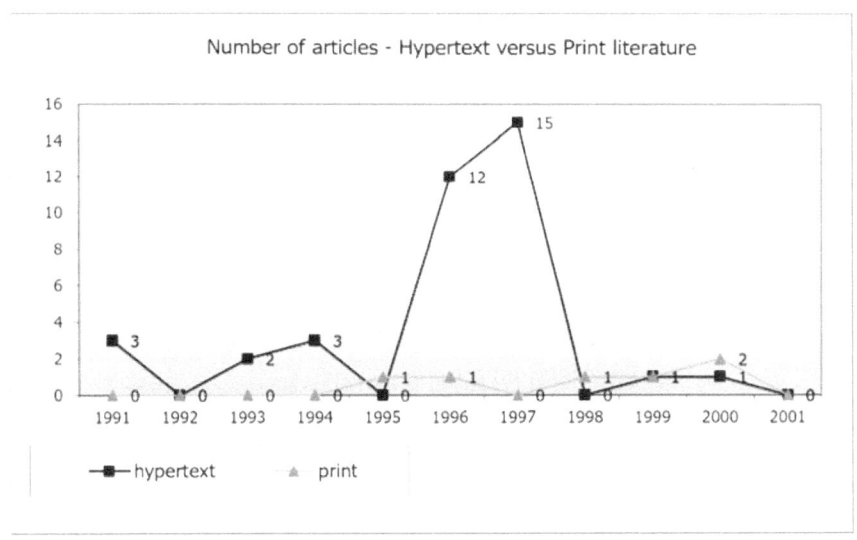

Table 2 - Hypertext poetics articles

The final confirmation that hypertext has turned into a metaphoric-technical term and lost its poetic glory was found in a "what's new" email from the Eastgate company, which turned to be their advertisement for moleskin notebooks and leather journals:

Florentine Journals[211]

We've just received a batch of truly impressive, hand-crafted leather desk journals from Florence.

These are permanently-bound, permanent books. They have great paper, great binding, great detailing. And, frankly, they're an indulgence.

Sometimes, a durable, functional journal is exactly you need. But some journals and notebooks are going to be your companions for a very long time:

- lab notebooks

- lecture notes

- your next novel

[...]

So, if you've got notes that will be on your shelf forever, not in a box in the attic, do take a look at these notebooks. (1.2.2005)

The Eastgate publishing company was one of the main forces that advanced hypertext publishing and research. Its turning to paper notebooks and journals attest to people's difficulties in changing their

---

[211] <http://www.eastgate.com/catalog/ItalianJournals.html>, 24.7.2016.

habits, thus paper and print is overriding the electronic text. However, as long as hypertext is the standard code of publishing and writing on the Internet it is here to stay.

In summation, it is obvious that some of the many promises, hopes and expectations that were pinned on hypertext were not realized, and hyper-literature stayed close to conventional norms of reading. At places where the expectations for innovations came true and caused a loss of significant narrative qualities, where a clear deviation from print conventions occurred, there is a compensation for the reader in the form of a creative game, the reader gets some interactive activities (interesting or boring, yet a game). However, this "game" depends on the linkage that creates the sequence of reading and that is hyper-literature's main innovation.

While in print literature there is only one fixed and undisputed sequence of text, hence of reading, hypertext presents multiple sequences. The multiple sequences are created by the author as he wrecks, breaks up intentionally and interrupts the narrative common model (print) into smaller parts and fragments the sequence into many small narrative pieces. Since this wreckage is premeditated by the author the combination of which results in different versions of the same narrative that may be compatible with each other or mutually exclusive, as was demonstrated in Emily's fate, in Moulthrop's *Victory Garden*, (did she come back alive or didn't she?). This is quite a change, a novelty, since the order in which the reader meets the texts is important to the overall meaning of the narrative (Poe, 1850 and Perry, 1979).

The hypertext technology enables the actual implementation of the theory of deconstruction: the text is no more a fixed and stable sequence that is controlled exclusively by the author who directs the narrative effects, its meaning and interpretation. It is a "sabotaged" text that is decentered and has to be re-constructed by its reader. The author is, of course, the one to prepare for the reader the optional connections by creating the links and the options of combining them so as to create narrative reading paths, and yet by the mere creation of the multi-options he gives up some of his undisputed control. Still, as long as there is no "high interactivity," where the reader can compose nodes of her own or add internal and external links to the text, the author is the one to prepare all the performative options and sees to it that all of them will have esthetic and emotional qualitative effects. Thus the reader's sensations of participation and the creative feelings are performative experiences and not reading experiences.

The experience of creativity and performance caused researchers to regard computer games as the continuity of hyper-literature, and as its development. In computer games too, the designer is the one to build the dramatic world and the player can act by the pre-designed rules and options that were laid for him. However ludologists (scholars of games studies[212]) did not see hypertext as their ancestor and they are trying to fend off any attempt to relate narratology to computer games.[213]

Hypertext turned into an arena of competition about order's sequentiality, coherence, meaning, causality etc. which is the materialization of the Derrida's critical concept of de-centralization of the narrative/tale/text. The reader can enter from various points of entries (after the initial "begin"); she can explore different places and leave through various other nodes (if there is no "exit"). What used to be in poetics a philosophical proposition and an interpretation proposal - has turned into a real and practical practice of de-centralization.

Hypertext allows a real avant-garde phenomenon: the abolition of the author's control (Barthes and the Derrida – "the death of the author"); the elimination of the "aura" of the genius creator, the artist (Walter Benjamin – "the author as producer"); the change from

---

[212] "Game studies" is the humanistic domain that refers to games as fictional symbolic artefacts and is not "Game Theory" that is a mathematical approach of games.

[213] See Jan Simon's article that refers to the rivalry between ludology and narratology: Simon, Jan. "Narrative, Games, and Theory," *Game Studies*, volume 7:1, 2007. Web document: <http://gamestudies.org/07010701/articles/simons>, 24.7.2016.

print to the digital world; the text being self-referential as it exposures the artistic devices by the linkage device and consequently becomes an exceptional model of defamiliarization of narratology principals and effects, so much that it is not "literature" in the regular meaning of the term but a genre in the narratology/narrativity field.

Hyper-literature did not reach the general public and remained the domain of its authors and academic researchers and almost perished. It can be found on the Internet as a kind of Choose Your Own Adventure stories where the reader chooses between some links. As technology progresses and the reader can hold the hypertext in his hand – pretty much as she holds a book (the appearance of the tablet), and as the readers are getting used to hypertext reading as it is the de-facto of the internet, which everyone uses today, hyper-literature may still rise and reach the public's notice.

This book realizes the transitional times, between printed texts and digitized ones, thus it should have been written in a hypertext format, not only because of its subject, but as one issue is connected to another in such a way that it was quite difficult to separate and present linearly. The gap between the subject matter and its presentation mode is an issue that was already commented on by Negroponte, (1995) that called this friction "the paradox of a book," and addressed it directly in his preface: "So why an old-fashioned book, Negroponte, especially one without a single illustration? Why is Vintage shipping *Being Digital* as atoms instead of bits, when these pages { . . .] can be so easily rendered in digital form, from whence they came?" (7) Though almost twenty years have gone by (Gunkel, 2003), since the Internet introduced hypertext as a writing and reading format, the transition from print to digital is not done yet. As a tribute to hypertext I decided to self-publish my book in a digital format.

Appendixes

Appendix A. - Victory Garden's structure

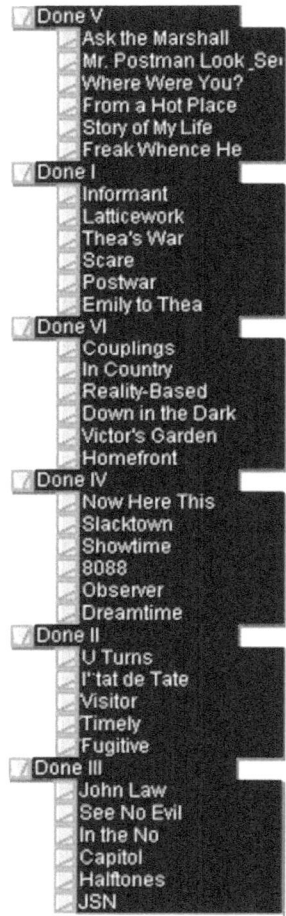

Figure 73 – *Victory Garden* outline view

This map shows the structure of *Victory Garden*, where the upper ordered list is the "volume" and the second level shows the "chapters" constructing each volume.

Appendix B. - Thea's letter – multiple versions

Node *Failure*

You were wrong to go, Emily, though I never asked if you'd considered alternatives. Why was that? I must have talked to a dozen kids who said they wouldn't go. But not you, kiddo. You knew what you wanted. Get the job done, you said.

It's the last thing I'd ever have said, Emily

How could you think this is okay? How could you go along with it?

How could you fail me

How could I

How

Node *War Games*

I thought you were wrong to go, Emily, and I still do, though I never asked if you'd considered alternatives. Why was that? I must have talked to a half dozen students who said they wouldn't go. But not you, kiddo. You knew what you wanted.

Get the job done, you said.

It's the last thing I'd ever have said, Emily, but you never sounded unsure. You knew. Get the job done, you say. Do your bit and come home.

But the job is immoral, evil, and wrong. It means willingly taking part in their war games ,their killing machines.

I can't believeThis

is such SHit...

Node *Hopeless*

I thought you were wrong to go, Emily, and I still do. Yet I never told you that. I never asked if you'd considered alternatives. I never told you what your options were, I never told you I'd back you up if you decided to refuse the orders.

Why was that? I must have talked to a half dozen students worried about the callups, men and women who said they weren't sure they ought to go. I did my bit, or at least I tried.

But you never sounded unsure, kiddo. Get the job done, you say. Do your bit and come home. When you said that, I guess I just looked into your eyes and decided it was hopeless.

No.

Node *No Resistance*

I thought you were wrong to go, Emily, and I still do. Yet I never told you that. I never asked if you'd considered resisting. I never told you what your options were, I never told you I'd back you up if you decided to refuse the orders.

Why was that? I must have talked to a half dozen students worried about the callups, men and women who said they weren't sure they ought to go. I explained it all to them, I got them in touch with the people who could really help.

But you never sounded unsure, kiddo. You were sure. Get the job done, you say. Do your bit and come home. When you said that, I guess I just looked into your eyes and decided it was your way, let it be.

Why didn't I try to change your mind? Why was I content to let you go? Why is it so hard to resist? If there's a moral failure here, it's as much mine as yours, Emily Ñ maybe more so. I just don't know.

Appendix C. - Branching of path In the beginning

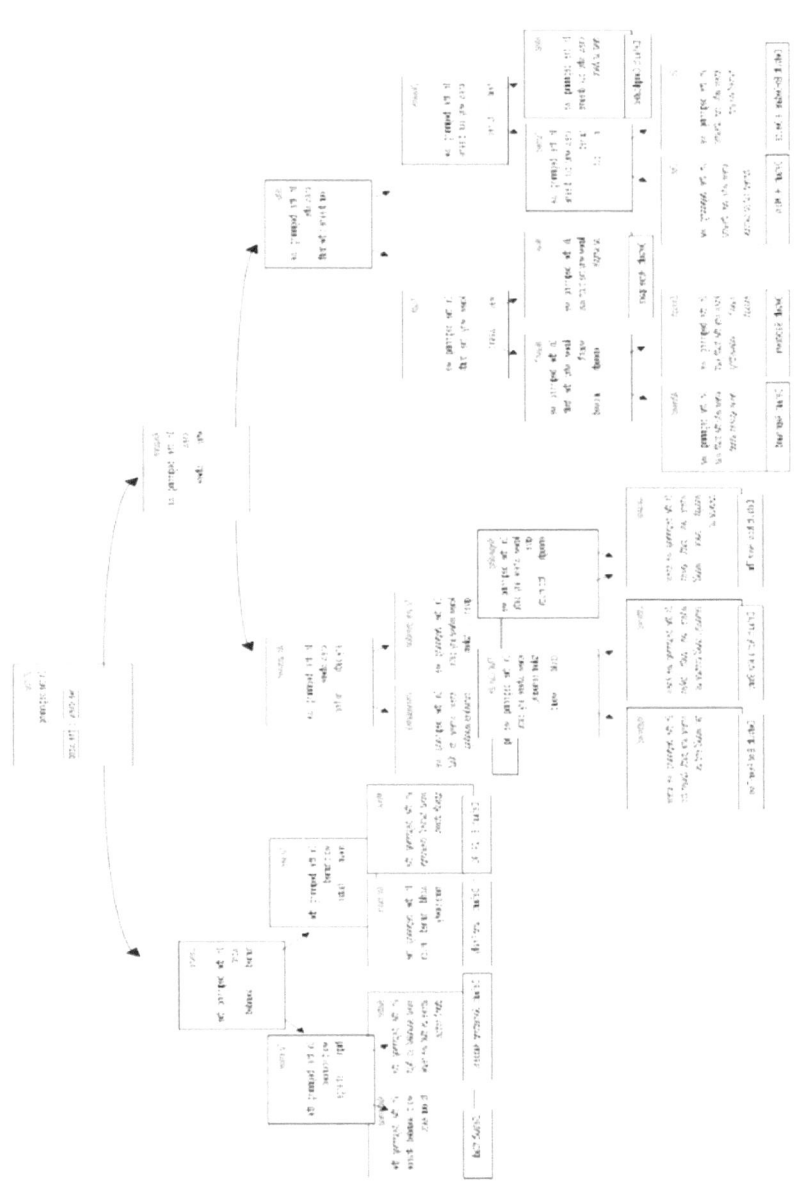

489

Appendix D. - Typography of node Time

Short time   *The shortest*

  A very brief interval

  No time even to know what was happening really

  Just a flash of light

   an ovenblast of heat

   and

Bibliography

Aarseth, Espen J. *Cybertext*. Baltimore and London: The Johns Hopkins University Press, 1997.

---. "Genre Trouble." *Electronic Book Review*, 21-5-2004. Web document: <http://www.electronicbookreview.com/thread/first person/vigilant>, 24.7.2016.

---. "We All Want to Change the World: The Ideology of Innovation in Digital Media." In *Digital Media Revisited*. Eds. Liestøl, Gunnar, Andrew Morrison, and Terje Rasmussen, Cambridge, Massachusetts: MIT Press, 2003, 415-439.

Ackoff, Russell L. "Towards a System of Systems Concepts. "Management Science 17, no. 11 (1971): 661-71. <http://www.jstor.org/stable/2629308>, 24.7.2016.

---, and Emery, F. E. and Brent D. Ruben. On Purposeful Systems: An Interdisciplinary Analysis of Individual and Social Behavior as a System of Purposeful Events. New Brunswick, N.J: Aldine Transaction, 2006.

Akutagawa, Tyunosuke. *Rashomon & Other Stories*. Trans. Takashi Kojima, Tokyo: Charles E. Tuttle Company, 1997 (1952).

Alsop, Derek. and Chris Walsh. *The Practice of Reading: Interpreting the Novel*. New York: St. Martin's Press, 1999.

Altitude Associates. *The Best of Cover Design: Books, Magazines, Catalogs, and More*. Massachusetts: Rockport Publishers, 2011.

Anonymous. *Laxdaela saga*. Trans. Magnus Magnusson and Hermann Palsson, Harmondsworth: Penguin Books, 1969.

Apollinaire, Guillaume. *Calligrammes: Poems of Peace and War (1913-1916)*. Trans. Greet Anne Hyde. Introduction by S.I. Lockerbie, Los Angeles, London: University of California Press Berkeley, 1980.

Aristotle. *Poetics*. Trans. by S. H. Butcher.

Ayckbourn, Alan. *The Norman Conquests* trilogy. Penguin Books, 1977 (1973).

Bailey, Kenneth D. Sociology and the New Systems Theory: Toward a Theoretical Synthesis. New York: state University of New York, 1994.

Baker, Nicholson. *The mezzanine*. New York: Vintage Books, 1988.

Ball, Don. ed. "To Read or not to Read: A Question of National Consequence." *Research Report #47*, produced by The Office of Research & Analysis in the National Endowment for the Arts, Washington DC, Nov. 2007.

Bardini, Thierry. "Bridging the Gulfs: From Hypertext to Cyberspace." *JCMC 3*:2, September 1997, web document: <http://onlinelibrary.wiley.com/doi/10.1111/j.1083-6101.1997.tb00069.x/full>, 24.7.2016.

Barth, John. *The End of the Road*. New York: Bantam Books, 1981 (1958).

---. *The Tidewater Tales*. New York: G. P. Putnam's Sons, 1987.

Barthes, Roland. "From Work to Text." In *Textual Strategies: Perspectives in Poststructuralist Criticism*. Ed. and Introduction Josue V. Harari, Ithaca, NY: Cornell University Press, 1979, 73-81.

---. *Image, Music, Text*. Trans by S. Heath, New York: Hill and Wang, 1988 (1977).

---. "The Death of The Author." In *Image, Music, Text.* Trans. R. Heath. New York: Hill and Wang, 1977, 155-164.

---. *The Pleasure of the Text.* New York: Hill and Wang, 1975 (1973).

---. *S/Z.* Trans. Richard Miller, New York: Hill and Wang, 1974 (1970).

Bay, Susanne. and Martina Ziefle. "Landmarks or Surveys? The Impact of Different Instructions on Children's Performance in Hierarchical Menu Structures." *Computers in Human Behavior*, Vol. 24:3, May 2008, 1246-1274.

Ben Shaul, Nitzan. Cinema of Choice: Optional Thinking and Narrative Movies. New York: Berghahn Books, 2012.

---. Hyper-narrative interactive cinema: problems and solutions. Amsterdam, New York: Rodopi, 2008.

Benjamin, Walter. "The Author as Producer." In *Reflections:Essays, Aphorisms, Autobiographical Writings.* Ed. Peter Demetz, Trans. Edmund Jephcott, New York: Schocken Books, 1978, 220-238.

Bennett, Maurice J. "The Detective Fiction of Poe and
	Borges." *Comparative Literature*, Vol. 35:3
	(Summer, 1983), Oregon: Duke University Press,
	262-275. Also:
	<http://www.jstor.org/stable/1770621>, 24.7.2016.

Berge, Kjell Lars. "Conflicts and Changes in Textual
	Norms." In *Symposium Collected Works
	NORDTEXT*. Ed. Charlotte Lindeberg, Pargas,
	Finland: Tidningsbokhandeln, 1992. Also:
	<http://www.eric.ed.gov/ERICWebPortal/detail?acc
	no=ED359746>, 24.7.2016.

Berners-Lee, Tim. *A Brief History of the Web*. Web
	document, 1993-1994.
	<http://www.w3.org/DesignIssues/TimBook-
	old/History.html>, 24.7.2016.

Bernstein, Michael. *Hypertext Gardens*. (1998), Web
	document:
	<http://www.eastgate.com/garden/Enter.html>,
	24.7.2016.

---. "The Bookmark and the Compass: Orientation Tools
	for Hypertext Users." in *ACM SIGOIS Bulletin,*
	Volume 9:4, Oct. 1988.

---. "Where Are the Hypertexts?" A presentation for the *1999 Hypertext Conference*. <http://www.eastgate.com/ht99/slides/Welcome.ht m>, 24.7.2016.

von Bertalanffy, Ludwig. "An Outline of General System Theory." *The British Journal for Philosophy of Science*, Vol. 1:2, 1950, 134-165.

Birkerts, Sven. "Portable Musing." *Atlantic Unbound*, September 10, 1998, <http://www.theatlantic.com/unbound/digicult/dc98 0910.htm>, 42.7.2016.

---. The Gutenberg Elegies: The Fate of Reading in an Electronic Age. New York: Fawcett Columbine, 1995 (1994).

Bleich, David. "Epistemological Assumptions in the Study of Response." In *Reader-response Criticism: From Formalism to Post-structuralism*. Ed. Jane P Tompkins, Baltimore: Johns Hopkins University Press, 1988, 134-153.

Bolter, Jay David. *Degrees of Freedom*. A web document: <http://www.uv.es/~fores/programa/bolter_freedom .html>, 24.7.2016.

---. "Topographic Writing: Hypertext and the Electronic Writing Space." In *Hypermedia and Literary Studies*. Eds. P. Delany and George P. Landow, Cambridge, Mass.: The MIT Press, 1991, 105-118.

---. *Writing Space*: *The Computer, Hypertext, and the History of Writing*. Hillsdale, New Jersey: Lawrence Erlbaum Associates, 1991.

---, and Joyce Michael. "Hypertext and Creative Writing." In *HYPERTEXT '87 Proceedings of the ACM conference on Hypertext ACM*, New York, NY, USA, 1987.

Bonder, Richard and Mark Chignell. "Dynamic Hypertext: Querying and Linking." *Computing Surveys*, vol. 31:4, 1999, Also: <http://www.cs.brown.edu/memex/ACM_HypertextTestbed/papers/39.html>, 24.7.2016.

Bookshelf 2000, Computer and Internet Dictionary. Microsoft Press 1997, 3rd Edition, Electronic Version.

Borges, Jorge Luis. *Collected Fictions*. Trans. Andrew Hurley, Penguin books, 1999.

Bostad, Finn. "*What Happens to Writing When Texts in 'A World on Paper' are Replaced by Messages in 'Virtual Space?'*" A research paper presented in a workshop in the congress of the Nordic Association for Semiotic Studies, 1994, Also: <http://coppock-violi.com/web/Finn_ToC.html>, 24.7.2016.

Bourdieu, Pierre. *Distinction: A Social Critique of the Judgement of Taste.* Trans. Richard Nice, Cambridge, Mass.: Harvard University Press, 1984.

---. *Language and Symbolic Power*. Ed. and introduced by John B. Thompson, trans. Gino Raymond and Matthew Adamson, Cambridge: Polity Press, 1991.

---. "The Forms of Capital." In *Sociology of Education*. Ed. Alan R. Sadovnik, New York: Routledge, 2007 (1986), 83-95.

Boyd, Brian. *Stalking Nabokov*. New York: Columbia University Press, 2011.

Brizendin, Louann. *The Female Brain*. New York: Broadway Books, 2006.

---. *The male brain*. New York: Three Rivers Press, 2010

Branwyn, Gareth. and Peter Sugarman. *Beyond Cyberpunk*. A *HyperCard* hypertext. 1991. Also: <http://www.streettech.com/bcp/>, 24.7.2016.

Bronwen, Thomas. "Stuck in a Loop? Dialogue in Hypertext Fiction." *Narrative* 15.3, 2007, 357-372.

Brooke, Collin Gifford. "Revisiting the Matter and Manner of Linking in New Media." In *Small Tech: The Culture of Digital Tools*. Eds. Byron Hawk, David M. Rieder and Ollie Oviedo, University Of Minnesota Press, 2008, 69 - 79.

Brooks, Cleanth. and Robert Penn. Eds. *Understanding Poetry*. New York: H. Holt, 1938.

---. *Understanding fiction*. New York: Appleton-Century-Crofts, 1959.

Brooks, Landon. "Hypertext and Science Fiction." *Science Fiction Studies*, Vol. 20:3 (Nov., 1993), 449-456. Also: <http://www.jstor.org/stable/4240286>, 24.7.2016.

Broos, Agatha. "Gender and Information and Communication Technologies (ICT) Anxiety: Male Self-Assurance and Female Hesitation." *CyberPsychology & Behavior*, Volume 8:1, 2005, 21-33.

Bukatman, Scott. "Virtual Textuality." *Artforum*, Jan 1994.
Also:
<http://jefferson.village.virginia.edu/~jmu2m/bukat
man.html>, 24.7.2016.

Bush, Vannevar. "As We May Think." *The Atlantic
Monthly*, July 1945.
<http://www.theatlantic.com/magazine/archive/194
5/07/as-we-may-think/3881/>, 24.7.2016.

Butt, John. and Kathleen Tillotson. *Dickens at Work*.
London: Methuen & Co. LTD, 1968.

Calvi, Licia. ""Lector in rebus": The Role of the Reader
and the Characteristics of Hyperreading."
*HYPERTEXT '99 Proceedings of the tenth ACM
Conference*, ACM New York, NY, 1999.

Calvino, Italo. *The Uses of Literature*. Boston: Mariner
Books, 1987.

Cambridge Dictionaries On-line
<http://dictionary.cambridge.org/>, 24.7.2016.

Carter, Locke M. "Arguments in Hypertext: A Rhetorical
Approach." In *HYPERTEXT '00 Proceedings of the
eleventh ACM on Hypertext and hypermedia*, 2000,
85 – 91.

Carroll, Lewis. *The Annotated Alice*. Introduction and notes by Martin Gardner, London: Penguin Books, 1970 (1960).

Chalker, Sylvia. and Edmund Weiner. *The Oxford Dictionary of English Grammar.* Oxford University Press, 1998.

Chandler, Daniel. *The Active Reader*. Web document, December 1995. <http://jcomm.uoregon.edu/~cbybee/j388_f08/active.html>, 24.7.2016.

Chatman, Seymour. *Story and Discourse: Narrative Structure in Fiction and Film*. Ithaca, New York: Cornell University Press, 1980.

Christie, Agatha. *The murder of Roger Ackroyd*. New York: Berkley Books, 2000 (1927).

Cohn, Dorrit. Transparent Minds: Narrative Modes for Presenting Consciousness in Fiction. Princeton, N. J.: Princeton University Press, 1978.

Conklin, Jeff. "Hypertext: an Introduction and Survey." *IEEE Computer* 20, 9 (Sep.1987), 17-41.

Coover, Robert. *Pricksongs & Descnats*. Suffolk: Picador, Pan Books, 1973 (1969).

---. "The End of Books." Web document in *The New York Times Book Review*. June 21, 1992. <http://www.nytimes.com/books/98/09/27/specials/coover-end.html>, 24.7.2016.

Corbett, Margery. and R. W. Lightbown. *The comely frontispiece: the emblematic title-page in England, 1550-1660.* London: Routledge & Kegan Paul, c1979.

Cortázar, Julio. *Hopscotch*. New York: Pantheon Books, 1966.

Coverley, M.D. *Califia*. Watertown MA: Eastgate Systems, 2000. (CD-ROM)

Craig, Alan B. et al. Developing Virtual Reality Applications: Foundations of Effective Design. San Francisco: Morgan Kaufmann, 2009.

Craig, R. T. "Communication Theory as a Field." *Communication Theory, 9* (2), 1999, 119-161. Also: <http://www.stes-apes.med.ulg.ac.be/Documents_electroniques/MET/MET-COM/ELE%20MET-COM%20A-8191.pdf>, 24.7.2016.

Culler, Jonathan D. "Literary Competence." In *Reader-response Criticism: From Formalism to Post-structuralism*. Ed. Tompkins, Jane P., Baltimore: Johns Hopkins University Press, 1988, 101-117.

---. On Deconstruction: Theory and Criticism after Structuralism. Ithaca: Cornell University Press, 1982.

cummings e. e. *Complete Poems: 1904-1962*. Ed. George J. Firmage, New York: Liverlight Publishing Corporation, 1991.

Danielewski, Mark Z. *House of Leaves*. New York: Pantheon Books, 2000.

---. *Only Revolutions*. New York: Pantheon House, 2006.

Daw David, "What Makes Siri Special?" *PCWorld,* Oct 25, 2011, wed document: <http://www.pcworld.com/article/242479/what_makes_siri_special.html>, 24.7.2016.

De Bono, Edward. *Lateral thinking: Creativity Step by Step*. New York: Harper & Row, 1973 (1970).

De Saussure, Ferdinand. *Course in General Linguistics*. New York: Philosophical Library, 1959 (1916).

De Vinne, Theodore Low. *The practice of typography*. New York: Oswald Pub. Co., 1902.

Derrida, Jacques. "Letter to a Japanese friend." In
    Derrida and difference. Eds. David Wood and
    Robert Bernasconi, Evanston: Northwestern
    University Press, 1988, 1-5.

---. Of grammatology, Trans. Gayatri Chakravorty
    Spivak, Baltimore: Johns Hopkins University
    Press, 1976

---. "Structure, Sign, and Play in the Discourse of the
    Human Sciences." In *The Structuralist
    Controversy: The language of Criticism and the
    Sciences of Man*. Eds. Richard Macksey and
    Eugenio Donato, Baltimore: John Hopkins Press,
    1972.

Dickens, Charles. *A Tale of Two Cities*. Penguin Classics,
    1994 (1859).

---. *Great Expectations*. Penguin Classics, 1996 (1860-61).

Dickey, William. "Poem Descending a staircase." In
    Hypermedia and Literary Studies. Eds. Delany P.
    and George P. Landow, The MIT Press, 1991, 143-
    152.

Drucker, Johanna. "Artists' Books and the Cultural Status
    of the Book". *Journal of Communication*, 1994,
    Vol. 44, Blackwell Publishing, 12-42.

---. The Visible Word: experimental typography and modern art, 1909-1923. Chicago: University of Chicago Press, 1994.

Durcan, Paul. *Give me your hand*, London: Macmillan, 1994.

Eaton, Jeanette. *Leaders in Other Lands*. Lexington MA: Heath, 1950.

Eco Umberto. *Semiotics and the Philosophy of Language*. Bloomington: Indiana University Press, 1986.

---. *The Limits of Interpretation*. Bloomington: Indiana University Press, 1994 (1990).

Edmonds, Molly. "Do men and women have different brains?" HowStuffWorks.com, 8 October 2008. Web document: <http://health.howstuffworks.com/human-body/systems/nervous-system/men-women-different-brains.htm>, 24.7. 2016.

Edwards, Benj. "A Brief History of Computer Displays." *PCWorld*, Nov. 2, 2010.

Ehrenreich, Ben. "The Death of the Book." *Los Angeles Review of Books*, 18th Apr 2011. Web document: <https://lareviewofbooks.org/article/the-death-of-the-book/>, 24.7.2016.

Eisenstein, Elizabeth. *The Printing Revolution in Early Modern Europe*. New York: Cambridge University, 1998 (1983).

Eliot, T.S. *The Waste Land and Other Poems*. Canada: Broadview Press, (1940) 2010.

Engelbart, Douglas C. "Collaboration Support Provisions in AUGMENT," *OAC '84 Digest*: *Proceedings of the 1984 AFIPS Office Automation Conference*, Los Angeles, CA, February 20-22, 51-58. Also: <http://www.dougengelbart.org/pubs/oad-2221.html>, 24.7.2016.

---, and English, William K."A Research Centre for Augmenting Human Intellect." *AFIPS Conference Proceedings of the 1968 Fall Joint Computer Conference*, San Francisco, CA, December 1968, Vol. 33, 395-410. Also: <http://www.dougengelbart.org/pubs/augment-3954.html>, 24.7.2016.

Evans, Christopher. *The Micro Millennium*. New York: Viking Press, 1979.

Even-Zohar Itamar. "Polysystem Theory." *Poetics Today*, Vol. 1:1-2, Special Issue: Literature, Interpretation, Communication (Autumn, 1979), 287-310. Also: <http://www.jstor.org/stable/1772051>, 24.7.2016.

Fanning, Christopher. "On Sterne's Page: Spatial Layout, Spatial Form, and Social Spaces in *Tristram Shandy*." *Eighteenth-Century Fiction*, Vol. 10:4, 1988, 429-450. Also: <http://post.queensu.ca/~cjf1/Fanning429-450.pdf>, 24.7.2016.

Faulkner, William. *Light in August*. New York: Modern Library, 1950 (1932).

Febvre, Lucien. and Henri-Jean Martin. *The Coming of the Book*. Trans. David Gerard, London and New York: Verso, 1999 (1958).

Federman, Raymond. *Double or Nothing*. Boulder: Fiction Collective Two, 1998 (1992).

Feller, Ross Alan. *Multicursal labyrinths in the work of Brian Ferneyhough*. D.M.A. Thesis, University of Illinois, 1994.

Fielding, Henry. The History of the Adventures of Joseph Andrews and his Friend Mr. Abraham Adams. New York and London: W. W. Norton & Company, 1958 (1742).

---. *Tom Jones, a foundling*. London: Penguin Books, 1994.

Fish, Stanley E. "Interpreting the Variorum" In *Reader-response Criticism: From Formalism to Post-structuralism*. Ed. Jane P. Tompkins, Baltimore: Johns Hopkins University Press, 1988, 164-184.

Fister, Barbara. *NDL 105: Books and Culture*. January 2011. Web document: <https://gustavus.edu/profiles/fister>, 24.7.2016.

Forster, E.M. *Aspects of the Novel*. London: Penguin Books, 2005 (1927).

Fowles, John. *The French Lieutenant's Woman*. Boston: 1st Back Bay, 1998.

Fragoso, Suely. "Understanding links: Web Science and hyperlink studies at macro, meso and micro-levels." *New Review of Hypermedia and Multimedia*, Vol. 17:2, 163-198, 2011.

Franzen, Jonathan. *The Corrections, a novel*. New York: Farrar Straus & Giroux, 2001.

Gabriel, Otto. and Andres von Brandt. *Fish Catching Methods of the World*. Oxford, UK: Blackwell Pub, 2005.

Gaggi, Silvio. *From Text to Hypertext*. Philadelphia: University of Pennsylvania Press, 1998.

Gardner, Colin. "Meta-interpretation and Hypertext Fiction: A critical response." *Computers & the Humanities,* 37:1, 2003, 33-56.

Genette, Gérard. *Narrative Discourse Revisited.* Trans. Jane E. Lewin, Ithaca: Cornell University Press, 1988.

Gladwell, Malcolm. "The Social Life of Paper." *New Yorker*, 25 Mar. 2002, 92-96. Also: <http://www.newyorker.com/magazine/2002/03/25/the-social-life-of-paper>, 24.7.2016.

Goddard, Linda. *Aesthetic rivalries: word and image in France, 1880-1926.* Oxford and New York: Peter Lang, 2012.

Golijan, Rosa. "The Ultimate Guide to Ebook Readers We Care About." *Gismodo*, Jan. 15 2010. Web document: <http://gizmodo.com/#!5445603/the-ultimate-guide-to-ebook-readers-we-care-about>, 24.7.2016.

Grafton, Anthony. *The Footnote: A Curious History.* London: Faber and Faber, 1997.

Green, Melanie C. "Transportation into Narrative Worlds: The Role of Prior Knowledge and Perceived Realism." *Discourse Processes*, 38:2, 2004, 247-266.

Gunkel, David J. "What's the matter with books?" *Configurations 11.3*, 2003, 277-303. Also: < http://muse.jhu.edu/article/173282>, 24.7.2016.

Gygi, K. "Recognizing the Symptoms of Hypertext...and What to Do About It." In *The Art of Human Computer Interface Design*. Ed. B. Laurel, Reading, MA: Addison-Wesley, 1990, 279-287.

Haigh, Thomas. "Remembering the Office of the Future: Word Processing and Office Automation before the Personal Computer." *IEEE Annals of the History of Computing* 28:4 (October–December 2006): 6-31. Also: <http://www.tomandmaria.com/tom/Writing/Annals 2006WP.pdf>, 24.7.2016.

Halasz, Frank. G. "Reflections on Notecards: Seven issues for the next generation of hypermedia systems." *Communications of the ACM,* July 1988, 836-852.

Hale Mike. "Drama at a Barbecue Leads Relationships to Fizzle." *New York Times*, Television Review, 15.2.2012. Also: <http://tv.nytimes.com/2012/02/15/arts/television/the-slap-on-directv.html>, 24.7.2016.

Harrison, Claire. "Hypertext Links: Whither thou goest, and why." *First Monday*, vol. 7:10, October 2002, <http://firstmonday.org/htbin/cgiwrap/bin/ojs/index.php/fm/article/view/993/914>, 24.7.2016.

Hartong Georg. *On the History of the Bookmark*. Web document: <http://www.duisburg.de/stadtbib/medien/bindata/bookmarkhistory.pdf>, 24.7.2016.

Hayles, Katherine N. "Electronic Literature: What is it?" *Electronic Literature Organization*, v1.0 January 2, 2007. Web document: <http://www.eliterature.org/pad/elp.html>, 24.7.2016.

---. "Print is Flat, Code is Deep: The Importance of Media-Specific Analysis." *Poetics Today*, 25:1, 2004, 67-90.

---. *Writing Machines*. Cambridge and London: The MIT Press, 2002.

Heffernan, James. *Museum of Words: The Poetics of Ekphrasis from Homer to Ashbery*. Chicago: University of Chicago Press, 1993.

Herrnstein Smith, Barbara. *Poetic Closure*. Chicago: The University of Chicago Press, 1970 (1968).

Hjelmslev, Louis. *Language: an introduction*. Trans. Francis J. Whitfield, Madison: University of Wisconsin Press, 1970.

Holland, Norman. "Unity, Identity, Text, Self." In *Reader-response Criticism: From Formalism to Post-structuralism*. Ed. Jane P. Tompkins, Baltimore: Johns Hopkins University Press, 1988, 118-133.

Hudson, Richard, "Language as a Cognitive Network." In *A Cognitive Approach to the Verb: Morphological and Constructional Perspectives*. Eds. Hanne Gram Simonsen and Rolf Theil Endresen, Berlin: Mouton de Gruyter, 2001, 49-72.

Humphrey, Robert. *Stream of Consciousness in the Modern Novel*. Berkeley: University of California Press, 1954.

Ihara, Rachel. Novels on the Installment Plan: American Authorship in the Age of Serial Publication, from Stowe to Hemingway. Ph.D. Thesis. The City University of New York, USA, 2007.

Imhof, Margarete et al. "Computer use and the gender gap: The issue of access, use, motivation, and performance." *Computers in Human Behavior*, Volume 23:6, November 2007, 2823-2837.

Iser, Wolfgang. "The Reading Process: A Phenomenological Approach." In *Reader-response Criticism: From Formalism to Post-structuralism*. Ed. Jane P. Tompkins, Baltimore: Johns Hopkins University Press, 1988, 50-69. First published in *New Literary History*, Vol. 3:2, 1972, 279-299. Also: <http://www.jstor.org/stable/468316>, 24.7.2016.

Jackson H.J. *Marginalia: Readers Writing in Books*. New Haven, Conn: Yale University Press, 2001.

Jaffé-Freem, Elly. *Alain Robbe-Grillet et la Peinture Cubiste*. Amsterdam: J.M. Meulenhoff, 1966.

Jakobson, Roman. "Closing Statements: Linguistics and Poetics." In *Style in Language*. Ed. Thomas A. Sebeok, Cambridge Massachusetts: MIT Press, 1960, 350–377.

---, and Pomorska, Krystyna and Rudy Stephen. *Verbal Art, Verbal Sign, Verbal Time*. Minneapolis: University of Minnesota Press, 1985

Jancovich, Mark. *The Cultural Politics of the New Criticism*. Cambridge University Press, 1993, 81-89.

Jefferson, Ann. *The Nouveau Roman and the Poetics of Fiction*. Cambridge: Cambridge University Press, 1985.

Jencks, Christopher. and David Riesman. *The Academic Revolution*. New Jersey: Transaction Publishers, 2002 (1968).

Johnson, Barbara. The Critical Difference: Essays in the Contemporary rhetoric of reading. Baltimore: Johns Hopkins University Press, 1980.

Johnson, Samuel. *The works of Samuel Johnson*. Vol. IX, London: S. and R. Bentley, 1820.

Johnson, Steven. "How the E-Book Will Change the Way We Read and Write." *The Wall Street journal*, April 21, 2009. Also: <http://online.wsj.com/article/SB123980920727621 353.html#articleTabs%3D> 24.7.2016.

Jones, Steven E. "Second Life, Video Games, and the
    Social Text." *PMLA*, Volume 124:1, January 2009,
    264–272. Also:
    <http://www.sjsu.edu/faculty/harris/DigLit_F10/Re
    adings/SJonesPMLA.pdf> 24.7.2016.

---. "The Book of *Myst* in the Late Age of Print."
    Postmodern Culture, Volume 7:2, January 1997.
    Also:
    <http://muse.jhu.edu/journals/postmodern_culture/v
    007/7.2jones.html>, 24.7.2016.

Joyce, Michael. *afternoon, a story*. Watertown MA:
    Eastgate Systems, 1995 (1987). (Diskette)

---. *Of Two Minds: Hypertext Pedagogy and Poetics*. Ann
    Arbor: University of Michigan Press, 1996.

---. *Othermindedness: The Emergence of Network Culture*.
    Ann Arbor: University of Michigan Press, 2000.

Kahn, John E. "The Protean Narrator, and the Case of
    Trollope's Barsetshire Novels." *The Journal of
    Narrative Technique*, Vol. 10:2 (Spring, 1980), 77-
    98. Also: <http://www.jstor.org/stable/30224991>,
    24.7.2016.

Keep, Christopher and Tim McLaughlin. *The Electronic Labyrinth*. Web document 1995, <http://www.iath.virginia.edu/elab/elab.html>, 24.7.2016.

Kenrick, William. "Review of Tristram Shandy." (1759) In *Tristram Shandy*. Stern, Laurence. Ed. Howard Anderson, New York, London: W. W. Norton & Company, 1980.

Kermode, Frank. *The Sense of an Ending*. London: Oxford University Press, 1966.

Kim, Hanhwe. and Stephen C. Hirtle. "Spatial Metaphors and Disorientation in Hypertext Browsing," *Behaviour and Information Technology*, Vol.14:4, 1995, 239-250.

Kitchin, Robert M. "Cognitive Maps: What are They and Why Study Them?" *Journal of Environmental Psychology*, Volume 14:1, March 1994, 1-19.

Knight, Dan. *Personal Computer History: The First 25 Years*. Web document: <http://lowendmac.com/lowendpc/history/index.shtml>, 24.7.2016.

Knights, L. C. Explorations: essays in criticism, mainly on the literature of the seventeenth century. London: Chatto and Windus, 1946.

Kolata, Gina. "Men and Women Use Brain Differently, Study Discovers." *The New York Times*, February 16, 1995. Web document: <http://www.nytimes.com/1995/02/16/us/men-and-women-use-brain-differently-study-discovers.html>, 24.7.2016.

Konrad, Hugo Jarausch. *The Transformation of Higher Learning 1860-1930.* Chicago: University of Chicago Press, 1983.

Kringelbach, Morten. and Vuust, Peter. and Geake, John. "The Pleasure of Reading." *Interdisciplinary Science Reviews*, Volume 33:4, December 2008, 321-335(15). Also: <http://www.kringelbach.org/papers/ISR_Kringelbach2008.pdf>, 24.7.2016.

Kruglanski, Arie W. and Donna M. Webster. "Motivated Closing of the Mind: "Seizing" and "Freezing"." *Psychological Review*, 1996, Vol. 103:2, 263-283.

Kunde, Brian. *A Brief History of Word Processing,
(Through 1986)*. Web document,
<http://www.stanford.edu/~bkunde/fb-
press/articles/wdprhist.html>, 24.7.2016.

Kurtz, Glenn. A. *From Work to Hypertext: Authors and
Authority in a Reader-Directed Medium*. 1997. Web
document: <http://glennkurtz.com/cgi-
bin/iowa/essays/work/index.html>, 24.7.20016.

Kurzweil, Ray. "*The Future of Libraries, Part 2: The End
of Books*." KurzweilAI.net August 6, 2001 (1992).
Web document: <http://www.kurzweilai.net/the-
future-of-libraries-part-2-the-end-of-books>,
24.7.2016.

Landow George P. *Definitions of Hypertext*. Web
document,
<http://www.cyberartsweb.org/cpace/ht/jhup/histor
y.htm>, 24.7.2016.

---. Hypertext 2.0: The Convergence of Contemporary
Critical Theory and Technology. Baltimore: The
Johns Hopkins University Press, 1997 (1992).

---. "Relationally Encoded Links and the Rhetoric of
Hypertext." *hypertext '87 proceedings Papers*,
November 1987, 331-343.

---, ed. "What's a Critic to do?: Critical Theory in the Age of Hypertext." In *Hypertext/Text/Theory*, Baltimore & London: The John Hopkins University Press, 1994.

---, ed. and P. Delany. *Hypermedia and literary studies.* Cambridge, Mass.: MIT Press, c1991.

Lanham, Richard A. *The Electronic Word.* Chicago: The University of Chicago Press, 1994 (1993).

Larsen, Deena. *Samplers.* Watertown MA: Eastgate System Inc., 1997. (Diskette)

Laszlo, Ervin. The Systems View Of the World: A Holistic Vision for Our Time (Advances in Systems Theory, Complexity, and the Human Sciences). New York: Hampton Press, 1996.

Laurel, Brenda. *Computers as Theatre.* Menlo Park California, Addison-Wesley, 1993 (1991).

Lawlor, William. *Beat Culture: Lifestyles, Icons, and Impact.* Santa Barbara: ABC-CLIO Inc., 2005.

Leavis, Q.D. *Fiction and the reading public.* London: Chatto & Windus, 1932.

Lessing, Gotthold Ephraim. *The Laocoon, and other prose writings of Lessing*. Trans. Edward Allen McCormick, Indianapolis, New York: The Bobbs-Merill Co., 1962 (1766).

Liestøl, Gunar. "Wittgenstein, Genette, and the Reader's Narrative in Hypertext." In *Hyper/Text/Theory*. Ed. G. P. Landow, Baltimore and London: The Johns Hopkins University Press, 1994.

Lodge, David. *Modern criticism and theory*. London: Longman, 2008 (1988).

Lord, Albert B. *The Singer of Tales*. New York: Atheneum, 1973 (1960).

---. *The Singer Resumes the Tale*. Ithaca and London: Cornell University Press, 1995.

Lund, Hans. Text as Picture: Studies in the Literary Transformation of pictures. Lewiston: E. Mellen Press, 1992.

Manguel, Alberto. *A history of reading*. :New York. Penguin Books, 1996

Margolin. Uri, "Experiencing Virtual Worlds: Observation to Co-Creation." *Poetics Today* 23:4, 2002, 707-717.

Marinetti, Filippo Tommaso. *Selected Writings*. Trans. R.W. Flint and Arthur A. Coppotelli, New York: Farrar, Straus and Giroux, 1972.

Marquez, Gabriel Garcia. *One Hundred Years of Solitude*. New York: Harper Perennial Modern Classics, 2006.

Mash, David. "The Death of the Book." *Mars Hill Review*. Web document: <http://www.marshillreview.com/extracts/mash.shtm>, 24.7.2016.

Matthews, Nicole. and Moody Nickianne. Eds. Judging a Book by Its Cover: Fans, Publishers, Designers, and the Marketing of Fiction. Aldershot/Burlington: Ashgate, 2007.

McAuliffe, Carmel. et al. "Optional Thinking Ability Among Hospital-treated Deliberate Self-Harm Patients: A 1-year follow-up study." *British Journal of Clinical Psychology* (2008), 47, 43–58.

McCabe, Heather. "Grrl Geeks Rock Out." *Wired magazine* (2.9.1999). <http://musiclub.web.cern.ch/MusiClub/bands/cernettes/Press/Wired.pdf>, 24.7.2016.

McHale, Brian. *Constructing Postmodernism*. London and New York: Routledge, 1992.

---. *Postmodernist Fiction*. London and New York: Routledge, 1987.

---. "Reader Response Theory," in *Routledge encyclopedia of narrative theory*. Eds. David Herman, Manfred Jahn and Marie-Laure Ryan, London: Taylor & Francis, 2005, 484-486.

McKnight, Cliff. and Andrew Dillon and John Richardson. *Hypertext in Context*. Cambridge: Cambridge University Press, 1991.

McLuaghlin, Tom. *Notes toward Absolute Zero*. Watertown MA: Eastgate Systems, 1995 (1993). (Diskette)

McLuhan, Marshall. *The Gutenberg Galaxy*. Toronto: University of Toronto Press, 1965 (1962).

---. *The Medium is the Massage*. New York, London, Toronto: Bantam Books, 1967.

McMillan, Graeme, "The Real 'You' Tube: *Choose Your Own Adventure*'s New Era." *Time Entertainment*, Jan. 09, 2013. Also: <http://entertainment.time.com/2013/01/09/the-further-adventures-of-you-the-multiple-possibilities-of-choose-your-own-adventure/#ixzz2Lk7ltCT2>, 24.7.2016.

Merivale, Patricia. "The Flaunting of Artifice in Vladimir Nabokov and Jorge Luis Borges." *Wisconsin Studies in Contemporary Literature*, Vol. 8:2, (Spring, 1967), Wisconsin: University of Wisconsin Press, 294-309.

Microsoft Encarta 96, Encyclopedia, CD-ROM

Mims, Christopher. "The Death of the Book has Been Greatly Exaggerated." *MIT Technology Review*, 21.9.2010. Web document: <http://www.technologyreview.com/blog/mimssbits/25783/>, 24.7.2016.

Monaghan, Patricia. *The Encyclopedia of Celtic Mythology and Folklore*. New York: Infobase Publishing, 2009.

Morrison, Toni. *The Bluest Eye*. New York: Vintage International, 2007.

Moulthrop, Stuart. *A Subjective Chronology of Literary Hypertext.* (14.4.2006) Web document: <http://www.people.vcu.edu/~mkeller/module/hypertext/docs/timelinemirror.htm>, 42.7.2016.

---. "Hegirascope". In *New River* Vol. 3, Ver. 2, October 1997. Also: <http://www.cddc.vt.edu/journals/newriver/moulthrop/HGS2/Hegirascope.html>, 24.7.2016.

---. "No War Machine." In *Reading Matters: Narrative in the New Ecology of Media*. Eds. Tabbi, Joseph. and Michael Wutz, Cornell University Press, 1997, 269-293. Also: web document, April 1995, <https://pantherfile.uwm.edu/moulthro/essays/war_machine.html>, 24.7.2016.

---. *Pax: An Instrument*, 2003. Web hypermedia: <https://pantherfile.uwm.edu/moulthro/hypertexts/pax/>, 24.7.2016.

---. *Radio Salience.* Playable multimedia first published in *New River* Spring 2007. Web document: <https://pantherfile.uwm.edu/moulthro/hypertexts/rs/>, 24.7.2016.

---. *Reagan Library*, Ver. 1.1, 2009 (1999). CD-ROM.
Also:
<https://pantherfile.uwm.edu/moulthro/hypertexts/rl
x/>, 24.7.2016.

---. *The Shadow of an Informand: An Experiment in
Hypertext Rhetoric*. First published in *Storyspace*
format, 1992. A printed version was published in
Writing on the Edge 4:1 (Fall 1992), Davis:
University of California. A web version was
published on November 1994,

---. "The Politics of Hypertext." In *Evolving Perspectives
on Computers and Composition Studies.* Eds.
Hawisher, Gail E. and Cynthia L. Selfe, Urbana:
National Council of Teachers of English, 1991.
253-271. Also known as "In the Zones: Hypertext
and the Politics of Interpretation." *Writing on the
Edge1*, no. 1 (1989): 18-27.
<http://www.jstor.org/stable/43158630>, 24.7.2016.

---. "Traveling in the Breakdown Lane. A Principle of Resistance for Hypertext." *Mosaic* 28:4, 1995, 55-77. Also: <https://pantherfile.uwm.edu/moulthro/essays/breakdown.html>, 24.7.2016.

---. *Under Language*, 2007. Digital poetry published in the *Iowa Review Web*: <https://pantherfile.uwm.edu/moulthro/hypertexts/ul/>, 24.7.2016.

---. *Victory Garden*. Watertown MA: Eastgate System Inc., 1991. (Diskette)

Murray, Janet. Hamlet on the Holodeck: The Future of Narrative in Cyberspace. Cambridge, MA: MIT Press, 1999.

Myers, Brad A. "A Brief History of Human-Computer Interaction Technology." *Interactions*, Volume 5:2, March/April 1998, 44-54.

Nabokov, Vladimir. *Lolita* (the annotated). Edited, with preface, introduction and noted by Alfred Apple, Jr. Penguin books, 1995.

---. *Pale Fire*. New York: Vintage International, 1989 (1962).

Negroponte, Nicholas. *Being Digital*. New York: Vintage, 1995 (1994).

Nell, Victor. "The Psychology of Reading for Pleasure: Needs and Gratifications." *Reading Research Quarterly*, Vol. 23:1 (Winter, 1988), 6-50. Also: <https://www.msu.edu/~dwong/CEP991/CEP991R esources/Nell-RdngPleasure.pdf >, 24.7.2016.

Nelson, Theodor Holmes. *Literary Machines 93.1*. Sausalito CA: Mindful Press, 1992 (1980).

Neumann, Fritz-Wilhelm. "Information Society and the Text: The Predicament of Literary Culture in the Age of Electronic Communication." In *Erfurt Electronic Studies in English*, strategy statement no. 6 (1999). Also: <http://webdoc.gwdg.de/edoc/ia/eese/strategy/neum ann/6_st.html> 24.7.2016.

Nielsen, Jakob. *Multimedia and Hypertext: The Internet and Beyond*. San Francisco: Morgan Kaufmann, 1995.

---. "The Art of Navigating through Hypertext." *Communications of the ACM* 33 March 1990, 296-310.

Nietzsche, Friedrich. *On The Genealogy of Morals and Ecce Homo.* Ed. Walter Kaufmann, New York: Vintage Books, 1989 (1887).

Norberg, Arthur L. "Changing Computing: The Computing Community and DARPA," *IEEEAnnals of the History of Computing,* Vol. 18:2, 1996, 40-53. Also: <http://gizmodo.com/391157/50-years-of-darpa-5-good-inventions-5-lousy-ones>, 24.7.2016.

Nyce, James M. and Paul Kahn. Eds. *From Memex to hypertext.* Boston: Academic Press, 1991.

Ong, Walter J. *Orality and Literacy: The Technologizing of the Word.* London and New York: Methuen, 1982.

Pape, Walter. "Happy Endings in a World of Misery: A Literary Convention between Social Constraints and Utopia in Children's and Adult Literature." *Poetics Today*, Vol. 13:1, (Spring, 1992), 179-196.

Pavić, Milorad. Dictionary of the Khazars: a lexicon novel in 100,000 words. New York: Vintage Books, 1988.

---. *The Glass Snail.* Web hypertext, 2003: <http://wordcircuits.com/gallery/glasssnail/>, 24.7.2016

Payne, David. The Re-enchantment of Nineteenth-Century Fiction: Dickens, Thackeray, George Eliot and Serialization. Basingstoke: Palgrave Macmillan, 2005.

Perelman, Bob. "Parataxis and Narrative: The New Sentence in Theory and Practice." *American Literature*, Vol. 65:2, 1993, 313-324. Also: <http://www.jstor.org/stable/2927344>, 24.7.2016.

Perec, Georges. *Life, a user's manual: fictions*. Trans. David Bellos, London: Harvill, 1987.

Perry, Menakhem. "Literary Dynamics: How the Order of a Text Creates Its Meanings." *Poetics Today*, Vol. 1:1-2, 1979, 35-64+311-361. Also: <http://www.jstor.org/stable/1772040>, 24.7.2016.

---, and Sternberg, Meir. "The King through Ironic Eyes: Biblical Narrative and the Literary Reading Process." *Poetics Today*, Vol. 7:2, 1986, 275-322. Also: <http://www.jstor.org/stable/1772762>, 24.7.2016.

Petroski, Henry. *The book on the bookshelf*. New York: A. A. Knopf, 1999.

Plant, Sadie. Beyond the Screens: Film, Cyberpunk and Cyberfeminism, Variant 14, summer 1993, 12-17. A paper presented at the ikon Gallery, Birmingham, during the Eighth Birmingham International Film and Television Festival, October 1992.

Plato. *Phaedrus*. Trans. Benjamin Jowett, Forgotten Books, 2010.

Poe, E. A. "The Philosophy of Composition." In *The Works of the Late Edgar Allan Poe*. Vol. II, 1850, 259-270.

Pollard, Alfred W. *Last Words on the History of the Title-page, with Notes on Some Colophons and Twenty-seven Fac-similes of Title-pages.* London: J.C. Nimmo, 1891.

Ponder, Cliff. *How to Read Using the Brain Correctly*, 1997. Web document: <http://www.learn-to-read-prince-george.com/read.html>, 24.7.2016.

Pool, Robert. "A History of the Personal Computer." In *Computers, Ethics, and Society.* Eds. Ermann, M. David. and Michele S. Shauf, New York: Oxford University Press, 1997, 91-101.

Price, Leah. "Introduction: Reading Matter." *PMLA* (2006). Also: <http://scholar.harvard.edu/leahprice/files/introduction_-_reading_matter.pdf>, 24.7.2016.

Propp, Vladimir. *Morphology of the Folktale*. Ed. Louis A. Wagner, Austin: University of Texas Press, 1968.

Randall, H Trigg. and A Lucy Suchman. "Collaborative Writing in NoteCard." In *Hypertext: Theory into Practice*. Ed. Ray McAleese, Bristol, UK: Intellect Ltd, 1999, 39-79.

Rettberg, S. *Destination Unknown: Experiments in the Network Novel*. Ph.D. thesis. Department of English and Comparative Literature, University of Cincinnati. Cincinnati, 2003. <http://retts.net/documents/rettberg_dissertation.pdf> 24.7.20016.

Richardson Brian ed. *Narrative Beginnings: Theories and Practices*. Lincoln: University of Nebraska Press, 2008.

---, ed. Narrative dynamics: essays on time, plot, closure, and frames. Columbus: Ohio State University Press, 2002.

Richardson, Samuel. *Pamela; or, Virtue rewarded.* Manchester: Russell and Allen, 1811.

Rimmon-Kenan, Shlomith. *Narrative Fiction: Contemporary Poetics.* London and New York: Routledge, 1983.

Robbe-Grillet, Allen. *Two Novels.* New York: Grove Press, 1965 (1959).

Rosello, Mireille. "The Screener's Maps: Michel de Certeau's "Wandermanner" and Paul Auster's Hypertextual Detective." In *Hyper / Text / Theory.* Ed. George P. Landow, Baltimore: Johns Hopkins University Press, 1994, 121-158.

Rudy, Willis. *The Universities of Europe, 1100-1914.* Rutherford: Farleigh Dickinson University Press, 1984.

Rüegg, Walter. Universities in the Nineteenth and Early Twentieth Centuries (1800-1945). Cambridge: Cambridge University Press, 2004.

Ryan, Marie-Laure. *Avatars of Story.* Minneapolis, London: University of Minnesota Press, 2006.

---. "Beyond Myth and Metaphor: Narrative in Digital Media." *Poetics Today* 23:4 (Winter 2002), 581-609.

---. Interview in the *dichtung-digital*
<http://www.dichtung-digital.de/Interviews/Ryan-29-Maerz-00/index2.htm>, 24.7.2016.

---. *Narratives as Virtual Reality*. Baltimore and London: The Johns Hopkins University Press, 2001.

---. *Possible Worlds, Artificial Intelligence, and Narrative Theory*. Bloomington and Indianapolis: Indiana University Press, 1991.

---, ed. *Cyberspace Textuality: Computer Technology and Literary Theory*. Bloomington and Indianapolis: Indiana University Press, 1999.

Ryman, Geoff. *Two Five Three*. Web Hypertext, 1996. <http://www.ryman-novel.com>. Last accessed: 24.7.2016.

Said, Edward W. *Beginnings: Intention and Method*. New York: Basic Books, 1975.

Saporta, Marc. *Composition No.1*. Trans. Richard Howard, London: Visual Editions, 2011 (1962).

Scholes, R. and R. Kellogg. *The Nature of Narrative*. London: Oxford University Press, 1968 (1966).

Sellen, Abigail. and Richard Harper. *The Myth of the Paperless Office*. Cambridge, Mass.: MIT Press, 2002.

Shabtai, Yaakov. *Past Continuous*. Trans. Dalya Bilu, London: Duckworth & Co, 1985 (1977).

Shannon, C. E. "A mathematical theory of communication." *Bell System Technical Journal*, vol. 27, 379-423, 623-656, July and October 1948.

Shaw, Lindsay H. and Gant, Larry M. "Users Divided? Exploring the Gender Gap in Internet Use." *CyberPsychology & Behavior*, December 2004, 5:6, 517-527.

Shawver, Lois. *Commentary on Wittgenstein's Philosophical Investigations.* Web document: <http://users.rcn.com/rathbone/lwtocc.htm>, 24.7.2016.

Shaywitz, Sally E. et al. "Functional Disruption in the Organization of the Brain for Reading in Dyslexia." *PNAS* vol. 95:5, March 3, 1998, 2636-2641.

Sherzer, Dina. "Serial Constructs in the Nouveau Roman." *Poetics Today*, Vol. 1:3, 1980, 87-106. <http://www.jstor.org/stable/1772413>, 24.7.2016.

Shields, Carol. *Happenstance*. Penguin Books, 1994 (1980).

Shklovsky, Victor. "Art as Technique." In *Russian Formalist*. Trans. Lee T. Lemon and Marion J. Reis, Lincoln: University of Nebraska Press, 1965.

Sholl, M. Jeanne. "Cognitive maps as orienting schemata." *Journal of Experimental Psychology: Learning, Memory, and Cognition*, Vol. 13:4, Oct 1987, 615-628.

Siegel, Daniel J. *The Developing Mind*. New York: Guilford Press, 1999.

Silliman, Ron. *The new sentence*. New York, N.Y.: Roof, 1987.

Simon, Jan. "Narrative, Games, and Theory," *Game Studies*, volume 7:1, 2007. <http://gamestudies.org/07010701/articles/simons>, 24.7.2016

Simson, Otto Von. *The Gothic Cathedral*. New York & Evanston: Harper & Row, 1962 (1956).

Slatin, John. "Reading Hypertext: Order and Coherence in a New Medium." In *Hypermedia and Literary Studies*. Eds. Delany, P. and George P. Landow, The MIT Press, 1991, 153-169. Also: <http://www.jstor.org/stable/377389>, 24.7.2016.

Sloane, N. J. A. and, A. D. Wyner Eds., *Collected papers of Claude Elwood Shannon.* IEEE Press, 1993.

Sloane, Sarah; *Digital fictions.* Stamford, Conn.: Ablex Pub., 2000.

Smith, J. B. and S. F. Weiss. "Hypertext." *Communications of the ACM*, 31:7, July 1988, 816-819.

Smith, Maureen. The U. S. Paper Industry and Sustainable Production: An Argument for Restructuring (Urban and Industrial Environments). Cambridge: The MIT Press, March 1, 1997.

Stephens, Julie A. *Anti-disciplinary protest: Sixties radicalism and postmodernism.* Cambridge: Cambridge University Press, 1998.

Sterne, Laurence. *The Life and Opinions of Tristram Shandy, Gentleman.* New York, London: W. W. Norton & Company, The Norton critical edition, 1980. (1759-1767)

Sternberg, Meir. *Expositional Modes and Temporal Ordering in Fiction.* Bloomington & Indianapolis: Indiana University Press, 1978.

---. "How Narrativity Makes a Difference." *Narrtive* vol. 9:2 (January 2001), 115-122.

---. "Ordering the Unordered: Time, Space, and Descriptive Coherence." *Yale French Studies* 61 (1981), 60-88.

---. "Telling in Time (I): Chronology and Narrative Theory." *Poetics Today* 11:4 (Winter 1990), 901-48.

---. "Telling in Time (II): Chronology, Teleology, Narrativity." *Poetics Today* 13:3 (Fall 1992), 463-541.

Stevick, Philip. *The chapter in Fiction*. Syracuse. New York: Syracuse University Press, 1970.

Strickland, Stephanie. *the Ballad of Sand and Harry Soot*. August 1999, <http://wordcircuits.com/gallery/sandsoot/frame.html>, 24.7.2016.

Tam, James. *Design and Evaluation of Web-based Dynamic Hypertext*. Ph.D. Dissertation, Department of Mechanical and Industrial Engineering, University of Toronto, 1997. Also: <http://www.collectionscanada.gc.ca/obj/s4/f2/dsk3/ftp04/Nq27738.pdf>, 24.7.2016.

Tavris, Carol. *The Mismeasure of Woman*. New York: Simon & Schuster, 1992.

The American Heritage Dictionary of the English
Language. Houghton Mifflin Company, 1992, 3rd
Edition.

Tepper, Steven J. *Why Do More Women Read Fiction?*
Center for Arts and Cultural Policy Studies,
Princeton University, 1998. Also:
<http://www.princeton.edu/~artspol/workpap/WP06
%20-%20Tepper.pdf>, 24.7.2016.

Theall D. F., "Beyond The Orality/Literacy Dichotomy:
James Joyce And The Pre-History Of Cyberspace."
Postmodern Culture, Volume 2:3, May 1992. Also:
<https://w2.eff.org/Net_culture/HTML/joyce_prehi
story_of_cyberspace.paper.html>, 24.7.2016.

Tillotson, Kathleen Mary. *Novels of the eighteen-forties.*
Oxford: Clarendon Press, 1956.

Tolva, John. *The Heresy of Hypertext: Fear and Anxiety in
the Late Age of Print.* 1995. Web document:
<http://www.ascentstage.com/papers/heresy.html#si
x>, 24.7.2016.

---, and Balcom David. "This is Your Brain on the
Internet." *Kairos 1.2*,
<http://english.ttu.edu/kairos/1.2/reviews/hegirasco
pe/review2.html>, 24.7.2016.

Tomashevsky, Boris. "Thematics." In *Russian Formalist*. Trans. Lee T. Lemon and and Marion J. Reis, Lincoln: University of Nebraska Press, 1965.

Tompkins, Jane P. Ed. *Reader-response Criticism: From Formalism to Post-structuralism*. Baltimore: Johns Hopkins University Press, 1988.

Tosca, Susana and Jill Walker. "Hypertext Criticism: Writing about Hypertext." *Journal of Digital Information*, Vol. 3:3, 2003. Also: <http://journals.tdl.org/jodi/article/viewArticle/116/115#>, 24.7.2016.

Tov, Emanuel. *Textual Criticism of the Hebrew Bible*. Minneapolis: Fortress Press, 2001 (1992).

Trollope, Anthony. *Barchester Towers*. New York: The New American Library of World Literature, 1963 (1857).

Tschichold, Jan. *The New Typography*. Trans. Ruari McLean, Berkeley: Univ. of California Press, 1995 (1928).

Vandendorpe, Christian. *From Papyrus to Hypertext: Toward the Universal Digital Library*. Trans. Phyllis Aronoff and Howard Scott, Champaign: University of Illinois Press, 2009.

Walsh, Richard. The Rhetoric of Fictionality: Narrative
Theory and the Idea of Fiction. Columbus: The
Ohio State University, 2007.

Webster, Donna M. and Arie W. Kruglanski, "Cognitive
and Social Consequences of the Need for Cognitive
Closure." *European Review of Social Psychology*,
Vol. 8:1, 1997, 133-173.

Weiland, W. J. and B. Shneiderman. "Interactive Graphics
in Hypertext Systems." *Proc. 28th Annual ACM DC
Technical Symposium*, 23, Aug. 1989, 23-28.

Weiss, Martin B.H. "Compatibility standards and product
development strategy: A review of data modem
developments." *Computer Standards & Interfaces*,
Volume 12:2, September 1991, 109-122.

Wells, Benjamin B. *Computer Revolution*. New York:
Nova Science Publishers Inc., 1997.

Whiteman Kaslow, Florence. Ed. et al. *Comprehensive
Handbook of Psychotherapy: Cognitive-behavioral
Approaches*. New Jersey: John Wiley & Sons,
2002, 303-304.

Whorf, B. *Language, Thought, and Reality: selected
writings of Benjamin Lee Whorf*. Cambridge, Mass:
The Massachusetts Institute of Technology, 1956.

Wiles R. M. *Serial Publication in England Before 1750*. Cambridge: Cambridge University Press, 1957.

Wittgenstein, Ludwig. *Philosophical Investigations*. Trans. G.E.M. Anscombe, Oxford: Basil Blackwell, 1968.

Woolf, Virginia. "The Love of Reading." In The Essays of Virginia Woolf Vol. 5: 1929 to 1932.

Wong, Linda. *Essential Study Skills.* Boston: Houghton Mifflin Harcourt, 2009.

Yankelovich, Nicole, Haan, Bernard J. Meyrowitz, Norman K. Drucker, Steven M. "Intermedia: The Concept and the Construction of a Seamless Information Environment," *Computer*, vol. 21:1, 81-96, Jan. 1988. Also: <http://research.microsoft.com/en-us/um/people/sdrucker/papers/intermedia1.pdf>, 24.7.2016.

Yates, Frances Amelia. *The Art of Memory*. Chicago: University of Chicago Press, 1966.

Yehoshua, Abraham B. *A Late Divorce*. London: Halban Publishers, 2006 (1984).

Yellowlees Douglas. Jane. *The End of Books – Or Books without End?* Ann Arbor: The University of Michigan Press, 2000.

---, "Gaps, Maps and Perception: What Hypertext Readers (Don't) Do." *Perforation 3* (Vol. 2). Also: <http://www.pd.org/topos/perforations/perf3/dougla s_p3.html>, 24.7.2016.

Žižek, Slavoj. For They Know Not What They Do: Enjoyment As a Political Factor. London: Verso, 1991.

www.ingramcontent.com/pod-product-compliance
Lightning Source LLC
Chambersburg PA
CBHW020427130626
46549CB00001B/17